THE HISTORY OF A CRICKET CLUB

Wagon Works
to Winget
1890 - 2005

by
C G MATTHEWS

Dianthus Publishing Limited

Published by Dianthus Publishing Limited,
The Pool House,
Kemble
Cirencester. GL7 6AD
Tel. 01285 770 239   Fax: 01285 770 896

ISBN 978-0-946604-26-5

Ron Thomas

*A good friend who introduced me to over 30 years of cricket
On The 'Wagon Works' Ground That has graced so many great cricketers*

VITAI LAMPADA
The Lamp of Life

*There's a breathless hush in the Close to-night -
Ten to make and the match to win –
A bumping pitch and a blinding light,
An hour to play and the last man in.*

*And it's not for the sake of the ribboned coat,
Or the selfish hope of a season's fame,
But his Captain's hand on his shoulder smote –
'Play up! play up! and play the game!'*

Sir Henry Newbolt
(1897)

Dianthus Publishing Limited

PREFACE

I began my cricketing career many years ago playing for Speech House CC in the Forest of Dean. I would play my game before going home via the local newsagent's shop to buy the Pink 'Un and read the reports of all the matches played during that previous week. The first report I would always look for was that of the Wagon Works Cricket Club which played at Tuffley Avenue, a ground that, when I was younger, I always dreamed of playing on. Little did I know that not only would I go on to play for the Wagon Works for many years and captain the side on numerous occasions, but I would also become President of the club, a position which I am still honoured to hold.

I recall one game during my captaincy when our opening batsman at the time, a young Charlie Matthews, approached me and asked to be dropped down the order because he was struggling for runs. I told him that not only would he open – but he would also face the first ball of the game. He struck that opening delivery for four and went on to make his first century for the club – a proud moment for both of us.

There have been many changes since the club was founded back in 1878, most lately the name change from the Wagon Works to Winget during the 60's and the ground being taken over by Gloucester City Council in the 90's. Yet the thrill of playing cricket on an arena graced by so many truly great players over the years remains as strong as it has ever been.

As the club celebrated its 125th Anniversary in 2002, it is apt that a record of times gone by should be written. Charlie Matthews has been researching and collecting material for this book for *10 years* or more and his dedicated work could not have been marked in a better way than the publication of this history which will, I am sure, bring back countless memories of seasons gone to players both past and present.

Stan Phelps

President, Winget CC

FOREWORD

"THE WAGGIES"

By Brian ("Bomber") Wells

I was hardly seventeen when I made my debut at the Gloucester Wagon Works ground for the "Nondescripts". I arrived at the ground courtesy of my mum's bike, already dressed in my whites and ready for action. I left the bike behind the pavilion - unlocked of course, for there was little fear of it being stolen in those days. It was a blistering hot day and I took shelter in the shade of the trees that stood in front of the pavilion. Then for the first time I took stock of the huge acreage that lay in front of me. To my left I noticed there were people playing tennis and then some 150 yards away, directly in front of me, I saw a large hut which I thought was the place where you could get refreshments, but I soon learnt that it was the second eleven's changing quarters. Some time later I learnt that the area running down from the first team ground was the second team's playing area. I also observed that there were outdoor practice nets running along the inside of the massive wall that still skirts the front of the ground. To my delight, the following season the "Nondies" used these same nets for our early season practice and they were first class as well. I soon discovered that behind the club house there was a magnificent bowling green. I found out where it was by chance really, when I hit a ball from the Works opening bowler, Vic Beamish, into the middle of it and Charlie Newman, who was keeping wicket, said to me "Now you're for it son, that's your week's pocket money gone for a burton". It wasn't until some time later that I found out that Charlie was the Wagon Works head groundsman. As for the game itself, I cannot honestly remember anything else about it except that it was over just after tea and we won easily. What I do remember clearly is that I went straight home and, whilst I was upstairs changing, my mother, who hadn't the vaguest idea about cricket or any other sport for that matter, prepared me a meal, which of course I downed so it wouldn't disappoint her.

Three of four years later I played for Gloucestershire on that same ground and what a thrill that was. So when Charlie Matthews asked me if I could write a foreword to his work and include thoughts of matches and characters I had played with and against on there, I was very happy to say yes. To start with, one of Gloucestershire's greatest characters in the 1950s was its own Secretary, Colonel Henson. He was always dressed immaculately and one could be forgiven in thinking he might well have stepped straight out of Burton's shop window. His dress for all occasions, whether it was hot, cold, wet or dry, was in the style of the country gentleman. Viyella check shirts, sports jacket, cavalry twill trousers, brown suede shoes and always wearing a County tie, the final touch being a silk handkerchief in his top pocket. At a slow military step he would circumnavigate the ground, checking on the gate men and on his way would nod or speak to every member of the County Club who was there. I'm sure his repartee with them would have made a good script for any music hall act. Behind his appearance was a man as hard a disciplinarian as you would find anywhere and he was emphatic that all County Cricketers should be impeccable in their manners and in their dress. For instance, if we got our flannels dirty during play we had to wear clean ones for the next period and Colonel Henson ensured this through the kindness of a laundry in Bristol, which cleaned all our cricketing clothes for nothing.

Against Northampton during the 1950?s the County Club experimented with the hours of play and, if my memory is correct, we started about 1.20 p.m. and played until 8.20½ p.m. - the idea being to encourage people to come in their droves after tea. For instead of the usual 2 hour stint from 4.30 to 6.30 p.m., with these experimental hours we took tea about 3.50 p.m. played for a couple of hours and then we had what the players jokingly called "the hot dog break". This consisted of hot sausage rolls, a cup of tea and lasted about 10 minutes, then we were back in action until 8.20 p.m. In fact the experiment was reasonably successful, but was never carried on with. On the first day of the game it was unbelievably hot and sticky and two or three of the Northants players who weren't taking part in the match decided to take off their shirts and enjoy the sun on their backs in the player's enclosure. What they didn't realise was that the Colonel, dressed like an English Squire even though the temperature was a mere 65°F instead of 85°F plus, was due to pass them at any moment. He actually did pass the enclosure, but then came back; presumably he couldn't believe his eyes. He enquired of them as to what they were doing in the enclosure. When they told the Colonel they were Northants players his moustache bristled, his eyes nearly popped out of their sockets and he reminded them they were representatives of their County - not holiday makers at Butlin's Holiday Camp, and they should put their shirts back on immediately - which without argument they did. I wonder what the old lad would have thought of today's new enlightenment!

Most of what I knew about the Wagon Works ground before I played on it, I had heard from listening to my father and his brothers discussing cricket. The exploits of Hammond, Parker, Goddard, Barnett and many others filled my head. One of their favourite stories - and it always seemed to be somewhat altered every time they told it, concerned Tom Goddard's benefit match against Notts. Legend has it that Tom was rather worried that the famous Notts attack of Larwood, Voce and Butler (surely a trio of County fast bowlers which has never been surpassed) would get the game over in two days, thus robbing him of the third day's gate. Now cricket stories, like a good wine, get better and better as they mature and most people insist that Tom confided in Wally Hammond about his worry and Hammond replied that there was nothing to worry about because they wouldn't get him out. History shows that Wally scored over 300 and Tom got his third day's gate and for those who watched the game and played in it have all told me it really was the innings of a colossus. Funnily enough I was always a bit sceptical about the story when a boy. So when I began playing for the County I made enquires amongst those players who played in that game as to whether it was a true story but not one person could tell me, other than to say that it had been an absolutely marvellous innings. When I went to play for Notts, I was really going straight to the horse's mouth because Harold Larwood was on holiday in Nottingham from Australia and I was able to ask him, forgetting of course that he hadn't actually played in the game. He couldn't confirm the story, but he did tell me that, earlier in the season on a green topper at the Bridge, Wally was none too well and Bill Voce was taking a fiendish delight in digging the ball into Wally's ribs. Harold told me that he warned Vocey that Wally would exact revenge one day. Later on I tackled Bill Voce and he confirmed Larwood's story and I like to think that Wally, on the Wagon Works ground, gained his revenge. Harold Butler, who died recently, did play in the game and he confirmed that Wally straight drove Bill Voce out of the ground and over the top of the houses in Tuffley Avenue for the biggest six he'd ever seen in his life. I asked Harold what was Bill's reply to that, and he said that he bowled the next one shorter outside the off stump making it almost impossible for it to be driven, so Hammond square cut it for six over the top of the dressing rooms. Thus you have two versions of a legendary story - which is correct I have no idea - does it matter, I don't think so - but one thing for sure is that it's still the greatest legend of the Wagon Works.

Dennis Compton, without doubt, was the greatest batsman I ever had the pleasure to bowl against at the Waggies. He scored a brilliant century with a bat borrowed from Tom Graveney who had scored an equally marvellous century the previous day with it. The pitch when Dennis batted was a slow turner and I bowled deliberately just short of a length at him, and with seven fielders on the leg side, he was unable to really get the ball away. I knew this would upset him because, like all great batsmen, he liked to dominate the situation or to get out in the process. When I thought he'd had enough, I bowled what can only be described as the perfect away swinger to him. It started in the air about six inches outside his leg stump so he instantly put his front foot down across the wicket and prepared to play his famous leg sweep. Even as he did, the ball swung from leg to middle and off. I thought instantly "that's done him". At the last moment, the genius in Compton picked out the swing and he called out "It's the bloody swinger Bomber," and seemingly with all the time in the world, he allowed the ball to come across him and somehow contrived to hit it for four through the covers. The umpire at my end was Frank Lee, one of the game's best officials, and he was just as amazed as I was. He said to Dennis, "If you'd missed that Compo, it would have knocked all three down". Dennis, with a laugh, pointed his bat at me and remarked, "That'll teach the bugger to bowl spinners".

Two of the most exciting games at the Waggies were against Surrey, one I played in and one I didn't. In the one I played in, we had just arrived at the Wagon Works from a three-match away tour. On winning the toss, I was given permission from George Emmett, our skipper, to go into Gloucester to get some bits and pieces for the rest of the side from Bill Hook's shop in Westgate Street. Bill and I had been players for the "Nondies" at one time and by the time we had stopped chin wagging, it was almost 12.30 pm. When I arrived at the gate in Tuffley Avenue, it was just gone one o'clock. "Hurry up Bomb," one of the gate men called out, "we've lost eight wickets." I thought he must be joking, but I didn't have to go far to find out that he wasn't and by the time I reached the changing room and padded up, Sam Cook had just got out, but there wasn't time before lunch for me to go in. Arthur Milton, who had opened the innings and was still there when I joined him after lunch, carried his bat all the way through and we added about 30 runs before I was out. By now the wicket was turning square and we bowled them all out before close of play. Unfortunately they had a 100 or more lead. So confident were Surrey about bowling us out for next to nothing on the Monday that they actually cancelled their hotel where they were to stay overnight. In those days, my house in Podsmead Road practically backed onto the Wagon Works and on the Sunday morning, I went across with my dog to have a word with Charlie Newman who was busily cleaning the boots and pads. I remarked to him that if we had a nice local shower to wet the surface of the pitch, just enough to put the heavy roller on it to help bind it together (pitches were not covered in those days), and, if we could make enough runs, it would make the game very interesting indeed.

Believe it or not we got the local shower. The heavy roller bound the surface together and Jack Crapp played the dangerous Tony Lock with his big right pad pushed well forward hour after hour, whilst Ron Nicholls played possibly one of his best ever knocks for the County to stay with him for a long time. "Lockie" must have appealed 50 times for l.b.w. against Jack and each time the umpire, a certain Harry Baldwin who had been a post-war Surrey professional, wasn't interested. The most interesting decision occurred for "Lockie" with the most magnificent piece of fielding off his own bowling. He had anticipated that Jack would try to pinch a single off him to keep the bowling and as quick as a flash he followed through, picked the ball up, pivoted, and threw Jack's wicket down with Jack still a few yards short of his destination. "Lockie", who was as elated as no man could have ever been cried out "How about that then?" "Not out," Harry replied, and, as Tony Lock stood there, he added with a grin, "keep your hair on 'Lockie' ". No one could believe it. He was so enraged that in his next over he literally threw a bouncer at Jack. Our unsuspecting Cornish left-hander was still pushing forward with his right pad as the ball soared over both his head and that of the Surrey wicket keeper Roy Swetman's outstretched hands, to almost go for six byes. We finally ended up with a lead of about 130 and whilst all this had been going on, the Surrey twelfth man had been ringing round the hotels of Gloucester for accommodation for the team for that night. The next day the pitch was a dust heap and Sam Cook and I rubbed the ball in the dirt to open our attack. I struck the first blow when Surrey had about 30 on the board with the final ball of the over and as we changed round I passed Harry Baldwin who said to me, "Your mate Sam must have a sore throat because he hasn't had an appeal yet." I told Sam about this and straight away in his next over, he rapped Bernie Constable, who must have been two yards down the pitch, on the pads. "How is that?" Sam appealed, and Harry replied "I'm sorry Bernie, that's out". The rest is history and we won by 11 runs. It was a hollow victory we all knew and when George Emmett offered his apologies to Stuart Surridge the Surrey skipper, he simply laughed and replied, "We're used to it George, he does us regularly twice a season like this".

The game I didn't play in was two days of the most exciting cricket one could ever wish to see and I only wish that I could have taken part in it. I was initially down to play, but it wasn't to be and it was probably the game that lost the County the chance of the Championship, for after that defeat we faded badly. It was a game in which the groundsman Charlie Newman got a great deal of unwarranted criticism for the state of the pitch. The fact was that he'd prepared the pitch in exactly the same way as he had done previously for 20 years. Unfortunately, 1959 was a very hot and dry summer and the playing surface broke up from the very first ball bowled. Yet ask anyone who was there what they thought of the game and they would tell you it was the most fantastic cricket they had ever watched and a match never to be forgotten. The following season I was playing Notts, and sadly returned to Gloucester when my first wife died to find that the "Waggies" had become "Winget" and soon after that it became Tuffley Park. A poor name I believe for such a distinguished ground - I would have thought "Hammond's Way" or something of that ilk, for we are talking about a piece of history, not a bit of wasteland.

INTRODUCTION

The Gloucester Wagon Works Company, from which the cricket club took its name, was formed in 1860 by a group of local businessmen. The company over the next 120 years changed its name three times with the cricket club following suit. The cricket team's first recorded outing was in 1878, although it is quite likely matches were played before this date. The town Ham was the venue for its early games, the same venue used by most local teams at this time. The late 1800s saw the team move its home matches to Hempsted and later, during the First World War, sub-leasd the Gloucester Spa Ground.

Towards the end of the war, the company purchased 33 acres of land off Tuffley Avenue, which was turned into what is today's sports ground. In 1923 the County moved its Gloucester Festival to the ground, away from the Spa, much to the disgust of two prominent Gloucester County Committee Members. The following pages are a historical account of the cricket club with references to matches and characters of the time, and also some facts concerning the ground's association with the County for some 69 years.

It is a tribute to the hard work of the groundsmen, who produced wickets not only for local players, but ones fit for County and Test Players alike and to the unsung heroes - the umpires, the scorers and the ladies and gentlemen who supplied the refreshments for tea.

What can be better than to play cricket on a fine summer's day on the Wagon Works ground , an arena that has been graced by the likes of Hobbs, Hammond, Procter, Goddard, Gavaskar and the many players of the club and its visitors? This is a club with a unique history.

THE EARLY YEARS

In 1860, four local Gloucester businessmen met to discuss the formation of a company to make wagons for the ever-increasing railway industry. The amount of railway lines had doubled in the country over a ten-year period and the coal industry was producing over 80 million tons of coal per year. The company did very well in its first year, building three hundred and thirteen wagons and employing over 360 hands.

As the company grew so did its workforce and, inevitably, the social side, with reports of several activities including bowls and rounders. The first mention of cricket was when the following report was placed in the Gloucester Journal in 1878:

"A match was played on the Ham on Saturday, between St. Catherines and eleven of the employees of the Gloucester Wagon Company. It resulted in victory for St. Catherines by one run and seven wickets. The play on both sides was very good and the bowling of Puttick for the Wagon Works eleven and of Warner, Barnes and Jackson of St. Catherines was very effective."

Although this is the first reported match of the Cricket Club, it is quite likely that matches were played well before this. Unfortunately the club has no records of those early years and we can only be grateful for local newspapers, namely the Gloucester Citizen and Journal, and to a lesser extent the Chronicle, for match reports placed in them. Between 1878 and 1890 it seems that the club played only occasionally. Home matches took place on the Town Ham, an area of ground near Westgate Bridge where most local teams played. The opposition at this time was mostly local villages, church teams and Gloucester firms. One match report was placed in the Citizen in 1880 when the club visited Coaley in the Forest. No result was given but it seems that Mr C Verrinder of the Wagon Works team played very well.

In 1887 the Company, and of course the Cricket Club, changed its name from Gloucester Wagon Company to The Gloucester Railway Carriage and Wagon Company. It was now producing carriages as well as wagons for the Argentine, South African and Indian railways, and for the British Government.

From 1890 the Cricket Club moved its home ground to Hempsted, renting grounds belonging to Mr Goulding of Newark Farm. The Cricket Club over the next ten years was to increase its playing force and by the end of the century, was running three sides. There were a number of players who stood out, including George Romans, a batsman who was to play eleven matches for Gloucestershire between 1889 and 1903. George later joined the City Club and was also a founder member of the Gloucester Old Boys Ruby Club. Others who made their mark were P Clissold, R Dere, G Dere, C Sysum, G Page, R Roberts, H Huggins, and F Proctor, whose two sons Eddie and Harold were to become outstanding players after the First World War. The following pages are match reports from 1890 - 1900. Home matches are sometimes referred to as played at Llanthony, but this is certainly the same ground. One unusual fact is that there is no record of any matches during 1894 in any of the local papers. This is, as yet, an unsolved mystery, though I am sure some matches were played during this time.

1890

Saturday 10th May - GRC & Wagon Co v. Y.M.R.I.S

The match resulted in victory for Y.M.R.I.S. by 84 runs.

Scores   Y.M.R.I.S. 105   GRC & Wagon Co. 21

W Palmer and W Hilton played well for the winners. The former scoring 55 runs in capital style and the latter performing the 'Hat Trick' in taking four wickets in four balls.

Saturday 10th May - GRC & Wagon Co v. Tyndale - Played at Barnwood

Scores GRC & Wagon Co. 16 and 40 Tyndale 15 and 50 for five wickets.

Saturday 17th May - St. Catherines v. GRC & Wagon Co

These teams met on the ground of the former in Sandhurst Lane. The game ended in a tie, both sides scoring 48 runs in their first innings, the Wagon Works in their second venture making 27.

Saturday 24th May - GRC & Wagon Co v. Arlington

Played on the ground of the latter and resulted in victory for the Wagon Works by eight wickets and 8 runs.

Scores   Arlington 53 (Smith 15, Lewis 13)
                GRC & Wagon Co. 61 for 2 (Wilkie Not Out 28 Mundy Not Out 14)

Miss Chadborn kindly provided the teams with refreshments during the match.

Saturday 7th June - Gordon Wanderers v. GRC & Wagon Co

Played at Llanthony and resulted in a win for the Gordon Wanderers by one run.

Scores Gordon Wanderers 28   GRC & Wagon Co. 27

Saturday 7th June - Brunswick v. GRC & Wagon Co

Played at Deans Walk the match resulted in victory for Brunswick on the first innings.

Scores Brunswick 45 and 45 (Jones 15, Reid 11) Wagon Works 28 and 42 (Hogg 9 , Stephens 14) Clutterbuck bowled well for the winners taking 11 for 28 in the two innings.

1891

Saturday 30th May - GRC & Wagon Co v. Northgate

Played at Longford and resulted in an easy win for the former by 74 runs.

The following batted well for the winners. P Clutterbuck (19), G Aston and H Huggins (17 each), and F Bailey (15), Clissold also bowled well with success taking 6 wickets for 7 runs. Cook for the losers took 5 for 17 runs.

GRC & Wagon Co 86   Northgate 14

Saturday 30th May GRC & Wagon Co v. St. James

This match was played at Longford and resulted in a win for the former by 80 runs.

W G Roberts (22) J Holford (21), A S Smith (14 N.O.) and Clissold taking 5 wickets for 9 and Clutterbuck 3 for 5 played well for the winners.

GRC & Wagon Co 44   St James 14

Saturday 27th June GRC & Wagon Co v. County Asylum

Played on the latter's ground and resulted in a win for the Wagon Co. F Clutterbuck batted and bowled well making 44 not out and taking 5 for 17 runs.

GRC & Wagon Co 128   Asylum 64

Saturday 4th July GRC & Wagon Co v. St. Catherines

At Longford it ended in a draw, St. Catherines batted first and scored 55. Weaver contributed 20, Brunsdon (10) and Collins (10) and their opponents lost 2 wickets for 11. Rain prevented the match being concluded. Wilkie bowled well for the Wagon Works.

Saturday 18th July GRC & Wagon Co v. Barnwood House

Played at Barnwood House, Wagon Works won by 57 runs, F Bailey and G Aston played well for 27 and 17 runs respectively, while Dr Souter was top scorer for the losers making 20.

Clissold for the winners took 7 wickets for 25 runs.

1892

Saturday 14th May - GRC v. Barnwood House

GRC & Wagon Co played against Barnwood House. Played at Barnwood, Wagon Works won by 15 runs. Clutterbuck and Aston for the Works made 14 and 10 runs respectively.

Wagon Works 58   Barnwood House 43

Saturday 21st May - GRC & Wagon Co v. St Mary De Lode

Played on the ground of the former, Wagon Works won by 14 runs.

H Huggins bowled grandly capturing seven wickets for only 3 runs. Bailey also bowled well taking 3 for 9.

Wagon Works 29   Mary De Lode 15

Saturday 28th May - GRC & Wagon Co v. County Asylum

Played on the Asylum ground, Wagon Works won by 14 runs. Dr Minahon and H Clissold were top scorers for the Works making 10 each. H Huggins bowled well taking 4 wickets for 6 runs.

Wagon Works 59   County Asylum 45

Saturday 11th June - GRC & Wagon Co 'A' v. Primitive Methodists

Played on Wagon Works ground, Primitive Methodists won by 28 runs.

Primitive Methodists 50   Wagon Works 'A' 22

Saturday 2nd July - GRC & Wagon Co v. St Lukes

Wagon Works won by 37 runs on their own field. W George 17, Dr Minahon 11 not out. P Clutterbuck for the Wagon Works took 7 wickets for 5 runs and performed the 'hat trick'.

Wagon Works 59   St Lukes 22

July - Post Office v. GRC & Wagon Co

Played on the Wagon Works ground. Post Office 35 GRC & Wagon Co 17. Mr Merryless provided refreshments during the match.

Saturday 10th September - GRC & Wagon Co v. Barnwood House

Played at Barnwood

Match drawn, greatly in favour of the visitors, the Barnwood team narrowly escaping defeat by the last wicket playing out time and still being 37 runs behind. For the Works team, principal scores were Barnes, Aston and Hedges making 14, 12 and 10 respectively, and Sysum making 16 not out.

Wagon Works 75 for 9 (innings declared closed). Barnwood House 38 for 9

1893

Saturday 10th June - Wagon Co v. Barnwood House

Gloucester Wagon Co v. Barnwood House

Played on the ground of the latter, resulting in a victory for the Works on the first innings by 6 runs.

Wagon Works 41 Sysum (20) and 77 for 8 wickets
Huggins (20), F Bailey (16), Roberts (10)
Barnwood House 35, Compton (11). Sysum bowled well for the Works, taking 6 wickets for 10 runs.

Saturday 9th September

Gloucester Carriage and Wagon Works against County Asylum, played on the Asylum ground and ended in a win for the home team.

Scores Asylum 90
Dr Johnson (39), F Stout (23), Hodgson (20), and the latter batted one man short.

Gloucester Wagon Works 20

The Asylum bowlers came out well, G Williams taking 5 wickets for 8 runs and Halford 3 for 12.
Sysum for the Wagon Works took 5 for 34 runs.

1895

25th May

Arlington against Glos R C & W Works was played on the ground of the latter resulting in a very easy win for Arlington.

Gloucester Railway Carriage and Wagon Works 48

Arlington 160 for 3 wickets
A F Hughes 82 not out
G Wakeman 30
J Lewis 29 not out
Hughes took 4 wickets for 19 runs and Long took 5 for 25.

8th June

Barnwood House played against Wagon Works at Barnwood and the visitors were defeated after an exciting finish by a narrow margin of 9 runs. The House batted first and ran up 90 runs. Compton with a hard hit innings and Dr Santar 17 being the chief scorers. For the loser's score of 81, good batting was shown by Thornett 25 and Roberts 23, whilst Dere was in fine form with the ball, taking 8 wickets for 29. Powell 4 for 14 and Dr Santar 4 for 20 came off best in this department for the House XI.

22nd June

County Asylum defeated the GRC & Wagon Works at Wotton by 26 runs, Asylum 77 Wagon Works 51. H Thornett 20, W Roberts 10, for Wagon Works.

15th July

GRC & Wagon Co played Norton at Norton, Wagon Works won by 7 runs. C Sysum played well for 17, also taking 6 wickets for 19 runs.

Wagon Works 46   Norton 39

After the match, the home team kindly entertained the visitors to tea

29th July

The return match between the GRC & Wagon Co and Arlington resulted in a victory for the Works team by 25 runs.

H Thornett and F Marton batted well, making 12 and 22 respectively. Clissold and Dere were successful with the ball, capturing 7 wickets for 17 and 3 for 10 respectively.

Wagon Works 53   Arlington 28

26th August

The GRC & Wagon Co travelled to Cainscross to play Cotswold Rangers. After a closely contested game, the Works team won by 10 runs. Dr Minahon batted well. G F Dere and C Sysum distinguished themselves with the ball, Dere taking 5 for 11 and Sysum 4 for 8.

Wagon Works 39   Cotswold Rangers 29

Gordon Wanderers 'A' 78 Wagon Works 'A' 43.

1897

Saturday 8th May

Wagon Works 'A' 152 for 6

R Dere 15, F Salcombe 35, R Burden 22, R Roberts 10, Dorn Not Out 24, F Padbury 17.

Haresfield 18 All Out

Saturday 15thMay

Bowden Hall 56 (R Dere 6 Wickets for 20 Runs)

Wagon Works Reserves 51 (H Jones 11, Brunsdon 12 Not Out)

Saturday 22nd May - Wagon Works v. Tirley

Played at Llanthony. The Wagon Works fielded a weakened team, being without the assistance of G Romans, G Page and H Huggins. Tirley were assisted by Davis, Hooper and Daunter of the Tewkesbury Club. Tirley batted first making 64, with Davis scoring 24. For the Works, S G Simpson and C Sysum made things a little lively, scoring 64 in 35 minutes. The final total was 105 for 9, with Simpson scoring 30 and Sysum 31.

Wagon Works 'A' v. Police

Played on the ground of the latter:

Works 'A' 96 (W Roberts 33, A Powell 28)

Police 53 (Lewis 13, Collett 10)

Saturday 29th May

The Gloucester Wagon Works journeyed to Chalford, but unfortunately the weather was anything but favourable for cricket. Chalford, winning the toss, decided to bat, but were unable to make a start for three-quarters of an hour owing to a downpour of rain. There was a terrific wind blowing all through the game, and from one end of the wicket it was almost impossible to get the ball up to the other. Chalford made 86 (Cland-Smith 22, H Pools 30, J Clissold 11), whilst the Works played out time thanks to H Dorn who made 29 not out, the final total being 68 for 9. Also for the Works, C Sysum bowled splendidly capturing nine wickets for 24 runs.

The Post Office 'A' gained a narrow victory over the Wagon Works 'A', the margin only being 9 runs.

Wagon Works 'A' 43 (F King 11). The wickets were shared by Clutterbuck (4 for 15) and Click (for 25).

Post Office 'A' 52 (Click 18). Padbury and Salcombe bowled well for the losers taking 6 for 19 and 3 for 10 respectively.

Saturday 5th June

The first match between the Post Office and Wagon Works was played at Hempsted, the game ending in a draw.

Wagon Works 129 for 3 (W D Palmer not out 66, T Murdock not out 26) Other scorers were W Roberts (10), S Simpson (8), G Romans (11).

The Post Office ended play on 53 for two wickets (Oldland not out 25, Minahan not out 2).

Wagon Works 'A' v. St. Lukes

Played at St Lukes Ground.

Scores: Works 'A' 80 (F Bailey 26, R A Roberts 20 not out)
            St. Lukes 60 (G Guy 14, J Stock 11)

Rev. Metcalf obtained seven wickets at a small cost, whilst R Roberts and H Jones obtained five and three respectively.

Saturday 12th June

Dursley defeated the Wagon Works at Hempsted by 51 runs. The visitors made 99 and the Works made 38. Romans for the Works obtained 5 for 13.

St. Catherines 34, Wagon Works 'A' 23

Played at Sandhurst. For St. Catherines, J Bevan captured 7 for 10 and Rev. Ryley 2 for 10. The Rev. Ryley batted well and for the Works, G F Dere bowled well.

Saturday 26th June - Tewkesbury v. Wagon Works

Played at Tewkesbury

Tewkesbury 56 (H Jessop 13, W Brotheridge 12) Wagon Works 96 (D Palmer 36), Hill (6 wickets) and H Jessop (3 wickets) bowled well for the Town Club, as did Palmer and Sysum for the Works.

Wagon Works 'A' v. The Exchange

Played at the Works ground, Works won by 72 runs.

Wagon Works 'A' 95 (Padbury 22, Dere 20, Roberts 15, Minahan 13). The Exchange 23, R Dere and R Roberts bowled well, each taking 5 wickets, and Padbury kept wicket well, taking 4 catches and allowing no extras.

Saturday 3rd July

The Wagon Works received a visit from Hasfield Court and gave them a good beating by eight wickets and 140 runs. The Hasfield men were all dismissed for 37, C. Sysum taking 3 wickets for 6 runs and W D Palmer seven for 25. On the works going into bat some good form was shown. W G Roberts and T Murdock opened the account, the latter being bowled with the total at 20. Palmer then joined Roberts and the pair defied all the bowlers until 154 was on the board, when Palmer was caught for a splendid 104, which embraced one 6, one 5 and thirteen 4s. The batsman had been an hour and three quarters making them and had not given a chance. G Page was the next comer and with Roberts played out time. The latter played very well and was at the wickets for two hours and a half for 40, whilst Page made 15.

Saturday 10th July

The Wagon Works visited Barnwood House and won handsomely by two wickets and 177 runs. The House representatives batted first, but were all dismissed for 68 (G F Hannam-Clark 27). Huggins and Sysum took 5 for 11 and three for 32 respectively, whilst Palmer had one for 20. The Works started none too well, losing Page and Dorn for 12. Simpson and Palmer took the total to 62, when the former was bowled for 20, whilst 2 runs later, Palmer was bowled for 24. George Romans and H Huggins played all the bowlers alike, Huggins eventually being caught for a well played 35. Romans continued to bat finely, and except for a difficult chance when on 82, there was nothing to mar his splendid innings of 106 not out, which included 26 boundaries. The batsman took an hour and a half to make his runs. W Roberts made 13, and when time was called, the Works had put together 246 for the loss of 8 wickets.

Saturday 17th July

Wagon Works A 46, H Jones (14)
Price Walker A 35, H Jones (6 for 14)
and R Roberts (4 for 16)

Saturday 24th July

The 'Citizen' reported the following results for the Wagon Works Team so far this season. Played 11, won 5, lost 4, and drawn 2.

Saturday 31st July

The Wagon Works played their return match with the County Asylum at Wootton. The visitors winning the toss, elected to bat with George Romans and T Murdock. The first wicket fell for 24, but Romans continued to bat finely and eventually carried his bat for 79, made without a blemish. W G Roberts also batted well for 32 not out. The Works put the closure into force, with the total at 140 for five wickets. Holford was the most successful bowler.
The Asylum played out time making 100 for five wickets P Stout (38), Dr Smyth (19), Dr Winters (13) and extras 17.

Saturday 7th August

The Post Office administered a crushing defeat to the depleted Wagon Works team at Buddings field by 104 runs and five wickets. Wagon Works batted first and were all out for 52. The officials finished the day on 156 for five.

Saturday 21st August

The Wagon Works had the Gordon Wanderers for opponents and won easily by eight wickets. The Works won the toss and decided to let the Wanderers have first innings. They were dismissed for 58 by R Dere, who bowled very well, taking eight wickets for 21. T Stephens made 18 and S Ball 13. The Works replied with 59 for the loss of 2 wickets, G Romans being not out 40 and G Page 12.

The match between Wagon Works A and Elmore was played on the ground of the latter, when time alone robbed the Works team of victory. Elmore batted first and made 58 and the Works replied with 56 for six when time was called. For the Works F King (24) and C Pallister (13) did well and, with the ball, R A Roberts (four for ten) and H Jones (five for 23) did well.

Saturday 11th September

Dursley and Gloucester Wagon Co. played at Dursley and the game resulted in a somewhat sensational win for the home team by 13 runs. The visitors brought a very strong scratch XI, including Stevens the Gloucester professional. Dursley batted first, but were dismissed for 48, chiefly through the splendid bowling of Stevens, whose analysis read 14 overs, 7 maidens, 9 runs, 8 wickets. T Lorrimer was the only double figure scorer with 13.
The Company started well, making 33 for two wickets, the remaining wickets however, fell for an addition of only 2 runs. W D Palmer batted well for 22 and was the only batsman who played the bowling with any confidence. Woolams and Williams bowled splendidly and divided the wickets.

* Stevens was the Gloucester City professional, who that season for the City took 92 wickets and contributed over 500 runs.

1898

Saturday 7th May

The Wagon Works played Stonehouse at Stonehouse and, after a most pleasant and exciting game, won by one run.
The President (Mr E Jenner-Davies) kindly lent his private ground for the match, but it was so soft that runs were difficult to obtain. The home team was very strong, Stroud and Wycliffe College being represented. The Works started with only 36, no one reaching double figures, whilst Stonehouse replied with 37 (Merrett 10). The Works did better in the second innings making 95 (F Moseley 25, G Page 24, F Goulding 19). Merrett and Perkins bowled well for Stonehouse, whilst Guy, Huggins and Palmer bowled well for the Works.

Saturday 28th May - Wagon Works v. Barnwood House

Match played at Barnwood.

Scores: Wagon Works 109, (D Palmer 31, C Sysum 15, G Page 13, R Roberts 10, F Proctor 13). Barnwood House 62, (D Palmer took 7 wickets for a small cost).

Saturday 4th June - Gloucester II v. Wagon Works

Played at the Spa, Wagon Works were dismissed for only 66. Gloucester II replied with 236 for 9. George Romans, who later joined the Works Club for a number of years, scored 131 not out.

Works Team: G Page, W D Palmer, F Goulding, S Simpson, F Proctor, G Ellis, T Murdock, C Sysum, R A Roberts, A Guy, W Powell

Saturday 11th June

Price Walker 89, Wagon Works 72
Played at Llanthony. For the Walkers Huggins made 23 not out and Ellis 24.

Saturday 2nd July

G W R Swindon 61, Gloucester R C & W Co. 59.

Played at Hempsted.

Saturday 9th July

The Wagon Works received a visit from the Stonehouse Club and defeated them for the second time this season. (The Wagon Works Club being the only one to beat their Saturday team this year). The Works compiled 90, thanks chiefly to C Sysum and D Minahan. The former hit merrily making 17 in one over, but was eventually caught for 30, whilst the latter was not out 14. Stonehouse replied with 56 (G Hale 22, F Moseley 13). R A Roberts and W D Palmer bowled well, the former taking three wickets and the latter four. Tea was supplied by the Works Club and the game was most pleasantly contested.

Saturday 16th July

A considerable amount of interest was taken by the rival teams in the meeting of St James and Wagon Works A at Llanthony, the Works having been the only team to defeat the Vicarage Fielders this season.

Wagon Works A 41 (W Powell) F Loveridge (7 for 15)
St James 46 (J Banks 11) F Padbury (5 wickets)

Saturday 23rd July

Norton Court v Wagon Works played at Norton, Wagon Works 133, (W D Palmer 45) (G Page 20) (H Huggins 14) extras 20.
Norton Court 30, W D Palmer (7 wickets for 8 runs)

Saturday 30th July

The Wagon Works played their return match with the Post Office on Budding's Field and beat them for the second time this season. Going in first, the officials made a good start, F G Clutterbuck and F C Oldlands putting on 35 for the first wicket, when the former was caught for 29, the latter for 13. The official's score realised 84. The Works started well, G Page and W D Palmer putting on 45. When time was called, the Works had totalled 159 for eight wickets (S Simpson not out 39, G Page 37, R A Roberts not out 15, H Huggins 15)

Saturday 13th August

In the match between Gloucester Exchange and the Wagon Works II, both sides claimed victory according to their respective score books.

Saturday 20th August

Upton St Leonards & Wagon Works A met at Hempsted before a good crowd of spectators. The feature of the game was the grand display of batting given by A P Birchall, who scored 58 in a total of 118 for Upton. G Guy for the Works taking four wickets for 2. In reply, Wagon Works were all out for 46 (H Lawrence 17) and F King (10) batted well.

1899

Saturday 6th May - Gloucester Railway Carriage and Wagon Company v. Dursley

Met at Dursley. The home team won by 73 runs. Dursley 112 for 6 declared. Wagon Works 29 all out.

The following was reported in the Citizen concerning fixtures the previous week. Mr W J Winters, Hon. Sec to the Gloucester Railway and Carriage and Wagon Co. Club writes that *No match was arranged with the GWR CC and their 2nd XI for Saturday. If any error was made it was by the secretary of the Great Western Club.*

Saturday 13th May - Gloucester Railway Carriage and Wagon Company v. Apperley Court

Played at Hempsted. Gloucester Railway Carriage & Wagon Company 47 Apperley Court 46 The Works won by just one run.

Gloucester Railway Carriage and Wagon Company 'A' v. Atlas

Played at Sandhurst. Gloucester Railway Carriage & Wagon Company 'A' 57 Atlas 31

Saturday 20th May - Stephenson & Co v. Gloucester Railway Carriage and Wagon Company

Played at Hempsted. The Works won by an innings and 78 runs. Gloucester Railway Carriage & Wagon Company 124 (Verrinder 35, Padbury 28, Pugh 19, Roberts 14) Stephenson & Co 16 and 30 all out

Carter took 6 for 6; Roberts took 8 for 12 including the 'Hat Trick'.

Saturday 29th July

Wagon Works v Apperley Court was played at Apperley and won by the Wagon Works by 45 runs.

Scores: Wagon Works 78, Apperley Court 33

G Page (32), W G Roberts (12) and A Carter (9) batted best for the Works and H Huggins (seven for 15) and H Jones (three for 12) were the best with the ball.

Saturday 5th August

Exchange v Wagon Works A played on the Works ground.

Scores: Wagon Works 45 Exchange 91

Saturday 26th August

Gloucester Wagon Works v Upton St Leonards was played at Upton and won by the Works by 53 runs and two wickets.

Scores: Wagon Works 86 for eight. D Minahan 16, G Page 13, F Page 13, F Wood 12, and G Verrinder (11) batted well.

Upton all out 33 G Ellis (6 for 16)

Wagon Works "A" Team v Barnwood 2nd was played at Hempsted and won by the Works "A" by 8 runs.

Scores: Wagon Works "A" 36, Barnwood 2nd 28.

1900 - 1910

The start of the new century was, for the club, similar in many respects to the end of the last, still fielding 3 teams. H Jones captained the club that won 10 of its 16 matches, G Page topped the batting averages and G F Dere the bowling. George Romans did not play due to County commitments, but the club did have the assistance of H. Hacker who had some County experience.

The list of Club Vice Presidents reads like a who's who of local dignitaries, including the Rt. Hon. C J Monk MP, Mr A Slater (the Earl of Ducie), Sir John Darlington, Sir Lionel Darell and R V Vassar-Smith. There were 46 in the full list and it is interesting to note the reason for supporting the club. Mr A Slater (the Earl of Ducie) was Chairman of the board of Directors and also president of the Cricket Club. Many of the others were railway enthusiasts and were probably encouraged to support the club. The club was in a good financial position, the Vice Presidents' fees brought in over £30, a very healthy sum when you consider its major expenditure was only 5 guineas, this being for the ground rent.

R Burden, a club member, carried out the groundsman's duties and was assisted by A Speck. 1900 also saw the introduction of cricket caps with the club emblem embroidered on, these were on sale for 1 guinea.

The 1901 season was once more successful, the first team again being captained by H Jones and winning 10 of its 15 completed matches. George Romans was available for a number of games and topped the batting averages at 24.66. In 1902 there was an attempt to introduce a Gloucester and District Cricket league. This only ran for a few seasons, the Works winning the inaugural first division title by a single point. The Works team at this time was not as strong as the City Club and only played the City's second eleven. The City was not allowed to enter their first team in the league due to the fact they employed a professional. The subscription to join the league in 1904 was 10 shillings and umpires' fees for each match were 2 shillings, while members' subscriptions to join the club were 3 shillings. It is interesting to note in the club accounts for this time that a new mower for the ground cost 7 pounds, three cricket balls 14 shillings, a set of stumps 3 shillings and 3 pence and a pair of leg guards 8 shillings and sixpence. The club side during the early 1900s played Apperly Court who had the assistance of Alf Dipper, who was later to become a stalwart of the County side, appearing 478 times for the County and once for England. C S Barnett, C J (Charlie) Barnett's father was also to play against the Club for Tewkesbury. Towards the end of the decade the club had a number of new faces showing good promise - Harry Perkins and Charlie Restall who were to become long serving members and also L Hamblin, Sam Roberts, L V Huggins, Alf Carter and A Whiley. In 1905 Mr T Arnold took over the groundsman's work from Mr Burden and the umpire in those days was Mr T Murdock.

Club cap and badge on sale in 1900 for one guinea

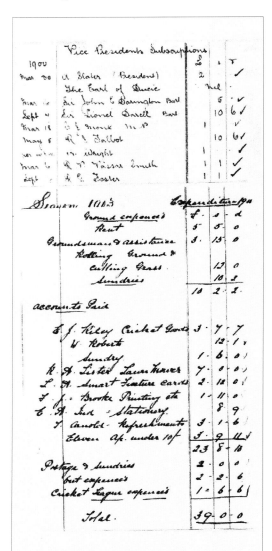

Top left: Extract from the secretaries' register 1900 listing a number of vice-presidents

1900

May 1900

Gloucester 11 v. Wagon Works at The Spa

The Wagon Works batted first and were all disposed of for 39 (D Minahon 16 not out). Smith took 5 wickets for 14, Jeans 4 for 5 and Whiston 1 for 13. Gloucester II passed their opponent's total with 5 wickets in hand and finished up with a score of 76. (I G Hunt 18, N Whiston 16, GS Morse 10). F Merrett took 3 wickets for 18, E Rust 3 for 20, S Allen 3 for 24 and Verrinder 1 for 4.

Wagon Works 'A' 120 (J Cox 53 for F Artus 19 G Collis 10)

St James 'A' 54, N Lewis batted well for St James, E Rust and G Collis shared the wickets for the Works.

Wagon Works Averages 1900

The past season has been a very successful one for the Works. Owing to the number of members, which is over 50 - three teams have been run. The first XI, under the Captaincy of H Jones, has played 16 matches with the following results: - 10 won, 5 lost and 1 drawn. Wins: Collins and Godfrey (2), Norton Court (2), King's Stanley (2), Nailsworth, Apperley, County Asylum and Upton. Lost: - Barnwood House (2), Gloucester A, Post Office and Roseleigh. Drawn: - Apperley. G Page and A Whiley have batted very consistently throughout the season. The highest individual score for the Club was 60 made by A Whiley against Collins and Godfrey, followed very closely by F Proctor 59 not out, and G Page 51. G F Dere has been in fine form with the ball, capturing 60 wickets at a cost of 5.81 runs each. Total runs scored for the Club: 1,318 for 143 wickets (average 9:21 per wicket) against 1,200 for 154 wickets (average 7:28 per wicket).

Batting Averages

	Inns	Not Out	Total Runs	Highest Score	Average
G Page	12	2	238	51	23.8
A Whiley	15	1	234	60	16.7
F Proctor	8	1	106	69	15.1
W Roberts	9	0	88	27	11.0
L Huggins	4	0	29	20	7.25
T Phelps	15	1	88	29	6.2

Bowling Averages

	Overs	Mads	Runs	Wickets	Average
G F Dere	173	45	401	69	5.81
A Whiley	55	6	147	21	7.01
H Jones	81.5	16	224	17	13.14
H Huggins	45.2	7	105	10	10.5
G Page	26.5	3	62	8	7.7

H S Hacker secured five wickets for 7 (including the hat trick) and C Verrinder 3 for 2.

The 'A' Team played 16 matches of which they won 10 and lost 6. Wins: Exchange (2), St. James' 'A' (2), King's Stanley (2), Ebley, Highnam, G.W.R. Stephens. Lost: G.W.R Oil Mill (2), Longford, Roseleigh 'A', Highnam. The chief batting averages were J Cost 14.8 and J Banks 11.81. In the bowling department, I Huggins took 25 wickets average 3.10, E Rust 30 at 4.7 and G Oullis 38 at 4.86.

The B team played 10 and won 4, lost 5 and drew 1. Wins: Barnwood House, Police St. Pauls, St. Lukes. Lost: Gloucester II, St. Pauls, Hempsted II, Atlas II. Draws: Hempsted II.

1901

Wagon Works Averages 1901

Played 15 Won 10 Lost 4 Drawn 1.

The teams defeated were Post Office (2), Apperley Court (2), Upton (2), Gloucester II, Nailsworth, County Asylum and Barnwood House. The losses were sustained from Norton (2), Gloucester II and Barnwood House. The drawn game was against the County Asylum.

The principal batting averages were:

G Romans 24.66, G Page 12.25, A Whiley 11, F Proctor 9.64, T Phelps 9.57, T Murdock 8.2 and L Huggins 7.75. G Page made the highest score of the season with 44.

The leading bowling averages were:

H Jones 37 wickets average 6.37, G F Dere 58 average 6.9, A Whiley 23 average 8.86, G Romans 11 average 10.81, G Page 5 average 12.8.

The 'A' team won the whole of their 12 engagements. Victories were secured over Ebley (2), Selsley (2), Stephens (2), Churchdown St. Marks, Cheltenham Exchange, Police, King's Stanley and Atlas. J Banks had the honour of scoring the highest individual score of 105 not out, heading the batting average with 19.88, followed by F Curtis 16.52, W Mason 12.16 and G Cullis 5.77, J Cox 15.11, W Roberts 14.75, W. Robinson 13.62. The bowling averages were H Turner 25 wickets average 2.92, E Rust 35 wickets average 3.02, G Cullis 42 wickets average 3.00.

Owing to his obtaining an appointment in Bristol, Mr F A Cowley, whose umpiring efforts have been greatly appreciated by the club, had to relinquish his duties as honorary secretary.

1902

Gloucester and District Cricket League

Post Office v. Wagon Works

This match, which decided the championship of the league, was played on the Post Office ground before a large number of spectators. Both sides were well represented. Brewer and Matthews were unable to play for the officials, whilst the Wagon Works had the able assistance of H S Hacker, the ex-City professional, for the first time in league cricket. Winning the toss the Wagon Works put the officials into bat, but so well did Dere (6 wickets) and Hacker (4 wickets) bowl, they were disposed of for 61 runs. The Works replied with 113, George Romans (46) Hacker (13) Whiley (13) Proctor (12) getting into double figures. By winning this match the Wagon Works became the first winners of the cup.

This match aroused considerable interest in local cricket, and was attended by the largest company ever seen at a match on Buddings Field. The game was keenly contested and good cricket was shown on both sides. Hacker's pace provided too much for the Officials, but Dere deserves great credit for his excellent bowling, which contributed in a great measure to the success of his team.

It is a curious coincidence that the Officials have three times been runners up in a cup competition, twice in football and once in cricket, but do not appear destined to attain the premier position. They, however, deserve credit for their efforts, playing the same team throughout the session.

First Division

	P	W	L	D	pts	For		Against	
						runs	wkts	runs	wkts
Wagon Works	8	5	2	1	11	764	71	537	80
Post Office	8	5	3	0	10	665	78	595	72
*Gloucester II	8	5	3	0	9	884	54	738	72
Longford	8	1	4	3	5	628	59	570	70
Oil Mills	8	1	5	2	4	297	75	780	59

* = Loses points for playing ineligible man

Second Division

	P	W	L	D	pts	For		Against	
						runs	wkts	runs	wkts
St Lukes	8	7	1	0	14	745	90	395	90
*High Orchard	6	4	2	0	8	381	70	286	70
Upton	7	2	3	2	6	383	65	507	80
Stephens	7	2	4	1	5	394	80	361	73
Highnam	8	0	5	3	3	435	80	660	72

* = Loses 2 points for playing ineligible man: awarded 2 points in lieu of cancelled match with Upton.

1903

Wagon Works Gloucester and District League

DIVISION 1

Fixtures for the Season, matches played at first named club's ground.

JUNE

6th	Gordon Wanderers v. Wagon Works
13th	Post Office v. Wagon Works
20th	Wagon Works v. Gloucester 'A'

JULY

11th	Inter League Match Gloucester v. Cheltenham
11th	St. Lukes v. Wagon Works
18th	Wagon Works v. Post Office

AUGUST

1st	Gloucester II v. Wagon Works
22nd	Wagon Works v. Gordon Wanderers

SEPTEMBER

5th	Winners of Gloucester League V. Winners of Cheltenham League

DIVISION 2

JUNE

6th	Wagon Works II v. High Orchard
13th	Wagon Works II v. Upton St. Leonards

JULY

4th	Wagon Works II v. Highnam
11th	Wagon Works II v. Gordon Wanderers II
18th	High Orchard v. Wagon Works II

AUGUST

1st	Upton St. Leonards v. Wagon Works II
22nd	Highnam v. Wagon Works II

Saturday 23rd May - Wagon Works v Barnwood House

Played at Barnwood

Scores: Wagon Works 129 Barnwood House 29. G Romans (62 not out), L Huggins and J Boucher batted well and H Turner (6 wickets for 10 runs) and E Rust (4 for 15) bowled well for the Works. Udal and Hacker did well for the House.

Wagon Works 'A' 107. (W Powell 61) Elmore 23, E Taylor (7 wickets for 11) bowled well for the Works. H Wixey and G Collingbourne were most successful for the losers.

Wagon Works II 60, Tabernacle 28. F Wood and F Robinson batted well and G Stone (7 for 14) and F Wood (2 for 3) bowled well for the Works.

Saturday 27th June - Wagon Works v. Apperley Court

Played at Apperley

Scores: Wagon Works 48, Apperley 35. G Romans (16), H Romans (11) and F Goulding (8) batted well for the Works. G F Dere (2 wickets for 4), H Jones (5 for 21) and H H Turner (2 for 8) bowled well for the Works and W Margrett and A Dipper for the losers. Batting in the second innings, the Works were dismissed for 63 (G Romans 20 not out).

22nd August

Highnam and Wagon Works II was played at Highnam, the home team winning by nine wickets.

Scores: Wagon Works 25 and 36, Highnam 54 and nine for one wicket. This was the return league encounter.
H P Ellis the Highnam captain, having won the toss, decided to put the visitors in on a drying wicket which favoured the bowlers and the innings was over for 25. Highnam replied with 54.

The Wagon Works going in again made 36 in their second venture, leaving Highnam 8 to get to win, and these were quickly made by O Surman and J Taylor. For the Wagon Works, W Robinson (11) and Powell (10) made the highest figures and, for Highnam, O Surman (10) and H P Ellis (22) did well with the bat and ball.
Tea was brought on to the field by the kindness of Mr and Mrs Ellis

1904

Saturday 7th May - Wagon Works v. St. Lukes

League match was played at Llanthony

Scores: Wagon Works 77 St. Lukes 53
St. Lukes batted first making 53 (F Collingbourne 11 and H Ellis 10). The works started badly losing 6 wickets for 24 runs, but a timely stand by J Banks (24) and T Phelps (14) put them in a safe position. A Whiley, L V Huggins bowled best for the Works. St. Lukes kindly entertained the Works to refreshments.

Saturday 14th May - Wagon Works v. Stroud Lypiatt

Played at Llanthony.

Scores: Wagon Works 67 for 7 (G Page 39 retired, J Boucher 11). Stroud Lypiatt 59 (H Smith 13, B Hulbert 14)
G F Dere took five wickets for 11 runs for the Works. Hulbert bowled well for the losers.

Gordon Wanderers 'A' met Wagon Works 2nd at Hempsted and, after a pleasant game, resulted in the following:

Gordon Wanderers 2nd 53 (R Oldham 14, R James 8, W. Ellis 8 Not Out). Wagon Works 2nds 30. F Stephens bowled well for the Wanderers taking seven wickets for a small cost. Taylor and Turner did best for the Works, the former doing the 'Hat Trick'.

Saturday 16th July - Tabernacle v. Wagon Works

Was played on the ground of the former club and resulted in an exciting finish, the home team winning by 4 runs.

Scores: Wagon Works II 32 Tabernacle 36

H Smith (7 for 13) bowled well

Saturday 23rd July - Wagon Works v. Matson

Played at Llanthony.

Scores: Wagon Works II 57 v. Matson 50

W Vickery showed good form for the Works with (32). Staite (18) and Mosley (11) did well for Matson.

Saturday 13th August - Wagon Works v. Apperly Court

Played at Apperley.

Scores: Wagon Works 88 Apperley Court 59

Apperley batted first making 59, J Rhymes making 12 not out and Captain Hasler 10. For the Works J Banks 4-18 and A Whiley 5-34 shared the wickets. T Phelps (29) and L V Huggins (22) took the score to 77 after losing 6 early wickets for 26. *A Dipper took 8 wickets for Apperley.

*A Dipper went on to play for Gloucestershire and one Test for England.

1905

Saturday 6th May - CITIZEN

This year the Citizen proprietors started giving 5 shillings to what the Editor considered the best batting and bowling performance of the week. J Smith of the Wagon Works received the first bowling prize taking 6 - 30 against Stonehouse.

Saturday 6th May - Wagon Works 113 v. Apperley Court

Played at Hempsted.

J Banks 35, G page 19, T Phelps 18 and W Sargent 12 batted well for the Works side and A Dipper 26, A Smith 10 did well for the losers.

H Turner took 6-12 for the Works and A Dipper also bowled well for Apperley Court.

Saturday 13th May - Wagon Works 115-6 Declared v. County Asylum 105 for 3

Played at Wotton.

H Dorn 54 not out. J Boucher 41 and A Whiley 34 batted splendidly for the Works and Dr. Smith made 56 not out.
B V Bruton scored 30 for the Asylum. L Huggins 2-18 bowled well for the Works.

Saturday 20th May Wagon Works 84-6 v. Gloucester 'A' 136-8 declared

Played at Hempsted - Match Drawn.

Fred Proctor 19 not out. A Whiley 13, G Page 16, J Boucher 10 batted well for the Works as did A Crouch 38 not out and F N Fox 31.

E P Smith scored 15 for the visitors.
 F Wood also bowled well for the Works

Wagon Works 'A' v. All Saints

Played at Cheltenham.

The match ended in a win for the Works. For the Works W Robinson 31,
J F Brookes 12, F Whitehead 15, batted well. A Burlton took 5-11 and F Artus 4-14.

Saturday 27th May - Wagon Works v. Collins and Godfrey   Played at Hempsted.

1905 Gloucester Railway Carriage and Wagon Co Ltd Cricket Club "A"team

G Stone (umpire) J T Brookes WJ Sargent J Welshman CE Brown FWhitehead L V Huggins (sec) S R Carter (Treasurer) F Artus A Burlton W J Robinson (Capt) E Taylor W Vickery H Underwood (scorer)
Played 15. Won 12, Drawn 2, Lost 1

The match ended in a good win for the Works by 5 wickets and 20 runs.

Wagon Works 125-5 J Banks 62, H Dorn 26 not out, T Phelps 14 not out, J Boucher 11 batted well for the Works, as did E Badham 16, H Jones 16, F Hooper 14 and W Moss 10 for Collins and Godfrey. F Wood bowled well for the Works.

Saturday 3rd June

On this day Jack Hobbs made 102 for Surrey v. Essex and Charlie Barnett 36 for Cheltenham v. Cirencester at the Victoria Ground, Cheltenham.

Wagon Works 'A' v. Upton St. Leonards

Match played at Hempsted.

Wagon Works 140-8 declared. A Whiley 76, J Boucher 23, E Hall 18, J Banks 10 batted splendidly for the Works.

Upton St. Leonards 74. S Matthews 23, P Simmonds 14, S Millard 10 not out, batted well for Upton. E Taylor bowled well for the winners.

Saturday 10th June

On this day George Dennett of Gloucestershire took seven Surrey first innings wickets. The old opponents Gloucester Post Office and Gloucester Wagon Works met at Buddings Fields and a keenly contested game resulted.

The Officials batted first and quickly lost seven wickets for 44 runs when F C Oldland 44, and Alec Matthews 16 not out doubled the score by excellent batting. The innings was declared when the century was reached and the 8th wicket fell.

The Wagon Works started disastrously, the first five wickets falling for no runs and the innings only reaching 29. The bowling and fielding of both sides was exceptionally good. Post Office 100 - 8 declared Wagon Works 29.

Saturday 17th June - Wagon Works v. Collins and Godfrey

Played at Tewkesbury - Match Drawn.

Wagon Works 130 H Perkins 24 not out, G Page 18, J Phelps 16, W J Robinson 15, J Boucher 12, H Dorn 12,   F Wood 11 were all in good form with the bat for the visitors. For the home side E Badham 31, C L Davey 17, H Jones 17 and W Bassett 12 did well. The visitors were kindly entertained to a smoking concert at the headquarters of the club after the match. A capital programme was arranged and a most enjoyable evening spent.

Saturday 24th June - Wagon Works v. Barnwood House

A pleasant game ended in a good win for the house by 30 runs. Barnwood House 142 Dr. Townsend 38, A Bewick 30, Rev. Hayden 17 batted well for the winners.

Wagon Works 112 J Banks 40, H Dorn 26, F Wood 12, A Bewick took the Hat Trick in taking 6 for 45 for the House.

Wagon Works 'A' v. Brockworth

Match played at Hempsted - Match Drawn

Wagon Works 'A' 136 E Taylor 48, F Golder 15, F Artus 12. Brockworth 52 for 9 A Gregory 16, D Selwyn 10 For the Works F Artus took 6-23.

Saturday 1st July - Wagon Works 'A' v. High Orchard

Played at Hempsted.

Wagon Works 'A' 44 J Boucher 12. High Orchard 30 S Summers 12. For the winners F Artus took 8-21.

Saturday 15th July - Wagon Works v. North Court

Played at Hempsted.

Wagon Works 160 H Perkins 33, G Page 28, E Hall 22, T Phelps 26, F Pugh 11, J Boucher 13 not out

North Court 99 J Shipman 21, F M Luce 19, S Freeman 13, A Whiley bowled well for the Works.

Wagon Works 'A' v. Upton St. Leonards

Played at Upton

Wagon Works 'A' 80 L Huggins carried his bat for 31 not out, W Sargent 21

Upton St. Leonards 33 F Artus 4 for 15

Saturday 22nd July - Gloucester II v. Wagon Works

Played at the Spa.

Afforded some excellent cricket, Gloucester won the toss and put the Works into bat. They started badly against good bowling by Summers, but an excellent innings by J Banks (55) totalled 125. At 5 o'clock Gloucester started their innings. Some dashing cricket was seen; they put on 80 in the first half hour, Smith claiming 63 with 12 fours and Sly playing beautifully for 54 not out. Peckover also hit 46, Gloucester totalling 214 for 4.

Saturday 5th August - Wagon Works II v. Hucclecote II

Match played at Hempsted.

Wagon Works II 67. J Boucher 21, C Brown 23, L V Huggins 14 batted well for the Works side.

Hucclecote II 34. E Rheam 10 not out batted well for the losers. W Vickery 6 for 18 and S Turner also bowled well for the Works.

Saturday 12th August - Highnam v. Wagon Works 'A'

Highnam 66 M Wixey 12, C Prosser 26 batted well for Highnam.

Wagon Works 'A' 67 for 5, W Robinson 26, W Vickery 22 not out. All batted well and F Artus did well with the ball.

The Works journeyed to Highnam with a weak side and two short, but fortunately were able to pick up two substitutes. The home team was very strong having the assistance of several outsiders. The Works' record was in danger, but splendid batting by Robinson and Vickery saved the side.

Saturday 2nd Sept - Brockworth Witcombe v. Wagon Works 'A'

The Wagon Works put the home side into bat and, with some good all round bowling, the home side only totalled 31. The Wagon Works fared even worse being all out for 25. Thus the Works lost their cherished record, this being their first defeat of the season.

1906

Saturday 5th May - Wagon Works v. Apperley Court

Played at Hempsted.

Scores: Wagon Works 62. J Boucher 24, *A Dipper took 8 wickets - rain stopped further play.

*A Dipper went on to play for Gloucestershire and appeared in one test for England.

Saturday 12th May - Hartpury House v. Wagon Works 'A'

Hartpury House easily defeated Wagon Works 'A' on the latter's ground.

Scores: Hartpury House 107. H Wood 32, J Simpkins 32. Wagon Works 'A' 37.   Sargent 18, Simpkins and Cogbill shared the wickets for Hartpury House, 5 for 10 and 5 for 17 respectively.

Wagon Works II 21. J Mansell 5 wickets for 7 and H A Wall 5 for 12. Stroud Road Primitive Methodists 28. A Coggins 14 for the Works and S Turner bowled well.

Saturday 19th May - Wagon Works v. Norton Court

Match played at Norton.

Scores: Wagon Works 129 - Norton Court 81

Lindsay Vears 35 not out, F Wood 23, F Artus 19, J Banks 15 and G Page 10 batted splendidly for the winners and for Norton Court, F Goscombe hit well for his 51, which included ten 4s. W Freeman made 15, J Boucher and F Gillender bowled well for their respective teams.

Saturday 2nd June - Barnwood House v. Wagon Works
Played at Barnwood.

Scores: Wagon Works 118 - Barnwood House 70

Lindsay Vears 32, F Wood 17, J Boucher 15 and A Burlton 14 not out, batted well for the Works and P H Ford 21, H Ford 16, Berwick 11 and Booth 10 for Barnwood House. The last wickets for Barnwood House fell for no runs.
H Perkins 5-19, including the 'hat trick', bowled well for the Works.
and H Howell for the losers.

Wagon Works 'A' v. Albert Flour Mills
Played at Hempsted.

Scores: Albert Flour Mills 53 - Wagon Works 'A' 63

G Allen 27 and L V Huggins 16 batted in good style for the Works and F Clutterbuck 13, E Simpson 10 and S Francis 10 for the Mills. F Artus and F Hancox took 6 wickets for their respective teams.

Saturday 16th June
Played at Hempsted.Gloucester II met the Wagon Works, but the game had to be abandoned. The Works had scored 49 for 8 wickets when the rain came on. L V Huggins was not out 19 and T Phelps contributed 18. F J Rust took 5 wickets for 21 and Renton 2 for 20.

Saturday 23rd June - Wagon Works v. Salmon Springs

Played at Stroud.

Scores: Salmon Springs 21 - Wagon Works 109

T Phelps 26, S Boucher 18 and J Welshman 12 batted best for the Works. J Banks 5-6 runs and J Welshman 3 for 12 runs bowled splendidly for the winners, as did F Foote for the losers.

Hucclecote II v. Wagon Works II

Played at Hempsted. Hucclecote won by 26 runs.

Scores: Hucclecote II 59. R E Rheam 15. Wagon Works II 33. J Long 6 for 12 and H Bircher 4 for 15 bowled well for the winners.

Saturday 30th June - Wagon Works 'A' v. Upton St. Leonards

Played at Hempsted.

Scores: Wagon Works 'A' 75 - Upton St. Leonards 45

H Jones 17, W Sargent 15, A Burlton 13 and F Artus 12 batted well for the Works, and S Millard 24, O Morris 10 for Upton. F Artus 5-22 and H Perkins 4-15 bowled well for the Works.

Saturday 7th July - Wagon Works v. Collins Godfrey

Played at Tewkesbury.

Scores: Wagon Works 206 for 8 Declared - Collins Godfrey 141 for 5

H Perkins 64, J Banks 31, W Holder 27, G Page 19, J Welshman 23 not out, T Phelps 11 not out batted splendidly for the Works and W Jackson 72, R Browning 29 not out, W Smith 11, M White 10 for the homesters. A capital concert was arranged for the visitors and a most enjoyable evening spent.

Saturday 21st July - Gloucester II v. The Wagon Works

Gloucester II gained an easy victory over The Wagon Works - played at the Spa.

Gloucester made 169. H J Weaver 62, W Henderson 33, L H Peckover 18, A H Adams 10 'extras' 32 and dismissed their opponents for 70, L Vears 35, J Welshman 18.

Wagon Works II v. King's Stanley Baptists
Played at Kings Stanley.
Scores: Wagon Works II 36 – King's Stanley 35.

The match ended in an exciting win for the visitors by 1 run. H Smith made 11 runs for the Works and C E Brown and W E Vickery shared the bowling.

1907

Saturday 4th May

Wellington and Co. opened their season with a victory over the Wagon Works II.

Scores: Wellington and Co. 64 Works 54. The highest scores for the winners were R Walter (18 Not Out) and A Veal (18), for the losers, Brown (23). R Walter bowled well for the winners and Welshman for the Works.

Good batting by Wagon Works 'A'.

Wagon Works 'A' v. Staunton and Corse was played at Hempsted and ended in a draw.

Scores: Wagon Works 'A' 102 for seven wickets (declared) Staunton and Corse 28 for 2 wickets. F Proctor (52 Not Out) batted in good style for the Works. H Hawkins bowled best for the visitors.

Saturday 18th May - Wagon Works v. Upton St. Leonards

Played at Upton.

Scores: Works 82. Upton 59. A pleasant game. C Savage 24, W Sargent 22 and A Carter 22 batted well for the Works and W F Chubb and Rev Helm for Upton. Archdeacon Scobell kindly entertained the teams to tea.

Saturday 25th May - Wagon Works v. Gloucester 'A'

Played at the Spa. Time robbed the Works of an easy victory.

Scores: Gloucester 'A' 123. Wagon Works 121 for 5 wickets. A H Romans 60, W D Henderson 22 and W H Fluck 19 batted well for Gloucester 'A' and J Boucher 47 not out, A Whiley 37, J Bank 20 for the Works. J Welshman bowled well for the Works.

Wagon Works 'A' v. Albert Flour Mills

Played at Hempsted.

Scores: Wagon Works 'A' 96 for 8 wickets declared. Albert Flour Mills 32 all out. S Roberts 24, E Taylor 23, Alf Carter 15 and L V Huggins 12 batted splendidly for the Works and W Foulkes 11 for the Mills. W Sargent 5 wickets for 9 runs and R Dere 4 for 20 bowled finely for the winners and A Hancox for the losers.

Wagon Works II v. Southgate

Played at Hempsted

Scores: Southgate 31. Wagon Works II 50. F Colebrook 26 for Southgate and S Beighton 19 and C E Brown 13 for the Works batted well. George Welshman 6 wickets for 17 bowled splendidly for the winners.

Saturday 3rd August - Wagon Works Outclassed

Barnwood House v. Wagon Works was played at Barnwood, the home team gaining a decisive victory.

Scores: Barnwood House 180 for four wickets (Norman Jones 64 Not Out, G Romans 48, K H Stratton 24, W Freeman 18, A Bannerman 15 Not Out). Wagon Works 20 all out. Norman Jones had eight wickets for 7 runs for the winners.

Wagon Works 'A' Victorious

Wagon Works 'A' v. Staunton and Corse was played at Staunton.Scores: Works 72, Staunton 22, W Sargent (40), W Vickery (17) batted well for the Works and W Sargent seven wickets for 11 bowled well.

Saturday 10th August - Wagon Works Win at Wootton

Wagon Works v. County Asylum was played at Wotton. The Works batting first compiled 157. The asylum responded with 54, The Works thus winning by 103 runs. G Allen (13), J Banks (16), T Phelps (20), E B Evans (25), A Whiley (29), E Turner (11) and L V Huggins (15) batted well for The Works, while C G Palin (38) was the only man to reach double figures for the Asylum. H Perkins (seven for 15) including the 'Hat Trick' and J Welshman (three for 2) obtained the wickets for The Works.

Hucclecote Beaten at Hempsted

Wagon Works II v. Hucclecote II was played at Hempsted.

Scores: Wagon Works II 73, Hucclecote II 18. G Welshman (19), S Beighton (12), batted well and G Welshman (six for 8) and W C Vickery (four for six) bowled well for The Works.

Gloucester Wagon Co and Wagon Co Ltd 1st Team 1907

S Lane (sec) TPhelps W Alien EEvans GPage S Carter W Winters T Murdock (umpire)
T Arnold (groundsman) R Brisland J Banks J Boucher H Perkins (captain) A Whiley
L V Huggins S Turner.   Played 14 Won 9 Drawn 3 Lost 2

1908

1st August - Wagon Works Splendid Win

Barnwood House 122 Wagon Works 151 for seven wickets at Barnwood.

For the Works, L V Huggins (75) played a superb innings, A Carter (25), J Banks (16), G Page, also did well.
H Perkins and A Carter did best with the ball for the Works.

Wagon Works 'A' 31 Hempsted 11. Played at Hempsted

For the winners R Dere (five wickets for seven) and W Sargent (four wickets for 4) bowled unchanged. For Hempsted, W Roberts took 5 wickets at small cost.

8th August - Wagon Works Beat The Asylum

For the second time this season, the Wagon Works proved too good for the County Asylum. Batting first The Asylum made 90. Dr. Smyth again played a not out innings of 37, Wrathall (13) and Rev. J B Chard (12) being the only other two to reach double figures. The Works replied with 132, thus winning by 42. For the Works, L Huggins (27), A Carter (26), J Banks (22) E Rust (20 Not Out) and W Vickery (17) batted well, while A Carter (five wickets for 19) was the most successful bowler. For the Asylum, C S Palin obtained eight wickets at a small cost.

Stroud Road Primitive Methodists v. Wagon Works II

Played at Hempsted.

Methodists win by an innings and one run. The Works could do little against the bowling of Mansell and Wall, the former taking four wickets for 10 runs, and Wall six wickets for 5, and were all out for 16. The Methodists replied with 52 (Wall 14, Prior 10). Batting a second time, the Works were dismissed for 35 (H Barnard 13). The Rev. W Shaw obtained 5 wickets for 10 runs and Mansell three for 11. For the losers, Dudfield and Taylor shared the wickets.

15thAugust - Wagon Works v. Wycliffe College

Played at Hempsted and resulting in a good win for the College.

Scores: Works 71 Wycliffe 92 for three wickets.

Wycliffe, on winning the toss, put the Works into bat, but they could only run up the total of 71. These were soon made by Wycliffe when they went out to bat and, at the call of time, the visitors had totalled 90 for three wickets. For the Works E B Evans (14), L V Huggins (14) and A Carter (11) were the only ones to reach double figures, while for the College Mr Evans 50 Not Out and J Lawson 20 Not Out batted excellently. Mr Evans also bowled well, obtaining seven of the Works wickets at a small cost.

Wagon Works 'A' v. Hartpury House

Played at Hartpury.

Scores: Works 45 Hartpury 21

For the Works, G F Dere (three for 5) and W Sargent (seven for 15) bowled well and A Speck (15 Not Out) and C Brown (10) did best with the bat.

22nd August - Fine Bowling By A Whiley

The Wagon Works easily defeated Apperley Court at Apperley. The Works batting first ran up a respectable total of 107, (A Carter 36, T Skipp 22 and J Boucher 17). Apperley replied with 40, the Works thus winning by 67 runs. None of the home batsmen reached double figures being all 'at sea' with the deliveries of A Whiley, who obtained the remarkable analysis of nine wickets for 12 runs. W Margrett and H Ball were the most successful bowlers for the losers.

29th August - Post Office and Wagon Works Draw

These old and keen opponents met on Budding's Field. The Post Office batting first ran up a total of 101 to which L T Barnes contributed 27, E T Huggins 21 and G Clutterbuck 15. The two first named carried the score from 2 to 60 before they were separated and batted in excellent style for their runs, each making some big hits.

G Clutterbuck got quickly to work and after scoring a 2, 3, 4 and 6, unluckily trod on his wicket.

The Wagon Works made a bad start losing five wickets for 28 when J Banks came to the rescue and played an excellent innings of 34 and saved the game for his side. Perkins was the best bowler for the Wagon Works while G Clutterbuck (six for 27) was the best bowler for the Post Office.

Scores: Post Office 101 Works 74 for nine.

1909

Saturday 1st May - League and Wagon Works Draw

Wagon Works v Gordon League was played at Hempsted. Scores: Wagon Works 124; Gordon League 91 for 4 wickets. The Wagon Works Club had prepared a splendid wicket for this match and going in first to bat found run getting fairly easy on such a good pitch. L Huggins (31) A Carter (23) J Boucher (20) L Vears (17) all batted very well. H Ellis bowled extremely well taking 6 wickets for 43 runs. The League found that runs were not so easy to find, G Brookes (21 not out) L Barnard (11) G Bourne (10) H Ellis (10) and J Welshman (12 not out) their top scorers.

Saturday 15th May - Wagon Works Successful

Wagon Works v Barnwood House was played at Barnwood. Works 123; Barnwood House 88.

Mr Field (26) and A Whiley (19) were the only players to find form for Barnwood House and once these had departed the House collapsed for 88.

The Works were never in any real danger and the runs required were hit off for the loss of 8 wickets. L V Huggins again showed good form, his 51 being a valuable one. J Banks (20) and W J Robinson (17) also batted well for the winners. H Perkins (5 for 26) and W Sargent (5 for 16) bowled well (the latter having all the runs hit from him before obtaining a wicket). Court (the ex-city professional) five, Bibby three and Whiley two shared the wickets for the House.

A Fine Sporting Finish

Primitive Methodists 109   Wagon Works 'A' 104

A very keen and pleasant game with a fine sporting finish. For the winners, useful scores were contributed by J Parsons (23), Price (21), Coggins (12) and Wall (10). For the Works, Sargent gave a fine exhibition of fierce driving and had hard lines in being out to a splendid catch by Ridel at point with the last ball of the match for a well hit 54. Ratcliffe (11) was the other chief scorer.

Allan (4 wickets for 15) and Wall (3 for 23) bowled well for Primitive while Sargent and Dere shared the wickets for the Works.

Saturday 12th June Wagon Works' Splendid Win

The Works obtained a good win by defeating Lydney at Lydney by 13 runs. Batting first the Works did none too well at the start, but with W Sargent (29), W J Robinson (15) and L V Huggins (11), they managed to reach 75. The home team expected to easily knock the runs off, but so well did H Perkins (6 for 22) and A Carter (2 for 10) bowl that they were dismissed for 62, Vick (12) being the only batsman to reach double figures. *H Jones (5 wickets) for a small cost was the most successful bowler for the home team.

*H Jones played one match for the County.

Midlands Narrow Victory

Midland Railway v Wagon Works 'A' was played at Hempsted. Scores: Midlands 59 Wagon Works 53. For the Midlands, W S Daniel scored 32 and A Hudson 10, and R Ellis bowled well taking seven wickets for 17. Sam Roberts (15) batted in good form for the losers, and the veterans Dere, Restall and Brown each took three wickets.

Saturday 3rd July

Wagon Works' Comfortable Win

The Wagon Works obtained their sixth victory of the season by defeating the County Asylum at Wotton. The Asylum batting first could do very little with the bowling of W Sargent (6 for 26) and H Perkins (3 for 12) and were all dismissed for 43. Spiller (11) and Marnam (10) were the only double figure scorers. The visitors obtained the runs necessary to win with 5 wickets in hand, and eventually ran up a total of 95, L Vears (20) W Vickery (15) A Carter (17) and L V Huggins (14). Letts (4 for 31) and Foster (3 for 17) were the most successful bowlers for the Asylum.

Saturday 23rd August

Wagon Works v. Nondescripts

Played at Hempsted. Scores; Works 45 Nondescripts 143. Winning the toss and batting first, the Works could do little against the bowling of W Egerton (6 for 26) and J P Barrett (4 for 11), only L V Huggins (15 not out) reaching double figures. The Nondescripts lost two wickets for 11 runs but E Davey and J P Barrett greatly improved matters and made the game safe. A long partnership between W Egerton and B Huntley added 80 runs, and then H Perkins, going on to bowl again met with success, taking altogether 8 wickets from 39 runs. The Nondescripts totalled 143 (W Egerton 44, B Huntley 37, E F Davey 21, P Barrett 10) winning easily by 98 runs.

A Match between Wagon Works 'A' and Hempsted was played at Hempsted, Scores; Wagon Works 'A' 61 (Restall 12, Turner 12). Hempsted 41 (Ford 24 not out, Hieron 8). The wickets were taken for the Works by W Burton, Dere and Hamblin, and, for Hempsted, Ford took 5 wickets for a small cost. The Rev Sinclair kindly entertained the visitors to tea.

Saturday 4th September

Wagon Works defeat Lydney

The Works obtained their second victory over Lydney this season by defeating them at Hempsted. On a pitch damaged by rain, the home team did well to compile a total of 93. W Vicary (27), G Brookes (23) and L Hamblin (18) batted well. Lydney started none too well, but a stand by the 5th wicket came in very useful and tails were up by the fall of the seventh wicket. The remainder did very little, however, and the innings finished on 75.

The Works thus won a keen, but well contested game by 18 runs. For Lydney, A E Vick (19), H Bowen (18) and G L Jones (10) were the principal scorers, while H Jones, W Jones and Grey (two each) shared the wickets. For the Works, H Perkins had 7 for 27.

Works in Form

Wagon Works 'A' v King's Stanley was played at King's Stanley.
Scores: Wagon Works 'A' 74 for 2 King's Stanley 56

For the Works, Restall (32) and Radcliffe (24). For King's Stanley, King (16) and Trigg (13) did well with the bat. The wickets were taken for the Works by Dere (5 for 26), W Burlton (1 for 14) and Roberts (1 for 7).

1910

Saturday 21st May

Wagon Works v Lydney

Wagon Works 108 Lydney 100 for 9 wickets at Hempsted. C Prior (50), T Jones (21) and R Radclyffe (11) were the main scorers for the Works. Lydney with 1½ hours to play, also scored well, and at the call of time were within eight runs of the home team's total with one wicket to fall. H Bowen (25), H Jones (25), D Grey (13) and J L Davis (10) were the top scorers for Lydney. H Jones also bowled well. A Carter (4 for 17) was the most successful bowler for the Works.

Wagon Works 'A' Win a Good Game

Lydney II 43; Wagon Works 'A' 69 at Lydney.
Both sides were well represented. S Roberts (13) and F Skipp (11) were the top scorers for the Works, while A Burlton (3 wickets for 8) and S Roberts (5 for 17) bowled well. Strike (15) was the top scorer for Lydney.

Saturday 11thJune

Wagon Works Draw with Wycliffe

Wagon Works 120 Wycliffe College 60 for 4 wickets, at Stonehouse. The Works batted first on a slow wicket and did well to obtain 120 runs. Wycliffe had about 80 minutes batting, but did not force the game, time being called at 6 o'clock. For the Works, L V Huggins (49), T Jones (26), J Banks (18), and L Hamblin (13) batted well, while W A Sibly (19 not out) and Perkins (11) did best for the College. Of the bowlers, Evans (5 for 27) and Perkins (4 for 36) obtained the Works' wickets. Sargent (2), Carter, and Roberts (1 each) did best for the visitors.

Sam Roberts at the club's Hempsted ground , 1910

Wagon Works 'A' Win Comfortably

Albert Mills (40), Wagon Works 'A' 101 at Hempsted.
Some good cricket was seen on a bad wicket. For the Works, T Skipp took seven wickets for 14 runs including the "hat trick". S Radclyffe (33) and F Proctor (23) batted well. G Smith (14) was top scorer for the Mills.

Y.M.C.A 52; Wagon Works II 38

At Hempsted for the Y.M, J Davis was top scorer with 10. R Eagles (6 wickets) and A Peglar (4 wickets) bowled well. W Clapton (10) and S Clapton (10 not out) did best for the Works. F Mansell did the damage for the Y.M.C.A, taking seven wickets for 21 runs.

Saturday 20th August - Wagon Works Teams All Win

Wagon Works v County Asylum was played at Wotton. Scores; Works 112 for 9 Asylum 32. The Works won the toss, but put the home team into bat. They were soon disposed of for the small total of 32, Dr Foster (20 not out) being the only batsman to show any form. The Wagon Works easily obtained the runs necessary to win and at the call of time had passed the century. H Perkins (27 not out), T Butler (18), C Prior (15), J Boucher (24) and G Brookes (14) being the principal run getters. For the Works, L A Hamblin (5 wickets for 11) and H Perkins (5 for 14) bowled well. While Hodgson (7 for 48) including the "Hat trick" did well for the Asylum. (9) was top scorer for the Court.

1911 - 1920

1911 continued in the same vein as previous years, but the fixture list was strengthening, if only slowly. The Club began playing further afield - Stroud, Lydney, Tewkesbury, Dursley and Sharpness to name but a few of the new venues.

The batting department during this time was in the hands of L Hamblin, L V Huggins, G Page and W Sargent, while the bowling was led by G F Dere, W Burlton, Harry Perkins and J Welshman.

The outbreak of war in 1914 was to curtail first class cricket for the duration, although some local matches were played, usually between companies supporting the war effort. These matches gave employees a break from the stresses of war and helped to raise both funds and morale.

The war in some ways helped the Wagon Works Club. The company sub-let the Spa Ground from the City Club in 1914 and continued to use the facilities until the end of hostilities. The decision was to see the end of the home fixtures at the Hempsted Ground because, in April 1918, the company purchased 33 acres of land in Tuffley Avenue from the Estate of Colonel Collett, a local businessman whose son played for both the City and County. This land was purchased for a little over £4000 and the following years were to see many changes, including bringing first class cricket to the Wagon Works Ground.

Thanks to the influence of a Mr John Parsons, ex-soldier John Brayshaw was given the job of converting these fields into a complete sports ground. In a pony and trap provided by the company, Brayshaw travelled the county to obtain materials for the new ground. With the help of Arthur Paish, a professional at the City Club and club member Harry Perkins, the clubhouse and pavilion were erected, the pair having been jointly purchased for £400.

During the early 1920s John Brayshaw returned to his hometown of Morcambe and sadly died in 1970. In 1919 Arthur Paish, a former veteran of 79 County appearances, was taken on as full time groundsman, a job he continued until his retirement in 1947. 1919 was also the year that 19 year-old Tom Goddard first played for the club. He was introduced by Harry Perkins, the two having worked together in the Bristol Road factory. It is also interesting to note that in 1914, a new addition to the company's board of directors was Mr Stanley Baldwin who, of course, was later to become Prime Minister.

1911

Saturday 13th May - Gordon League v. Wagon Works

Gordon League opened their season with a match against the Wagon Works and, after a good game, won by 35 runs. The Works batted first and were all dismissed for 60. G Brooks (16), H Perkins (12) and J Jones (11) were the chief scorers, on the League going into bat. So well did the Works bowl that they had five wickets down for 20 runs. J Welshman (24) and W Vinson (17) then made a capital stand, scoring 27 for the next wicket before the latter fell to a good catch by Hambling. H Ellis then quickly got 29 by clean hitting, the innings closing for 95.   F Mansell (five wickets for 20) and J Welshman (three for 3) were the best bowlers for the League, whilst W Sargent (five for 19) did best for the Works. The fielding of both sides was good, several good catches being brought off.

Saturday 20th May - Wagon Works Beat Eastington

The Wagon Works met and defeated Eastington at Hempsted. Batting first, the Works ran up the respectable total of 84. L Hamblin (21), W Sargent (17) and S Roberts (14) were the principal scorers. Eastington replied with 54, thus being defeated by 30 runs. W Capel (10) was the only batsman to reach double figures. H Perkins (five for 13) and L Hamblin (three for 5) bowled well for the home team, while P Tudor (four for 30) and C Capec (three for 30) did best for Eastington.

G F DERE'S HAT-TRICK

Wagon Works A v. Upton was played at Upton.

Scores: Works A - 52   Upton - 27

Upton won the toss and batted first, but could make little headway before the grand bowling of G F Dere (six for 18, including the hat-trick) and W Burlton (four for 7), only F Chubb (14) batting well. The Works started badly but thanks to the batting of G Brown (15 not out) and G F Dere (9), they reached the score of 52. S Millard took six wickets for Upton.

Saturday 10th June - Wagon Works 156 for Six Wickets declared

(L V Huggins 52 not out, G Page 37, W Sargent 13, S Roberts 13 not out). County Asylum 69 for nine wickets (Spiller 19, E G Palin 12). H Perkins six for 24 and T Jones two for 10 bowled well for the Works, whilst Hodgson 4 for 43 bowled best for the Asylum.

All Saints 172 (Platt 68 not out, Philpotts 30, Adams 21). Wagon Works II 33 (Philpotts five for 15, Beard four for 18)

Huntley 118 for 5 wickets (H Poyner 50, S Humpherson 41). Wagon Works A 65 (F Skipp 26), J Moon four wickets for 12, S Bray three of 6.

Saturday 29th July - Wagon Works 85 for Nine Wickets declared Lydney 34 for 2 Wickets

Rain greatly interfered with play. For the Works, G Brookes (31), C Brown (18) and A Carter (11) did best with the bat, whilst J L Davis (17 Not Out) did best for the home team. I Gray (3 for 17), W Jones (three for 9), H Jones (three for 2) and H Perkins (two for 13) did the bowling for their respective sides.

1912

Saturday 11th May - Gloucester Wagon Works 101, Butter-Row 26

<u>At Hempsted </u>- The Works opened the season easily defeating the Stroud League Champions. For the Works, L V Huggings (32), G Brookes (18), L Hamblin (13), F Turner (10) and T Burden (13 Not Out) were the principal run getters. The visitors could do little with the bowling of H Perkins (seven wickets for 9) and T Jones (three wickets for 12). M Ayres (seven for 19) was the most successful bowler for Butter-Row.

<u>Gloucester Wagon Works 'A' 150</u> - (P Speck 39, W Moore 37 Not Out, G Griffin 24, C Restall 13, G Dere 11)

All Saints 31 on the Town Ham

R Dere (five wickets for 18 runs) and W Moore (four for 9) bowled well for the winners.

On the 15th April 1912 Disaster Struck the Titanic. The following was reported in the Citizen on Saturday 11th May. *That the fund opened by the Lord Mayor of London on the night of May 11th had already amounted to £250,000. Also that 100 guineas had been collected amongst passengers of the Titanic's sister ship, 'The Olympic', on her last voyage.*

Saturday 27th July - Wagon Works 121 for Five Wickets Declared

(H Perkins 47, E Adams 41 and G Turner 20)

Cinderford White Rose 27, H Perkins took seven wickets for 5 runs and W Sargent three for 15. John Buffry (3 for 36) and E Buffry (2 for 5) were the most successful with the ball for the losers.

(A M Mills 48, E Brindle 1, A J Thomas 14)

Wagon Works A 95 for 8 wickets (L Hamblin 34, P Davis 26, A Long 12 Not Out and W Moore 10 Not Out).
L Hamblin bowled well for the Works, taking 5 wickets for 6 runs.

1913

Saturday 31st May - Gloucester Wagon Works v. Dursley

Dursley 100 for 8 (H Berkley 16, W Harris 17, W A Smith 22, Atkin 13) For the Works, T Jones took 4 for 25.

Wagon Works 58 for 4 rain stopped play (C Prior 20, A Whiley 17, S Roberts 9 Not Out)

Gloucester Wagon Works 'A' v. Huntley

Played at Huntley.

Huntley 60 (C Restall 7 for 20, G F Dere 2 wickets for the Works). Wagon Works 'A' 67 (Restall 39) Mr F Jones took 6 for 14 for Huntley.

Saturday 26th July - Wycliffe College v. Gloucester Wagon Works

Wycliffe College 157 for 8 (I Godfrey 13, T M Sibley 33, W Thomas 14, J S Evans 48)

Wagon Works 41 for 6 (C Prior Not Out 13, E Ruck 19) For the Works, H Perkins with 4 for 55 was the most successful bowler.

Saturday 1st August - Gloucester Wagon Works v. Sharpness

Played at Sharpness

Gloucester Wagon Works 107

For the Works, W Sargent Not Out 28, E Adams 27, G Turner 14 batted well.

Sharpness 85 (O T Shurman 25, G W Smith 11) For the Works, Welshman took 8 for 37.

Saturday 9th August - Gloucester All Saints v. Gloucester Wagon Works

Played at Hempsted.

All Saints 48 (A Bayliss 10, H Hughes 12 Not Out).

Wagon Works 98 (C Prior 15, E Ruck 33, J Boucher 15).

Bowling for the All Saints, Hayes took 6 for 45 and Shepherd 2 for 5. For the Works, H Perkins bowled well taking 7 for 14 including the 'Hat Trick'. Also Sargent 1 for 15 and Roberts 1 for 11 did well.

1914

Saturday 2nd May - Wagon Works 106, Gloucester A 39

Played at Hempsted, the principal run getters for the Works were H Perkins (22), W Sargent (20), C Prior (15), L Hamblin (11) and T Jones (16 Not Out), while H Perkins (five for 14) and W George (four for 17) also bowled well. J L Woolley (six for 30) and Dr Creese (two for 23) did best for Gloucester A.

Longhope 68 - Wagon Works A 60 - Played at Longhope

For the home team, E Constance (20) and H Hall (16) played well, and E Constance (six wickets for 14) did best with the ball. For the Wagon Works, G Turner (17), H Salt (12) and W Brown (10 not out) were the most successful.

Saturday 13th June - Branwood House 74, Wagon Works 120 for Eight Wickets

Played at Barnwood. For the Works, W Burlton obtained seven wickets for 16. Burlton (36), C Prior (14) W Sargent (14), S Roberts (18 not out) and T Jones (10 not out) batted well for the winners.

Wagon Works A, 88 (W Holland 24 and W Pegler 20) Hartpury House 45 (R Sysum 26 not out) for the Works, W Pegler (seven wickets for 12) and W Brown (two wickets for 12) bowled well.

Saturday 4th July

Wagon Works gained their seventh victory of the season by defeating All Saints (Cheltenham) at Hempsted. Batting first, the Works made 90 (L Hamblin 28 not out), H Perkins (25), W Sargent (13). All Saints replied with 41 H Bayliss (13 not out), Kilminster (three for 15) and Eden (two for 15) did best with the ball for the visitors, while W Burlton (seven for 14) and H Perkins (three for 15) bowled unchanged for the Works.

All Saints II (Cheltenham) 63 (E Herbert 14, E Chuffe 12)

Wagon Works A 129 for Eight Wickets (J Banks 70 not out), L Price 20 and H Head (13 not out) for the Works, W Brown took eight wickets for 29 runs.

1915

With the outbreak of war a year earlier, the conflict in France was taking its toll on the country with most sporting events being cancelled due to men enlisting in the armed forces. The City clubs' fixtures were cancelled and, because the GRC & Wagon Works Co. was engaged in the war effort manufacturing wagons and munitions, the company sub-let the Spa Ground for certain fixtures for the duration of the war.

Men, of course, were enlisting to fight for their country, but it was soon discovered that perhaps it would have been wiser for some to remain as so many skilled workers were being lost from manufacturing industries. The GRC & Wagon CO was no exception and the following article was placed in the Gloucester Journal.

Wagon Works' Night Gang At The Front

A correspondent has handed to us for reproduction a photographic group which is of special interest at the present time, having regard to the need for munitions workers and the complaint that so many skilled men were, in the early months of the war, induced to enlist, whereas their services would have been so much better employed on war works. The group comprises of what was a complete night gang at the Wagon Works, and all but one are now serving in the 1/5th Gloucesters.

In this old Newspaper cutting from left to right are:
Standing: Lce-Corp. J Perris, Sergt. Proctor, Sergt. J Mutloe and Lce-Corpl. Wakefield.
Kneeling: Pte. H Jones and Pte F Barnard.

1916

There are no reports of matches that were played by the works side on the Spa Ground during 1916. All reports were of the war effort, although some games were played. The club unfortunately has no records of these.

An interesting article appeared in The Citizen during the summer of 1916. In a letter to his parents, a Mr Watts of the 1/5th Gloucesters wrote:

The people at home will be pleased to hear that we can find time during our four days from the trenches to indulge in a little sport. On Thursday afternoon a cricket match was arranged and played between A and D companies. Of course the pitch was not "first class", but a very enjoyable and interesting game was the result. It was a rather novel game, for in the next field there was a battery of artillery blazing away. The game had been in progress for about ten minutes when the Germans began shelling a small village not a quarter of a mile away, yet the game proceeded as if it was being played on the Spa at home. The finish was very exciting and everyone enjoyed the afternoon's change. The kit used had kindly been sent out by friends in Gloucester, a gift that was much appreciated.

SCORES: A company 72 all out,   D company 52 all out.

The A company included Capt. G.F Collett and Capt. H.C.B Sessions from the city club and it seems very likely that one or two players were from the Wagon Works team.

1918

1914 - 1918 Wagon Works Sub-Let the Spa from Gloucester

Saturday 8th June

Rodborough visited The Spa to play The Wagon Works 1st Team and won a good game by 30 runs. Rodborough batted first and compiled 76 (W Dredge 17, W Elderkin 16 and W Lusher 11). The Works started disastrously, losing 4 wickets for 6 runs, but Brown (25) improved matters. Redston (5 for 19) and W Elderkin (5 for 26) bowled splendidly for Rodborough and Whiley (6 wickets) did best for the losers. This is The Works' first defeat.

Railway Carriage and Wagon Co Ltd Cricket Club 1918

G F Dere (umpire) L V Huggins H H Turner A Elliot J Watkins GTurner J Banks L Smith (scorer)
R Roberta P Bloodworth A Whiley C Brown (captain) J MacGregor (president) H Perkins H Bamard
H Wheatley L Price (sec) front row A Paish S Roberts

1919

Saturday 3rd May

Wagon Works 1st XI 121 for 5 (A Paish 59 not out, F Cresswell 24 not out, H E Perkins)

Sunningend 1st XI 68 (H Wixey 17 not out) Best bowling figures; H E Perkins (6 for 25) for the Works. Wagon Works won by 53 runs at Tuffley.

Wagon Works 'A' 120 (P Speck 37, J Gwinnet, S Roberts, G Smith 11)

Sunningend II 58 (A Bayliss 15, A Prince 14 not out), Best bowling figures; W Berriman (6 wickets for 15), L Whiley (3 for 13) for the Works; and D Hardy (4 wickets) for Sunningend at Cheltenham.

Wagon Works 'B' Team 48 (Winston 15, Crowther 12.

The Templars Cheltenham 57 (W Brown 10 not out, A Stubbs 10). Templars won by 9 runs. Best bowling figures; Eagles 6 for 17, H Wheatley, 3 for 14 for the Works at Cheltenham.

Saturday 17th May

Wagon Works 'A' 144 (L Whiley 34, J Gwinnet 32, F Skipp 28 not out, W Peglar 12)

Bradley Court 69 (R E Abbot 14, Hodson 12) A Burlton 4 for 36, W Berriman 3 for 14, T Skipp 2 for 3 bowled well for the Works. Macado took 6 wickets for Bradley Court. Match played at Bradley Court, the Works won by 75 runs.

Saturday 21st June

Wagon Works1st XI 166 for 7 Dec' (P Speck 45, W Brown 22, P Bloodworth 22, L Hamblin 16, H Turner 16, H E Perkins 12 not out)

Cheltenham 'A' 69 (R Elmes 11, A E Trigg 10). Best bowling was H E Perkins (5 for 26) for the Wagon Works. Match played at Tuffley, the Works winning by 97 runs.

Wagon Works 'A' 81 (T Skipp 25, A Burlton 11, T Burden 16, C Sysum 10 not out)

Cinderford 56 (G Phelps 13, O Phelps 12, J Hall 11). For the Works, R Eagles (8 for 20) bowled well.

Wagon Works 'B' 65 (W Melling 26, F W Proctor 17)

Cinderford White Rose 65 (W Morgan 10, W Buffry 11), at Cinderford, match ending in a tie.

Saturday 28th June

Bradley Court 173 (R Abbot 88, J Welman 50)
Wagon Works 'A' 187 for 6 (T Burden 78 not out, J Gwinnet 31, C Sysum 26)
Sysum for the Works taking 7 for 28, played at Tuffley Avenue.

Saturday 5th July

Wagon Works 1st XI 178 (W Sargent 45 not out, A Paish 25, G Turner 23, H H Turner 21, H E Perkins 16, W Brown 13)

Sunningend Works 110 (Brinmore 16, Bellamy 41). For the Works, W Sargent (6 for 35) and H Perkins (4 for 17) bowled well, Bellamy for Sunningend took all 10 wickets.

Saturday 26th July - Wagon Works' Fine Win!!

At Tuffley Avenue

The Works recorded a fine victory over Ross by 216 runs. The visitors collapsed completely before the bowling of H Perkins and W Sargent, the whole side being out for 29 (H West 10). Seven of the team failed to score. The bowlers' analyses are worthy of reproduction.

H Perkins	4 overs	1 maiden	10 runs	6 wickets
W Sargent	3 overs	0 maiden	12 runs	4 wickets

The Works made light work of the target and passed the Ross total for the loss of 2 wickets. When stumps were drawn, the Works had scored 245 for 9 (Hamblin71 with ten 4s) Paish (52 with eight 4s) and Perkins (56 not out, seven 4s).

Saturday 16th August

Wagon Works 1st XI 180 for 6 (L Hamblin 67, H E Perkins 44)

Barnwood House 155 for 8 declared (Wooley 52, Hayward 21 not out). For the Works, H Perkins (4 for 49) bowled well, the Works won by 4 wickets and 25 runs, played at Barnwood.

Saturday 23rd August

Gloucester Wagon Works 75 (G Turner 22, A Paish 12)

Cheltenham 'A' 86 (J Brain 33 not out). Match played on the Victoria Ground, Cheltenham.

On this day Lord George Hamilton, President of Kent C.C.C, unveiled a fountain that had been erected on the St Lawrence Ground, Canterbury, in memory of the members of the Kent Cricket Team who fell during the war.

Saturday 30th August - Wagon Works' Good Performance

Gloucester Wagon Works completed a pronounced victory over the Bristol Carriage and Wagon Co. at Tuffley Avenue by 162 runs. Batting first, the home side reached a total of 194 for 9 wickets, when the innings was closed (G Turner 43, L Hamblin 35, A Paish 31, W Sargent 21, W Brown 15, H Perkins 16, T Burden 13.) The Bristol team completely collapsed before the bowling of Perkins (6 for 28) and W Sargent (4 for 14). Perkins took his first five wickets for 2 runs.

Wagon Works 'A' 60 (W Peglar 19, T Skipp 14).Northgate 68 (R Beard 20 not out) For Northgate, H Clissold took 7 for 12 runs and, for the Works, A Burlton took 3 for 12. Match played at Sandhurst.

Saturday 13th September

Wagon Works 186 for 6 declared (H E Perkins 99, T Burden 40, and S J Roberts 24)

Gloucester 'A' 76 for 4 (Dr Cress 25 not out, W Barnett 17 and Bretherton 13) Match drawn.
On this day Alf Dipper, playing for Gloucester City 1st, XI made 102 not out. This gave him a final aggregate for the season of 915 runs from 13 innings, 7 not outs, at an average of 152.5.

WAGON WORKS' SPORTS CLUB

CRICKET SECTION

The following are the averages for the past season. Prizes were awarded by Mr and Mrs McGregor to players who had played in 75% of their respective team's matches and obtained the highest number of points. These were awarded to: Messrs H E Perkins, L A Hamblin, J T Skipp, C H Sysum, R G Eagles, W Mellins and G V R Stanley.

FIRST TEAM AVERAGES

BATTING

	No of Inn	Times not out	Highest score	Total runs	Avg
Batting					
A Paish	15	3	83	402	33.50
H E Perkins	14	2	99	338	23.16
L A Hamblin	16	0	71	304	19.00
W Sargent	11	1	45*	149	14.90
P W Speck	13	2	45	142	12.90
C E Brown	12	8	30*	112	12.44
W A Brown	15	3	22	134	11.16
G A Turner	14	0	43	154	11.00
P Bloodworth	15	1	22	113	8.07
H H Turner	11	3	21	63	7.87

BOWLING

	Runs	Wickets	Avg
H E Perkins	364	60	6.06
W Sargent	352	49	7.18
P Bloodworth	94	12	7.69
H H Turner	134	17	7.88

Seventeen matches were played of which 11 were won, 2 drawn and 4 lost. The victories were as follows: - Sunningend (2), Rodborough Dean Close, Ross, Wycliffe College, Bristol Wagon Co.' (2), Cheltenham 'A', Dursley, Barnwood House. The two drawn games were with Ross and Gloucester A, whilst defeat was suffered from A.O.D., Rodborough, Cheltenham A and Dursley.

1920 – 1929

The Twenties were to be much like cricket in general for the Works' team, a 'Golden Age' that was to see many improvements - a new ground, an improved fixture list, a number of new players and, in 1923, the introduction of County Cricket with Lancashire being the first visitors.

The players to make their mark at the club were ex-county players Arthur Paish, Tom Goddard (when county duties allowed) and the brothers, Harold and Eddie Proctor. Also to the fore were Bert Watkins, a wicket keeper who was later to play for the County and Leslie Smith, a fine opening bat, who was later to become President of the club. Others were Albert Hopcroft, a fine wicket keeper and batsman who was to have a county trial in 1928 and EJ (Dick) Stephens who was to play 216 matches for Gloucestershire in the not-too-distant future.

By 1927 the Works' team was able to field the brothers Jim and Frank Stephens, who, over the next 30 years, were to become great stalwarts of the club - Jim an all rounder and Frank, an excellent opening bowler and no mean bat. In later years, Jim was to become chairman and president of the club and Frank, a quiet man, assistant groundsman. The start of county cricket in 1923 brought many stars to the ground, one being the legendary Jack Hobbs who played there in 1925 for Surrey, scoring 52 and 3 not out and Harold Larwood who, in 1928, scored his second highest first class score of 101 not out for Nottinghamshire v. Gloucestershire, and also unusually bowled 25 overs for 52 runs without taking a wicket.

Gloucestershire also played Essex in 1925, C.W.L. Parker taking 9 for 44 and 8 for 12 in the game.
The Wagon Works' fixture list really began to expand, the team taking on the city team's first eleven in addition to Hereford, Cheltenham, Worcester and Ross to good effect. The facilities at the ground in Tuffley Avenue were likewise being improved. The 1920 recession enabled the Works' employees to build an eight-foot wall along the Avenue end – this project was carried out due to the foresight of the Works' Manager, J McGregor. Many of the Works' coal wagons were not sold, but hired to companies instead - the income generated from this enabling the company to stay solvent over a difficult period.

It can be noted that when the county moved its fixtures away from the Spa Ground in 1923, George Romans of the city club, who had played for the Works at the turn of the century, resigned from the county committee in disgust at the decision.

In 1927, Albert Hopcroft took over the captaincy from H Brown, who had captained the club for the previous three seasons. This decision was to be significant in the club's history as he was to captain the first eleven for a record sixteen seasons. In 1925 the club side, as you will see, lost only two of its twenty matches and in 1926, this was improved to only one loss in eighteen outings, Hopcroft distinguishing himself with a batting average of thirty-five. Hopcroft's early success at club level led to his selection for the Gloucestershire club and ground to play Monmouthshire at Newport in 1928.

The following match reports refer to E J (Dick) Stephens as E J Stephens and his relative, E J Stephens as J or Jim, as he was more commonly known.

1920

Saturday 8th May - Wagon Works 1st X1 99 v. Gloucester A X1 49

Played at Tuffley Avenue
Wagon Works 1st X1 99 (W Sargent 23, T W J Goddard Not Out 19, H E Perkins 12). Gloucester A X1 49 (Barnes 13, Fowler 10). H E Perkins 6 for 20, for the Works and Weare, for Gloucester, bowled well.

Wagon Works A X1 15 v. Tuffley & Whaddon 13

Eagles (4 for 3) and Sysum (5 for 9) bowled effectively for the Works, as did Long (4 wickets) for Tuffley & Whaddon.

Wagon Works B X1 29 v. Cam 35

Played at Cam. Cox for Cam and Berryman for the Works bowled well.

Saturday 5th June - Wagon Works 1st X1 102 v. Wye Valley 87

Played at Hereford.

For the Works, (Paish 24, T Burdon 21, H Perkins 15, W Sargent 14) were the highest scorers and H Perkins (6 for 22) and P Bloodworth (4 for 22) bowled well for the winners. For Wye Valley, Dowers 28 and Mashford batted well.

Saturday 22nd July -Wagon Works 1st X1 v. Ross 1st X1

The Wagon Works played their return match with Ross at Tuffley Avenue on Saturday, the game resulting in an easy victory for the Works. Batting first, Ross were dismissed for 90 (H West 20, G Hone 16, H J Packer 14). The Works were 98 for 5 when time was called. P Bloodworth 38 Not Out, W Sargent 14 Not Out, R Burden 11 and Extras 16 were the highest contributors. With the ball, C Brown (3 for 27), R Eagles (2 for 9), W Sargent (3 for 33) and P Bloodworth (2 for 27) all did well.

Wagon Works A X1 85 v. Bradley Court 38

C Sysum 7 for 20 bowled extremely well, and also with the bat, contributing 39 runs for the Works' side assisted by C Merrett with 21.

Wagon Works A X1 61 v. Old Patesians 33

For the Works, T Skipp 17, L Smith 13, R Eagles 11 did well with the bat, as did O Bloodwood 10 for Old Patesians. Sysum for the Works took 8 for 14, including 4 wickets in successive balls. Match played at the Works' Ground.

Wagon Works B X1 v. Cinderford White Rose

For the Works, (Guy 22 and Beniman 10) batted well and, with the ball, (Beniman 6 for 23 and Shellswell 4 for 9) did well.

Wagon Works Juniors 59 v. 1/5th Gloucester Juniors 48

Played at the Works, C Taylor 17 and W Clark 13 and Proctor 6 for 23 did well for the Works.

1921

Whit - Monday 16th May - Gloucester Wagon Works 45 - Bristol Avonside 48

Played on the Works Sports Ground.

For the Works, P Bloodworth (22), L Smith (12) batted well and H E Perkins took 7 for 13 runs. For Avonside, H Groves (14) and H Smith (5 wickets for 23) did best.

Saturday 21st May - Gloucester Wagon Works 1st XI 127 - Cheltenham 'A' 28

Played at Cheltenham.

For the Works, A Paish (51), W Sargent (35) and P Bloodworth (15) were the principal scorers, while Percy Bloodworth who took 7 wickets for 6 runs (including the 'Hat Trick') was practically unplayable. For Cheltenham, T Deavall took 8 wickets for 28 runs.

Saturday 11th June - Gloucester Wagon Works 97 - Gloucester Nondescripts 59

Played on the Works Sports Ground.

Batting first, The Nondescripts could do little with the Works' bowling and were dismissed for the small total of 59. (G Collingbourne 15 and T Hall 13 Not Out). The Works obtained the necessary runs to win for the loss of 5 wickets. A Paish (25 not out), L Hamblin (20), W Morris (16) and H Brown (10) did well for the winners. H E Perkins (7 wickets for 14) and S Roberts (3 for 42) bowled unchanged for the home team.

Wagon Works 'B' Team 56 - Wycliffe College II 31

Played at the Works Sports Ground. For the Works, L Price (17), W Trigg (11) and R Sheliswell (10) batted well and R Sheliswell (4 wickets) bowled well.

Saturday 23rd July - Wagon Works 204 for 8 Declared - Gloucester II 65

Played on the Works Sports Ground.

For the winners, A Paish (54 not out), T Burden (49), L Whiley (29), T Goddard (19), H E Perkins (14) batted well, while H E Perkins (7 wickets for 30) and T Goddard (3 for 29 were in good form with the ball. For Gloucester II, C F Crooms, H Colwell and H A Gardner were the principal scorers.

Wagon Works 'B' Team 112 - 2nd County Asylum 89

Played at Coney Hill. For the Works, W Trigg (37), F Proctor (15), S Roberts (14), L Watkins (12), F Merrett (12 not out) all batted well and W Berriman (8 wickets for 20 runs) was the most successful bowler.

Saturday 30th July - Gas Works Cheltenham 110 - Wagon Works 'A' Team 90

There is no recorded fixture for the Wagon Works' 1st team on this date but The Citizen reported that Arthur Paish played for the City Club in a match against Cheltenham. In that game, George Romans, the ex Wagon Works player scored 13 and eighteen-year-old Wally Hammond opened the batting, though being dismissed for only 3.

Wagon Works 'A' Team 143- Bradley Court 45

Played at the Works Sports Ground.

For the Works, W Morris (27, C Merrett (20), H Hanman (17), L Smith (15), G Turner (13), A Carter (11), R Eagles (14 not out) batted well, while A Carter (5 wickets for 18) was the most successful bowler.

Wagon Works 'B' 92 - Huntley 55

Played at the Works Sports Ground.
For the Works, E L Blackford (21), A Watkins (15), S Roberts (12) E Brown (10) batted well and W Berriman took 8 wickets for 28.

Saturday 3rd September - Wagon Works 92 for 6 wickets – Metropolitan Works (Saltley) 25
Played at Saltley.

For the winners, A Paish (38 not out), W A Brown (12 not out) and E R Lewis (10) batted well, while H E Perkins (6 wickets for 9 runs) and T Goddard (2 for 11) were in good form with the ball.

Wagon Works 'A' 158 for 7 Wickets - YMCA 50

Played at the Works Sports Ground.

For the Works, H Brown (73 not out), S J Roberts (38), J Harris (21) W Morris (10) batted well and W Peglar (6 wickets for 21) and R Eagles (4 for 16) did equally as well with the ball.

Wagon Works 'B' 72 for 9 Wickets - Cam 51

Played at Cam.

For the winners, A L Hayden (23) and J Madeley (10) batted well. In the bowling department W Berriman took 6 wickets for 22 runs and R Sheliswell 4 for 15.

Saturday 10th September - Wagon Works 1st 177 for 6 (declared) Ross CC 46

For the Works, H Brown (44 not out), L Hamblin (38), J Winters (37), E R Lewis (20), W Sargent (10 not out) did best with the bat, while T Goddard (6 for 23) and H Perkins (3 for 14) bowled extremely well.

Wagon Works 'B' 97 Eastington II 38

For the Works, L Hayden (20), R Sheliswell (17), F Proctor (14 not out) and T Skipp (13) batted well, while W Berriman (6 for 11) and R Sheliswell (2 for 4) accounted for Eastington's low score.

1922

Saturday 13th May - 1922 Wagon Works v. Barnwood House

Scores: Wagon Works 144 - Barnwood House 53. For the Works, A Paish (42 not out), L H Whiley (24), L Smith (22) and S Strebor (22) batted well, while *T Goddard (5 for 23) and A Paish (3 for 0) did well with the ball.

*T W J Goddard played several representative matches for Gloucestershire during 1922 and from then until his retirement in 1952. During his career for the county, Goddard played 558 matches taking 2,862 wickets. He also appeared 8 times for England, his best bowling performance being 6 for 29 against New Zealand at Old Trafford.
splendidly.

Saturday 20th May

Gloucester Wagon Works Sports Club (Cricket section) 1st Team Season 1922

A E Harris (scorer) P Ryder E L Blackford T E Goddard E R Lewis G F Dere (umpire) H Brown L E Smith L H Whiley W A Brown* H E Perkins** A J Paish A Watkins
(*Vice-Capt and assistant Hon-Sec) (**Capt and Hon Sec)

Gloucester Wagon Works Easy Win at Thornbury

The Works visited Thornbury and recorded a fine win. Going in first, the Works batted consistently, and the innings realised 125, H Brown, especially showing good form. W Curtis, who bowled unchanged for Thornbury, took four wickets for 34 runs. Thornbury started disastrously, losing two wickets before scoring, and the later batsmen offered little resistance. The side were all dismissed for 19. T Goddard (4 wickets for 9) and H Perkins (4 for 10) bowled with deadly effect.

Scores: Wagon Works 125 - Thornbury 19. (L C Smith 12, H Brown 23, A Paish 13, J Winters 10, T Goddard 18, S J Roberts 11, W A Brown 11): Thornbury 19.

Tyndale v. Wagon Works Juniors

Scores: Tyndale 103 - Wagon Works Juniors 26. W Cresswell (30 not out) and W E Dance (24) were the best for Tyndale for whom N Taylor took 8 wickets for 5 runs, and at one period had 7 for 0 runs - a capital achievement on the Works ground.

Gloucester Wagon Works 'A' v. Mitcheldean Sports Union

Played at Tuffley,

The Works made 133 for 8 declared (H Hanman 30, Joe Harris 29, T Butler 25, W Morris 14), Mitcheldean were then dismissed for 50 (F Grove 15, R C Abbott 12, F S Pardoe 11). For the Works, W Peglar (5 wickets for 25) and A Carter (4 for 23) shared the bowling.

Saturday 27th May - Wagon Works v. Tewkesbury

Played at the Works Sports Ground.

Scores: Wagon Works 138 Tewkesbury 140 for 5. For the Works, S Roberts (38), H Perkins (32), P Ryder (24 not out) and A Watkins (17) batted well. For Tewkesbury* C S Barnett (51 not out), W Margrett (31), J Willis (26) scored consistently and J Godwin (4 wickets for 32) was the most successful bowler.

C S Barnett was the father of Gloucestershire & England player C J Barnett.
 (3 for 26) were the most successful bowlers. For the Gas Works, P Bellamy (36), C Butler (17), J Cocks (15) and J Franklin (16 not out) were the principal scorers.

Saturday 24th June - Wotton Under Edge v. Wagon Works

Played at The Sports Ground, Tuffley Avenue.

On this day A Dipper made his second century of the match for Gloucestershire.

Scores: Wotton Under Edge 38 - Wagon Works 132 for 6. For the Works, L H Whiley (72), and H Perkins (5 for 23) were in fine form with bat and ball

Saturday 8th July - Inter Works Cricket

Gloucester Wagon Works 99 for 4 declared v. Metropolitan Works (Saltley) Birmingham 39. L H Whiley (34), H Brown (29), L Smith (14), J Winters (12) batted well for the winners, whilst T Goddard (5 wickets for 20) and H Perkins (3 for 17) bowled well. Holbard (2 for 30) was most successful with the ball for the visitors.

Saturday 15th July - Wagon Works v. Thornbury

Played at the Sports Ground, Tuffley.

Scores: Wagon Works 102 - Thornbury 74.

For the Works, T Goddard (32) H Brown (20) and J Winters (10) batted well. A Paish (5 for 20) and T Goddard (5 for 32) shared the wickets. Thornbury: J Hodges (16) batted well and * E M Grace (3 for 57) bowled well.

E M Grace was the nephew of the great W G Grace, and son of E M Grace, W G's older brother who appeared with W G in the first ever test match in England against Australia at the Oval in 1880.

Saturday 26th August - Wagon Works v. Ross

Played at Ross.
Scores: Wagon Works 127 - Ross 63.

For the Works, H E Perkins (48), P Ryder (14), E R Lewis (12) and A Paish (11) batted well, while T Goddard (4 for 25) and H Perkins (4 for 23) shared the wickets. For Ross, G W Stevens (19 not out), A J Wilden (4 for 39) and Martin (4 for 43) being the most successful bowlers.

Wagon Works 'A' v. Old Patesians

Played at Cheltenham.

Scores: Wagon Works 'A' 149 - Old Patesians 100. For the Works, A Carter (49), J Harris (40) and W Morris (27) were in good form with the bat, and Steve Proctor (4 for 17) and A Carter (4 for 40) were the most successful with the ball. For the Old Patesians, A W Mann (22), K Wilson (20), F Mann (19), B Howman (11) and H Spinks (16) were the chief scorers.

Saturday 2nd September - East Gloucestershire v. Wagon Works

Match played at Charlton Park, East Gloucestershire.

Scores: East Gloucestershire 33 - Wagon Works 60. East Gloucestershire batted first on a very soft wicket and it soon became apparent that runs would be difficult to get. With the exception of H C Blair-Sessions, who batted well for 20, no one offered any resistance to T Goddard (5 for 13) and H E Perkins (3 for 19). The Works obtained the necessary runs with 6 wickets in hand, thanks to some good batting by L H Whiley (14) and J Winters (10). H Bell Howarth (4 for 28) and Morse (3 for 15) were the most successful bowlers for East Gloucestershire.

1923

**Saturday 2nd June**

COUNTY CRICKET AT THE WAGON WORKS GROUND

AN AUSPICIOUS OPENING

An interesting day's cricket, a real summer afternoon, and a splendid attendance-the gate receipts amounted to £144 representing, with members of the County Club and the Wagon Works Sports Club, a crowd of something like 3,000-combined to make the opening day of County cricket at the Tuffley Avenue enclosure an auspicious one. What the final returns from the match with Lancashire will be, compared with the Spa, cannot be approximately surmised, but it may be safe to assume that after Saturday's experience the County Executive, with the kind permission of the Directors, will allocate further matches to the Wagon Works Sport Ground for another season. The fear in some quarters that the cricketing public would not take the trouble to go to Tuffley to see a match was removed by the satisfactory attendance on Saturday and, with improved transport facilities of getting to the ground, there is no reason why the patronage should not be considerably increased. As to the suitability of the enclosure for county cricket, there was no disagreement on this point; the playing field itself was in splendid order and the pitch excellent. The lack of a pavilion or covered stand was commented upon; but should county cricket be firmly established at Tuffley, this provision would no doubt be favourably considered by the Directors of the Wagon Company, in conjunction with the Gloucestershire Club.

During luncheon Mr R E Bush, the President of the County Club, cordially thanked the Directors of the Company for so generously placing the ground at the disposal of Gloucestershire. They had followed the example of Fry's and Packer's at Bristol in doing so free of charge, and their action was deeply appreciated. He also complimented the ground staff upon their work. Mr J J Macgregor, Managing Director, briefly replied.

GODDARD'S BOWLING PERFORMANCE

The cricket on Saturday furnished some interesting features, chief of which was the success obtained by the junior members of the Gloucestershire team. T Goddard, the Wagon Works bowler, is being given a good trial this season and in this match, the local professional delighted his friends with a really fine performance. Six wickets for 41 runs represented his afternoon's work - the best thing he has done for the county since the opening match with Surrey at Bristol. Goddard hit the stumps on five occasions, and made the ball nip so quickly off the pitch that he took a lot of watching. A missed opportunity of a stumping robbed the Gloucester man of the "hat trick".

Saturday 16th June - Swindon Olympic 141 - Wagon Works 73 for 5 Wickets

Played at the Sport Ground, Tuffley.

For the Works, H Brown made 28, J Winters 26 not out and H Brown took 7 for 35 runs, match drawn.

Wagon Works 'A' and Tewkesbury 'A' met at the Sports Ground, Tuffley Avenue, the Works winning by a small total of 6 runs. The Works made 130, W Morris 49 which included 2 6s and 5 4s, R Howell 12, and S Smith 11. Also for the Works, W Peglar 5 for 38, R Howell 2 for 13 and A Carter 2 wickets bowled well. Tewkesbury replied with 126 all out with Warner top scoring on 43. bowled well.

Saturday 18 August - Gloucester Wagon Works v. Hereford CC

This match was played at Hereford and though play continued until 7:30, a draw resulted. The Works, winning the toss, batted first on a fast wicket and, thanks to splendid batting by H Brown and A Paish, were able to declare at 194 for 9 wickets. Hereford made a capital start, the first 4 wickets putting on 113, but after the dismissal of H K Foster, R E Bailey and Colonel Thornycroft, the rate of scoring quietened down, and the end came with Hereford 50 runs behind and only 2 wickets in hand.

Colonel Thornycroft 3 for 30 and H Leveson-Gower 3 for 70 were the most successful bowlers for the home team and for the Works, A Paish 4 for 24 and H Brown 2 for 26.

Wagon Works						**Hereford C C**					
Brown	c	Gower	b	Croome	58	Foster	c	Bloodworth	b	Proctor	33
Blackford			b	Williams	9	Stephens			b	Brown	10
Smith	st	Bailey	b	Gower	0	Bailey			b	Brown	34
Merrett			b	Gower	4	Thorneycroft	c	H Brown	b	Paish	26
Bloodworth			b	Gower	0	Crooms			b	Paish	12
Paish	not out				50	Leveson-Gower	c	Winters	b	Paish	9
Winters			b	Thorneycroft	19	Kedge			b	Bloodworth	5
Proctor	c	Bailey	b	Thorneycroft	5	Ashton	c	Smith	b	Paish	4
Watkins	c	Croome	b	Thorneycroft	6	Procter	not out				1
Brown			b	Williams	4	Willimas	not out				5
Procter	not out				1						
	EXTRAS				38		**EXTRAS**				5
	Total (for 9 wickets declared)				194		**Total (for 8)**				144

In this match Hereford included H K Foster, a former Worcestershire player and also H Leveson-Gower, a former Oxford University and Surrey captain who also captained England in South Africa for 3 matches in 1909-10. He was knighted in 1953.

Saturday 1st September - Gloucester Wagon Works v. Evesham

Played at the Works Sports Ground.

Scores: Evesham 69, F J Bailey 17, A Nicholls 15. Wagon Works 72 for 6, H Brown 17, T Goddard 16 not out. For the Works, T Goddard took 4 wickets for 22.

Newent v. Wagon Works 'A'

Played at Newent.
Newent 55, J M Scott 13, A Carter took 7 wickets for 27 and P Bloodworth 3 for 12. The Works 'A' 85, F Cresswell 19 not out, H Hanman 12.

1924

Saturday 28th June - Gloucester Wagon Works v. Herefordshire

Played at the Works Ground at Tuffley and won by the visitors by 4 wickets who successfully chased the host's score of 128 all out.

For the Works, Ryder's 66 included one 6 and twelve 4s. HK Foster played a fine innings for Herefordshire and just missed the century by 4 runs. In his attractive display, he hit fifteen 4s.

Wagon Works 'A' defeated the Gas Works at Cheltenham by 39 runs. Batting first, the Gas Works could do very little against the splendid bowling of A Carter (5 wickets for 28) and W Peglar (5 for 30) and were all out for 58 runs (F Brewster and C Voyce 13). The Works made a poor start, 3 wickets falling for 15 runs, but A Carter 26, H Hanman 20, W A Brown 18 and G Turner 11 improved matters and the total reached 97.

Cam 121 - Wagon Works 'B' 56

Played at the Works Sports Ground.

For Cam, G Jackson 29, C Reeves 28, L Jones 18 were the principal scorers and F Tockwell 6 wickets and G Tockwell 4 wickets, were in good form with the ball. H Banks 14 and G Green 12 were top scorers for the Works and E Draper, 5 wickets for 44, bowled well.

Saturday 12th July

The inter works match between The Gloucester Wagon Works and The Metropolitan Carriage and Wagon Works Co was played at Birmingham, the Gloucester team winning by 2 wickets.

Scores: Metropolitan Works 61 all out. H Proctor 3 for 18, Winters 3 for 13, W Brown 2 for 14. Gloucester Works 65 for 8, L Blackford 10, A Paish 14, H Brown 16 not out. For the Metropolitan Works, W Andrews took 5 for 22.

Cavendish House (Cheltenham) visited the Wagon Works Sports Ground to oppose the 'B' team and proved successful by 16 runs. The homesters batted first, but could do little against the bowling of F Ricketts and H Smith, W Mellings 22 and L S Price 16 being the only batsmen to reach double figures as they were dismissed for 77. The visitors replied with 86, H Draper being the Works' best bowler.

Saturday 9th August - Wagon Works v. Ross

Played on the Works Sports Ground - Match Drawn.

ROSS						Wagon Works					
R E Abbot	st	Watkins	b	Paish	27	H Brown	lbw		b	Roff	28
WF Jackson	c	H Proctor	b	Blackford	1	E Proctor			b	Ellis	3
JH Moore	c	Howell	b	Paish	9	Blackford	st	West	b	Roff	2
RW Roff			b	H Brown	84	LC Smith	Not out				22
HN Thomas	st	Watkins	b	Paish	7	R Howell	Not out				7
FE Ellis	Not out				22						
HR Jefferies	Not out				2						
	EXTRAS				4		EXTRAS				18
	Total (for 5 declared)				156		Total (for 3 wickets)				80

L.C. Smith was later to become Sir Leslie Smith and Cricket Club President

Wagon Works 'B' 63, R Meredith 17 not out. Ross 'B' 27. For the Works, E Hale 4 for 7, and R Meredith 4 for 11 bowled well. Played on the Works Ground.

1925

Saturday 2nd May

Gloucester Wagon Works 'A' opened the season at the Sports Ground, Tuffley Avenue, against Tewkesbury 'A'. The Works batted first scoring 106 for 4 wickets declared with J Condwick 45 not out, H Hanman 33 and S Smith 14 being the principal scorers. Tewkesbury 'A' replied with 62 all out, E Hale 7 wickets for 21 runs and A Carter 2 for 20 being the leading wicket takers.

Saturday 30th May - Gloucester Wagon Works Defeat Stroud

Played at Stroud.

The Works made a poor start, the first 2 wickets fell for only 3 runs, and although Goddard and Hopcroft improved matters 8 were down for 54. E Proctor and Blackford made a determined stand for the 9th wicket adding 78 runs in 80 minutes. For Stroud, G Wedel 5 for 29 and H J Huggins 4 for 47 shared the wickets. Stroud commenced in similar fashion, half the side being out for 20 runs. Dr Munden and C Carter, however, put on 59 for the 7th wicket, the former hitting 9 4s, but when the last wicket fell the home side were 17 runs behind. T Goddard 5 for 44 and H Proctor 3 for 32 were the most successful bowlers.

*George Wedel for Stroud was aged 25 in 1925 and between then and 1929 he played 45 matches for Gloucestershire, scoring over 500 runs and taking 51 wickets. Also in the Stroud team was H J Huggins, an ex Gloucestershire player who, between 1901 and 1921 played more than 200 matches for the County, scoring over 4000 runs and taking 584 wickets. In 1925 he was aged 48.

Wagon Works						Stroud				
H Brown	lbw		b	Huggins	0	H Evans	c	Paish		0
LC Smith	b	Huggins			5	F Poole	Lbw	Proctor		7
R Howell	c	Simons	b	Wedel	0	A L Crowe	b	Goddard		1
T Goddard	b	Wedel			16	G Wedel	b	Goddard		12
AJ Paish	lbw		b	Wedel	2	H J Huggins	b	H Proctor		0
A Hopcroft	b	Wedel			19	GW Holloway	b	H Proctor		6
J Winters	b	Wedel			2	Dr M Munden	c	Paish	b	H Brown	46
F Merrett	Run out				5	CR Carter	b	Goddard		27
E Proctor	b	Huggins			30	LE Farmiloe	b	Goddard		0
E Blackford	b	Huggins			42	FG Betts	b	H Brown		2
H Proctor	not out				1	E H Simons	Not out			8
	EXTRAS				9		EXTRAS			5
	Total				131		Total			114

Saturday 27 June – Wagon Works beat Gloucester
Played at the Works Sports Ground.

Wagon Works defeated Gloucester by 7 wickets. The feature of the match was the bowling of W Brown who took 6 Gloucester wickets for 19, and the wicket keeping of A Hopcroft who, besides taking two sharp catches, did not give away a single extra.

GLOUCESTER CITY						WAGON WORKS			
AV Wybrow	c	Proctor	b	Brown	47	L Smith	retired hurt		1
FJ Benbow	lbw		b	Proctor	4	E Proctor	b	Bull	10
Loveridge	b	Blackford			2	R Howell	b	Bull	10
EC Rogers	b	Brown			11	A Hopcroft	b	Wybrow	7
P Tilley	c	Hopcroft	b	Brown	0	A Paish	not out		32
W Seabrook	c	Hopcroft	b	Brown	0	H Brown	not out		34
A T Voyce	b	Brown			14				
M Lulham	b	Brown			0				
G Scott	b	Paish			19				
H J Hyett	lbw		b	Brown	8				
A Bull	not out								
	Total				106	EXTRAS			20
						Total (For 3 Wickets)			114

For Gloucester, W Seabrook, a young talented player, took part. He eventually played one county match in 1928. Also playing for Gloucester was A T Voyce, the well-known Gloucester and England rugby player.

Gloucester 'A' v. Wagon Works 'A'

Played at the Spa.

The Works batted first and ran up a good score of 168. J Condick 55 not out, A Carter 37, P Bloodworth 21and L Perkins 16 all did well. Gloucester 'A' reached 112 for 7 with S Bennett 21 being top scorer. For the Works, E Hale took 5 for 45.

Saturday 11th July - Wagon Works Comfortable Win

Played on The Sports Ground.

METROPOLITAN WORKS							WAGON WORKS						
Downs	b	Proctor				0	L C Smith	b	Andrews				2
Andrews	b	Proctor				10	J Condick	b	Downs				8
Turner	b	Proctor				0	R Howell	c	Downs	b	Andrews		10
Brookes	b	Blackford				0	J Winters	c&b	Dixon				58
Haynes	b	Blackford				0	AJ Paish	not out					52
Brookes	c	Blackford	b	Proctor		10	H Proctor	lbw		b	Comely		2
Childs	c	H Brown	b	W Brown	33	F Merrett	not out					16
Dixon	b	W Brown				11							
Comely	b	W Brown				7							
Davis	not out					0							
Jackson	b	W Brown				0							
	EXTRAS					6		EXTRAS					9
	Total					77		Total (for 5)					157

W A Brown (4 for 15)   H Proctor (4 for 31)   E Blackford (2 for 16)

Saturday 11th July

Wagon Works 'B' 56 - W Berriman 18, Blaisdon 56, Pember 15. E Stephens, for the Works, (6 for 10).

E Stephens was only 16 in the above match. He went on to play for the county as a batsman between 1927 and 1937, making 216 appearances, scoring 4593 runs and taking 29 wickets. Also on this date, W R Hammond scored 61 for the Gloucester Nondescripts.

***Sir Jack Hobbs and Andy Sandham opening the batting for Surrey v
Gloucestershire on the Wagon Works ground 1925***

Saturday 25th July - Wagon Works win at Worcester

Played at the County Ground at Worcester.

The Works had first use of a good wicket, but the batting generally was not up to the usual standard and the whole side was out for a moderate 124. The homesters made a promising start, 50 being hoisted for the loss of 3 wickets. Little resistance was offered afterwards though and the last 7 wickets fell for just 28 runs.

WAGON WORKS

L Smith	Hit Wickets	b	Rabjohns		14
E Proctor	b	Roberts			0
R Howell	b	Boulter			13
J Winters	c	Osborne	b	Boulter	27
A Paish	b	Clarke			5
H Brown	b	Rabjohns			18
A Hopcroft	not out				17
L Blackford	b	Rabjohns			0
F Merrett	run out				2
W Brown	c&b	Rabjohns			1
H Proctor	c	Rabjohns	b	Roberts	15
EXTRAS					**12**
Total					**124**

D Rabjohns 4 for 85

WORCESTER

S Collier	b	W Brown			42
R Townsend	st	Hopcroft	b	Blackford	3
C Smith	c	H Brown	b	Blackford	0
C Davis	lbw		b	W Brown	9
J Clarke	lbw		b	H Brown	2
L Warren	b	H Brown			0
A Boulter	b	H Brown			0
W Roberts	b	Blackford			13
D Rabjohns	c	Paish	b	H Brown	8
P Osborne	not out				1
T James	c	H Brown	b	Blackend	0
EXTRAS					**4**
Total					**82**

L Blackford 4 for 18

For the Works, Jim Stephens took 3 for 9.

Saturday 16th August Wagon Works beat East Gloucestershire

EAST GLOUCESTERSHIRE

KA Woodward	st	E Proctor	b	Paish	50
EL Vulliamy	c	Brown	b	Paish	36
Hawarth	st	Proctor	b	Paish	2
HH Hords	st	Proctor	b	Paish	2
MB Moore	c	Condick	b	Paish	5
HC Jackson	c	Smith	b	Paish	2
LD Morse	c	Brown	b	Paish	5
C Jessop	not out				
LS Smith	c	Perkins	b	Paish	0
JL Fawcett	b	Peglar			0
PR Clauss	Absent				0
EXTRAS					**21**
Total					**123**

A Paish 8 for 38, including the 'Hat Trick'

WAGON WORKS

LC Smith	c	Bell-Hawarth	b	Morse	16
J Winters	c	Morse	b	Bell-Hawarth	74
AJ Carter	b	Morse			26
AJ Paish	not out				4
W Peglar	b	Bell Hawarth			0
EF Proctor	not out				1
EXTRAS					
Total					**121**

L Blackford, J Condick, W Perkins, H Proctor and WA Brown did not bat

A SPLENDID SEASON - RESULTS AND AVERAGES

With a greatly strengthened fixture list, the premier XI of the Wagon Works Cricket Club enjoyed a most successful season, only two defeats being sustained in 20 matches. The form all-round was excellent, and in the batting averages, six members of the team secured an average of over 20. The bowling figures too reveal the strength of the attack. In batting, the team averaged 21.5 runs per wicket, as against 11.7 by opponents.

1st XI Played 20, Won, 11; Lost, 2; Drawn 7

		AGAINST		FOR	
Opponents	Result	Runs	Wkts	Runs	Wkts
Tewkesbury	Drawn	121	6	97	3
Hereford	Ab'nd -	-		88	5
Evesham	Won	88	10	108	4
Ross	Drawn	193	6	103	5
Stroud	Won	114	10	131	10
Stinchcombe Stragglers	Won	57	10	204	8
Nondescripts	Won	69	10	152	4
Worcester	Drawn	96	5	219	3
Ross	Lost	187	5	170	10
Evesham	Drawn	119	6	195	9
Gloucester	Won	105	19	116	3
Worcester	Won	82	10	124	10
Metro Works (B'ham)	Won	77	10	107	5
Hereford	Won	52	10	95	3
Thornbury	Lost	129	8	118	10
Headess Cross	Won	60	10	165	10
Chelt. Nondescripts	Won	14	7	120	8
East Gloucester	Won	125	10	126	4
Stroud	Ab'nd	88	7 -	-	
Gloucester	Ab'nd -	-		19	0
		1765	**150**	**2451**	**111**

BATTING

	Inns	Not Out	Highest Score	Runs	Average
A J Paish	15	9	76*	373	62.1
T W Goddard	6	1	50*	140	28.0
A E Hopcroft	13	5	64*	218	27.2
L C Smith	18	3	81	351	23.6
J Winters	11	1	74	251	23.1
R Howell	13	0	79	280	21.5
H Brown	14	4	50	183	18.3
F Merrett	11	2	34*	122	13.5
E Procter	15	3	33	151	12.6

*Signifies not out

BOWLING

	O	M	R	W	A
T W Goddard	87	29	179	29	6.1
W A Brown	122	29	253	33	7.8
A J Paish	41	8	141	13	10.3
H Procter	130	27	367	20	12.6
H Brown	79	10	263	20	13.1
E L Blackford	91	21	272	14	19.4

'A' TEAM
Played, 17-Won, 9; Lost, 5; Drawn 3

BATTING

	Inns	Not Out	Highest Score	Agg	Avrg
J Condick	15	4	76*	275	25.0
P Bloodworth	11	1	55	324	24.9
H Banks	10	1	85*	193	21.4
G Turner	10	2	19	92	11.5
W Pegler	8	1	23	0	11.4
A Carter	12	0	37	128	10.7
L Perkins	14	1	17	80	6.2
W Parry	14	3	14*	67	6.1
H Hanman	17	1	33	88	5.5
E Hale	10	3	25*	35	5.0

*Signifies not out

BOWLING

	O	M	R	W	A
E Hale	138	27	326	52	6.3
P Bloodworth	76	23	139	20	6.9
W Pegler	61	12	120	14	8.6
L Perkins	91	15	219	25	8.8

'B' TEAM

Played 14-won 6, lost 7; drawn 1. C Merrett 71 runs, average 14.2 and A Sysum 119 runs, average 13.2 headed the batting averages, while the successful bowlers were: J Stephens 23 wickets, average 5.9; G Court 19-6.4; W Berriman 48-6.7; and P Webber 23-7.3

'C' TEAM

Played 14-won 4, lost 8; drawn 2. Batting: R Holford 64 runs, average 12.8; L Baldwin 73-10.4. Bowling: C Restall 34 wickets, average 4.1; V Bullock 31-4.5; R Holford 15-8.3.

1926

Saturday 22nd May - Gloucester Wagon Works v Hereford

Played at Hereford. The home team batted first on a good wicket, but could only muster 80 runs, H Proctor having the capital analysis of six wickets for 25 runs. The Works obtained the necessary runs for the loss of eight wickets. Scores

HEREFORD						WAGON WORKS				
Capt R L Green			b	Proctor	0	H Brown		b	Harborne	22
F Powell			b	Proctor	6	L Smith	lbw	b	Owens	5
Dr Ward-Power	lbw		b	W Brown	11	R Howell	lbw	b	Crees	25
Dr Crees	c	Howell	b	Proctor	2	J Winters	lbw	b	Green	31
Col Thornycroft	c	Winters	b	Proctor	21	A Hopcroft	lbw	b	Owens	18
E Collier	lbw		b	Proctor	1	F Merrett		b	Crees	0
B Harborne			b	Proctor	0	E Proctor	run out			13
T Owens		Run out			16	L Perkins		b	Thorneycroft	0
H Thorne		Run out			5	W Brown	not out			17
H Munroe		Not out			0	H Proctor	not out			10
T Perks	c	Howell	b	Winters	4					
		Extras			**14**			**Extras**		**6**
		Total			**80**			**Total (for 8 wickets)**		**147**

Wagon Works 'A' v. Cadbury's

Wagon Works 'A', 114 for 8 wickets declared (A Carter 32, C Poolman, 26 not out, E Stephens 18, H Banks18)

Cadburys 63 for four wickets (J Wellings 26) on the Works Sports Ground. For the Works, E Stephens took three for 17.

Sunday 23rd May Wagon Works v. Nondescripts

WAGON WORKS						NONDESCRIPTS					
H Brown	c	Collingbourne	b	Benbow	51	T Burns	lbw		b	Proctor	0
L C Smith	st	Clarke	b	Burns	12	W Clarke			b	Proctor	0
R Howell	b	Burns			29	G G Wooley	c	Proctor	b	Brown	8
J Winters	b		b	Hill	46	F Benbow			b	Brown	1
A J Paish		Not out			37	J Benbow			b	Proctor	0
A Hopcroft		Not out			11	W Prior	c	Hopcroft	b	Brown	1
		EXTRAS			**11**	H Pollard	st	Hopcroft	b	Brown	10
		Total (for 4 declared)			**195**	J Hill	c&b	Smith			7
F Merrett, E F Proctor, L Perkins, W A Brown, H Proctor did not bat						G Collingbourne		not out			29
						G Savage		not out			0
								EXTRAS			**10**
								Total (for 8 Wickets)			**66**

MATCH DRAWN

Saturday 29th May - Wagon Works v Ross

Played on the Sports Ground, the home team lacked the services of Paish and Hopcroft, but won an entertaining game by 56 runs.

Wagon Works 159   H Brown (40), H Banks (35), W A Brown (21), J Winters (17), E Stephens (16).
Ross 103   H Meredith (25). W A Brown, for the Works, took 5 wickets for 28.

Wagon Works C team 54 L Mundy (14 not out)
LonghopeII 21, Charlie Restall bowled well taking 7 wickets for 9 runs.

Saturday 31st July - Gloucester well beaten by the Wagon Works.

Gloucester City have accomplished some good performances this season and have shown a considerable improvement on last year's form, but they failed badly against the Wagon Works, being easily defeated at the Sports Ground by five wickets and 52 runs. Against an accurate and well-varied attack, the City batsmen gave a feeble display, of which the only feature was a resolute innings of 32 which included five 4s, by G P Pennington. Pennington was a Somerset County Rugby forward, and he had been making big scores for Weston Super Mare. He has come to live in Gloucester and the City Club will be glad of his assistance. The Wagon Works knocked off the 128 runs required to win in an hour and a half for the loss of three wickets. J Winters made top score with 57, but it was a lucky and streaky knock and the best batting was shown by the opening pair, H Brown and E Stephens. For the Works, H Brown took three wickets for 19, H Proctor three for 24, J Winters two for 15, W A Brown one for 22, and L Blackford one for 39. The Wagon Works again have a nicely balanced team this year and one which must still be one of the very best in the northern part of the county. The wealth of bowling talent at the disposal of the captain (H Brown) is shown by the division of Gloucester's wickets. The fielding is excellent and the batting, if not brilliant, would appear to be very sound.

Scores:
Gloucester 127 all out G P Pennington (32), N Browning (22), P Tilley (19)
Wagon Works 179 for five, H Banks (40), J Winters (57), H Brown (32), E Stephens (31).

**During August, the club was to run its first recorded cricket week,
playing the following three fixtures on the sports ground.**

Saturday 3rd August

Wagon Works 165 for nine dec (H Brown 50, E Stephens 12, R Howell 20, L Smith 22, E Proctor 20, W Brown 17, L Blackford 10); Stinchcombe Stragglers 74 for four (W L Neale 11, G Grey 27, L Owen not out 16) match drawn.

Sunday 4th August

Headless Cross 104 Wagon Works 188 for five (E Stephens 28, R Howell 24, L Smith 50, L Perkins not out 26)
For The Works, L Blackford took three for 19.

.Monday 5th August

Gloucester 190 all out (G P Hollingworth 54, J E Coates 36, R N Loveridge 31) Blackford four for 63, Smith two for 24. Wagon Works 153 for 3 (E Stephens not out 72, A Paish not out 43), Ball two for 46, match drawn.

Saturday 21st August - Gloucester v Wagon Works

The Wagon Works suffered their first defeat of the season when they met Gloucester at the Spa. This was the third time the two sides had met this season. The first game went in The Works' favour, and in the second, there was no result. In dismissing the visitors for the small score of 75 the City did extremely well, thanks mainly to some fine bowling by W Seabroook who emerged with the excellent analysis of 5 wickets for 22. A great contrast was seen when the Wagon Works batted, for their fielding was of a very poor description, several chances being missed and it was seldom that a ball was picked up cleanly. Paish, for The Works, took 6 for 40.
Wagon Works 75 all out (A Hopcroft 36, E Stephens 10) Gloucester 155 all out (J W Morris 38, W Seabrook 34)

Wagon Works II 139 (W Peglar 56, A Carter 46, A W Lewis six for 45)

Gloucester II 142 for eight (A Ault 34, J S Dilks 23)

Saturday 11th September - Worcester v Wagon Works

Played at Worcester

Wagon Works						Worcester					
H Brown	c	Clarke	b	Rabjohn	12	S Collier	Not out				40
A Hopcroft	b	Boulter			26	A Heaton	c	H Brown	b	Goddard	8
E Stephens	c	Harber	b	Rabjohn	54	W Roberts	b	W Brown			13
J Winters	lbw		b	Rabjohn	11	R Townsond	c	Hopcroft	b	Godard	3
A Paish	Not out				35	J Clarke	b	Goddard			15
T Goddard	b	Harber			0	C Smith	Run out				3
H Banks	b	Harber			10	P Osborne	Run out				6
R Howell	lbw		b	Harber	13						1
	EXTRAS				16		Total (for 5 wickets)				89
	Total (for 7 declared)				177						

Match Drawn

Gloucester Railway Carriage and Wagon Co Ltd Cricket Club 1st Team 1926

L Smith A Hopcroft W Brown H Proctor LPerkins FMerrett J Winters H Brown
R Howell   A Paish   E Proctor

Photographed at Hereford

1927

May

The County Festival came to the Works Ground in early May, Yorkshire being the first visitors and their side included England players Herbert Sutcliffe, Percy Holmes and Wilfred Rhodes. Gloucestershire were well beaten by an innings and 21 runs, the highlights of the match were Sutcliffe and Holmes' record opening partnership and Hammond's century.

The 284-run opening partnership by Sutcliffe and Holmes became the highest opening first class stand made on the ground. Wally Hammond made 135 in 3½ hours, but it was not enough to stave off defeat.

Six years later Holmes and Sutcliffe were involved in another record opening partnership, this time against Essex at Leyton. The pair scored 555, Sutcliffe made 313 and Holmes 224 and it remains Yorkshire's highest opening stand to this day.

Wilfred Rhodes took 4187 first class wickets in his career, Sutcliffe made 149 first class centuries while Holmes hit 67.

Mr R. Parry, one of the umpires in this match, met with a serious accident whilst officiating on the Monday morning. Parry was maimed during the 1st World War and wore an artificial leg. This naturally handicapped his movements and, in trying to avoid a collision with Sutcliffe who was completing a quick single, he slipped and fractured the stump to which the artificial limb was attached. He was conveyed to Gloucester Royal Infirmary and Mr. A. Paish, ex county player and groundsman of the Wagon Works, carried out the umpiring duties for the remainder of the game.

The gate receipts for the match were approximately £250, of which £178 was taken on the Saturday when the attendance was estimated at 3500.

Cricket Club being presented with the pavilion clock by the Works Dance Commitee 1927

Saturday 28th May - Wagon Works v. Tewkesbury

Played at the Sports Ground, Tuffley. The visitors, on a good wicket, compiled the useful total of 186, J L Brain, after being missed early on, batting well for 58 which included one six and eight 4s. A Paish (four for 54) and H Brown (three for 52) were the most successful bowlers for the home side. With one hour and fifty minutes to obtain the necessary runs, the Works started splendidly, H Brown putting on, with his partner Hopcroft, 57 in 36 minutes for the first wicket. Howell contributed valuable runs and he and Brown added 66 for the second wicket. H Banks and Brown obtained the last 82 runs in 32 minutes with Brown completing his century before stumps were drawn. Most of his runs were obtained in front of the wicket, chiefly by hard driving and well placed shots to the on side. Scores:

Tewkesbury 186 all out (J L Brown 58, L Barnett 40, and *C J Barnett 23)
Wagon Works 215 for 3 (H Brown 100 not out, A Hopcroft 34, R Howell 21, H Banks 45)

*C J Barnett was only 16 when this match was played; he went on to play 424 matches for Gloucestershire and was capped 20 times by England.

Saturday 9th July - Wagon Works v. Metropolitan Works (Saltley)

Wagon Works						Metropolitan Works			
H Brown	c&b			Fowler	29	W Andrews	b	Stephens	13
A Hopcroft	run out				12	J Jefferies	st	Hopcroft b Blackford	0
D Howell	c	Bryant	b	Down	5	J Down	b	Stephens	24
A Paish	c	Chilos	b	Fowler	0	A Hurdman	lbw	b Brown	1
J Condick	b	Andrews			14	H Wilkins	c& b	Paish	2
E Proctor	b	Childs			12	J Thomas	c	Hopcroft b W Brown	6
C Poolman	not out				27	A Childs	not out		3
S Smith	b	Andrews			18				
EXTRAS					10	**EXTRAS**			1
TOTAL (for 7 declared)			127			**TOTAL** (for six wickets)			50

Match Drawn

Wagon Works A 139, (A Evans 55 not out, A Newman 22, F Stock 15, A J Carter 12).
Metropolitan Works A 73 for nine wickets (S Smith 22, Hodgson 19) played at the Sports Ground Tuffley; match drawn. For the Wagon Works, G Welshman took six wickets for 22 runs.

Saturday 16th July - Swindon v. Wagon Works

Played at Swindon

Swindon						Wagon Works				
S Whittaker	c	E Stephens	b	Goddard	11	H Brown	c&b		Hoare	12
G Wood	lbw			Winters	34	A Hopcroft	b	Wood		13
E Nash	b	J Stephens			2	E Stephens	b	Wood		0
Rev Hoare	c	Winters	b	Goddard	1	R Howell	lbw		b Willis	17
N Litten			b	Goddard	0	A Paish	st	Nash	b Wood	12
T Sutton	not out				7	J Winters	c	Litten	b Willis	2
P Pillinger	b	Winters			0	T Goddard	c	Hoare	b Willis	3
F Glastenbury	b	Goddard			0	C Poolman	not out			3
E Besant	run out				0					
F Binnie	c	J Stephens	b	Goddard	0					
A Willis	c	Blackford	b	Goddard	0					
EXTRAS					3	**EXTRAS**				3
TOTAL					58	**TOTAL**	(FOR 7)			65

Goddard 6 for 18
Match won by Wagon Works by 3 wickets

A Willis 3 for 7

1928

Saturday 5th May - Wagon Works v. Ross

Played at the Works Sports Ground.

Wagon Works received an early setback, Brown being well taken at the wicket with only 11 runs scored. The third wicket partnership between Hopcroft and Banks easily produced the finest cricket of the match. Altogether the stand realised 134 runs in 54 minutes and was finally terminated when Banks was caught off Morgan. Hopcroft scored 86 before finally being caught by B L Watkins, a former Works player, his score including 10 4s.

WAGON WORKS				ROSS				
H Brown	c Watkins b Roff	3	B L Watkins	lbw		b Paish	50
A E Hopcroft	c Watkins b Baynsham	86	H J Wilding	c	Banks	b Stephens	25
C Poolman	c Roff b Morgan	21	P S Morgan	c	Paish	b Stephens	3
H Banks	c Lane b Morgan	70	R W Roff	c	Proctor	b Paish	4
J Winters	lbw b Baynsham	31	B Baynsham	not out			23
E F Proctor	not out	16	J Lane	not out			6
F Stock	not out	7	A C Jerard			b Stephens	10
	EXTRAS	19		EXTRAS			3
	TOTAL(FOR 5 DECLARED)	253		TOTAL (FOR FIVE)			124

A J Paish, W A Brown, S T Smith, J Stephens (3 for 28) and J Stephens did not bat. A Paish (2 for 28)

MATCH DRAWN

Ross 'A' 117, (G Kearsey 36, E Turner 17)

Wagon Works 'A' 139, (A Evans 45, A Mayhew 23, E Hale 14, W Bourne 10 not out) For the Works, A Carter (3 for 11) and E Hale (3 for 35) bowled well.

Wednesday 30th May - Wagon Works v. Nondescripts

Played on the Sports Ground, the Works batted first with H Brown and A Hopcroft putting on 141 for the first wicket. Brown's final total of 131 was compiled in two hours and ten minutes.

WAGON WORKS				NONDESCRIPTS				
H Brown	c Stephens	b Pollard	131	T Burns	b	Mountney		4
A Hopcroft	c Gillespie	b Benbow	46	F Benbow	run out			50
F Stock	run out		9	E Paish	c	Hopcroft	b Mountney	2
J Winters	b Burns		6	J Stephens	c	Hopcrof	b W Brown	42
C Poolman	not out		36	F Carr	st	Hopcroft	b Paish	20
A Evans	not out		15	R Goddard	b	Mountney		4
	EXTRAS		12	H Pollard	b	Mountney		7
	TOTAL (for 4 declared)		255	G Collingbourne	c	Mountney	b Paish	9
				A Gillespie	b	H. Brown		0
				E Hancock	not out			0
				W Clark	not out			1
				EXTRAS				5
				Total (for nine)				140

For the Works, Mountney (4 for 41) and Paish (2 for 29) were the most successful bowlers.

Saturday 19th July - Nondescripts beat the Wagon Works

WAGON WORKS					NONDESCRIPTS			
H Brown	b Hawker		5	F Benbow	c W Brown	b H Brown	22
A Hopcroft	lbw	b Burns	27	W Prior	b W Brown		0
R Howell	b Hawker		0	A Wybrow	c Banks	b Howell	90
A H Evans	b Burns		10	T Stephens	c J Stephens	b Paish	5
A J Paish	run out		2`	F Voyce	not out		57
F Stephens	b Hawker		8		**EXTRAS**		**6**
H Banks	b Hawker		16		**TOTAL**	(FOR 4)	**180**
C Poolman	b Hawker		2				
J Stephens	b Hawker		4		**Nondescripts won by 6 wickets**		
W A Brown	not out		4				
G Welshman	lbw	b Burns	4				
	EXTRAS		**1**				
	TOTAL		**83**				

F Hawker 6 for 24.

* On this date the following report was placed in the Citizen: "Tom Goddard's selection for the England team to visit South Africa has afforded the greatest satisfaction to his old clubmates of the Gloucester Wagon Works CC."

Saturday 11th August - Wagon Works v. Swindon

T GODDARD IN FORM

In this match at Swindon, the Works lacked the services of A Hopcroft, H Brown, F Stock and L Mountney, but had the assistance of Tom Goddard. The fixture was set apart for the benefit of Mr Pugh the groundsman, and a large crowd was present when the Works took first knock on a good wicket.

Winters showed capital form for his 62, which included a 6 and six 4s and E Proctor and C Poolman assisted him to put on 86 for two wickets. Subsequently, Goddard and Paish materially helped the scoring and by the tea interval the innings was declared closed for the loss of six wickets. For Swindon, Wood bowled consistently, taking four wickets for 56 runs.

Swindon never looked like obtaining the necessary runs, but by sound batting managed to play out time. Wood again distinguished himself by making top score and being undefeated. Goddard bowled splendidly, taking five wickets for 41

Scores:

Wagon Works 179 for six declared E Proctor (15) J Winters (62), T Goddard (34), A Paish (33); Swindon 108 for seven G Wood (20 no) Goddard (five for 41).

Saturday 18th August - Wagon Works Good Win at Monmouth

The Wagon Works visited Monmouth and won by 78 runs. Batting first, the Works compiled 182 for 4 wickets in an hour and three-quarters. The partnership of Banks and Paish had realised 115 when the latter retired. Banks hit one 6 and eleven 4s and Paish eight 4s. With two hours to bat Monmouth played for safety, but fine bowling by Paish brought about a definite result, the whole side being dismissed for the moderate total of 104. For the Works, Paish (six for 45), Welshman (two for 19) and Winters (one for 8) secured the wickets.

Scores:

Wagon Works 182 for four declared
H Banks (68), A Paish (51), E Proctor (32)
Monmouth 104 all out

1929

Saturday 28th April Wagon Works v. Swindon

H Banks Opens With a Century

For the opening match of the season at Tuffley, Swindon provided the opposition. Batting first on an easy-paced wicket, the home batsmen scored at a good rate, and although H Brown was run out at 23, Proctor and Winters carried the score to 60 before the second wicket fell. Banks then joined Proctor and the rate of scoring increased, Banks especially hitting with great vigour.

Despite various bowling changes, the pair were not separated until they had added 119 runs, Proctor being taken at square leg for a sound 56. Banks, who had over-hauled his partner, still scored at a great rate and reached his century with a huge drive which cleared the ring. He was dismissed soon afterwards, having scored 107 out of 144 runs in 56 minutes. His best hits were two 6s and fifteen 4s. The innings was then declared closed, 204 runs having been scored in an hour and fifty minutes.Swindon, with two hours to bat, took matters carefully, Poppitt in particular batting very cautiously and at the drawing of stumps was still undefeated. The match terminated at 7.30 in a draw, only seven wickets having fallen for the 342 runs scored. For the Works, A Paish took one for 17, L Mountney one for 17 and E J Stephens one for 30. For Swindon, A E Lloyd had two for 36, and E B Lloyd one for 23.

WAGON WORKS					SWINDON			
H Brown	run out			13	G Wood	b	Stephens	9
E Proctor	c	Williams	b A Lloyd	56	G Poppitt	not out		43
J Winters	lbw		b E Lloyd	22	AE Lloyd	c	Paish b Mountney	28
H Banks	b	A Lloyd		107	N Litton	b	Paish	18
FW Stock	not out			4	E Lloyd	Not out		35
	EXTRAS			2		**EXTRAS**		5
	Total (for 4 declared)			204		Total (for 3 wickets)		138

Sunningend 75 (Arpin 11, Harvey 10); Wagon Works 'A' 76 (N Cole 14 not out, L Ireland 14). At Cheltenham the Wagon Works won an exciting game by 1 run. For the Works, E Hale took 4 for 25, A Newman 3 for 10 and H Hemmings 2 for 9 and for Sunningend, Stratford, Arpin and Miller were most successful.

Wagon Works 'B' entertained Sunningend II at the Sports Ground. The visitors batted first and compiled 98 runs (H Wacroft 14, A Osbourne 12). The home team had reached 61 for three wickets when stumps were drawn. J Brookes batted splendidly for the Works, being 40 not out at the close. H Robinson did best with the ball for Sunningend, whilst L Daniels was the most successful bowler for the Works.

Gloucester Railway Carriage and Wagon Co Ltd Cricket Section 1st Team 1929 Played 19 Won 9 Lost 4 Drawn 6

L V Huggins A J Paish E Proctor J Winters T Goddard H Brown G Welshman A H Evans
H Brown (scorer) GPoolman PF Stock (joint hon sec) H Banks (vice captain)
A E Hopcroft (captain) W A Brown (joint hon sec) EJ Stephens LMountney H E Perkins (chairman)

Saturday 4th May - Stroud's fine performance

The Works lost to Stroud at Tuffley by five wickets. The Works won the toss and batted first. With only 5 runs scored, Hopcroft was bowled, but H Brown and Evans raised the total to 61 before Evans left after a sound display. With 103 on the board for the loss of three wickets a good total seemed assured, but the remaining batsmen, taking risks in endeavouring to obtain runs quickly, were soon disposed of and the innings aggregated the moderate total of 151. H Brown carried off the batting honours for a well-played 54.
The visitors, with an hour and three-quarters to bat did not attempt to go for the runs at the start and were behind the clock until Braybrooke opened out. Runs afterwards came at a good pace, but the score was within 6 of victory when Braybrooke's splendid effort ended by him playing hard on to his wicket. The game terminated in an exciting manner, the winning hit being made on the stroke of time.

For Stroud, G Wedel took three wickets for 41 and A L Crowe three for 55, while for the Works, J Winters two for 43, H Brown one for 11 and L Mountney one for 14.

WAGON WORKS

H Brown	c	Blen	b	Crowe	54
A Hopcroft	b	Crowe			2
A Evans	run out				24
H Banks	b	Crowe			18
FW Stock	b	Wedel			10
J Winters	c&b	Cullimore			16
E Stephens	b	Wedel			3
EF Proctor	c	Betts	b	Wedel	4
AJ Paish	not out				8
W Brown	run out				3
L Mountney	run out				0
EXTRAS					3
Total					145

STROUD

FJ Betts	b	Mountney			25
N Cullimore	run out				12
A Braybrooke	b	Winters			73
R Redstone	c	Evans	b	H Brown	19
G Wedel	lbw		b	Winters	8
JD Blen	not out				10
Dr Munden	not out				3
EXTRAS					2
Total (for 5 wickets)					152

Saturday 11thMay - Wagon Works v Nondescripts

Played at Tuffley on Saturday, this game ended in a draw. The scoring was never very brisk owing to the keen fielding of both sides.

For the Works, A Paish, E Proctor and A Hopcroft batted well, and T Burns and the Stephens brothers showed the best form for the visitors. T Burns 2 for 35 H Pollard 1 for 20 and F Hawker 1 for 47 were the most successful bowlers for the Nondescripts, and W Brown 2 for 30, L Mountney 1 for 16 and J Stephens 1 for 27 for the Works.

WAGON WORKS

H Brown	lbw		b	Hawker	6
AHopcroft	c	Meadows	b	Burns	24
BF Proctor	run out				32
H Banks	c	J Stephens	b	Pollard	16
J Paish	not out				33
H Evans	b	Burns			15
F Stock	not out				2
EXTRAS					19
Total (for 5 wickets)					147

NONDESCRIPTS

J Benbow	c&b	W Brown			13
Paish	b				1
K Smith	run out				3
Stephens	c	Hopcroft	b	Mountney	14
Stephens	lbw		b	W Brown	16
Burns	not out				42
J Pollard	not out				11
EXTRAS					3
Total (for 5 wickets)					103

Saturday 18th May   *Wagon Works v Ross*

Ross had the advantage of batting first on a good wicket at Tuffley. Meredith was bowled off his pads with the first ball sent down. With only 15 runs scored, Watkins was easily caught and bowled, but Rolf and Wilding produced a lively stand and added 58 for the third wicket.

The Works batsmen showed indifferent form, the first three wickets falling for 17 runs. Hopcroft and Paish added 34 for the fourth wicket and, later Poolman showed some confidence, but eight wickets were down for 88 runs. Stephens and Brown, by steady batting, added 24 runs and although stumps were not drawn till 8 o'clock, the game remained unfinished. For the Works, Paish took three wickets for no runs, W A Brown four for 43, and J Stephens two for 44, while and for Ross, F E Ellis had four for 18, F Hill three for 54 and P S Morgan two for 16.

ROSS

RWP Roff	c	Hopcroft	b	Stephens	35
H Meredith	b	Stephens			0
BI Watkins	c&b	W Brown			8
AJ Wilding	c	Hale	b	W Brown	53
W Baynham	c	Stephens	b	W Brown	13
PS Morgan	c	Evans	b	W Brown	11
J Lane					10
G Home	c	Hale	b	Paish	10
AC Gerard	c	H Brown	b	Paish	0
F Hill	lbw		b	Paish	0
FE Ellis	Run out				0
	EXTRAS				
Total (for 5 wickets)					**145**

WAGON WORKS

H Brown	c	Roff	b	Ellis	2
AE Hopcroft	c	Jerrard	b	Ellis	30
J Winters	lbw		b	Ellis	1
H Banks	st	Watkins	b	Hill	0
AJ Paish	lbw		b	Morgan	18
FW Stock	b	Hill			1
AH Evans	c	Lane	b	Hill	7
C Poolman	b	Ellis			13
E Stephens	lbw		b	Morgan	19
WA Brown	Not out				8
E Hale	Not out				4
EXTRAS					13
Total (for 9 Wickets)					**116**

Saturday 25th May - Wagon Works v Lydney

Owing to the late arrival of the visitors, a start was not made until 3 o'clock at Tuffley. Lydney batted first, and by good batting totalled 174 runs for the loss of half their wickets. Grey, Elliott and S Jarrett all batted with confidence. With just over an hour and a half left to bat, the Works forced the pace, 95 runs being scored in an hour for the loss of 4 wickets. The next three wickets fell quickly, however, and the game ended tamely in a draw. H Brown batted well for his runs, and A Evans also was in good form. For Lydney, B Woolridge (5 wickets for 27) bowled effectively.

LYDNEY

P Grey	c	Brown	b	Winters	80
J Berthon	lbw		b	Mountney	14
C Rosser	run out				0
G Elliot	c	Banks	b	Stephens	68
S Jarrett	not out				25
H Thomas	c	Winters	b	Mountney	0
W Cornock	not out				8
EXTRAS					13
Total (for 5 wickets declared)					**178**

WAGON WORKS

H Brown	c	Cornock	b	Woolridge	39
E Proctor	b	Elliot			12
AH Evans	not out				26
J Winters	c	Cornock	b	Woolridge	0
A Hopcroft	st	Rosser	b	Woolridge	16
AJ Paish	b	Woolridge			9
FW Stock	b	Elliot			1
J Stephens	not out				3
EXTRAS					12
Total (for 7 wickets)					**127**

Saturday 1st June

Gloucestershire played Worcestershire on the Wagon Works Ground

The ground receipts were £225, which up to that date had only been beaten once when Surrey played and Jack Hobbs was the main attraction. The gate number was 5000.

Saturday 8th June - Easy win for Wagon Works

Wagon Works visited St Paul's College, Cheltenham and won easily. The wicket was on the soft side and appeared likely to assist the bowlers. The Works, batting first, made a good start ,despite the fact that the ball frequently got up awkwardly, and 38 runs were scored before H Brown edged one to first slip. Hopcroft showed sound defence, and with Evans added 69 runs for the fourth wicket. The innings was declared closed at the useful score of 161 for the loss of five wickets, thanks chiefly to Hopcroft and Evans, who both exceeded the half century, the former hitting nine fours and the latter eight.

Rain delayed the resumption considerably, but eventually it was possible to continue. The Collegians however, on the rain-damaged pitch, offered little resistance to the bowling of W Brown and A Paish, the whole side being disposed of for 43 runs. Brown took seven wickets for 11 and Paish three for 17.

WAGON WORKS					ST. PAUL'S COLLEGE				
AE Hopcroft	lbw		b	Ainsworth 52	T Edwards	c	Welshman b	W Brown	4
H Brown	c	Cameron b		Matthews 16	C Hudson	c	H Brown b	W Brown	7
E Proctor	b			Matthews 7	W Green	c	Paish b	W Brown	14
HS Banks	c	Ette b		Matthews 7	R Holiday	b	W Brown		0
AH Evans	not out			57	CR Bough	c	Paish b	W Brown	1
AJ Paish	c	Riseley b		Ainsworth 1	R Ainsworth	st	Hopcroft b	Paish	8
FW Stock	not out			3	G Ette	c	Hopcroft b	W Brown	1
					W Hollis	b	W Brown		0
					O Cameron	lbw		b	Paish	0
					R Matthews	c	Hopcroft b	Paish	6
					R Risleley	not out			0
EXTRAS				18	**EXTRAS**				2
Total (for 5 wickets declared)				161	Total				43

Gloucester Railway Carriage and Wagon Co Ltd Cricket Section "A" Team Season 1929 Played 14 Won 8 Lost 6

F Stephens E Hale F Brisland G Welshman W A Brown (joint hon sec) A Mayhew J Brookes A E Evans H Smith (umpire)
H E Perkins (chairman) C Poolman F Stock (joint hon sec) G Croft A Carter (capt) A Hemmings W Bourne N Cole F Cresswell

WAGON WORKS WELL BEATEN AT TEWKESBURY
SOUND INNINGS BY C S BARNETT

The Wagon Works visited Tewkesbury and lost by seven wickets. Morrison and Young, who opened the bowling for Tewkesbury, were in good form on a wicket to their liking, and although the first Works' pair put on 21, half the wickets fell for 39. Banks, however, showed more confidence and, with the assistance of Proctor, added 30 runs for the sixth wicket. Three further wickets fell quickly however, and nine men were out for 84 runs. The last wicket proved troublesome. Mountney defended well and helped Brown to add a useful 38. Morrison and Young bowled unchanged, the former taking five for 56 and Young five for 49.

The home side, with the wicket playing a lot faster, obtained the necessary runs for the loss of three wickets, Barnett and Chatham scoring 81 before being parted, the old county player completing a sound 53. Brown (two for 30) and J Winters (one for 18) secured the wickets.

WAGON WORKS					TEWKESBURY					
H Brown	c	Goodwin b	Morrison	14	C Barnett	b	Winters			59
A Hopcroft	b	Morrison		4	C Chatham	lbw		b	W Brown	35
AH Evans	b	Young		2	E Morrison	c	Banks	b	W Brown	3
AJ Paish	c	Smith	b	Young	7	P Smith	not out				9
HS Banks	c	Morrison b	Young	28	St Freeman	not out				8
J Winters	lbw		b	Morrison	1						
EF Proctor	b	Morrison		9						
FW Stock	b	Young		5						
E Stephens	c	Herridge b	Young	0						
WA Brown	not out			30						
L Mountney	b	Morrison		5						
	EXTRAS			**12**		**EXTRAS**				**11**
	Total			**119**		**Total for 3**				**125**

Saturday 13th July

At Wagon Works

Metropolitan Works (Birmingham) 105 all out.
Wagon Works A Hopcroft 42 E J Stephens 27 not out.

Saturday 20th July

Wagon Works Beaten at the Sports Ground

Nondescripts 175 for 8 declared, T Stephens 75, E Paish 32.
Wagon Works 60 all out A H Evans carried his bat for 22 not out.

Saturday 27th July - Stroud v. Wagon Works

Played at Stroud. Wagon Works 201 for 6 H Brown 58 A Hopcroft 59, J Winters 42 not out. Strouds 130 for 5, G Wedel run out 46, Welshman and Brown 1 for 12, Stephens 2 for 45.

Saturday 24th August - Wagon Works beat the clock – Fast Scoring By Banks and Brown

The return match played at the Wagon Works, Tewkesbury 158 C Chatham 72, C S Barnett 30.

Wagon Works 159 for seven, H Brown 54, H Banks 57.

Saturday 7thSeptember

Tom Goddard Again - 9-42 Against Swindon

Swindon						Wagon Works		
G Wood	Lbw		b	Goddard	16	A Hopcroft		12
ER Hart	c	Goddard	b	Brown	0	H Banks		33
A Lloyd	b	Goddard			51	A Evans		26
W Liton	lbw		b	Goddard	0	T Goddard	Not out	22
P Pillinger	b	Goddard			16	A Paish		7
JB Lloyd	c	Hopcroft	b	Goddard	18	J Winters	Not out	13
G Tinsley	b	Goddard			0			
R Stone	c	Banks	b	Goddard	12			
R Stevens	lbw		b	Goddard	0			
R Knapp	Not out				13			
G Brunger	b	Goddard			0			
	Extras				13	**Extras**		27
Total					139	(4 wickets)		140

1930 – 1939

The County Festival at the works' ground that had been so successful from 1923 continued with great players, not only from Gloucestershire but all the leading counties, playing there.

In 1931 the New Zealand Tourists were the visitors, Surrey in 1932 and 1939, Yorkshire in 1933, 1935 and 1938 and Lancashire four times during the decade. Sussex made the trip in July 1930 and included Maurice Tate and the legendary K.S. Duleepsinhji, though Gloucestershire won the match by an innings.

Charlie Barnett, who had played against the Works Team for Tewkesbury a few years earlier scored 94 and Tom Goddard on his home ground took two for 40 and five for 54. K.S Duleepsinhji, who had a week earlier scored a century for England at Lord's was out comparatively cheaply in both innings, scoring only 17 and 11. His first class career would have lasted much longer had it not been for ill health, for in only seven full seasons he played in 12 tests, scoring 3 centuries and averaging 58.

Tom Goddard was to hold his benefit match on the ground in 1936 against Nottinghamshire. Legend has it that Goddard was concerned that because of the low first innings' scores, the match would not last the full four days and his 'purse' would duly be affected. Goddard expressed his concern to Wally Hammond who it is said replied, "Don't worry Tom, I'll bat all day if necessary". Hammond did bat for over 6 hours making 317, his highest total for Gloucestershire and the highest score ever made on the ground. For the Works side, Albert (Hoppy) Hopcroft continued to captain the first eleven throughout the 30's and was one of the mainstays of the batting during that time. A.E (Bert) and A.H (Tripey) Evans, Harold Banks, Charlie Poolman and the Stephens brothers all compiled useful runs, whilst Frank Brisland, L Parsons, A Mountney and Harold Proctor, along with Frank Stephens, each bowled extremely well. Towards the end of the decade two names making their way into the first eleven were Vic Beamish, a very good all rounder and Frank Barber, a fine spin bowler. A name that should be remembered at this time is that of Charlie Restall. He captained the junior side, or 'C' eleven as it was known, for many years and along with groundsman and ex–county player Arthur Paish, was very successful in the coaching of younger players. Charlie Restall, after retiring from playing and coaching in later years was to be seen helping Arthur Paish and latterly Charlie Newman with the groundsman's duties. During the early 1930s Restall, a generous man, encouraged players in his team by rewarding those who took a 'Hat-Trick' or made scores of 50 or more, with a shilling – a tidy perk in those days.

In 1934 the fixtures again included the town sides of Stroud, Ross, Tewkesbury and Malvern along with arch rivals The Nondescripts. Of the nineteen matches played that year, 12 were won, 5 drawn, and only 2 lost, Albert Hopcroft finishing with a batting average of 28.8. In 1935 Mr Peter Smith took over the position of Treasurer from Mr W.A. Brown who had held the position for several years, only to hand over the reins in 1938 to Mr E.J. Jennings. 1938 was not as successful as previous seasons, only 7 of the 22 games played being won, while unusually 10 were drawn. Skipper Hopcroft completed his tenth season as captain with a batting average of 23.61. Frank Stephens captained the newly formed evening team successfully, while the 'B' Team was led by Mr C. Webber, taking over from Mr J.A. Carter.

The County Club throughout these years was grateful to the Wagon Works for the free use of the ground and its facilities and also the first class pitches prepared by Arthur Paish and his assistants.

Towards the end of 1931 a new chairman of the company was appointed and during his time in office, he played a pivotal role in helping the company out of recession. Leslie Boyce, who was the M.P. for Gloucester, soon became the cricket section's new President and in later years went on to become the Lord Mayor of London.

In May 1939 the cricket team's first eleven match at Lydney was held up while the Prime Minister's train passed by – Neville Chamberlain being on his way to visit Viscount Bledisloe. Ironically, war was soon to be declared, plunging the country and sport into deep depression.

1930

Wednesday 7thMay

Gloucestershire started their game against Lancashire on the ground and chasing a total of 215, were dismissed for only 54. Only two players reached double figures, one player being E J (Dick) Stephens of the Wagon Works Club.

Saturday 21stJune

County Professional Assists Wagon Works
Goddard Seven for 27

For this match, the home side included Tom Goddard the County Professional, but Tewkesbury lacked the services of C S Barnett (Charlie Barnett's father) and A T Young.

Batting first, the Works totalled 149, thanks mainly to H Brown, B Howely and A Evans. E G Morrison bowled well for the visitors taking four for 46, C Chatham had 3 for 52 and R Linnell 2 for 15.

Tewkesbury made a poor start, two wickets falling for two runs. Although Morrison, Chatham and Mustoe improved matters, a further collapse ensued, and the whole side was dismissed for 63. Goddard's bowling was instrumental in bringing about the result, his seven wickets only costing 27 runs. J Stephens took one for 11, and G Welshman one for 14.

WAGON WORKS

H Brown	lbw		Morrison	35
A Hopcroft	b		Morrison	5
JR Howell	c Simms	b	Morrison	26
AH Evans	c Neale	b	Chatham	36
EF Proctor	c Hitchman	b	Morrison	6
F Stephens	b		Linnell	10
J Winters	c Morrison	b	Linnell	8
WA Brown	c Chatham			9
T Goddard	run out			4
E Stephens	c Hitchman	b	Chatham	0
G Welshman	not out			0
EXTRAS				10
Total				**149**

TEWKESBURY

AP Barnett	c Goddard	b	J Stephens	0
RH Green	lbw Goddard			0
C Chatham	b Goddard			11
R Morrison	b Goddard			21
RT Mustoe	c H Brown	b	Welshman	13
T Hitchman	b Goddard			4
B Freeman	b Goddard			0
H Warner	c H Brown	b	Goddard	6
C Neale	run out			0
WC Simms	c&b Goddard			0
R Linnell	not out			
EXTRAS				6
Total				**63**

Saturday 21st June

Wagon Works 'C' 53 (C Brown 21, S Russell 10)
Williams and James 151, (R Doyle 73, L Oakley 23 and R Miller 22) R Miller (five for 20) and S Hancocks (three for 15) were the successful bowlers for the winners.

Stroud Brewery 119 for five wickets (C Watkins 37, R E Griffiths 19, R Wager 20 not out)
Wagon Works 'B' 103 (A Matthew 33, L S Price 24, A Bloodworth 14) S Harding bowled well for the winners, whilst W Parry captured three wickets at a small cost for the losers. Played at Tuffley Avenue Sports Ground.

Saturday 12thJuly - Wagon Works Lose at Birmingham

The Gloucester Wagon Works visited Birmingham for their annual match with the Metro-Cammell Works. The home side batted first and thanks to Down and Fowler, the innings realised the useful total of 147, the former especially giving an excellent display. For the Gloucester Works W Brown (six for 38), J Stephens (three for 28) and G Welshman (one for 21) secured the wickets. The visitors commenced promisingly and had scored 65 for the loss of two wickets. The third wicket fell at 83, when H Brown was bowled after a fine knock of 41. Subsequently a rot set in, and, although Banks and W Brown improved matters and played out time, it was agreed to continue and the Gloucester team failed by 15 runs. For the home side, Caulkett took five wickets for 35, and Fowler two for 26.

Metro Cammell Works					Wagon Works				
J Gibbons	b	W Brown		1	H Brown	b	Fowler		41
W Mountford	c	Paish	b J Stephens	13	AH Evans	b	Caulkett		9
J Down	b	J Stephens		71	F Stephens	c	Down	b Wiggins	13
C Resney	b	Welshman		5	A Hopcroft	b	Fowler		16
G Fowler	b	W Brown		34	C Poolman	c	Down	b Caulkett	1
W Sullivan	b	W Brown		9	HS Bank	b	Down		23
R Kempson	b	W Brown		1	AJ Paish	b	Sullivan		4
R Harris	b	W Brown		0	G Welshman	b	Caulkett		0
L Caulkett	c	F Stephens	c J Stephens	2	F Brisland	b	Caulkett		0
N Wiggins	c	Brisland	c W Brown	5	WA Brown	b	Caulkett		13
F Routledge	not out			4	R Stephens	not out			0
	EXTRAS			2		**EXTRAS**			12
	Total			147		**Total**			132

Metro Cammell Works 'A' 137
(Hodgson 33, Leg 24, James 23, Harris 17)

Wagon Works 'A' 108
(J Brookes not out 31, A J Carter 24, E Proctor 10, E Hale 10)
For the Works E Hale took four wickets for 16 and A Carter two for 33 and for Birmingham, Hodgson captured seven for 33.

Wagon Works 'B' 151
(Eamer 32, Parry 24, W Trigg 22)

Cam II 114
Harris 36, R Brindle 25, C Nicholls and W Berriman bowled well for the winners.

1931

Saturday 9thMay - Wagon Works v. Nondescripts

Played on the Works' Sports Ground.

The visitors, winning the toss, put the Works in to bat on a wicket likely to assist the bowlers. This policy was justified as the home side, in less than an hour, lost half their wickets for 34 runs. However Evans, Banks and Jim Stephens pulled the game round and a respectable score resulted. For the Nondescripts, Benbow (3 for 35) and Wybrow (3 for 39) bowled well.

The visitors never looked like losing the game, but steady bowling kept the rate behind the clock and at 8 pm an enjoyable game ended in a draw. For the Works, Paish (1 for 14) and W Brown (1 for 26) were the most successful bowlers.

WAGON WORKS						NONDESCRIPTS					
H Brown	c&b	Carr			6	F Benbow	c	Poolman	b	Paish	31
A Hopcroft	st	Voyce	b	Benbow	12	D Meadows	c	Paish	b	W Brown	1
F Stephens	c	Voyce	b	Burns	9	A Wybrow	c&b	H Brown			16
C Poolman	c	Burns	b	Benbow	3	F Voyce	run out				32
A Paish	c	Hawker	b	Benbow	0	F Stephens	not out				38
A Evans	st	Voyce	b	Wybrow	22	F Hawker	b	Mountney			4
H Banks	b	Wybrow			36	K Burns	not out				5
J Stephens	not out				41						
G Welshman	b	Burns			5						
W Brown	c	Voyce	b	Wybrow	2						
L Mountney	b	Hawker			4						
		EXTRAS			9			EXTRAS			9
		Total			149			Total (for 5)			136

Saturday 29thMay - Wagon Works' Good Win

The Works had the best of a low scoring game at Tetbury. Batting first, the home side fared poorly, losing six wickets for 29 runs. Only A Cocks showed any resistance and he and A W Cook were the only batsmen to score double figures.

The Works found run getting no easy matter but proceeding steadily, obtained the necessary score for the loss of seven wickets.

TETBURY						WAGON WORKS					
A W Cook	c	Evans	b	Brisland	11	A Evans	b	Prout			7
J Parry	c	Evans	b	Mountney	2	J Stephens	c	Braine	b	Prout	18
Dr M Braybrooke	c	Banks	b	Mountney	4	H Brown	b	Prout			10
P Prout	b	Brisland			2	A Paish	c	Braybrooke	b	Prout	4
W Eldridge	c	Mountney	b	Brisland	2	H Banks	b	Prout			0
W Dyer	b	Mountney			5	A Hopcroft	lbw		b	Brown	38
A Cocks	b	Brisland			21	C Poolman	lbw		b	Brown	11
E Brown	c	J Stephens	b	W Brown	7	F Stephens	not out				6
A Braine	b	Brisland			4						
A Edwards	Not out				2						
		EXTRAS			9			EXTRAS			1
		Total			78			Total (for 7 wickets)			95

Bowling: Brisland 6 for 23, Mountney 3 for 30

Bowling: Prout 5 for 39, Brown 2 for 10

Saturday 11th July - Wagon Works B v Cam II

At the Works ground, Tuffley Avenue
Scores: Wagon Works B 142 for 8, (L Evans 53, R Gladwin 36, L Price 20). Cam II all out 50.

Saturday 18th July - Wagon Works v Lydney

Played at Tuffley Avenue. Wagon Works defeated Lydney on the Works Sports Ground by 17 runs. The visitors, batting first, fared only moderately on a wicket affected by rain, and were dismissed for 93 runs. For the Works, H Brown (three for 14), H Proctor (three for 25), and A Paish (two for 19) secured the wickets.
The home side, after losing the first wicket without a run scored, batted steadily, the total standing at 79 for four wickets, but a further four wickets fell before the runs necessary for a win were obtained. The total eventually reached 110, J Stephens being top scorer with 36.

For Lydney, L Martin took six wickets for 22.

Saturday 1st August - Wagon Works Win At Ledbury

The match was held at Ledbury with the Works winning by five wickets. The last eight Ledbury wickets fell for a mere 20 runs, Proctor during this period taking seven for 9. Hopcroft's wicket keeping was also a feature, he having a hand in the dismissal of five batsmen (two stumped and three caught). Banks' 53 not out included two 6s and five 4s.

Scores: Ledbury 112 (A Heaton 34), Wagon Works 138 for five (J Stephens 27, H Banks not out for 53, F Brisland 19, F Stephens not out 11)

1932

Victory for the Works

The annual match with Kendrick and Jefferson's (West Bromwich) was played on the Sports Ground. Batting first the visitors fared only moderately, and half their batsmen were dismissed for 18 runs. Freeman, Burlton and Cook showed more confidence later, but the total only reached 66. For the Wagon Works, Mountney bowled finely, capturing 5 wickets for 13 runs, and Brisland took 3 for 13.

The home side appeared to be in difficulties at one period, losing 7 wickets for 53 but, thanks to Mountney and Paish who added 38 runs for the 8th wicket, a win was obtained by 25 runs with 2 wickets in hand. For the visitors, JR Burlton (3 for 19) and W Hartshorn (3 for 31) were the most successful bowlers.

Kenderick and Jeffersons 66, T Freeman (20), S Cook (12), J Burlton (12)

Wagon Works 91 for 8, L Mountney (22), A Hopcroft (13), A J Paish (17 not out)

Saturday 11th June - Wagon Works on Top

The Works had the assistance of Tom Goddard and Dick Stephens, the County professionals, against Ross. Batting 1st, the visitors had scored 204 for the loss of 8 wickets at the tea interval. Evans showed excellent form in scoring 61, and Goddard, who hit a 6 and five 4s, quickly knocked up 44. The home side, with the exception of Roff and Cox, found Goddard's bowling too much for them. The Ross captain however batted splendidly and deservedly reached the half-century. Goddard took 7 wickets for 50 runs and Preece for Ross took 4 for 62.

WAGON WORKS						ROSS					
E Stephens	lbw		b	Meredith	18	RWP Roff	b	Goddard			51
HS Bank	c	Preedy	b	Preece	12	H Cook	b	Goddard			0
C Poolman	b	Preece			0	GR Preece	run out				3
AH Evans	c	Footett	b	Peachy	61	H Meredith	c&b	Goddard			10
H Brown	b	Woodwiss			15	C Peachy	c	F Stephens	b	Goddard	9
A Hopcroft	lbw		b	Meredith	6	S Woodwiss	lbw		b	Goddard	1
F Stephens	c	West	b	Preece	13	PS Morgan	b	Brisland			3
T Goddard	b	Preece			44	D Cox	c	Banks	b	Proctor	23
H Proctor	not out				14	H West			b	Goddard	1
L Mountney	not out				11	J Footett	b	Goddard			2
						SG Preedy	not out				7
			EXTRAS		10			EXTRAS			11
			TOTAL (for 8 declared)		204			TOTAL			121

F Brisland did not bat

Works Win by Seven Wickets

The Wagon Works proved easy winners in the annual match with The Metropolitan C C at Saltley, Birmingham. The Metropolitan team fared moderately and the side was dismissed for 115. For the visitors, H Brown bowled effectively, capturing eight wickets for 48 runs. The Gloucester Works experienced little difficulty in obtaining the runs, Evans and Jim Stephens, in a spirited partnership, put on 91 in an hour, the latter hitting two 6s.

Metropolitan Works 115, A Edwards (15), H Brown (8 for 48)
Wagon Works 137 for 3, A Hopcroft (8), A Evans (42), J Stephens (55), C Poolman (19), E Proctor (9), F Stephens, H Brown, W Brown, H Proctor, F Brisland and L Mountney did not bat.

Saturday 13th August

Works beat Ross

Ross visited the Sports Ground and batted first on a fast track. The first three wickets fell with only four runs scored, but Meredith and Roff added 50 runs for the fourth wicket, and Peachy improved matters further. The score totalled 120 for 5 wickets, but then another collapse occurred and the remaining batsmen could only muster eight runs between them.

J A Brooks accomplished a sensational bowling performance for, in the space of 12 balls, he took 5 wickets for one run including the 'Hat Trick' and had the full analysis of 6 for 13. H Proctor took 3 for 48 and H Brown one for 17.

The Works, with plenty of time, batted consistently and passed their opponent's score with only three wickets down. Hopcroft, F Stephens and Poolman showed good form. For Ross, G Sainsbury had three wickets for 53. J A Brookes is the son of Mr J T Brookes, Chairman of the Gloucester Rugby Football Club, and has only been promoted to the 1st XI for the last two matches.

Scores:
Ross 128, H Meredith (54), C Peachy (22),
Wagon Works 162 for 5, F Stephens (51), C Poolman (31), A Hopcroft (26), H Brown (17), H Banks (15).

Saturday 20th August

Wagon Works draw with Cheltenham

Heavy scoring characterised the game between the Wagon Works and Cheltenham at the Sports Ground. The Works batted first on an excellent wicket and made a splendid start, Hopcroft and Evans putting on 70 runs in 50 minutes for the first wicket. Two further wickets fell sharply, but when Banks joined Evans the rate of scoring increased and the total reached 160 before another wicket fell. Evans batted very soundly for his 57 which included six 4s, while Banks, who obtained his 60 in 35 minutes, hit three 6s and five 4s. The innings was declared closed at the tea interval, having occupied just over two hours. For Cheltenham, Woof (3 for 74), Bowen (2 for 38) and Yiend (1 for 42) secured the wickets.

The visitors, with two hours to bat, made a poor start, Ince and Jordan both being dismissed with only 8 runs scored. Hedges then joined Lewis in a stand that yielded 124. The old Oxonian played a dashing innings and obtained 94 of those runs in 70 minutes, reaching the boundary on 12 occasions. When time was called Cheltenham still required 56 runs with 4 wickets in hand. For the Works, E Proctor bowled well, taking 4 wickets for 34 runs.

Scores:
Wagon Works 216 for 7 declared. Team: A Hopcroft, A Evans, Poolman, H Brown, H Banks, H Smith, F Stephens, J A Brookes, A Paish, C Mountney, H Proctor.
Cheltenham 161 for 6. F Lewis (37), Hedges (94)

On this day in a match at the Oval, Surrey played Yorkshire and the following was reported:

Bowes' persistence in dropping the ball short when faced by Hobbs caused a minor 'breeze'. In one over three successive balls, abnormally short, flew over Hobbs' head, and the Surrey player, after apparently voicing a protest walked down the pitch to a point a few feet from the bowler's end and patted the turf with his bat. Bowes failed to upset the great batsman and Hobbs scored 90 out of 135 in two hours.

Saturday 12th September

CENTURY BY STEPHENS

Lydney failed badly at the Sports Ground and the whole side was dismissed for 31 runs. Tom Goddard and H Proctor bowled unchanged, taking 3 wickets for 12 runs and 7 for 16 respectively. The Works obtained the necessary runs for victory without losing a wicket and subsequently Dick Stephens and H Smith indulged in some free hitting, putting on 140 runs in 55 minutes. The county professional had the satisfaction of topping the century and was undefeated at the close having hit two 6s and seven 4s.

WAGON WORKS

J Stephens	lbw		b	Elliot	9
E Stephens	not out				114
H Smith	st	Hiron	b	Martin	58
C Poolman	not out				10
Extras					**10**

E F Proctor, H Brown, F Stephens, A H Hopcroft, A J Paish, H B Proctor, T Goddard – Did Not Bat

Wagon Works   **201 for 2**   **Lydney 31**

1933

Saturday 11th May

Wagon Works had a splendid win at Lydney. Good batting by A Evans, J Stephens, C Poolman and F Stephens allowed the Wagon Works to declare at the tea interval with 179 for 6, C Holmes 4 for 46 was the home team's best bowler. Lydney were all out for 110. J Stephens 4 for 22, J Brookes 2 for 12, H Brown 2 for 21, F Stephens 1 for 5 and H Proctor 1 for 30 shared the wickets for the winners.

Lydney 110 all out

WAGON WORKS

A Hopcroft	lbw		b	Elliot	3
A Evans	c	Elliot	c	Holman	32
J Stephens	lbw		b	Holman	24
E Stephens	c	Richards	b	Dunford	11
H Banks	c & b	Holman			2
C Poolman	not out				47
F Stephens	not out				46
Extras					**8**
Total				**179 for 6 declared**	

Saturday 1st June

Playing at Thornbury, the Works won by one wicket and 20 runs. H Proctor took 5 wickets for 36 including the "hat trick" for the winners. For Thornbury, Pullen had 4 for 24 and Jackson 4 for 32.

WAGON WORKS

A Hopcroft	c & b	Jackson			20
J Stephens	c	G Pullen	b	F Pullen	0
A Evans	b	G Pullen			27
H Smith	c	Thompson	b	Jackson	4
C Poolman	lbw		b	G Pullen	1
H Banks	not out				22
H Brown	c	Wicks	b	Jackson	0
E Proctor	b	G Pullen			0
F Brisland	b	G Pullen			0
B Hale	b	Pullen			0
L Hale	c	Potter	b	Jackson	4
Total				**83 for 9**	

Monday 1st July

In a keen draw at Cheltenham, the Wagon Works beat St Paul's College by 5 runs. Batting first, the College could do little against the bowling of H Proctor who came out with the average of 8 wickets for 12 runs. F Brisland also bowled well, taking the other 2 wickets for 6. The Wagon Works fared better than the home team going into bat, but collapsed when the second wicket partnership was broken. For the College, Workman took 6 for 14, Linnel 2 for 9 and Brown 1 for 11.

St Pauls   44

WAGON WORKS

J Stephens	b	Brown			1
A Evans	c	Holley	b	Workman	15
H Smith	c	Brown	b	Workman	3
C Poolman	lbw	Workman			0
L Smith	c & b	Linnel			1
H Brown	lbw		b	Workman	5
A Hopcroft	c	Brook	b	Linnel	0
A Mountney	not out				
F Brisland	c	Jones	b	Workman	4
H mProctor	c	Middleton	b	Workman	0
Total					**49**

Saturday 6th July

Metro Cammell Birmingham batted first against the Wagon Works at Tuffley, but W Sullivan and C Ramsey were the only ones to stand up against the bowling of H Brown and H Proctor. Brown took 6 wickets for 31 and Proctor 2 for 26. The Wagon Works passed the visitor's total of 110 with only 3 wickets down.

A Hopcroft batted well for 76.

For Metro Cammell Wiggins took 3 for 58.

Metro Cammell 110 all out

WAGON WORKS

J Stephens	b	Wiggins			6
A Hopcroft	lbw	Wiggins			76
A Evans	b	Fowler			8
F Stephens	b	Caulkett			22
H Smith	not out				42
H Banks	c	Gibbons	b	Wiggins	21
H Brown	not out				5
	Extras				**16**
	Total				**196 for 5**

Saturday 27th July

Wagon Works gained a splendid win over the Nondescripts at the Sports Ground by 120 runs and 4 wickets. Wagon Works 240 for 6 wickets.

Nondescripts 120 All Out

WAGON WORKS

A Hopcroft	lbw		b	Wybrew	39
J Stephens	c & b	Hawker			47
F Stephens	b	Hawker			10
A Evans	lbw		b	Hawker	0
H Banks	c	Hawker	b	Voyce	78
H Smith	b	Benbow			5
C Poolman	not out				36
V Maly	not out				6
	Extras				**19**
	Total				**240 for 6** H Proctor, H Brisland, H Brown did not bat

1934
Saturday 5th May

WAGON WORKS START WELL

Nondescripts, opening the season with the Wagon Works on the Sports Ground, at first found runs hard to get. T Banks however began to show good form and was unlucky to be run out after he had scored a useful 43. J Hill also batted well for 18 not out, the Nondescripts declaring with 124 for 8.

Wagon Works went for the runs, the first wicket putting on 47 before A Hopcroft was caught for 27. J Stephens (66 not out) and A Evans (31 not out) put on 76 for the third wicket. F Carr (2 for 39) for the Nondescripts and H Proctor (3 for 32) and H Brown (2 for 28) for the Works bowled well.

Scores:
Nondescripts 124 for 8 declared T Burns (43), J Hill (18 not out).
Wagon Works 131 for 2 J Stephens (66 not out), A Hopcroft (27), C Poolman (2), A Evans (31 not out), Extras (3).

Saturday 19th May - Stroud v. Wagon Works
Played at Stroud.

Stroud					Wagon Works				
MH Cullimore	st	Hopcroft	b	Brown	57	J Stephens	b		Cullimore	5
JR Nicklin	b	Stephens			32	A Hopcroft	c&b		Cullimore	55
GA Wedel	c	J Stephens	b	F Stephens	76	A Evans	b		Harris	0
F Harris	c&b	Mally			9	C Poolman	c&b		Cullimore	7
CR Carter	b	Brisland			3	F Stephens	lbw	b	Wedel	3
L Cordwell	c	J Stephens	b	F Stephens	0	H Banks	b		Wedel	38
VJ Venables	b	F Stephens			0	H Smith	b		Wedel	4
FG Betts	not out				2	H Brown	b		Wedel	10
MM Murden	not out				4	V Mally	not out			1
						H Proctor	not out			1
		Extras			13			Extras		2
		Total (for 7 declared)			196			Total (for 8)		126

Wedel 4-33
Cullimore 3-55   F Brisbane Did Not Bat
F Stephens 3-29

Saturday 26 May

BRILLIANT CENTURY FOR WAGON WORKS

Wagon Works defeated Lydney on the latter's ground by 140 runs. The Works lost 2 wickets for 8 runs but Frank Stephens and H Banks quickly hit 91 in 39 minutes at which point Banks was caught out for a vigorous 52 which included four 6s and three 4s. With a total of 223 for 7 wickets the innings was declared closed, the runs being made in just 109 minutes. F Stephens remained undefeated with 135 not out made in 104 minutes. He gave a brilliant exhibition of stroke play and hard hitting, his score including two 6s and sixteen 4s.

With nearly 2 ½ hours to bat, Lydney made a bad start by losing two wickets for 5 runs. The Works' bowlers were always on top, and, assisted by several smart catches, the home team were dismissed for a total of 83. H Proctor had two wickets for 15; H Brown two for 24; J Stephens three for 18; G Welshman two for 9 and Brisland one for 14. S Jarrett (five for 79) bowled well for Lydney.

Wagon Works A v Lydney A

Played at the Sports Ground (Gloucester)

Lydney 'A' 110 All Out. A Wilcox (35), S Jackson (18), J Allsop (10) and D Drew (10). Bowling, (5 for 45),
T. Bradbury (3 for 24), V Maly (1 for 9) and A Evans (1 for 10).
Wagon Works 'A' 183 for 6. E Proctor (66, ten 4s), J Lane (51 not out), Mansell-Davis (28), A Bloodworth (16). Bowling: H S Hopkins (2) and D Drew (1) took the most Lydney wickets.

Saturday 2nd June - Wagon Works Do Well At Home

Wagon Works

J Stephens	b	Rodway	98
A Hopcroft	lbw	b Mustoe	36
F Stephens	b	Mustoe	0
H Banks	b	Chatham	2
A Evans	not out		106
H Smith	not out		28
Extras			**12**
	Total (for 4 Declared)		**282**

Tewkesbury

S Freeman	lbw	b	F Stephens	13
Dr Sheppard	lbw	b	Brisland	12
C Chatham	not out			53
R Padfield	st	Hopcroft b	Proctor	16
W Mustoe	lbw	b	Brisland	8
E Green	lbw	b	Welshman	5
E Neale	not out			5
Extras				**22**
Total (for 5)				**134**

Match Drawn

Saturday 31st June - Wagon Works defeat Malvern

Played at the Sports Ground, the Wagon Works gained an easy victory over Malvern. The visitors were dismissed for 69 due to fine bowling by Brisland 4 for 21, Brookes 2 for 13, Proctor 3 for 20 and Welshman 1 for 5. The Works put on 64 for the first wicket, Hopcroft making 72 in seventy minutes, while Banks gave a brilliant display of forcing cricket to complete his century in only 64 minutes, including one 5 and sixteen 4s.

Wagon Works 'A' v. Nailsworth

Wagon Works 'A' 238 for 7 declared, A E Evans 56, P Smith 38, V Maly 34, G Roberts 29 not out, E W Hale 23, E Proctor 25, M Davies 13.
Nailsworth 103 for 9, D Hall 46, C Ball 26 not out. Bowling, T Bradbury 6 for 16 and V Maly 3 for 24

Saturday 17th September - Wagon Works v. Lydney

The Works batted in bright style, and thanks to F Stephens who scored 87 (fourteen 4s), A Evans 31 (four 4s) and Tom Goddard 60 in 18 minutes (eight 4s and two 6s), the total reached 214. Ledbury lost 3 wickets for 24, but good batting by Clarke 69 (one 6 and six 4s) managed to save the game. Goddard took 4 wickets and Brookes 3.
The cricket section of the Wagon Works had a successful season under A Hopcroft who had captained the team for 7 years. A Evans 2, H Banks and F Stephens recorded centuries during the season, while F Brisland bowled splendidly.

The record was 19. Won 12, Lost 2, Drew 5

	INNS	NOT OUT	RUNS	HIGHEST SCORE	AVERAGE
A Evans	16	5	591	125	53.72
F Stephens	17	1	518	135	32.37
A Hopcroft	17	1	461	75	26.33

1935

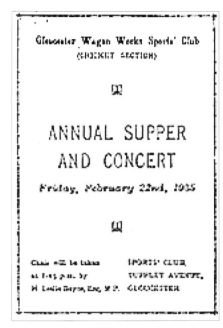
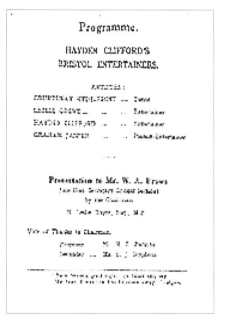

Saturday 15th June   - *Tom Goddard in Form For Wagon Works*

Tom Goddard, the Gloucestershire cricketer assisting the Wagon Works against Malvern at Malvern, secured eight wickets for eleven runs and, in his first over, dismissed three batsmen lbw without conceding a run.

Batting first on a tricky pitch, Wagon Works lost their first three wickets for eight runs, but thanks mainly to Banks and Hopcroft, were able to declare at 53 for 9. Malvern fared even worse than their opponents. Thanks to the brilliant bowling of Goddard, the visitors won a low -scoring game by 23 runs.

Wagon Works						Malvern					
J Stephens	st	Mann	b	Evans	2	H Winstanley	lbw		b	Goddard	0
F Stephens	c	Burton	b	Evans	4	J Evans	lbw		b	Goddard	3
V Maly	c	Parker	b	Evans	1	P Whitton	lbw		b	Goddard	0
H Banks	st	Mann	b	Evans	13	R Phelps	b	Goddard			0
J Lane	b	Paytor			5	G Burton	c	Banks	b	Brisland	0
A Hopcroft	run out				20	L Mann	b	Goddard			10
A Evans	c	Evans	b	Cridland	2	M Dubois	c	Brookes	b	Goddard	5
J Brookes	c	Whttion	b	Evans	4	L Cridland	b	Goddard			0
L Parsons	b	Cridland			0	F Paytor	run out				2
F Brisland	not out				0	R Parker	c&b	Goddard			3
						A Wolfe	not out				2
			Extras		2			Extras			5
			Total (for 9 dec)		53			Total			30

T Goddard did not bat

Saturday 29th June Wagon Works' Batsmen In Form

Wagon Works gained a nine wickets victory over Ledbury at Ledbury. The home team started poorly, losing two wickets for two runs in the first over against the fast bowling of Brookes and Brisland. Good batting by Beach and Smith improved the score and the innings eventually realised 132. Left with 88 minutes to get the runs, Stephens and Hopcroft put on 94 before the former was bowled for a stylish 44. Hopcroft hit twelve 4s in his brilliant innings of 86 not out. For the Works, Brookes took two wickets for 22, H Proctor four for 39, Brisland three for 23 and F Stephens one for 19.

Ledbury: 132 All Out   (W Beach 47, J Smith 25, W Lawrence 15)

Wagon Works: 158 for 1 (J Stephens 44, A Hopcroft not out 86, C Poolman not out 24)

Wagon Works II: 137 All Out (G Roberts 50, M Wellman 11, G Court 19, B Evans 18, P Smith 15)

Tyndale: 142 for 6 (K Keck 44), (S Davies 23) F Smith (two for 23)   Played at the Sports Ground.

Saturday 6th July

Wagon Works Beat The Clock

Wagon Works won a splendid match at Tetbury. Tetbury declared after scoring 131 runs in 2½ hours for three wickets. Left with ninety minutes to get the runs, the Works went all out to 'Beat the Clock' and won with about four minutes to spare. Stephens and Maly batted so well that 105 were on the board in seventy-three minutes. Stephens' 56 included six 4s. H Banks and Evans did some smart running between the wickets and the total at the drawing of stumps was 134 for five.

TETBURY				WAGON WORKS				
J Parry	b	Brookes	12	J Stephens	b	Clarke		56
M Braybrooke	not out		55	A Hopcroft	c	Chapman b	Cox	9
R Cook	b	Brisland	0	V Maly	lbw	b	Clarke	34
P Prout	b	Brookes	32	H Banks	run out			18
T Astill	not out		23	A Evans	b	Cox		2
				J Lane	not out			0
				F Brisland	not out			4
Extras			9	Extras				11
Total (for 3 declared)			131	Total (for 5)				134

Saturday 13th July - Wagon Works v Metropolitan Cammell (Birmingham)

Inter-Works match played on the Works Sports Ground.

METROPOLITAN CAMMELL					WAGON WORKS					
H Swinfield	run out			11	J Stephens	st	Realey	b	Down	75
H Wilkins	b	Brookes		52	F Stephens	b	Wilkins			21
G Fowler	b	Parsons		32	C Poolman	st	Realey	b	Down	9
J Down	c	J Stephens	b Brisland	60	H S Banks	st	Realey	b	Down	2
L Alexander	not out			38	J A Lane	c	Wilkins	b	Trueman	9
					V Maly	not out				7
					A H Evans	not out				0
		Extras		8			Extras			9
Total (for 4 dec')				201			Total (for 5)			132

Match Drawn

Saturday 17th August - Wagon Works' Good Performance

Gloucester Wagon Works accomplished a splendid performance in defeating Tewkesbury on the Wagon Works Sports Ground by 105 runs. The home side made a good start, Hopcroft and Maly putting on 70 runs in 43 minutes in a bright partnership before the latter was caught. Banks hit 4 boundaries in his first over, and with Hopcroft raised the score to 129 before Hopcroft was bowled for a vigorous knock of 70 made in an hour. Banks hit 36 runs in 33 minutes (including seven 4s) and the Works declared at 206 for nine, made in less than two hours.

With 2½ hours to get the runs Tewkesbury made a fair start, the opening pair putting on 33. Barnett batted in attractive style for his 41 (eight 4s), but against brilliant bowling by Frank Stephens (8 for 46), were all out for 101.

1936

Saturday 2nd May   Drawn against Wagon Works

Gloucester Nondescripts started the season with a drawn game against Gloucester Wagon Works. Nondescripts put on 20 for the first wicket, had five down for 85 and declared with 147 for 7.

Wagon Works lost 3 for 35, and when time was called had made 79.

NONDESCRIPTS

F Benbow	b	Brooks			4
F Voyle	c	Brooks	b	Barber	15
A Walden	lbw		b	Maly	16
T Stephens	c	Brooks	b	Barber	44
E Taylor	b	Brooks			15
R Cooper	c	Brooks	b	Banks	4
E Paish	c	Poolman	b	Barber	24
J Stephen	Not Out				16
	EXTRAS				9
	Total (for 7)				147

Edwards, Russell and Gillespie did not bat

WAGON WORKS

J Stephens	lbw	Stephens			12
V Maly	c	Walden	b	Stephens	7
F Stephens	lbw		b	Benbow	10
C Poolman	c	Gillespie	b	Cooper	26
H Banks	b	T Stephens			12
J Lane	Not Out				4
J Bell	Not Out				7
	EXTRAS				1
	Total (for 5)				79

W Nicholls, G Roberts, J Brooks, F Barber did not bat

Saturday 9thMay

Stroud Draw with Wagon Works

WAGON WORKS

J Stephens	st	Dash	b	Cullimore	10
A Hopcroft	c	Clutterbuck	b	Atkinson	11
V Maly	c	Endacott	b	Atkinson	0
C Poolman	run out				13
H Banks	st	Dash	b	Endacott	57
F Stephens	hit wicket		b	Endacott	16
J Lane	b	Mills			13
L Parsons	b	Lynch			21
F Brisbane	b	Mills			0
F Barber	not out				4
J Brooks	b	Lynch			0
	EXTRAS				19
	TOTAL				164

STROUD

M Cullimore	lbw		b	Barber	20
J Nicklin	b	Brooks			0
G Wedel	c	Maly	b	Brooks	5
M Clutterbuck	lbw	Brisland			1
L Cordwell	c	Hopcroft	b	Brisland	30
N Smith	c	J Stephens	b	Brisland	0
J Endacott	b	Barber			6
R Mills	not out				21
D Dash	lbw	B Barber			9
	EXTRAS				1
	TOTAL (for 8)				93

Rev. Father O'Lynch and G Atkinson Did Not Bat

Saturday 16th May

Brothers in fine stand

Gloucester Wagon Works were unlucky not to force a victory against Ross on the Sports Ground. The Works made 225 for 5 declared, Ross replying with 153 for 9. The Stephens brothers' stand of 91 runs before J Stephens was bowled for a vigorous 84 was the highlight, this made in 1½ hours.

Frank Stephens and V Maly hit so hard that the Wagon Works were able to declare after 2½ hours. Ross lost 4 wickets for 19 runs when drizzle set in and the Wagon Works had to field and bowl with a wet ball. Beach and Webb made good for Ross and raised the score to 94 before Webb was well caught by Brooks. Beach continued to bat well but was eventually caught for a well-played innings of 75. Ross lost nine wickets, but managed to survive and make a lucky draw.

For the Wagon Works, Barber took 3 for 19 and Brooks 3 for 39. For Ross, Beach took 2 for 51 and Hill 3 for 50.

Wagon Works 'A 'V.Ross 'A' at Ross

Ross 'A' 48, D Brown 5 for 16
Wagon Works 'A' - 52 for 4 Proctor 21 Not Out

Gloucester Wagon Works Cricket Club 1st Eleven 1936
Record. ...Played 16....Won 10....Drawn 6

H Brown   W A Brown   APaish   HEPerkins
(Scorer)   (General Secretay)   (Coach)   (Chairman)
WNicholls AHEvans JCLane FBrisland FH Stephens I Parsons WMelling (umpire)
JABrookes HS Banks* AEHopcroft* E J Stephens F A Barber
*(vice captain) **(captain)

1937

Saturday 1st May - Wagon Works v. Nondescripts

Gloucester Nondescripts gained a splendid victory over the Wagon Works by 80 runs. The Nondescripts lost their first two wickets for 30 but F Benbow, joining F Voyce carried the score to 85 when the former was lbw. With help from T Stephens, F Voyce, with a useful score of 47 carried the total to 114 before the next wicket fell. A Walden (22) helped to carry the score to 156.

The Wagon Works lost the first two wickets for 16 and half the side was out for 48, the rest carrying the total to 76, F Stephens (14) and A Evans (17) being top scores. C Buffrey (3 for 3), F Carr (4 for 21) and F Benbow (2 for 21) for the Nondescripts and F Stephens (6 for 42), J Lane (1 for 10) and J Stephens (1 for 14) for the Works did well with the ball.

Saturday 8th May - Wagon Works v. Lydney

In an exciting finish on the Wagon Works Ground, the home side defeated Lydney by one wicket. Lydney found runs hard to get against steady bowling and were all out for 130, having batted over 2½ hours. Hiron, Wherett and Carter batted well.

With 100 minutes in which to get the runs the Wagon Works lost three wickets for 19, but Banks hit out well and helped to carry the score to 54 before being bowled. Lane batted in a forceful manner for 51. When the last over was called three runs were needed for victory and Mountney, who batted very well, made the winning hit with two balls to spares.

For Lydney, Wherett (4 for 34), Howells (2 for 27), G Wooldridge (2 for 48) and J Wooldridge (1 for 10) shared the wickets and Parsons (3 for 17), Barber (3 for 33), F Stephens (3 for 43) and Lane (1 for 14) bowled well for the winners.

Sunday 16th May - Wagon Works v. GWR Swindon

Gloucester Wagon Works gained a brilliant victory over GWR Swindon at the Works Sports Ground. Swindon batted for 3 hours for 140 for nine declared.   Left with 1½ hours to compile the runs, the Wagon Works lost J Stephens at 21, but Hopcroft and Banks took the score to 57. The pair went for the bowling whole-heartedly, and when time was called Banks was just four runs off his century. Swindon sportingly played on for Banks to reach his hundred. Wagon Works 217 for 2, H Banks 108 not out, F Stephens 60 not out.

Saturday 22nd May - Wagon Works v. Morris Motors

Played at the Sports Ground.

Wagon Works batted first and scored 158 for 8 declared, J Stephens (51), F Stephens (18) and J Lane (30 not out) being the main scorers. Morris Motors replied with 103 for 2 until rained stopped play.

Saturday 29th May - Stroud Draw With The Wagon Works

Played at Tuffley Avenue.

Stroud 154 – 6 declared. M H Cullimore 62, F Barber 3 for 31

Wagon Works 98 for 7 J Lane 27.

Saturday 13th June - Lydney foiled by the clock

Lydney had the better of a drawn game against the Wagon Works at Lydney. Rosser and P Grey for Lydney batted well against steady bowling. The Wagon Works lost five wickets for 23 runs, but Hopcroft and Lane pulled the game round and managed to stave off defeat. For Lydney, Woolridge took three wickets for 19 and Jarrett three for 43.

Lydney					
W Whereatt	c	Hopcroft	b	Brookes	4
G Wooldridge	lbw		b	F Stephens	0
E Hiron	b	J Stephen			17
C Rosser	c&b	Lane			72
R Carter	c	Bloodworth	b	J Stephens	0
T Garland	lbw		b	F Stephens	6
R Aldridge	b	Brookes			16
P Grey	not out				37
S Yateman	c	Lane	b	Evans	5
S Jarrett	b	Banks			8
Extras					**7**
Total (for 9 declared)					**172**

E Gillo did not bat

Wagon Works					
A Hopcroft	Not out				37
J Stephens	c	Gillo	b	Jarrett	8
F Stephens	lbw		b	Wooldridge	1
H Banks	b	Jarrett			0
C Poolman	b	Wooldridge			2
A Evans	c	Wooldridge	b	Jarrett	1
J Lane	lbw		b	Wooldridge	47
A Bloodworth	Not out				0
Extras					**1**
Total (for 6)					**97**

J Brookes, L Mountney and F Banks did not bat

Saturday 19th June - Gloucester v. Wagon Works

Played at Tuffley Avenue Sports Ground.

Gloucester City 191 for 9 declared A V Wybrow 69.

Wagon Works 143 for 7 (in 110 minutes) J Lane 52, C Poolman 39 not out.

Saturday 26th June - Brilliant Wagon Works Stand

A brilliant stand by C Poolman and H Banks, who made 63 and 68 respectively, beat Malvern at Malvern.

Wagon Works 190 for 5 declared

Malvern 110 all out, Parsons 2-20, Barber 1-26, J Stephens 2-27.

Saturday 17th July - F Stephens' All Round Performance

Metro Cammell 74 all out, F Stephens 5 – 20, Parsons 5 – 40. Wagon Works 93 for 9, F Stephens 29

Saturday 31st July - Wagon Works v. Malvern

Played at Tuffley Avenue.

Wagon Works 149 all out. F Stephens 34. Malvern 117 all out. Barber 4 – 34.

On this day Wally Hammond scored his 127th century, 110 v Somerset at Bristol, overtaking W G Grace's record.

Saturday 7th August - Wagon Works Draw at Tetbury

Tetbury 181 for 7 declared. M Braybrooke 87, F Stephens 3 – 49. Wagon Works 126 for 4, J Stephens retired hurt 38.

Saturday 11th September - Wagon Works v. Bourton Vale

Played at Tuffley Avenue.
Wagon Works 199 for 8, F Stephens 91. Bourton Vale 93 for 6.

Tom Goddard's final analysis for the season for Gloucestershire was:

O	M	R	W	AV
1,336	329	3730	222	16.50

1938

Saturday 30th April - Gloucester Wagon Works v. Stroud

Stroud and Gloucester Wagon Works figured in a drawn game on the Works Ground. After a slow start, Stroud declared after 2.5 hours batting at 190 for 4. Smith and Dash both batted well. Left with 1 hour and 50 minutes batting, Wagon Works went for the runs and at one stage looked like forcing a win, but a breakdown in the middle order spoilt their chance. J Stephens, Poolman and Lane batted well. Stroud made some fine catches and Wedel was on good form with the ball.

STROUD						WAGON WORKS					
W Cullimore	lbw	B Stephens			10	C Poolman	run out				35
H Smith	st	Horcroft	b	Banks	86	J Stephens	c	Chew	b	Cullimore	39
L Cordwell		B Phillips			6	H Banks	c	Gardner	b	Wedel	8
D Dash	st	Hopcroft	b	Bell	54	E Stephens	c	Smith	b	Wedel	5
G Wedel	not out				11	J Lane	not out				39
D Pink	not out				8	F Stephens	lbw		b	Wedel	0
						T Phillips	c	Cullimore	b	Wedel	4
						J Bell	st	Dash	b	Endacott	10
						A Evans	not out				12
		EXTRAS			15			EXTRAS			17
		TOTAL (for 4 Dec)			190	Match Drawn		TOTAL (for 7)			171

Saturday 7th May - H Banks Scores 52 - Wagon Works Foiled by Lydney

WAGON WORKS						LYDNEY					
J Stephens	c	Grey	b	Thomas	12	P Grey		J Stephens		F Stephens	0
C Poolman	c	Powell	b	Thomas	38	D Carter	c	Banks	b	F Stephens	1
F Stephens	lbw		b	Gilo	5	W Hastie	c	Evans	b	F Stephens	2
J Lane	st	Carter	b	Jarrett	27	E Hirma	run out				45
H Banks	c	Carter	b	Jarrett	52	R Aldridge	lbw			F Stephens	1
J Bell	c	Hirma	b	Aldridge	5	W Thomas	b	Brown			31
A Evans	c	Aldridge	b	Jarrett	0	C Rosser	not out				10
H Philipps	lbw		b	Aldridge	0	K Powell	b	Philipps			2
W Brown	not out				4	T Garland	not out				2
A Bloodworth	not out				16						
		EXTRAS			16			EXTRAS			12
		TOTAL (for 8)			169			TOTAL (for 7)			106

F Barber did not bat   E Gilo and S Jarrett did not bat

Wagon Works figured in a drawn game at Lydney. The Works batted first and after 2 hours reached 169 for 8 before declaring. Banks, Poolman and Lane all batted well. With less than 2 hours to get the runs Lydney started badly, losing 4 wickets for 15, but plucky batting by Hiram and Thomas enabled Lydney to save the game. For the Wagon Works, F Stephens took 4 for 20 and S Jarrett had 4 for 76 for Lydney.

Saturday 14 May   Dick Stephens Three short of a century

GLOUCESTER AND WAGON WORKS IN DRAWN GAME

A drawn match resulted between Gloucester and the Wagon Works at the Spa. The Wagon Works were undistinguished except for E Stephens, who was unfortunate to miss a century, his innings including ten 4s and occupying two hours. With seven wickets down for 154 the Works were not too safe, but Hopcroft and Beamish, aided by some luck added 34 and the innings was declared. Hyett took 2 for 56, Ball 2 for 40 and Hawker 3 for 31, but the latter could not bowl at his normal pace.

Gloucester could not score fast enough to make the runs in the 110 minutes left for play. Morland and Wybrow made a good start and Hawker raised hopes with some quick runs, but the score was only 95 for 4 with half an hour left. Hayward and Romans put on 49 without further loss in that time but the game was left drawn. Beamish took 1 for 18, Pearce 2 for 40 and Barber 1 for 34.

WAGON WORKS					GLOUCESTER					
E Stephens	b	Hawker			97	AV Wybrow	c	Beamish	b	Pearce	27
C Poolman	c	Wybrow	b	Hyett	0	SJ Morland	b	Beamish			37
A Bloodworth	lbw		b	Ball	12	HM Cairns		Terry	b	Pearce	4
H Banks	b	Ball			5	F Hawker	b	Barber			19
J Stephens	b	Hawker			28	FA Hayward	not out				22
F Stephens	lbw	Hawker			0	M Romans	not out				26
A Hopcroft	not out				19						
V Beamish	not out				16						
	EXTRAS				10		EXTRAS (for 4 wickets)				9
	TOTAL (for 7)				187		TOTAL				144

E M Sessions, G Elliot, S Hyett and S Taylor did not bat.

Saturday 28th May - Wagon Works Defeat Worcester

Worcester 103 all out (F Stephens 3 for 27, A Phillips 3 for 34)

Wagon Works 104 for 5 (H Banks 52, C Poolman 16)

Saturday 21st May - Gloucester's Exciting Victory

Gloucester gained an exciting victory over the Wagon Works on the Sports Ground. With one over to go Gloucester needed 10 runs to win. Hayward obtained 7 off the first 3 balls and Shelly 1 off the 5th. Hayward hit the last for 4 to end the match.

Spectators were entertained by an interesting day's cricket in fine weather. It was unfortunate that Stephens and Goodard were unable to play for the Works owing to injury, but Hopkins was included in the side. Twelve a side was played.
The Works lost 2 wickets for 27, but Poolman and Banks batted well against some good bowling. Poolman left at 69 and Banks, who hit 2 6s at 98. Bell also hit well, but Hopkins stayed an hour and enabled the score to reach 186. Barnett had 1 for 6, Sinfield 3 for 89, Hawker 4 for 51 and Wybrow 3 for 24.Gloucester had just over 2 hours to bat and scored steadily. Barnett made some beautiful shots before skying one from J Stephens. Wybrow hit well and Sinfield batted stylishly, but both were out in the same way from skiers. Hawker failed and 6 wickets went down for 131 with only 29 minutes left. The last 2 overs produced 29 runs of which Hayward, who had previously been subdued, made 23. Parson had 2 for 48, J Stephens 2 for 35 and Barber 3 for 24.
The wicket keeping on both sides was worthy of mention, Sessions conceding one bye and Hopcroft none.
There was a good crowd and a collection for Sinfield's benefit realised £6 16s.

GLOUCESTER

C Poolman	b	Hawker			36
J Stephens	b	Barnett			0
J Lane	lbw		b	Sinfield	7
H Banks	c	Wybrow	b	Hawker	49
F Stephens	b	Hawker			6
A Hopcroft	b	Hawker			0
J Bell	st	Sessions	b	Wybrow	35
V Hopkins	not out				31
A Phillips	lbw		b	Sinfield	5
W Nicholls	b	Wybrow			0
L Parsons	st	Sessions	b	Wybrow	14
F Barber	b	Sinfield			1
		EXTRAS			2
		TOTAL			186

WAGON WORKS

C Barnett	c	Nicholls	b	J Stephens	34
Wooley	c	F Stephens	b	Parsons	11
A Wybrow	c	Lane	b	J Stephens	34
R Sinfield	c	Phillips	b	Barber	36
M Romans	lbw		b	Barber	6
C Hayward	not out				41
F Hawker	b	Barber			0
Healey	b	Parsons			17
Colley	not out				6
		EXTRAS			4
		TOTAL (for 7)			189

B Sessions, H Hyett and S Morland did not bat

Saturday 4th June - Tetbury Lose Race With Clock

WAGON WORKS

C Poolman	run out				7
A Hopcroft	b	Bailey			30
J Bell	c	Astill	b	Witchell	19
H Banks	c	Cox	b	Bailey	19
A Evans	b	Smith			1
F Stephens	b	Cox			49
W Nicholls	b	Witchell			4
L Evans	b	Witchell			1
J Stephens	not out				
L Parsons	not out				
		EXTRAS			4
		TOTAL (for 8)		167	

TETBURY

Dr Brambrooke	c	F Stephens	b	Barber	11
T Astill	b	J Stephens			31
H Witchell	not out				32
C Taylor	b	Parsons			46
A Cook	not out				4
		EXTRAS			10
		TOTAL (for 3)			134

Saturday 9th July Wagon Works Travel to Oxford - Drawn Game with Morris Motors

Gloucester Wagon Works journeyed to Oxford for their match with Morris Motors, the result of which was a draw.

Morris Motors batted first and started well, making 100 for the loss of only 2 wickets, but a collapse followed and they lost 5 wickets for the addition of 45 runs before the declaration was made.

The Works had one and three quarter hours in which to get the runs, but found Phipps bowling too well to take liberties and a drawn game was inevitable.

Phipps bowled 18 overs for 21 runs taking 3 wickets. For the Works, J Stephens (33), and H Banks (17) were top scorers.

On this day Gloucester City played Elders and Fyffes of Bristol. Included in the Elders team was Charlie Newman who was later to become the Wagon Works head groundsman after Arthur Paish retired. Elders and Fyffes were all out for 50, Charlie Newman being the only batsman to reach double figures (18).

Saturday 13th August

WAGON WORKS' BIG VICTORY

Wagon Works won the toss and put the visitors in. Ross at once found runs were hard to get against steady bowling and good catching and after slow batting for two and a half hours were all out for 130. Wagon Works' opening pair made a good start. Dick Stephens was in fine form and he made 57 runs out of the first 68 before being bowled. Banks treated the bowling mercilessly and in one over from Roff he hit 26 runs. He batted in brilliant style and made the winning hit, Wagon Works winning by eight wickets. For the winners, Stephens had 5 wickets for 32 runs, Brown 2 for 29 and Pearce 2 for 29.

ROSS					WAGON WORKS					
D West	lbw		b	Briscano	30	E Stephens	b	Knowley			57
R Roff	b	Stephens			5	C Brown	c	Reevestucker	b	Roff	17
L Newton	b	Pearce			17	H Banks	not out				57
W Constance	b	Stephens			3	A Hopcroft	not out				6
R Webb	c	Beamish	b	Brown	15						
H Knewley	c	Stephens	b	Brown	14						
N Nicholas	b	Pearce			14						
H Down	b	Stephens			14						
S West	c	Horcroft	b	Stephens	3						
T Reevestucker			b	Stephens	9						
C Peachey	Not out				9						
EXTRAS					7	EXTRAS					2
TOTAL					136	TOTAL (for 2)					139

A Bloodworth, F Brisland, C Poolman, V Beamish, L Evans, W Brown and W Pearce did not bat.

Saturday 20th August - Record Aggregate for Wagon Works

Swindon GWR batted first on the Wagon Works Ground and found runs hard to get against steady bowling by the home side and were at one stage 8 wickets down for 105 runs. The last batsmen hit out hard though and the score eventually reached 165, leaving the Works one and three quarter hours to get the runs. Beamish bowled well taking 6 wickets for 45. Brown had 2 for 36. C Poolman batted very well at the start of the Wagon Works innings and then Banks took charge of the game, and hitting out brilliantly, scored 87 in an hour which included 14 4s. Banks has now scored 726 runs in 16 completed innings, which is a club record for any season. Proctor rendered splendid help with a score of 31 runs and the Wagon Works won with about 5 minutes to spare.

1939

Saturday 6th May

WAGON WORKS PUT LYDNEY IN AND WIN. MATCH STOPPED TO CHEER PREMIER.

Putting Lydney in to bat on a soft wicket proved a successful move by the Wagon Works' captain and the Forest Side was all out for 60.

The Works lost five wickets before passing the Forest Team's score. They were eventually dismissed for 144.
The match was stopped on the arrival of the Premier on his way through the park to visit Viscount Bledisloe. The Premier raised his hat and smiled in acknowledging the cheers of the players.

Lydney 60   _Wagon Works 144_

The Premier was of course Neville Chamberlain. Viscount Bledisloe is well known in International Rugby as the man whose name is on the Cup when New Zealand play against Australia. Viscount Bledisloe was Governor General to New Zealand when the first match took place in 1931.

Saturday 13th May - GRC & W Co. v. Bristol Schoolmasters

Wagon Works made a sporting offer to Bristol Schoolmasters on the Sports Ground. The Schoolmasters hit up 241 for 5 declared and the home side had a wicket to fall when time was called. They offered to play another quarter of an hour to give the visitors a chance of victory, but the Schoolmasters declined.

For the Schoolmasters, Knapton had 2 for 39, Dewfall 2 for 21 and Wells 2 for 13 and for the Wagon Works, F Stephens took 2 for 60 and Beamish 2 for 53.

Schoolmasters 241 for 5 Declared   _Wagon Works 133 for 9_

GRC & W Co. v. Metro Cammell (Birmingham)

The start between the two teams at the Sports Ground was delayed by rain and it was decided to play 18 overs a side.

The visitors in 18 overs totalled 108 and the Works 116 for 5 in 15 overs.

Saturday 22nd July - GRC & W Co. v. Nondescripts

The Nondescripts were well beaten at the Sports Ground. The Works were lucky enough to win the toss and put the Nondescripts in to bat, the policy paying off. J McIntire was in fine form, receiving excellent assistance from V Beamish and F Stephens and the Nondescripts were all back in the Pavilion for 82.
McIntire had 4 for 11, Beamish 3 for 25 and Stephens 2 for 25. The Works acquired the necessary runs for the loss of 4 wickets, mainly due to an excellent knock of 48 not out by F Stephens. T Price took 2 - 17.

1940 - 1949

The war years (1939 - 1945) were to curtail a great deal of sport in Britain and all first class cricket during this period was abandoned as all hands were put to the war effort.

The Wagon Works Company continued to produce rail trucks of different varieties, but more and more branches moved over to producing armaments in the form of shell cases and ammunition boxes. In 1940 the Company was asked to build and test Churchill Tanks, which they did, producing 764 tanks over the course of the war.

The Company was visited twice during the war by Queen Mary, who spent this period of time living at Badminton.

The Cricket Club continued to play a number of matches each year - these were played against local firms, a welcome break during hostilities. In 1944 Albert Hopcroft was presented with a watch by Mrs Boyce, the President's wife, for his 16 years as club captain.

Tom Goddard arranged several games during the war years on the Works ground and brought a number of first class players along, with all profits from these matches going to the R.A.F. Benevolent fund. Arthur Paish retired as head groundsman in 1947 after 29 years' loyal service. His position was taken by Charlie Newman who had previously spent several years on the ground staff at Lord's.

A match took place in 1945 between the Australian Air Force and the R.A.F. Six of the Australians had been included in the Australian test side that had played England at Lord's a few weeks before. One of these was the great Australian all rounder, Keith Miller.

The Cricket Club's main source of funding during this time came from a rugby guesser which was organised amongst the Works' employees. This was very successful and the winning numbers were Gloucester Rugby Club's scores in the winter and Gloucestershire C.C.C.'s scores during the summer months.

In 1948 the death of Mr J.J. MacGregor was announced. MacGregor had been Managing Director of the Wagon Works and was the Cricket Club's President from 1918-1932. 1946 was a historic year for Mr H.E. (Harry) Perkins, having reached 45 years association with the Cricket Club as both player and chairman.

There were a number of new faces showing promise after the war, although it was to be a number of years before the club was back to the strength of the 1930s. The newcomers included Charlie Newman, Wally Lodge, P Phillips, Brian Cummings, R Hamblett, Les Priest, K Hooper, George Woodridge, Doug Swift, Tom Salter and Alan Pugh. Two young players also to come along in 1948 were Jackie Corbett and schoolboy Eric Stephens, son of Jim Stephens. Eric remembers that in 1948 the club had an away fixture at Colwall. Transport was a coal lorry from the Works that had been brushed clean, with planks of wood put across for seating. On arrival at the ground Eric was asked to play as the team was a player short. It was a hot day and Eric's uncle Frank bowled throughout the Colwall innings. Unfortunately, after the match the local hostelry had run out of beer and the team had to travel to the Prince of Wales Pub in Staunton for some much-needed refreshment.

1949 was a difficult year for the club, the first eleven winning only four of its 20 matches, 8 being lost and 8 drawn. 2 were cancelled due to bad weather. The batting averages were topped by Vic Beamish with 23.91 and the bowling by L. Priest with 8.9.

1949 was also the year in which Graham Hale made his first team debut for the club against Colwall, and a person who no one seems to remember, but who played one game against Worcester, making 2 runs, a Mr A Stutlz.

1946 – G. Romans died.
1948 – A. Paish died.

1940

During 1940 the Battle of Britain took place. Although the Wagon Works fielded a regular side, many players were working for the Works in helping the war effort. Records are not that good due to most of the local papers reporting news of the battles in France. The ground was used on many occasions for fitness training by the Works' employees and army units.

Wagon Works 'A' v Tyndale

Match played on the Sports Ground, Tyndale winning by 49 runs. For Tyndale, the following batted well; E. Comley (34), S. Baldwin (28). The most successful bowlers for Tyndale were G. Allison (4-13) and R Beard (4-23) and, for the Works, L. Parsons (3-38).

Scores: Tyndale   106
        Wagon Works 'A'   57

Saturday 15th June -Gloucester City v Wagon Works

No result.

Friday 28th June - Article in the Citizen

It was reported that Don Bradman had enlisted in the Air Force in Perth. On this day a report in the Citizen recounted that Germany had lost 74 aircraft in the last 6 days.

Saturday 13th July

Gloucester Strollers visited the Wagon Works Sports Ground to meet the 'A' team and won by 9 runs. The Wagon Works were dismissed for 74 (A.E. Evans 13, J. Wheeler 12, G. Roberts 11, P. Smith 10, J. Williams 6 for 30).

Strollers 83 (B. Lidiard 24, D. Newman 21).

1941

Saturday 14th June - Gloucester v. GRC & W Co.

Gloucester defeated the Wagon Works by 144 runs to 106, but a slow outfield kept the scoring down. Gloucester lost 4 wickets for 23, but P. Nicholl (33) and Hitches (21) raised the score to 85, later batsman helping the score along to 144, Kirton (28) and Whitfield (17 N.O.) were the better scorers. Barber took 5 for 44 and J Stephens 2 for 26 whilst Parsons, 2 for 16, also bowled well.

The Wagon Works also started badly, losing 4 for 33, then Banks (27) and Swift (24) added 44. The later batsmen however, failed against the bowling of Hyett and Brown and the score only reached 106. Brown had 4 for 62 and Hyett 6 for 40.

Saturday 13th July - Gloucester v. GRC & W Co.

Played on the Spa ground, Gloucester made 155 for 6 when rain stopped play. J Stephens had 2 for 25, Barber 2 for 58 and Beamish 2 for 20.

Saturday 9th August - GRC & W Co. v. Gloucester.

Played at the Works Ground Tuffley, good bowling by J and F Stephens in a high wind caused the collapse of Gloucester and only Brown (69 with 8 fours) made a stand after being missed early on. The innings realised 112, J Stephens taking 8 for 51 and Beamish 2 for 5. J Stephens (46) and Hopcroft (24) set the Works on the way to a win. Later wickets began to fall, but Gloucester's score was passed with 6 wickets down. Waddington took 4 for 41 and Elliott 1 for 34.

Gloucester Railway Carriage and Wagon Company Cricket Club 1st Eleven 1941

D Swift V Beamish L Priest E Jennings G Roberts P Hopkins
Jim Stephens   F Barber A Hopcroft A E Evans   H Banks L Parsons

1942

Report in *the Citizen,* 6th June 1942, commenting on a game at the Wagon Works Ground.

THE ONLY FIRST CLASS CRICKET MATCH THIS SEASON

ROYAL AIR FORCE
v
GLOUCESTERSHIRE

(In aid of the R.A.F. Benevolent Fund)

at the
WAGON WORKS SPORTS GROUND TUFFLEY AVENUE

(By Kind Permission of the Wagon Works Sport & Social Club)

SATURDAY JUNE 13TH 1942

Hours of Play 12 noon - 8 p.m. Luncheon 1.30 - 2.15 p.m.
RAF Band Will Play Selections During The Day

Admission 2/6d and 1/3d Car Park 1/-

SUPPORT A GRAND CAUSE

Saturday 2nd May - Glouceser Wagon Works v. RAF

RAF 99 All Out. Barnes 37, Hunt 15 Not Out, F Barber 3 for 11, J Stephens 3 for 25, V Beamish 2 for 15

Wagon Works 52 All Out. F Stephens 10, *Nutter 6 for 18 in 7 overs

*Albert Nutter played County Cricket for Northamptonshire.

Saturday 9th May - Gloucester Wagon Works v. Optimists CC

Optimists CC 107 All Out. S Griffith 43, L Priest 3 for 24, E A Evans 4 for 8

Wagon Works 111 for 9. G Roberts 48, V Beamish 20, Griffith 5 for 27.

Saturday 16th May - Gloucester Wagon Works v. Tuffley Sports

Played on the Sports Ground.

Tuffley Sports 86 All Out. E Brunsdon 27, T Hancock 16.

Wagon Works 117 for 6. H Banks 60, T Salter 24 not out, A Hopcroft 13 not out. Bowling – S Gill 6-1-3-42

Saturday 6th June - Gloucester Wagon Works v. Gloucester City

Wagon Works 67 All Out. V Beamish 16. Bowling – Wooley 3-0-11-4

Gloucester 40 for 5. C Cockrill 20 not out. Bowling – Beamish 7-0-17-4

Saturday 20th June - Gloucester Wagon Works v. Rotol Airscrews

Played at the Sports Ground.

Wagon Works 84 All Out. D Swift 19, A Hopcroft 17, T Salter 7. Bowling – J Lacey 10-1-25-8

Rotol 47 All Out. C Bloxome 13, G Brown 7. Bowling – V Beamish 8-1-5-14, Phillips 6-2-21-4

1943

Saturday 24th July

At the Wagon Works Sports Ground, which had become an Annual Fixture during the War

Gloucestershire vs. Royal Air Force

The Gloucestershire team was arranged by Tom Goodard. The match was drawn.

RAF 216 Gloucestershire 182

Sunday 25th July

Tom Goddard's XI V War Industries XI

War Industries Team Comprised of:

G G Wooley, S Munnery, P C White (Beaven & Son), V Beamish, G Birch, C Poolman (G.R.C & W Co.), E Dwyer, E Comley (Morelands), C Cockerell, F Walden (G.A.C.), R Wakefield (Fielding & Platt), R Medcroft, J Marshall (Rotol), R Gladwin (Griggs & Co.), R Yardley (William Gardners & Son), W Brind (G.W.R.).

Tom Goddard's Team defeated War Industries by 203 runs. They scored at the rate of 130 runs an hour and finished on 279 for 4 declared, War Industries 76.

Albert Hopcroft receiving a gold watch from the wife of the president, Sir Leslie Boyce, in 1943 after captaining the club for 16 seasons

1944

Saturday 24th June - GRC & W Co. v. Tuffley Sports

Played at Tuffley Avenue. Tuffley batted first and were all out for 141. The Wagon Works replied with 92 all out, with only 5 minutes of play remaining.

Saturday 22nd July - GRC & W Co. v. Gloucester Harlequins.

Gloucester Harlequins batted first making 153 for 5 declared. GRC & W Co. were 57 all out.

Saturday 5th August - Tuffley Sports v. GRC & W Co

Played on Tuffley's ground. Tuffley Sports 96 all out. GRC & W Co. 161 for 5.
V Beamish (75), D Medcroft (31), A Hopkirk (16), J Stephens (15) and R Medcroft were the main scorers.

Saturday 12th August - GRC & W Co. v. Glos Corporation (Electricity Department)

Gloucester C.E.D. 134 for 8 declared. GRC & W Co. 104 for 6. Match drawn.

1945

Saturday 26th May - GRC & W Co. v. Gloucester Corporation (Electricity Department)

Wagon Works: 145 (F Stephens 78 Not Out). V Beamish (15), F Miller (13), G Roberts (11).
Gloucester Corporation (Electricity Dept.) 129 All Out.
Match played at Tuffley Avenue.

Sunday 22nd June - GRC & W Co. v. Gloucester Harlequins

Wagon Works: F Stephens (31), G Roberts (24), V Beamish (16), were top scorers.
For the Harlequins: R Harris took 4 for 23, S Edwards 2 for 21 and W Wren 2 for 27.
Harlequins: 74 for 7. Match Drawn.
Played on the Wagon Works Ground.

Saturday 29th June - GRC & W Co. v. Tuffley Sports

Played at Tuffley Avenue. Interference by rain was mostly responsible for a drawn game.
Tuffley declared on 95 for 8. The Wagon Works replied with 61 for 3.

Saturday 4th August - Gloucester Corporation (Electricity Department) v. GRC & W Co

Gloucester Corporation (Electricity Dept): 55 All Out.
Wickets fell to F Stephens (6 for 19) including "The Hat Trick" and V Beamish (4 for 29).
Wagon Works: 97 All Out
F Walden (40), B Evans (12), R Ryland (11) and L Priest (10 Not Out).

SPORTING END TO R.A.F. MATCH
Saturday 2nd June - Played at the Works Ground
Edrich's brilliant bowling

There was a sporting finish to the match at the Wagon Works Ground, Gloucester on Saturday, in which the Royal Air Force beat the Royal Australian Air Force by 16 runs.

Left with two and a half hours to get 175 runs, the Australians made a gallant effort to win, but Warburton and Edrich bowling fast in the rain beat them with ten minutes to spare.

After a most confident start by Washbrook and Brooks for the R.A.F, and a particularly bright knock by Edrich, Ellis, the Australian's left handed spin bowler, proved too dangerous on a drying pitch in the afternoon for the R.A.F. to make anything like a big score.

Edrich, in fact, was the only batsman who could do anything with him. He hit one ball on to the club building for a beautiful six and took quite a number of fours. Squires might have been able to pile up a few for the R.A.F. for he played confidently, but was unluckily run out. After Cristofani had Edrich caught at the wicket, Ellis, bowling with the wind, soon ran through the remaining batsmen. His four wickets cost 39 runs.

Australia's Bad Start

The Australians lost two wickets in a very bad start. Edrich had Craig lbw, and Miller, one of the Australian's best batting hopes, was out first ball to a brilliant catch by Warburton in the slips off Edrich. Miller meant to drive the ball, but it struck the corner of his bat and flew like a bullet to Warburton who held it.

Almost at the end of the innings he brought off a similar catch to dismiss Workman, who made a sound 68 and very nearly carried his bat. It was Workman and Pettiford who built up the Australian's score, putting on 87 runs for the third wicket. Pettiford was enterprising, and except for a hard chance to Edrich and an easy catch to Warburton at mid on which got him out, his 44 was as sound an innings as Workman's.

Cristofani, in a do or die innings, made a run a minute until he was caught by Brooks at extra cover with a brilliant back handed catch, high up with one hand. Williams, another Australian batting hope, was clean bowled by Warburton, who got Roper the same way with the next ball. Stocks stopped the hat trick by taking a single, and he and Workman continued to steal singles in a desperate effort to win the game.

Fast Bowling in the Wet

When Edrich knocked Stocks' off stump flat, the Australians had 25 runs to get in 20 minutes and two wickets in hand. It did not seem too difficult and Workman restored confidence with a couple of good drives off Edrich, but Warburton's second brilliant catch sent him back with the total still 17 short of the R.A.F. score. Ellis made a single, and then Edrich rounded off a splendid patch of fast bowling on the wet pitch by smashing Semey's wicket and so winning the game. Edrich's five wickets cost only 26 runs, while Warburton took 4 for 52.

R.A.F.

C Washbrook	lbw		b	Roper	50
D Brooks	b			Miller	41
R E S Wyatt	lbw		b	Ellis	4
W J Edrich	c	Sismey	b	Cristofani	36
R S Squires		Run Out			16
P A Makenzie	lbw		b	Ellis	1
L Warburton	b	Ellis			0
W E Jones	lbw		b	Cristofani	6
R Oakes	lbw		b	Ellis	5
J S Buller	b	Miller			8
P Jackson		Not Out			3
		Extras			5
		Total			175

R.A.A.F.

J A Workman	c	Warburton	b	Edrich	68
H Craig	lbw		b	Edrich	4
K R Miller	c	Warburton	b	Edrich	0
J Pettiford	c	Warburton	b	Jackson	44
R M Stanford	b	Warburton			0
N R Stocks	b	Edrich			3
R G Williams	b	Warburton			0
D R Cristofani	c	Brooks	b	Warburton	28
S J Sismey	b	Edrich			2
A W Roper	b	Warburton			0
R S Ellis		Not Out	1		3
		Extras			9
		Total			159

Above is the RAF team which defeated the Royal Australian Air Force at the Wagon Works Ground by 175 runs to 159. From left to right are (front row): F/Sgt C.Washbrook (Lancs and England), F/O RES Wyatt (Warwick and England), S/Ldr W J Edrich DFC (Middlesex and England), F/O R S.Squires (Surrey), F/Sgt D Brookes (Northants); (back row): Mr E C Rogers (organiser of the match), LAC J S Butler (Worc), LAC Warburton (Lancs), S/Ldr. B.A. Mackenzie DSO DFC (Hants), S /Ldr A E R Gilligan, Sgt R Oakes (Sussex), F/Sgt P Jackson (Worcs) and Mr G Court (umpire)

The Australian team, from left to right, are (front row): F/0 R S Ellis, F/0 D. R. Cristofani, F/Lt. A W Roper, S/Ldr. S J Sismey, F/Sgt. J A .Workman and F/0 R. M. Stanford DFC; (back row): F/Sgt H. Craig, P/0. J Pettiford, W/0 R G Williams, F/Lt K D Johnson, F/0 K R Miller and N R Stocks. Ellis, Sismey, Workman, Stanford, Williams and Miller were members of the Australian team who played in the Test Match at Lord's.

1946

Saturday 4th May 1946 - Century Stand for the First Wicket

The Wagon Works, on their own ground, defeated Fielding & Platts by seven wickets. The latter batted first and scored 167 (Hinton 60, Millington 20, Bircher 22). The Wagon Works replied with 169 for 3 (F Stephens 60, T Roberts 44, Banks 37, Pullman Not Out 15). Stephens and Roberts put on 106 for the first wicket for the Works, for whom F Barber took 4 for 24. The three Work's wickets were shared by W Pick (2 for 27) and Millington (1 for 35).

Saturday 18th May - Wagon Works v. Colwall

Score: Colwall 216 for 4 declared

(*H Horton not out 101) V Beamish (1 for 21) P Phillips (1 for 23)

Wagon Works 132 for 4 (F Stephens 63, V Beamish 37) H Brazington (1 for 13) Match Drawn.

*H Horton went on to play County Cricket for Worcestershire and Hampshire.

Saturday 25th May - GRC & W Co. v. Amorpheans

The Wagon Works batted first against Amorpheans at Tuffley, and in 1½ hours, totalled 182 for the loss of 4 wickets. Frank Stephens, scoring 102 not out in 1 hour 45 minutes without giving a chance, was well supported by V Beamish (31) and J Stephens (30). The Amorpheans were left with the same time to get the runs as the Works, and at the time of drawing stumps, were 88 for 4 wickets.

Saturday 27th July - Wagon Works Lose at Lydney

Lydney 158 for 8   GRC & W Co. 49 All Out

Saturday 3rd August

A fine knock by J Lane who scored 72 runs when they were badly needed was a feature of the Wagon Works innings against Swindon GWR at Swindon.
The match was drawn. Wagon Works declared with their score of 179 for 9, at the close Swindon GWR had reached 146 for 4. Batting first on a fast true wicket, the Works started rather shakily losing 2 wickets for 8. The 6th and 8th wickets put on 44, and 57 respectively, and placed the visitors in a more favourable position. J Lane's chanceless innings was mainly responsible, excellent hooking and driving characterised his display. Swindon failed by 33 to reach the Works total.

Wagon Works 179 for 9 declared. J Lane (72 Not Out) B Evans (24), F Stephens (17), H Banks (15), G Roberts (14), W Artus (12), Swindon 146 for 4.

1947

Saturday 3rd May - GRC & W CO V Tewkesbury

In their opening match of the season, Wagon Works gained a fine win over Tewkesbury by 8 wickets.

Wagon Works 122 for 2, Tewkesbury All Out in 1½ hours for 56.

Wagon Works A H Evans (66 Not Out), C Poolman Run Out (4), H Banks C Neal 6 Robinson (18), C Newman Not Out (30), Extras 4 Total 122 for 2.

Saturday 17th May - GRC & W Co. v. Colwall

Wagon Works gained an easy victory over Colwall by 8 Wickets on the Wagon Works Ground. Colwall were all out for 113, Wagon Works 127 for 2.

Saturday 31st May - GRC & W Co. v. Gloucester City

Rain spoiled Gloucester's chance of beating the Wagon Works on their ground. Gloucester needed 3 wickets to win with 11/2 hours play left, when rain fell heavily enough to stop play. The City put up their best score to date, 192 for 8 when Hawker declared. Wagon Works 105 for 7, rain stopped play.

Wagon Works A H Evans (44 Not Out), C Poolman (1), C Newman (10), F Stephens (8), R Watts Run Out (1),
V Beamish (1), H Banks (27), J Stephens (2), Extras (6).

Saturday 5th July - GRC & W Co. v. Metro Cammell (Birmingham)

Wagon Works defeated Metro Cammell Works at Tuffley by 5 wickets. The visitors lost a wicket with the 2nd ball, but after the dismissal of Hudson who made 29, very little opposition was met until the last pair put on 32.
Evans and Watts opened confidently for the Wagon Works, the latter being out to a brilliant caught and bowled by Fowler, who held a sharp rising drive above his head one handed.
Wagon Works lost four more wickets before scoring the necessary runs. The Wagon Works' most successful bowler was Frank Stephens who captured 5 for 31.

Metro Cammell 105, Wagon Works 115 for 5.

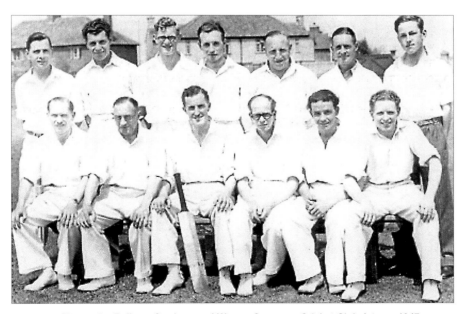

Gloucester Railway Carriage and Wagon Company Cricket Club A team 1947
L Evans C Pearce R Beamish D Swift P Phillips Webb (umpire) B Smith
M Wellman A E Evans R Mansell-Davies R Hamblett J Wheeler G Woodridge

1948

Saturday 12th June - Wagon Works v Tewkesbury

The Wagon Works home match against Tewkesbury was drawn. Tewkesbury batted first and were soon scoring freely against Stephens and Lodge. After Nottingham went at 36, bowled in Barber's first over, the scoring quietened down and with 6 down for 85, Tewkesbury appeared to have lost their good start. But F.C. Fort and N. Warren hit hard and Tewkesbury were able to declare at 169 for 9 after 2½ hours.

Left 1½ hours to obtain the required score, the Works looked as though they may have got the runs while C. Newman and C. Poolman were together, but Newman went at 29 and Poolman, who scored 52, received indifferent support and the Works were 105 for 7 when stumps were drawn.

For the Works, Barber took 5 for 34 and for Tewkesbury Hodges took 4 for 7.

Tewkesbury 169 for 9　　　　　　　　*Wagon Works*

C. Newman	c	Warren	b	Bassett	12
C. Poolman	c	Neal	b	Nottingham	52
F. Stephens	c	Robinson	b	Hodges	9
P. Phillips	b	Hodges			11
J. Wheeler	c	Nottingham	b	Hodges	4
B. Watts	Run out				4
A.E. Evans	b	Hodges			4
G. Roberts	Run out				0
M. Wellman	Not out				
				Extras	**3**
				Total	**105**

Saturday 10th July Wagon Works v Nondescripts

The Nondescripts won their game against the Wagon Works by 9 runs in a very low scoring match, the bowlers on both sides being on top throughout. For the Nondescripts*, B. Wells took 4 for 10 runs and Hayward, 4 for 12. The Wagon Works' best bowlers were F.Stephens 5 for 32 and Pearce 4 for 20. The fielding on both sides was first class and nothing was given away.

Nondescripts 65 all out　　　　　　　*Wagon Works*

C. Newman	c	Hayward	b	Wells	13
B. Watts	lbw		b	Hook	3
P. Phillips			b	Adams	0
F. Stephens			b	Wells	10
V. Beamish			b	Hayward	5
C. Poolman			b	Hayward	0
T. Wheeler	lbw		b	Wells	4
W. Lodge	c	Hill	b	Hayward	0
J. Moore	st	Walden	b	Hayward	0
D. Jewell	Not out				9
W. Pearce			b	Wells	0
				Extras	**7**
				Total	**56**

*B Wells went on to play for Gloucestershire and Nottinghamshire

Groundstaff preparing the Square for County Cricket in 1948
From left to right Charlie Newman Frank Stephens Charlie Restall and Mr F Boon

1949

Saturday 28th May

The game between the Nondescripts and Wagon Works was one of the most interesting between the old rivals for many years. The Works' captain, on winning the toss, put the Nondescripts in and his policy was soon justified as the visitors lost Walden before a run was scored. After this wickets fell rapidly, only Voyce of the first eight batsmen faced with the bowling of Beamish and Lodge, batted with any confidence. After the fall of the 7th wicket Strand and Wells came together with only 30 runs on the board and a change came over the innings. Strand ,a young new member, kept his wicket intact for 40 minutes, while Wells attacked the bowling hitting three 6s in his 33 runs. After these two were out, the last wicket pair of Hayward and Hill put on a further 27.

When the Works batted, their opening pair went for the runs immediately, Newman being particularly severe with the bowling. After his departure, well caught on the boundary by Adams, wickets fell fast and the Works had lost 9 wickets for 79 runs when the last pair came together. These two, Lodge and Parsons, batted steadily and the score slowly mounted towards victory.

For the Works, Beamish took 5 for 46 and Lodge 2 for 24 and for the Nondescripts Hayward took 6 for 46 and Wells 2 for 55.

Nondescripts 101 all out, Wagon Works 125 all out, P Phillips (8), C Newman (32), V Beamish (0), B Cummings (3), C Poolman (0), K Hooper (6), R Hamblett (1), A.H.Evans (12), H Taylor (15), W Lodge (21), M Parsons (27)

Saturday 16th July - Rotol v Wagon Works

A fine opening knock by G Birchall, who was only one short of a half century when he was bowled, was a feature of the game whent-tri Rotol entertained the Wagon Works.

After Brown and Davey had returned to the Pavilion, the Rotol middle order was easily disposed of, until Jennings stepped in to con tribute a bright 25.

Below full strength the Wagon Works batted only 43 minutes before rain stopped play with their score at 62 for 4. Rotol 134, Wagon Works 62 for 4.

Saturday 23rd July - Wagon Works In Exciting Tie

After an innings packed with excitement, Gloucester Wagon Works had to be content with a tie when they entertained Witney. The visitors lost their first 3 men for 39, but subsequent batsman hit out, Priest retiring with a bleeding nose and Bishop carrying his bat for 45 and the innings was declared at 164 for 6.

Losing Newman before a run was scored, the Works' representatives then hit out, Hamblett, Phillips and Beamish making excellent contributions. With the minutes slipping by, Evans brought the scores level but failed to get a winning hit before time was called.

Wagon Works' Scores. C Newman (0), R Hamblett (21), M Parsons (4), P Phillips (34), L Priest (9), F Stephens (14) V Beamish (44), A.H. Evans (20), A.E.Evans (1) Total 164 for 7.

Saturday 30th July - Wagon Works v Tewkesbury

At tea time, the Works declared at 170 for 8, Corbett having carried his bat for a useful 24. Tewkesbury were left with 2 hours, and apart from Moses and Pitman, they faired poorly at Tuffley and finished on 144 for 7.

Saturday 7th August - Wagon Works v Westinghouse Brake

Although they lost their first wicket for 10 runs, the Wagon Works finally reached 261 before they declared with one wicket left to fall when they entertained Westinghouse Brake.

The visitors replied with a respectable 165 for 5 before the close.

1949 FIRST ELEVEN AVERAGES

BATTING　　　　　　　　　　　　　　　　　　　*BOWLING*

	Inns	Runs	H/Score	Ave	Name	Overs	Runs	Wkts	Ave
V. Beamish	12	287	72	23.91	L. Priest	31.66	89	10	8.9
F. Stephens	11	221	53	20.09	M. Parsons	53	184	15	12.26
A.H. Evans	10	174	51	19.33	J. Corbett	11	51	3	17
P. Phillips	20	345	68	18.15	F. Barber	99	258	15	17.2
C. Newman	17	268	43	15.76	V. Beamish	165	504	29	17.37
C. Poolman	15	204	87	15.69	D. Mortimer	15	59	3	19.66

P Phillips was to take 7 catches and wicket keeper Charlie Newman made 4 stumpings.

1950 -1959

The new decade brought a number of changes to the club: spin bowler Frank Barber took over the captaincy of the first eleven from A.H (Tripey) Evans while the second eleven were to see Harold Simms take on the skipper's role from A.E Evans. 1950 also brought about the introduction of a Sunday team, with P. Philips honoured with the chance of captaining the side in its inaugural season.There were two centuries scored during the 1950 season, the first by Charlie Newman and the second a week later by George Woodridge, a fine 129 against old adversaries Westinghouse Brake (Chippenham) on the Sports Ground.The club also recorded it,sfirst win over Worcester City since before the war winning by 5 wickets in July.

During the early 50s the players' wives made tea for the teams, in particular Mrs Hamblett, Mrs Taylor and Mrs Swift. Doug Swift recalls cycling to Bill Dawe's fruit and vegetable shop in Bristol Road to pick up the salad items and take them to the ground before the start of play. Towards the end of the 50s these duties were taken over by Eric and Edna Ford. W (Bill) Morris umpired for the first eleven for much of the 50s until his sad death in 1959, and Bill Aubrey was the scorer after umpiring throughout the 1940s.

The senior players Frank Barber, Doug Swift, Charlie Newman, Vic Bramish, Brian Cummings, Lewis Deane, along with comparative new boys Jack Corbett, Graham Hale, Ken Newman and Roy Morley made up the majority of the first XI. Also supporting the club at this time were stalwarts Tom Salter, who took up umpiring due to a knee injury in the late 50s, and his wife Dolly who scored for the club from the end of the Second World War until well into the 70s.

Doug Swift had an excellent season in 1952, amassing 573 runs at an average of 38, while Lewis Deane bowled splendidly, taking 67 wickets at an average of 11.00. Dick Hamblett took over the captaincy in 1953 from Frank Barber after three seasons in charge and the club organised its first ever tour, taking them for a long weekend to South Wales.

The team travelled by coach to play Porthcawl on the Saturday, unfortunately the game was cancelled due to Porthcawl double booking, although Doug Swift and Lewis Deane did manage to play, turning out for Porthcawl.

On Sunday a second coach carried wives and family to Barry Island for the tour's second game, no record of the match remains, although the tour was a success and a further tour took place in 1958.

In 1951 Harry Perkins received a presentation to mark his 45-year association with the club on the occasion of his retirement as Chairman. He had been a club stalwart since well before the First World War, serving as a player, captain, chairman and committee member.

1955 was a sad year for the club when Sir Leslie Boyce, who had been Cricket Club President since 1931, sadly died. He was Chairman of the Gloucester Railway and Carriage Company and, in this position, was also Cricket Club President. He was born in Sydney Australia, fought at Gallipoli in the First World War, being nearly buried alive until a gravedigger found he was still breathing. After the war he went to Oxford University and became a barrister, joined the company on the Board of Directors and also became a leading financier. He was elected MP for Gloucester and became the Lord Mayor of London in 1951. Also, in 1955, it should be noted that Her Majesty Queen Elizabeth II visited the company for a tour of the factory.

Wally Lodge topped the batting averages in 1956 with 22.23 scoring 335 runs, and Denis Mortimer the bowling with an average of 3.81, although Roy Morley took most wickets, 53 in total.

Club Captain Doug Swift averaged 26.09 in 1957, topping the batting averages and Roy Morley topped the bowling with 9.6,7 taking in total 53 wickets. The club had an extremely good season in 1957, playing 20 games and only losing 2, wicket keeper Brian Cummings completing 10 stumpings.

The 50s also brought many test stars to the Works ground, some of whom became cricket legends of the time. Teams included Middlesex, Surrey, Kent and Lancashire, playing in the traditional Gloucester Cricket Festival. Surrey were the visitors in 1951 and their side included Tony Locke, Jim Laker, and EA Bedser, Laker taking 8 wickets during the game which Surrey lost by 5 wickets.Middlesex were Festival visitors in 1952.England test legends Edrich and Denis Compton were in the team, Compton scoring 82 in his first innings and 25 in his second.

In comments made to the press after the match, Denis Compton said "The pitch gave no assistance at all to the bowlers, and compared with many wickets, the ball came through too easily and slowly". He added "Any good batsman who so desired, and who took no chances, could stop there all day. In fact" he continued "The wicket was so perfect it was too good".

Surrey were back again in 1956 when, along with the Bedser twins Eric and Alec and Jim Laker, was England Captain Peter May who scored a modest 8 and 34. Also in that same year Middlesex returned, this time in his only innings Denis Compton scored 47. Both Peter May and Denis Compton were to join forces later in the year to play against Australia in August for the last test of the series at the Oval. May scored 83 not out and 37 not out, Compton 94 and 35 not out in a rain affected drawn match.

The Works team was to see two newcomers in 1959, Stan and Eileen Phelps from Speech House in the Forest of Dean. Both, over the coming years, were to become splendid servants to the club both on and off the field, indeed both still continue today, Eileen as first team scorer and Stan as Club President and sometimes as umpire.

1959 brought a change in captaincy, Doug Swift standing down to Des Yearsley after four years in charge of the first eleven, and Derek Turner taking over from George Billingham in skippering the second eleven. The first eleven had a poor season, winning only 3 of their 17 games, although they did reach the final of the Gloucester 20 over knock out losing out to Nondescripts.The second eleven did rather better, winning 7 of their 12 completed matches. The Sunday XI under the captaincy of Nigel Barker recorded the best set of results, winning 11 of their 22 fixtures.

1950

Saturday 17th June - Lydney V Wagon Works

Played at Lydney.

Lydney set Wagon Works a hard task, but the Gloucester Team accepted the challenge and won by a boundary hit off the fourth ball of the last over to secure a well-deserved win.

Winning the toss, Lydney elected to bat on a fast wicket. Although Aldridge started shakily against Beamish and Stephens and survived an appeal for L.B.W, he did his side good service by scoring 42 before missing a straight delivery from Woodridge.

Ron Hock quickly scored 64 before being run out by a smart return from Cummings. The innings was declared closed at 175 for 8, after being at one time 139-2.

The Works had just under 2 hours in which to get the runs and set about the job from the start. Wickets were sacrificed and at 35-4 the position looked grim, but a fine 119 run partnership followed between V. Beamish (75) and D. Swift (62). They batted superbly and pushed on quickly at nearly two runs a minute during their time together.

Hooper and Hamblett carried on their good work and Hooper went halfway down the wicket for the four that gave the Works victory.

Lydney 175 for 8   R. Aldridge 42, R. Hook 64, Bowling: F. Stephens 3-46, W. Lodge 1-11, G. Woodridge 1-28.

Wagon Works 177 for 7   V. Beamish 75, D. Swift 62, Bowling: B Peglar 6-66, L. Jenkins 2-61.

Saturday 24th June - Wagon Works v South Gloucester

Played on the Wagon Works Ground.

After electing to bat first South Gloucester lost the initiative and were finally beaten by Gloucester Wagon Works by 7 wickets. Beamish 3-21 and Stephens 3-14 played a big part in breaking down South Gloucester's resistance and Woodridge 1-21, Hooper 2-5 and Barber 2-7 completed the work, the visitors being dismissed for 91.

A brilliant not out innings by Beamish was scored, his 59 being the highlight of the Works' batting display.

South Gloucester 91 all out

Wagon Works 120 for 4 - V. Beamish 59 not out, B. Cummings 28, C. Newman 15. Bowling - Dewick 2-27.

Three Club Stalwarts E J (Jim)Stephens Harry Perkins and W A (Bill) Brown
pictured outside the Bowls Pavilion in 1950

Saturday July 1st - Wagon Works v Worcester

Wagon Works registered their first post-war win over Worcester by 5 wickets.

WORCESTER

P.Neal	c	Cummings	b	Hooper	21
A.Weston	b	Beamish			1
T.Winwood	b	Lodge			63
M.Weaver	st	Newman	b	Lodge	7
K.Humphries	Not Out				28
E.Tinkler	c&b	Beamish			8
P.Richardson	st	Newman	b	Barber	6
J.Spilsbury	c	Lodge	b	Barber	2
T.Neel	Not Out				2
	EXTRAS				**2**
	TOTAL(FOR 7 DEC')				**145**

WAGON WORKS

G.Woodridge	c	Sub	b	Tinkler	9
P.Phillips	c	Tinkler	b	P.Neal	41
V.Beamish	c	Winwood	b	Spilbury	30
B.Cummings	b	Jones			30
C.Newman	Not Out				24
D.Swift	b	Jones			1
R.Hamblett	Not Out				4
	EXTRAS				**11**
	TOTAL (FOR 5)				**150**

Saturday 19th August - Wagon Works v Westinghouse

Put in to bat on a moist wicket at Tuffley Avenue, Wagon Works were able to declare on 237 for 3. The man behind this impressive total was George Woodridge, whose 129 not out followed a century by Charlie Newman in the Works' previous match. The latter contributed 23 not out, and Frank Stephens with 53 and Brian Cummings with 28 gave useful support.

Westinghouse were dismissed for 108, their best performance being put up by A. Edwards with 38. F. Stephens completed a fine all round display by taking 7 for 34.

WAGON WORKS

F. Stephens	b	Durbridge			53
A. Purdy	c&b	F. Dunn			3
G. Woodridge	Not Out				129
B. Cummings	c	Hemmings	b	Durbridge	28
C. Newman	Not Out				23
			EXTRAS		1
			TOTAL (for 3 dec.)		**237**

WESTINGHOUSE

108 ALL OUT

F. Stephens 7 for 34

1951

Saturday 27th May

Wagon Works 'B' 100 (A Pugh 29, K Stephens 14, S Priest 12)   Rotol 'A' 49

Wagon Works 'A' 73 (J Moore 20, H Sims 15, F Dudley 13)   Swindon British Rail 'A' 92

Saturday 23rd June - Lydney vs. Wagon Works

After a somewhat uncertain start in their home match with Gloucester Wagon Works, Lydney accumulated a total of 193 for 2, but could not win, the visitors getting 139 for 5 to force a draw.

Lydney 193 for 2 (K Rossiter 40, J C Morgans 73 not out, R Hook 61 not out) Bowling: W Lodge 1-24, (J Corbett 1-66).

Wagon Works 139 for 5 (D Swift 42, C Newman 82) Bowling L Jenkyns 2-31, (E Beeley 2-16).

Saturday 30th June - Hamblet and Cummings Save Works

Winning the toss and batting first at the Wagon Works ground, visitors Dowlais, a visiting team from the Principality, started strongly and 70 runs were on the board before the first wicket fell. Despite frequent changes of bowling subsequent batsmen continued to score freely, and eventually a declaration was made with the score at 163 for 4.

Wagon Works fared disastrously on going to the wicket, three batsmen being back in the pavilion with only 17 runs registered. Useful stands by B Cummings and R Hamblet saved their side, a drawn match resulting:

Dowlais 163 for 4 dec (A Morgan 51, K Pike 39 not out). Bowling: (Mortimer 1-9, K Hooper 1-15)
Wagon Works 82 for 6 (R Hamblett 24 not out, B Cummings 24). Bowling: (C Richards 4-21)

Wagon Works 'B' 153-9 (B Bourne 54, N Barker 35, J Wildy 17 not out, G Fivash 17, W Boseley 13)
Rotol 'B' 95 for 4. (R Roderick 35 not out). Bowling: (B Bourne 2-18, K Pearce 1-12)

The Gloucester Citizen reported that this was Gloucester's hottest day of the year so far, reaching 80° in the shade.

Sunday 1st July - Wagon Works vs. National Smelting Co

Wagon Works Sunday XI and National Smelting Co. (Bristol) drew their match at the Works ground, the home side's 9th wicket pair managing to hold out to avoid defeat.

National Smelting Co 168 for 7 dec (R Allen 65, R Wring 35) Bowling: (K Hooper 5-38)
Wagon Works 113 for 8 (R Hamblett 31, W Lodge Not Out 47)

Saturday 7th July - Archdales (Worcester) vs.Wagon Works

Visiting Worcester, Wagon Works were well beaten by Archdale's who ran up the score of 179 for 8 before declaring. The Works were soon in trouble and were dismissed for 100.

Archdale's 179 for 8 Britton 73
Wagon Works 100 All Out G Woodridge 23, J Corbett 20 Bowling Taylor 5-38, Rudge 3-24

On this day Brian (Bomber) Wells took 6 for 29 for Gloucestershire Etceteras against Lydney.

Wagon Works 'A' 144 (T Salter 39, H Taylor 29). Bowling: Jenkins 5-34
Lydney 'A' 131 for 6 Bowling: K Pearce 3-38, D Woodward 1-33, L Priest 2-30

The Citizen reported on this day that a Gloucester District Eleven was to play a Bristol District Eleven in aid of Gloucestershire player Jack Crapp's benefit. Included in this side were three players from the Wagon Works team, Doug Swift, Charlie Newman and Brian Cummings.

Wagon Works 'B' 73 (G Fivash 26, B Bourne 26)   Permali 111 (A Preece 48) Bowling: (A Pugh 4-31).

Sunday 8th July

Wagon Works 81 (A Pugh 27), T Salter 24)   Woodpeckers 85 for 8 (D King 20)
Bowling: A Pugh 2-14. Limited to 18 overs

Saturday 14th July - Westinghouse Brake Co. vs. Wagon Works

Westinghouse 183 for 2 dec (J Hopkins 100 not out). Bowling: G Woodridge 2-32
Wagon Works 136 for 8 (D Mortimer 27 not out)

Wagon Works 'B' 60 (A Pugh 22, N Barker 14)
Twyning 62 for 4 (L Townsend 32) For Twyning F Lewis took 7 for 21

Saturday 21st July

Wagon Works 'A' 156 for 3 (T Salter 62, A E Evans 42 not out)
Rotol 'A' 128 All Out

Wagon Works 166 (W Lodge 77, K Hooper 37)
Old Elizabethans 91 for 7

Saturday 18th August - Gloucestershire Etceteras Too Strong for Wagon Works

Wagon Works 79 all out. (B Cummings 24, W Lodge 18). Bowling: Harbin 4-23, Wilshaw 3-13
Gloucestershire Etceteras 148 for 5 (*R B Nicholls 34) Bowling: D Mortimer 2-35
*R B Nicholls later played many years for Gloucestershire. Tom Goddard captained the Etceteras team.

Saturday 9th September

Wagon Works Sunday team 83 (W Lodge 30 not out. D Young 17) Barry 94
Wagon Works 'B' 100 (T Salter 60, L Priest 27)
Upton St. Leonards 51 all out

*Mr G Brinkworth (General Manager) presents a gold watch to Harry Perkins on his retirement
from the chairmanship after 45 years' connection with the club. February 1951*

1952

Saturday 10th May

Wagon Works v Gloucester City – played on the Works Sports Ground
Gloucester City 128 for 9 (W. Moreland 34, F. Pickett 27) Bowling: - (Mortimer 3-19, Deane 3-22, Beamish 2-36, Barber 1-11)
Wagon Works 83 all out (D. Swift 14, G. Woodridge 12) Bowling: - (Heritage 4-12, Pickett 3-22)
Citizen's verdict on the match: The man-in-the-street's idea of a Saturday afternoon local match.

Gloucester City III 30 (M. Riddiford 7-10, M. Gough 3-19)
Wagon Works III 38-8 (M. Riddiford 14 not out)

Wagon Works 4th XI 49 (S. Russell 16)
Fielding's Apprentices 52-7 (P. Macey 4-10)

Mine (Author's) Birthday, the day I was born.

Sunday 11th May

Gloucester Wayfarers 75 (R. Carr 3-7, D. Swift 3-14, D. Turner 2-9, K. Hooper 2-16)
Wagon Works Sunday XI 77-7 (D. Swift 23, R. Hamblett 17, L. Deane 15)

Monday 12th May

Wagon Works IV 57 (P. Hoyes 12, Eric Stephens 10 not out)
Rotol IV 85 (K. Newman 3-20)

Wagon Works Painters 28, Coach Shop 85

Saturday 31st May

Wagon Works v Archdales (Worcester) – played on the Sports Ground

Wagon Works 127 for 4 Dec (D. Swift 71 not our, G. Hale 4, G. Woodridge 9, B Cummings 6, W. Lodge 17, R Hamblett 16 not out)
Archdales 62 (L. Deane 6-19, D. Mortimer 3-27) L. Deane bowled throughout hitting the stumps 5 times.

Saturday 28th June - Another Wagon Works victory.

Gloucester Wagon Works gained another good victory when they entertained Lydney. Apart from D. Brown who hit brightly to score 73 and R.C. Aldridge (23), Lydney's batsmen failed against the accurate bowling of L. Deane (7-27), Beamish (1-41) and Lodge (2-1).
The Works made a bad start, but a fine innings by Woodridge, well supported by Hale and Beamish, ensured victory.
Lydney 122 (D. Brown 73, L. Deane 7-27)
Wagon Works 124 for 3 (G. Woodridge not out 65, Beamish not out 22, Hale 16, P. James 2-17)

Saturday 12th July

Won with 10 minutes to spare Westinghouse Brake applied their name determinedly to their innings against Gloucester Wagon Works and despite welcome acceleration of a third wicket partnership, reached only 146-4 at tea time after nearly 2½ hours on an easy paced wicket.
Beamish and Deane bowled steadily for the Works and took 1-55 and 1-39 respectively, but it was Lodge's spinners that met with the most success, bringing him 2-18.
Wagon Works, with less than 2 hours left to bat started disastrously, losing Hale and Woodridge with only 2 runs on the board.
A splendid stand of 94 between Swift and Cummings however retrieved the position, and with the other batsmen forcing the pace the Works gained a fine victory by four wickets with ten minutes to spare.

Westinghouse Brake 146 for 4 Dec' (A.E. Cleverley 52 not out, Lodge 2-18)
Wagon Works 148 for 6 (D. Swift 49, B. Cummings 54, C Newman run out 11, W. Lodge not out 15)

Sunday 20th July

Wagon Works win race for victory.

Gloucester Wagon Works Sunday XI raced against the clock to gain a splendid victory over Barry.

The visitors declared on 151 for 9, leaving the Works 110 minutes to get the runs.

High spot of the Works innings was a fighting stay by Dick Hamblett (Capt) who hit 67, and a fine half century by D. Young.

Barry 151 for 9 Dec' (G. Hillier not out 55, M. Riddeford 4-33, D. Turner 2-17)

Wagon Works Sunday XI 157 for 4 (D. Young 55, R. Hamblett not out 67, T. Salter not out 3)

Saturday 26th July

Swift scores ton for Wagon Works

Wagon Works 201 all out (D. Swift 111, B. Cummings 24, G. Woodridge 18)

Dowlais 111 for 8 (W. Lodge 3-21, F. Stephens 1-10, R.Carr 1-13)

PRESIDENT	Sir Leslie Boyce	COLOURS Navy & Blue
HON SECRETARY	H D Swift	

The 1952 season was the most successful campaign since 1936. The club's performance reflected the results of coaching and the influx of young members. Approximately 100 matches were played of which 80 reached a conclusion, thus fulfilling the club's intention to limit the number of drawn games to a minimum. The Worcester game was indicative of this policy. The second X1 won 8 of 17 matches played, drew 3 and lost 6. An interdepartmental league was run during the season (8 teams participating when two matches were played on Tuesday and Thursday evenings.) Another point of interest was the running of a Sunday X1 which had a very successful season. The cricket table is to be further enlarged.

1st X1 AVERAGES

	WICKETS	AV	RUNS	AVE
F A M Barber (Capt)	1	20		
H D Swift			573	38
B Cummings			342	23
W Lodge	13	14	174	17
C Newman			225	16
V Beamish			96	16
F Stephens			100	14
R Hamblett			107	13
D Turner			45	11
G Woodridge			155	11
L Deane	67	11	86	11
R Carr				

2nd X1 AVERAGES

	WICKETS	AV	RUNS	AVE
H E D Simms (Capt)	15	12		
F Dudley			91	10
H Taylor			156	22
A Webb			156	14
K Pearce	25	10	159	12
T Salter			162	11
W Boseley			61	10
D Young			86	10
D Woodward	29	9		
D Turner	20	5	109	15
N Barker				

1st X1 matches Sat, WON: Rotol 58, 63, Worcester 160, 160-2, Archdales 127-4*, 148-6, Rotol 125, 132-5, Colwall 156, 128, Tewkesbury 51, 47, Worcester O.B. 149, 79. Drawn Colwall 144-8*, 101-6, Witney 130-4, 201, Dowlais 110-8, 164-5*, B.R.W.R. Swindon 81-6. LOST: Worcester, Gloucester, Witney, B.R.W.R. Swindon, Lydney.

1953

Saturday 23rd May - Works have a bigger shock than City

In the first three overs at the Spa Wagon Works took three wickets for six runs to give Gloucester City Cricket Club their biggest shock of the season. City skipper, Pat Nicholas, steadied the team with a useful 20.

The City star though was J Courtice, who contributed a delightful variety of strokes to stop the rot and to enliven the game. With his personal score at 42 he was caught and bowled by Corbett. By that time, however, he had saved the City's self-respect. The Works' most dangerous bowler was J Corbett who took 4-44.

Gloucester City 149 for 8 DEC (J Courtice 42, R.G. Nicholls 34, J Corbett 4-44)
Wagon Works 44 all out (B Steward 17-5-22-5)

Saturday 6th June -Works Beat Tewkesbury

Played on the Wagon Works ground

Tewkesbury 119 all out (L Deane 5-48, D Mortimer 2-16, V Beamish 2-19)
Wagon Works 121 for 5 (B Cummings 58 not out, C Newman 27, W Lodge 10 not out)

Sunday 7th June - Wagon Works Avoid Defeat

In a tense atmosphere bowlers Terrett and Corbett played out time at the Sports Ground to thwart Dowlais in their efforts to force a win against the Works.

The Welshmen, who would have fared badly but for an invaluable knock by Reader, left the Works just over 100 minutes to get the runs. Beamish and Newman tried hard to score quickly but on their dismissal wickets fell at frequent intervals, though Lodge and Deane offered stout resistance. Beamish, who sent down 20 overs, kept an immaculate length and captured four Dowlais wickets for 33.

Lodge had 3-18 in nine overs while Deane took 2-22
Dowlais 110 all out (H Reader 42)
Wagon Works 90 for 9   (C Newman 24)

Saturday 13th June - Wagon Works Win by 6 Wickets

Bright and consistent batting, following equally steady bowling, gave Wagon Works a splendid win over visitors Old Elizabethans (Worcester) by 6 wickets. A devastating opening spell by pace bowler Jackie Corbett, ably supplemented by Vic Beamish, set the Old Boys side rocking on their heels and with half their wickets gone for only 30 runs, a rout appeared imminent. But Bingham proved a stumbling block to the Works and when he was joined by EIT, the innings was given the impetus it so sorely needed.

The adventurous EIT provided the most spectacular batting of the match, and his short but merry knock included several tremendous drives, one of which soared high over the boundary. Bingham, however, was mainly responsible for saving his side from complete collapse and he was unlucky to miss his half century. Billingham and Beamish gave the Works a useful start and a good stand by Swift and Newman added 46, before the former was caught in the deep.

Old Elizabethan	123 all out	(Corbett taking 4 wickets)
Wagon Works	124 for 4	(D Swift 38, C Newman not out 26, L Deane not out 20)
Wagon Works 'A'	144 for 7	(N Barker 52, G Haze 45)
Stroud Brewery	62 for 8	(K Pearce 5-20, D Woodman 2-17)

Saturday 27th June - Wagon Works Thwarted by Fine Stand

At 6.30pm on the Sports Ground, Colwall's score in reply to the Wagon Works 'big total of 192-6 dec', stood at 43-6. They seemed doomed to a crushing defeat, but an hour later when stumps were drawn, the visitors had 116 on the board with the seventh wicket pair still together. Earlier, Vic Beamish for the Works had hit two sixes and six fours in his innings of 68 and he received splendid support from Newman and Lodge.

Wagon Works 192 for 6 dec (Beamish 68,Lodge 36 not out, Newman 32,G Billingham 15,J Horton 3-42)
Colwall 116 for 7 (J Horton not out 75, G Berry not out 14, J Corbett 4-45, L Deane 2-25)

*J Horton played 59 times for Worcestershire between 1934 and 1938, he died in 1998.

Saturday 25th July - Exciting Win for Wagon Works

In a thrilling finish Wagon Works defeated Shirehampton, (Bristol) at the Sports Ground by four wickets in the last over of the day. With rain preventing any play until 4.15, Shirehampton, after a slow start, had 58 on the board without loss. The introduction into the attack of young leg-break bowler, Roy Morley, making his debut with the 1st eleven, brought a remarkable change to the state of the game.
In seven overs he took 4-24 and when Shirehampton declared, they had lost five wickets for 127. Left with 1½ hours to get the runs, the Works made an indifferent start and lost both opening batsmen for 21. A superb forcing innings of 67 from acting captain Doug Swift however, put his side right back into the fight and when he was caught on the boundary, only eight runs were needed for victory and one over left.
Amid great excitement Jackie Corbett hit these off with two sparkling drives to the boundary. Deane and Terrett also played fine innings for the Works and gave their skipper splendid support.

Shirehampton 127 for 5 dec (R Morley 4-24, G Billingham 1-19)
Wagon Works 128 for 6 (D Swift 67, L Deane 17, G Terrett 16 not out)

Gloucester Railway Carriage and Wagon Company Cricket Club embark on their first tour to South Wales in 1953

1954

Saturday 1st May - Thrilling win for Wagon Works

An exhilarating display of batting with Vic Beamish leading the way enabled the Wagon Works to beat Ledbury, and the clock, at the Sports Ground and gain their second successive victory. Taking first knock Ledbury batted steadily, but found Lewis Deane again in grand form, six of their batsmen falling victims to his wiles at a cost of only 30 runs. Beamish and Des Yearsley gave good support and the visitors were forced to continue their innings after the tea interval.
With rain threatening, the Works went for the runs at a cracking pace and passed the visitors' total with only four wickets down in 79 minutes. Beamish reached his half-century in just over half an hour, Gough, Swift and Billingham also used the long handle with telling effect.

Ledbury 129 all out (L Deane 6-30, B Beamish 2-25, D Yearsley 2-29)
Wagon Works 142 for 4   (V Beamish 56, M Gough 28, G Billingham 17, C Newman 9 not out, K Trevarthen 14 not out).

During this week Tom Tyler, voted Hollywood's leading cowboy star in 1942, died aged 50. His films included "Hellfire", "The Tenderfoot", "Cheyenne" and "San Antonio". Also showing at Gloucester's Hippodrome Cinema was "The Moon is Blue" starring William Holden, David Niven and Maggie McNamara.

Saturday 3rd July - Another Works Victory

Scoring nearly twice as fast as their opponents, Wagon Works, weakend by the absence of several regular players, gained a splendid away win over Tetbury by six wickets.
Acting captain Vic Beamish, who bowled nine overs without success but conceding only 15 runs, handled his attack cleverly, and despite several promising stands the Tetbury batsmen were never allowed to settle down. Over two hours batting brought them only 112 runs with Deane, Morley and Lodge all bowling well. It took the Works only 100 minutes to knock off the necessary runs, thanks chiefly to the splendid batting of Mike Gough and Ken Trevarthen. The latter, in particular, gave a polished display and was unlucky to be bowled two short of his half century. He reached the boundary eight times.

Tetbury 112 all out (E Davenport 29, L Deane 4-46, R Morley 3-23, F Stephens 1-13)
Wagon Works 115 for 4   (M Gough 32, K Trevarthen 48, F Stephens 13)

Saturday 10th July - Close Escape for Wagon Works

A splendid fighting innings by Wally Lodge enabled Wagon Works to force a draw against Westinghouse Brake at the Sports Ground, though the visitors were unlucky to be thwarted of victory.
Fielders clustered in a ring round the batsmen in the last two overs, but young Roy Morley gallantly helped Lodge to hold the fort. Batting first, Westinghouse started slowly but as they opened out, runs came at a good rate, Day providing the backbone of their respectable total.
Morley bowled his leg spinners cleverly and deserved even better figures than 4-38, while Beamish also kept a steady length. With two hours to get the runs, Wagon Works lost three wickets quickly and though Gough and Woodridge put them back into the game with a valuable fourth wicket partnership, the rate of scoring dropped as the innings progressed.

Both Newman and Deane pulled muscles and were forced to bat with runners.

Westinghouse Brake 158   (Beamish 3-41, Deane 1-23, Lodge 1-24, Morley 4-38)
Wagon Works 127 for 9   (Gough 32, Woodridge 17, W Lodge 22 not out)

Monday 26th July - Easy Victory for Wagon Works

Consistent batting and a grand unchanged bowling spell by acting captain Vic Beamish and veteran Frank Stephens, gave Wagon Works an easy victory by 65 runs over the touring side, Haverfordwest, on the Sports Ground.

Works, taking first knock, were given an excellent start by Frank Stephens and George Billingham who put on 64 for the first wicket. Three more batsmen including Billingham went for the addition of 23 runs, but then another fine stand by Charle Newman and Jim Stephens enabled Works to declare at 127-6.

Haverfordwest's batting collapsed completely against Beamish and Stephens and despite two minor stands they were bundled out for 62, Charlie Newman making two stumpings and a fine catch.

Wagon Works 127-6   (Billingham 38, Stephens 25, Newman not out 27, J Stephens 11)

Haverfordwest 62   (Beamish 6-19, F Stephens 4-27)

Saturday 14th August - Works First Saturday Defeat

Poor fielding and inconsistent batting brought Wagon Works their first Saturday defeat of the season when they lost away to Old Elizabethans by four wickets. Taking first knock, Works lost wickets quickly and with three falling at the same score, they had lost half their batsmen with only 11 runs on the board.

Ken Trevarthen however, batted steadily, and with good support from Graham Terrett and Derek Turner the Works eventually reached 87 with Turner's innings a mixture of watchfulness and aggression, his 23 including a six and thirteen singles.

Wagon Works 87

Old Elizabethans 88 for 6   (Morley 3-25, Terrett 2-23)

Club President Sir Leslie Boyce presenting Doug Swift
with a barometer for his services to the club in 1954

1955

Saturday 30th April - Wagon Works v Woodpeckers

Played on the Works Sports Ground. Brian Cummings batted extremely well and was the backbone of the Wagon Works' innings, scoring 69 not out including eight 4s and a six and reached his fifty in an hour. He was supported by Vic Beamish who scored a quick fire 34, including 3 fours and 2 sixes.

Wagon Works 182 for 7 declared (Cummings 69 not out Beamish 34)

Woodpeckers 41 all out (Roy Morley, seven for 12 runs taken in 5.1 overs, including the 'Hat Trick')

Saturday 14th May - Wagon Works v Nondescripts

Played on the Sports Ground.

Nondescripts 109 for 8 Declared.

Wagon Works 84 all out (Beamish 34)

Saturday 10th June - Wagon Works v Dowlais

Played on The Sports Ground.

Dowlais 69 all out (R. Morley 6 for 18)

Wagon Works 75 for 0 wickets (G.Billingham 35 n.o. W. Lodge 38 n.o.)

Sunday 19th June - Wagon Works v Colwall

Played on the Sports Ground.

Wagon Works 119 for 7 Declared (R. Hamblett 40 not out).

Colwall 57 for 9 (D. Mortimer 5 for 6)

Saturday 25th June - Wagon Works v Tewkesbury

Played on the Sports Ground.
A remarkable last wicket stand between leg spinner Roy Morley and fast bowler Des Yearsley enabled Wagon Works to build up a total of 149 and beat Tewkesbury by 15 runs.
When the gallant pair became associated, the Works had lost nine men with only 85 runs on the board and their chances of victory seemed slender. Morley and Yearsley however refused to be overawed by the dominance of the Tewkesbury attack and though runs came occasionally from unintended shots, both players also produced a number of splendid drives that would not have disgraced accomplished batsmen. It was Morley who carried on the good work when Tewkesbury made their reply. A productive third wicket partnership between Coutts and Collins caused the Works some anxiety, but Morley dismissed both batsmen, and apart from a bright knock by J. Bourton, the Tewkesbury innings disintegrated.

Morley finished with 4-32, while Yearsley, who bore the brunt of the opening attack, bowled far better than his figures suggest.

Wagon Works 149 (Morley 28 not out, D. Yearsley 31, D. Mortimer 16, D. Swift 17).
Tewkesbury 134 (Coutts 43, Collins 42)

Saturday 29th July - Colwall v Wagon Works

Played at Colwall.

Wagon Works 171 for 8 (K. Newman 21, T. Salter 20, K. Trevarthen 20, L. Swift 21, L. Deane 21)

Colwall 86 (C. Dominey 34).

Bowling: Yearsley 3-16, Deane 3-23, Yearsley 3-36.

Sunday 30th July - Wagon Works v Conveyors (Ready Built)

Played at the Sports Ground.

Wagon Works 159 (K. Newman 51)

Conveyors 120 (T. Simms 63)

Bowling: D. Mortimer 2-38, G. Terrett 4-20, K. Newman 2-35, A. Pugh 2-25.

Monday 1st August - Wagon Works v Baldwins (Swansea)

An eighth wicket partnership of 58 between Graham Terrett and Des Yearsley enabled Wagon Works to total 135 in their August Monday home match against Baldwins (Swansea). This was not enough, for the Welshmen passed their target with only three wickets down.

Wagon Works 135 (G. Terrett 42, D. Yearsley 25, C. Newman 32, K. Newman 20)

Baldwins 137 for 3 (C. Pilot 65)

Bowling: Yearsley 1-35, Terrett 1-33, Newman 1-34.

Saturday 27th August - Wagon Works v Lydney

Played on the Sports Ground

LYDNEY						WAGON WORKS					
K.Rossiter	c	C.Newman	b	Yearsley	4	G.Billingham	b	O'Driscoll			11
W.Whereat	c	Gough	b	Yearsley	4	K.Newman	Run Out				31
R.Nicholas	lbw		b	Yearsley	29	M.Gough	c	Rossiter	b	Whereat	21
V.Jordan			b	Yearsley	40	C.Newman	b	O'Driscoll			12
W.Stone	c	L.Swift	b	Morley	0	D.Swift	b	Whereat			4
J Allopp	c	Yearsley	b	Morley	2	G.Woodridge	run out				4
T.Jones			b	Morley	28	L.Swift	not out				5
H.O'Driscoll	c	Bailey	b	Morley	4	R.Morley	not out				5
L.James	c	C.Newman	b	Mortimer	1	EXTRAS					6
P.James	lbw		b	Morley	10	TOTAL (FOR 6)					99
P.Gerrard	not out				1						
		TOTAL			123						

Bowling: Morley 5-48, Yearsley 4-15, Mortimer 1-18

Mortimer, Yearsley, Bailey did not bat.
Bowling: O'Driscoll 2-27, Whereat 2-42

1956

Saturday 5th May - Wagon Works v Ledbury

Played on the Works Sports Ground

Wagon Works 41 (K. Newman 15 not out)

Ledbury 102

Saturday 12th May - Wagon Works v Tetbury

Played on the Works Sports Ground

Wagon Works 135 for 8 Declared (W. Lodge 48, D. Yearsley 20 n.o.)

Tetbury 51 all out (Morley 8 for 36)

Saturday 19th May -Wagon Works v Hoffman's

Played on the Works Sports Ground

Hoffman's 142 for 9 (Deane 3-32, Yearsley 3-28, K. Newman 3-28)

Wagon Works 121 for 7 (W. Lodge 56)

Monday 21st May - Wagon Works Beaten

Despite a splendid partnership of 78 for the fifth wicket between Charlie Newman and Tony Webb, a Wagon Works XI were beaten by visiting Gorseinon in their bank holiday match at the Sports Ground by three wickets.
Works lost their first four batsmen for only 49 runs, though Ken Newman, Charlie's son, hit 26. Charlie Newman and Tony Webb both passed their half-centuries in a free scoring stand, Newman reached the boundary seven times in his 62, while Webb also batted stylishly in compiling 51 and the home side totalled 162.
Gorseinon's batting had a note of consistency, and with only one batsman failing to reach double figures, they passed the Works' score with only seven men out.
The losers' most successful bowlers were Graham Terrett (3-50) and Ken Trevarthen (2-14).

Saturday 26th May -Tewkesbury v Wagon Works

At Tewkesbury

Tewkesbury 74 (R. Morley 6-25)   Wagon Works 78 for 8

Saturday 23rd June - Wagon Works v Colwall

Played on the Sports Ground
Colwall 117 (Deane 3-28, Bailey 3-28, Morley 2-20)
Wagon Works 123 for 3 (D, Swift 69 not out)

Saturday 7th July - Wagon Works v Marle Hill

Played on the Sports Ground

Marle Hill 177 for 8 Declared (Yearsley 2-56, Morley 5-54)

Wagon Works 178 for 5 (W. Lodge 54, G. Hale 66)

Saturday 21st July

Wagon Works made a bold, but unsuccessful bid to beat Westinghouse at the Sports Ground when they scored 126 for 5 in reply to the visitors' 132 for 6 declared.

One of the features of the match was the opening spell of bowling by the Works' Lewis Dean, his first eight overs were all maidens and in nearly an hour he conceded only seven runs. Wally Lodge set the pace for the Wagon Works with a stylish half century, and though desperate efforts were made to hit off the last few runs still required in the last over, the visitors' attack proved equal to the occasion.

Caught on a spinner's pitch, Wagon Works 'A' came unstuck against Westinghouse 'A' and lost by 37 runs.

The home side compiled 124, the only bowler to cause them any worry being Cyril Woodridge who claimed 5-34.

Works were all out for only the second time this season for 87. Also in trouble were Wagon Works 'B', well beaten by Civil Service 'A' by 53 runs.

Saturday 28th July - Wagon Works v Lydney

Failure to cope with the spin of Roy Morley led to Lydney's defeat on the Sports Ground at the hands of Wagon Works, six wickets the final margin.

LYDNEY					WAGON WORKS				
D Thomas	b	Morley		28	W Lodge	c & b		James	32
R Powell	b	Dean		0	G Hale	lbw		b	Johnson	2
G Johnson	c	Lodge	b	Dean	16	K Newman	c	Jordan	b	James	32
J Morgans	lbw		b	Lodge	0	M Gough	c	James	b	Morgan	9
V Jordan	c	Deane	b	Morley	5	P Cummings	Not out			2
W Stone	c&b	Deane		23	K Trevarthan	Not out			13
M Jarrett	b	Deane		6					
L Nicholas	st	Cummings b	Morley	0					
L James	b	Morley		7					
B Horspool	not out			8					
		EXTRAS	6			EXTRAS	12	
		TOTAL	101			TOTAL	102	

Deane 4-28, Morley 5-15   D. Swift, L. Deane, A. Pugh, R. Morley and D.Bailey did not bat. P. James 2-26, Morgans 1-7

Saturday 18th August - Wagon Works v Tewkesbury

Played on the Sports Ground

Wagon Works 86 (K. Newman 21, M. Gough 23)

Tewkesbury 87-6

Season 1956
Gloucester Wagon Works Cricket Club 1st X1
Order of Batting Averages
Qualification 9 Innings

NAMES	INNINGS	TIMES NOT OUT	RUNS	MOST IN INNINGS	AVERAGE
W Lodge	15	-	335	56	22.33
D Swift	15	2	260	69 not out	20.00
D Yearsley	12	5	130	30 not out	18.57
K Newman	17	4	241	35 not out	18.53
K Trevarthen	12	5	98	28 not out	14.00
M Gough	15	3	165	35 not out	13.75
G Hale	9	-	112	66	12.44
B Cummings	10	2	52	23 not out	6.50
R Morley	10	1	49	14	5.44

Order of Bowling Averages
(Qualification 10 Wickets)

NAMES	OVERS	MAIDENS	RUNS	WICKETS	AVERAGE
D Mortimer	23.5	8	42	11	3.81
L Deane	160.5	53	286	36	7.94
R Morley	149.4	24	457	53	8.62
D Bailey	88	15	269	21	12.81
D Yearsley	143	28	393	14	28.07

		Score of own side	Score of Opponents
Matches Played	19	Total Runs - Wickets	Total Runs - Wickets
Matches Won	8	1795 - 125	2018 - 165
Matches Lost	6		
Matches Drawn	4		
Matches Abandoned	1		

AVERAGE RUNS SCORED   AVERAGE RUNS CONCEDED
Per Wicket   ... 14.36   Per Wicket   ... 12.23

Total Number of Catches taken.... 50 - D Yearsley took 8

1957

Saturday 4th May - Wagon Works v Ledbury

Played at the Sports Ground:

Ledbury 45 all out (D Turner 5 for 22 R Morley 4 for 6)

Wagon Works

W Lodge	not out		11
K Trevarthen	lbw	Ward	0
C Newman	b	Ward	10
B Cummings	not out		15
	Extras		**12**
Total (for 2 wkts)			**48**

Saturday 11th May - Wagon Works v Tetbury

Played at the Sports Ground

Tetbury all out 93 (D Yearsley 5-18, D Turner 3-33, Mortimer 1-15, Morley 1-23)

Worgan Works 95 for 5 (K Trevarthen 32 Inc a six and 3 fours, H D Swift 35 Not Out)

Wagon Works 'A' gained victory over Tetbury 'A' at Tetbury by 46 runs after they had been dismissed for 98, Tom Salter top scoring with 26. Tetbury were then shot out for 52.

Saturday 18th May - Close Thing for Wagon Works

On a rain-damaged pitch at Stonehouse, visiting Wagon Works kept their unbeaten record when they accounted for Hoffmanns by the narrow margin of four runs in a match in which the bowlers were always on top. Taking first knock the Works were struggling from the start against some fine bowling by Paul Egan and Len Blick and lost their first three wickets quickly. But then skipper Doug Swift and Ken Newman improved matters and with George Woodridge and Keith Pearce also resisting bravely they reached 73, the eighth wicket adding an invaluable 18 runs with Roy Morley giving Pearce good support. Hoffmanns fared even worse at the outset, several early wickets falling to the speed attack of Jackie Corbett and Derek Turner and when leg-spinner Roy Morley took over the batsmen found runs even more difficult to obtain, though Len Clutterbuck batted resolutely for a splendid 21 which included three boundaries before falling victim to the persistent Morley, whose five wickets cost him 20 runs in only six overs. Fast bowler Jackie Corbett, the Gloucester rugby centre, had even better figures, while Turner deserved more regard than his analysis shows.

Bowling:	Corbett	4-15
	Turner	1-16
	Morley	5-20
	Mortimer	0-14

Saturday 25th May – Wagon Works v Old Elizabethans

Played at the Sports Ground

Old Elizabethans 103 – Bowling Corbett (0 for 21), Yearsley (3 for 15), Turner (1 for 13), Pearce (1 for 17), Morley (5 for 26)

Wagon Works 104 for 3 – W lodge (33), G Hale (4), K Newman Not Out (33) D Yearsley (6), D Swift Not Out (24)

Saturday 8th June – Wagon Works v Westinghouse

At the Sports Ground

Westinghouse 138

Wagon Works 99 for 4 W Lodge (57), G Hale (9), B Cummings (1), D Swift (13), C Newman Not Out (17)

Saturday 15th June – Wagon Works v Tewkesbury

Played at the Sports Ground

Tewkesbury 195 for 6 Bowling R Morley (3 for 48), Bailey (2 for 46)

Wagon Works 144 for 3 W Lodge Not Out (68), K Newman (8), K Trevarthen (25), C Newman (2), B Cummings Not Out (44)

Saturday 16th June – Wagon Works Sunday XI v Nondescripts

At the Sports Ground

Wagon Works Sunday XI 99 K Newman (25), M Gough (30)

Nondescripts 101 for 2 Bowling Bailey (2 for 25)

Saturday 22nd June – Wagon Works v Colwall

At the Sports Ground

Colwall 148 for 9 declared Bowling Morley (4 for 29), Bailey (2 for 28), Turner (2 for 37), Pearce (1 for 21), Lodge (0 for 19)

Wagon Works 74 for 8

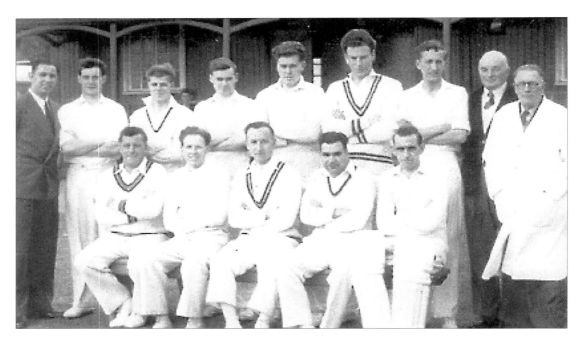

Gloucester Railway Carriage and Wagon Company Cricket Club 1957

G Billingham G Hale K Pearce R Morley K Newman D Bailey D Turner W Brown W Morris (umpire)

C Newman G Woodridge D Swift (c) W Lodge B Cummings

Saturday 27th July

Works win and keep record v Lydney

Having taken first knock at the Sports Ground on an easy-paced pitch, Lydney no doubt had high hopes of inflicting on Wagon Works their first defeat of the season.

These hopes soared higher at the tea interval when, chiefly by dint of a spendid knock of 80 from Johnny Morgans, they were able to declare at the comforable total of 150-5 after two hours and 20 minutes batting. But they had under-estimated the prowess, determination and quality of the Works' batsmen. In a mere 105 minutes the home side had passed the Lydney total in the face of a keen attack, despite the fact that they had lost eight wickets in their quest for the runs. Lydney lost two wickets for 13, but Johnny Morgans and schoolboy Trevor Wintle provided a resolute combination of youth and experience. Even the well-flighted leg-spinners of Roy Morley posed few problems in the air, until he beat and bowled Wintle for an invaluable 19.

Superb Display – John Allsopp executed several neat, but powerful shots in a compact little innings, but his admirable assistance was overshadowed by Morgans who completely dominated the batting. When he was stumped within sight of his century he had hit seven fours in a superb display. Wagon Works quickly made their intentions only too clear; there were to be no safety-first tactics. Graham Hale went early, but Wally Lodge and Brian Cummins strode purposefully onward to the point where skipper Doug Swift took over and practically clinched matters with a polished knock that fell just short of the half-century.

Lydney: W Whereat b Corbett 5; V Jordan c Woodridge b Yearsley 4; T Wintle b Morley 19; J. C Morgans st Cummings b Yearsley 80; J Allsopp b Yearsley 22; M Jarrett not out 6; T Tompkins not out 1; extras 13; total (for 5 dec) 150 M Purvis, LG James, P James and A Smith did not bat.

Bowling: Corbett 1-27; Yearsley 3-38; Turner 0-8; Bailey 0-22; Morley 1-42.

Wagon Works: W Lodge c and b; L.G James 36; G.S Hale lbw b; J James 9; B Cummings b Whereat 33; H.D Swift c and b; L.G James 48; C Newman; st Wintle b; L.G James 1; D Yearsley run out 2; G Woodridge c; Morgans b; L.G James 8; D Bailey c; Allsopp b; Smith 4; J.J Corbett not out 5; D Turner not out 0; extras 7; total (for eight) 153. R Morley did not bat.
Bowling: Smith 1-35; P James 1-36; Whereat 1-18; Morgans 0-17; Tompkins 0-13; L.G James 4-27.

Saturday 24th August – Lydney v Wagon Works

Played at Lydney

Lydney 157 for 4 Bowling D Yearsley (2 for 40), W Lodge (2 for 13)

Wagon Works 112 for 8 W Lodge (34), G Hale (5), D Swift (48), D Bailey (3), D Turner (0), B Cummins (0), N Barker (4), D Yearsley (0), G Woodridge not out (0), J Corbett not out (0), extras 18.

Season 1957
Gloucester Wagon Works Cricket Club 1st X1
Order of Batting Averages
Qualification 10 Innings

NAMES	INNINGS	TIMES NOT OUT	RUNS	MOST IN INNINGS	AVERAGE
D Swift (Captain)	15	4	287	48	26.09
W Lodge	16	3	314	68 not out	24.15
C Newman	13	1	215	60	17.91
D Turner	12	4	126	35	15.75
B Cummings (wicket Keeper)	18	2	237	41 not out	14.81
K Newman	11	2	115	33 not out	12.77
G Woodridge	13	3	106	25	10.60
J Corbett	10	2	80	36	10.00
G Hale	10	-	89	26	8.90

Order of Bowling Averages
(Qualification 10 Wickets)

NAMES	OVERS	MAIDENS	RUNS	WICKETS	AVERAGE
R Morley	156.1	9	513	53	9.67
D Yearsley	128.5	30	340	29	11.72
D Turner	106.5	6	369	28	13.17
J Corbett	101.2	19	283	13	21.76
D Bailey	80.3	9	275	12	22.91

Matches Played	20		Score of own side	Score of Opponents
Matches Won	9		Total Runs - Wickets	Total Runs - Wickets
Matches Lost	2		2031 - 131	2376 - 162
Matches Drawn	8			
Matches Abandoned	1			

AVERAGE RUNS SCORED
Per Wicket 15-50

AVERAGE RUNS CONCEDED
Per Wicket 14.66

Total Number of Catches taken   63 -   B Cummings took 9
                                                 B Cummings stumped 10.

1958

Saturday 3rd May - Wagon Works v Hereford

Played at Hereford

Wagon Works 143 for 9
W Lodge (53), B Cummings (27), K Newman (33)
Hereford 92 for 3 - Rain stopped play
Bowling Yearsley (1 for 17), Morley (1 for 23), K Newman (1 for 18)

Saturday 10th May - Wagon Works v Tetbury

Played at Tetbury

Wagon Works 156 for 6 declared
W Lodge (31) N Barker (19), B Cummings (32), K Newman (21), H D Swift (0), C Newman (34), D Turner (8), L Swift (8)
Tetbury 99 for 7
Bowling J Corbett (2 for 25), D Yearsley (1 for 9), R Morley (3 for 41), K Newman (1 for 22)

Saturday 17th May - Old Elizabethans v Wagon Works

Played at Worcester

Wagon Works 40 all out   K Newman (12)
Old Elizabethans 41 for 2 K Newman (2 for 26)

Saturday 7thJune - Westinghouse Brake v Wagon Works

Played at Chippenham

Westinghouse 167 for 6
Wagon Works 107 for 7 K Newman (44), including a six and five fours.

Saturday 14th June - Tewkesbury v Wagon Works

Played at Tewkesbury
Tewkesbury 164 for 7 declared. D Yearsley (2 for 33)
K Newman (1 for 33), R Morley (3 for 41), W Lodge (1 for 3).
Wagon Works 81 all out.

Saturday 21st June - Wagon Works v Colwall

Played at the Sports Ground

Wagon Works 145 for 4 declared W Lodge (50), K Newman (7), D Swift (34), K Trevarthen (27), C Newman (12), D Yearsley (6)
Extras (7).

Colwall 91 for 8 Yearsley (5 for 22), Morley (2 for 24), K Newman (1 for 7), Salter (0 for 1), Corbett (0 for 19)

Wednesday 16th July

SURPRISE K.O. WIN BY FIELDINGS

Emerging from the early tactics of defiant defence, and accelerating suddenly to a high gear of almost arrogant aggression, Fieldings defeated the well-fancied Wagon Works by six wickets at the Spa last night in the semi-final round of the Gloucester Cricket knock-out cup competition.

WAGON WORKS

N Barker	b	Poole		0
W Lodge	lbw		b Williams	20
K Newman	c Williams	b Poole		8
C Newman	b Poole			0
B Cummings	c Woodward	b Poole		0
K Trevarthen	c&b Poole			2
HD Swift	c McCreesh	b Poole		13
GS Hale	not out			12
R Carr	b Williams			1
EXTRAS				8
TOTAL(for 8)				**64**

Bowling -Poole 6-24 Williams 2-32

FIELDINGS

V Butcher	b	Corbett		1
J Haines	c	Carr	b Yearsley	0
L Pilkington	not out			33
H Smith	lbw	Corbett		3
L McCreesh	lbw		b Yearsley	20
R Woodward	not out			1
EXTRAS				7
TOTAL(for 4)				**65**

Bowling - Corbett 2-15 Yearsley 2-43

Fieldings now meet Shire Hall in the final

Saturday 19thJuly Wagon Works openers put on 98

Some remarkable twists and turns of fortune featured in the match at the Sports Ground between the Wagon Works and Old Elizabethans (Worcester). The home side eventually ran out winners by seven wickets, thanks mainly to a splendid opening partnership by Wally Lodge and Nigel Barker.

OLD ELIZABETHANS

DG Payne	b	Yearsley		0
RK Lancy	b	Yearsley		0
TH Clarke	lbw		b B Corbett	0
C Shaw	b	Yearsley		3
S Robinson	c&b	Newman		35
A Hill	run out			6
G Taylor	b	Newman		59
R Homan	not out			18
L Elt	st	C Newman	b K Newman	5
W Smith	b	K Newman		3
J Bursten	b	Hale		0
EXTRAS				7
TOTAL				**136**

Bowling

Corbett	1-28
Yearsley	3-9
K Newman	4-18
G Hale	1-5

WAGON WORKS

N Barker	b	Shaw		54
W Lodge	not out			61
K Newman	c	Smith	b Bursten	10
K Trevarthen	c	Payne	b Bursten	4
C Newman	not out			4
EXTRAS				3
TOTAL(for 3)				**93**

GS Hale, F Stephens, R Carr, J Corbett, R Morley and D Yearsley did not bat.

Season Summary

With an increased number of playing members no difficulty was experienced in fielding three Saturday teams as well as a Sunday XI.

The first team played 20 matches sustaining only two defeats, although the 'A' team were not so successful, but the 'B' XI had a reasonably good season and won half the matches played. The Sunday XI had a creditable record considering the strength of the opposition met. A short Whitsun tour was arranged and despite bad weather which interfered with fixtures it was socially very enjoyable. Roy Morley had another good season, taking 53 wickets for an average of under 10 runs a wicket and he, along with Ken Newman, was honoured by being selected for the County Club and Ground Side. The interdepartmental league was won by William Gardner & Sons; the M.S.E team were runners up. The annual dinner and dance attracted 170 members and friends and was a big success.

Season 1958
Gloucester Wagon Works Cricket Club 1st X1
Order of Batting Averages
Qualification 10 Innings

NAMES	INNINGS	TIMES NOT OUT	RUNS	MOST IN INNINGS	AVERAGE
W Lodge	14	4	516	96 not out	51.60
K Newman	17	2	391	82 not out	26.06
N Baker	18	-	300	54	16.66
K Trevathen	10	1	113	29	14.77
C Newman	14	2	144	34 not out	12.00

Order of Bowling Averages
(Qualification 10 Wickets)

NAMES	OVERS	MAIDENS	RUNS	WICKETS	AVERAGE
K Newman	114.1	13	324	23	14.08
D Yearsley	133	36	257	18	14.27
J Corbett	122.3	28	301	20	15.05
R Morley	157.1	12	563	37	15.21

Matches Played	19	Score of own side	Score of Opponents
Matches Won	5	Total Runs - Wickets	Total Runs - Wickets
Matches Lost	7	2058 - 132	1989 - 121
Matches Drawn	6		
Matches Abandoned	1		

AVERAGE RUNS SCORED AVERAGE RUNS CONCEDED
Per Wicket 15.59 Per Wicket 16.43

Total Number of catches taken - 38
C Newman stumped 10

1959

Saturday 2nd May – Works Beaten by Hereford

Accurate spin bowling by Hereford's J Chadd and K Edward skittled out Gloucester Wagon Works for only 59 on Hereford racecourse. Despite good bowling by R Carr, who took 2 for 45, Hereford scored freely and the side was able to declare at tea with the score at 123 for 5.

HEREFORD				WAGON WORKS	
EL Jenkins	lbw	Carr	18	W Lodge	5
A Mitchell	b	Morley	37	G Woodridge	6
R Jones	b	Carr	11	D Swift	6
P Harrison	lbw	Corbett	27	A Webb	9
B Smith	b	Corbett	17	G Farmer	5
J Cadd	not out		5	A Salter	0
				H Taylor	5
				R Carr	3
				R Morley	9
				J Corbett	0
				D Mortimer	1
EXTRAS			8	EXTRAS	7
TOTAL			123	TOTAL (for 3)	56

Saturday 9th May

It was a batsman's day at Tuffley Avenue when the Wagon Works met Lydney. During the 4 hours 30 minutes of play, the teams amassed a total of 314 runs in a drawn game.

WAGON WORKS					LYDNEY				
W Lodge	Not out			62	D Thomas	c	Morley	b Yearsley	83
N Barker	b	L James		41	R Nicols	c	Webb	b	10
D Swift	c	Brown	b Smith	32	J Wiltshire	c	Morley	b Yearsley	30
K Newman	b	D Thomas		4	T Tomkins	b	Yearsley		13
A Webb	not out			3	W Whereat	c	Swfit	b Yearsley	2
					A Smith	not out			2
					P James	not out			1
	EXTRAS	24				EXTRAS	7		
	TOTAL	166				TOTAL	148		

D Thomas 1-11
A Smith 1-37
L James 1-19

D Yearsley 4-45
J Corbett 1-37

Saturday 23rd May - Tail Enders Rescue Wagon Works

Wagon Works were saved from a rout by their tail-end batsmen when they met Old Elizabethans at Worcester, where a keenly contested game ended in a draw.

Only Nigel Barker and Mike Gough showed any confidence earlier in the innings, and Works' position looked hopeless when their first six wickets had gone for a mere 46 runs.

Their last four batsmen - Reg Carr, Roy Morley, Jack Corbett and skipper Des Yearsley, all of whom are the recognised bowlers, came to the rescue and between them scored more than half the visitors' final total of 132.

Although left with plenty of time to get the runs, Old Elizabethans were soon in trouble against the hostile Works' attack, Corbett bowling particularly well.

But a splendid half century by Wheeler enabled the home side to recover, and when stumps were drawn they needed only four runs for victory with two wickets in hand.

Wagon Works 132 for 9 (N Barker 22; R Carr 13; R Morley 25; JJ Corbett 21 not out; D Yearsley 16)
Old Elizabethans 129 for 8 (Wheeler 50; Corbett 4-36; Yearsley 2-21; Morley 1-27; Carr 1-27)

Saturday 6th June - Works Draw

In an effort to beat both the weather and their visitors, Wagon Works skipper Des Yearsley made a sporting declaration when they met Westinghouse (Chippenham) on the Sports Ground.

The declaration was made after only 82 minutes batting and with the score at 125 for 3.
Although Westinghouse were given exactly the same time to get the runs they were soon struggling against the varied Works' attack, leg spinner Roy Morley proving particularly hostile, and at the close had only reached 63 with six wickets down.

WAGON WORKS					WESTINGHOUSE	
N Barker	not out			67	63 for 6	
H Taylor	run out			19	Morley	4-17
MG Gough	b		Day	15	Salter	1-10
K Newman	c	b	Vizor	22	Yearsley	1-17
G Hale	not out			1	Carr	0-16
					Newman	0-3
		Extras		1		
		Total		125		

Gloucestershire, led byTom Graveney take to the field at The County Festival August 1959

Gloucestershire v Surrey

Played at Gloucester on 26th, 27th August 1959   Surrey beat Gloucestershire by 89 runs

Surrey

Batsman	First innings				Second innings			
JH Edrich	b		Cook	45 (2)	c	Milton	b Allen	14
ABD Parsons	c Meyer	b Smith		7 (1)	c	Milton	b Cook	0
KF Barrington	c Milton	b Smith		12 (4)	c	Milton	b Cook	49
MJ Stewart	lbw	b Allen		7 (5)	c	Brown	b Mortimore	29
DGQ Fletcher	c Brown	b Allen		0 (6)			b Mortimore	0
R Swetman	c Smith	b Cook		13 (7)	c	Brown	b Mortimore	11
D Gibson	c Nicholls	b Allen		8 (3)			b Cook	0
EA Bedser	not out			23	c	Milton	b Cook	8
GAR Lock	lbw	b Cook		1	c	Young	b Cook	16
JC Laker	c Smith	b Allen		0	lbw		b Mortimore	3
AV Bedser *		b Allen		11	not out			0
EXTRAS	(1b 3)			3	(1b 1)			1
TOTAL				130	TOTAL			131

Gloucestershire

Batsman	First innings			Second innings		
DM Young	c Stewart	b Laker	8	b Laker		6
CA Milton	c Stewart	b Laker	12	b Lock		6
RB Nicholls	c A Bedser	b Lock	2	c Stewart	b Laker	1
TW Graveney	c Swetman	b Lock	31	b Lock		0
DG Hawkins	c Swetman	b Lock	0	st Swetman	b Laker	0
JB Mortimore	c Parsons	b Laker	13	c AV Bedser	b Lock	0
AS Brown		b Laker	0	c Lock	b Laker	5
DA Allen	c Lock	b Laker	16	not out		18
DR Smith	c Barrington	b Lock	2	lbw	b Laker	28
BJ Meyer	c Edrich	b Lock	17	run out		0
C Cook	not out		0		b Laker	0
EXTRAS						7
TOTAL			101	TOTAL		71

Gloucester	O	M	R	W	O	M	R	W
Smith	17	5	37	2				
Brown	3	1	5	0				
Mortimore	18	14	9	0	23	14	28	4
Allen	19.5	8	43	5	13	6	36	1
Cook	15	6	33	3	27.3	12	66	5

Surrey	O	M	R	W	O	M	R	W
AV Bedser	2	0	7	0				
Gibson	1	1	0	0				
Laker	21	7	53	5	15	6	27	6
Lock	23.2	13	32	5	15	6	37	3
EA Bedser	4	0	9	0				

Fall of Wickets

	S 1st	G 1st	S 2nd	G 2nd
1st	17	13	0	7
2nd	35	22	0	13
3rd	45	22	58	13
4th	45	32	77	13
5th	70	45	79	13
6th	93	45	102	22
7th	109	82	111	26
8th	110	82	111	66
9th	119	84	131	71
10th	130	101	131	71

Umpires: CS Elliott and Davies * The above match decided the County Championship, the game being well remembered by many as a classic.

1960-69

Perhaps the decade that was to see most overall change was the 1960s. The company and cricket club made two name changes in 1963 and 1967. The introduction of the Three Counties Cricket League came about in 1968 and a very sucessful six-a-side competion began in 1963.

Mike Gough took over the captaincy of the first eleven in 1960, a position which was only to last one season. He later joined the City Club for a number of seasons, but unfortunately died at a comparatively early age.

The club reached the final of the Gloucester 20 over knock-out competition in 1960, losing a low scoring but eventful final to Dowty-Rotol. 1960 was also the year that saw two club stalwarts hang up their boots after many seasons playing - Wally Lodge and club groundsman and coach Charlie Newman, who was still to score one more century, 107, against Westinghouse 'A' in May.

It is without doubt that if any cricketer was asked what he would like to achieve on the cricket field, it would be either to hit a century, six sixes in an over, or, for a bowler, certainly to take all ten wickets. This was achieved by J Clements playing for the Works 'A' team against Tewkesbury 'A' on the 29th July 1961, though ironically he was on the losing side by 6 runs. His final analysis was 10-45; fortunately a record of the match was kept by Tewkesbury as no scorecard remains in club records.

The first of the two name changes came about in 1963 when the Gloucester Railway Carriage and Wagon Co, so called for over 100 years, was bought by the Winget Group of Rochester. The company was to become known as Gloucester Engineering, a subsidary of the parent company. This title remained only until 1967 when the name Gloucester Engineering was dropped in favour of the parent group, to become Winget Gloucester.

The club's six –a-side tourament began in 1963. This competition became very sucessful for over 13 years, bringing together many local sides in addition to some from further afield. As many as 200 cricketers representing over 30 sides and playing on the club's three pitches, the first and second XI pitches while the third ground was the one sometimes used by the Robinswood Hill club at weekends. Apart from the winners' and runners' up trophies there were over 30 other presentations, ranging from highest batting aggregate to most wickets taken, and from most sixes hit to most catches held etc, etc. All the presentations were donated by the club's sports and social section and their sponsors.

These competions were very successful, starting at 10.00am and not finishing until sometimes past 6.00 in the evening, the final always attracting a large crowd. The Works team often had a strong side and won the competition in 1968 and 1969, beating some highly fancied opposition.

The 1966 season was a very sad time for the cricket fraternity in general. On the 22nd May the legendary TWJ (Tom) Goddard died at the age of 66. He was undoubtedly the finest player to come from the Works team and his first class record speaks for itself.
He started out on his county career in 1922 as a fast bowler, but was not very successful until BH Lyon persuaded him to become an off spinner. His height, large hands and long fingers suited this type of bowling and between 1922 and 1952 he claimed no fewer than 2862 first class wickets. Goddard played 558 county matches for Gloucestershire in addition to representing his country on eight occasions. Only one Gloucestershire player has ever taken more wickets than Goddard - C.W.L Parker, who claimed 3170 wickets having played in 602 matches. Other records Goddard achieved were 5 wickets in an innings no fewer than 246 times, and he took the hat-trick on six occasions.

Not a product of the Wagon Works club but a name that is synonymous with the Works Ground, is that of WR Hammond who passed away in 1965. His score of 317 in 1936 was the highest first class score on the ground and Hammond's highest score for Gloucestershire.

The backbone of the Works side, whether it was Wagon Works, Gloucester Engineering or Winget during the early 60s, were the likes of Farmer, Stephens, Phelps, Newman, Morley, Hale, Salter and Corbett and later in the decade, the names of Jones, Smart and Worrall would be added, bringing together a rather formidable team.

The 1965 season will be well remembered in that two young South Africans appeared for the county club and ground side on the Works Ground when playing against the Works team. These two were none other than Barry Richards and Mike Procter who, over the coming years, were to become arguably the finest cricketers of the time. The county club and ground had the better of a drawn game, the highlight of which was Procter's 119 scored in 69 minutes. Tony Salter had the honour of bowling Procter with Tony Smith taking Barry Richards' wicket. Also representing the club and ground side was David Shepherd, who was to go on and play 282 matches for Gloucestershire, scoring over 10,000 runs and reaching a highest score of 153. After retiring from county cricket in 1979, Shepherd became a well-respected county and test umpire.

The Winget Club joined the Three Counties League in its inaugural season in 1968 along with the other founder members, Worcester City, Hereford, Tewkesbury, Cirencester, Ross and Abergavenny. The league allowed the club to play further afield than in the past and was believed to be instrumental in bringing new players to the club, notably in later years.

1968 was also the year that I joined the club, a year I remember well, playing on the ground that had graced so many truly great players.

I joined the company in May as an apprentice, and it was my good friend Cliff Thomas's father Ron, who appeared one day at the apprentice school's large sliding door. Ron, knowing I enjoyed cricket, offered to pick me up that evening and take me to the ground for net practice, an offer I eagerly accepted.

On arrival at the ground Ron introduced me to the players that were to become very good friends and colleagues over the years - Ken Newman, Roy Morley, Tony Salter, Stan Phelps, Graham Hale, Tony Webb, Jack Corbett and many others. I changed into my cricket kit and walked to the nets that were adjacent to the wall in Tuffley Avenue. After bowling a few overs I was asked to put the batting pads on and select a bat: kit was supplied in those days, not like now when everyone has their own. I took guard and played a few shots and it was then that I became aquainted with the club groundsman and coach, Charlie Newman, who said to me, 'Play each ball on its merit', words I have always remembered. Charlie became a very good friend to all the players, as did his assistant, Frank Stephens, both of whom had played and been associated with the club for many seasons. My first game on the first XI square was a Sunday match, I am not sure of the opposition, but it was a lovely sunny day and I will always remember walking out and thinking how lucky I was to play where all those great players had played before me.

Over the coming seasons I got to know many fine cricketers from our club and other sides, playing with or against them and enjoying every moment.

Ken Newman topped the 1968 batting averages with 30 plus after scoring 698 runs, and Brian Worrall claimed 40 wickets with a bowling average of 14.1. In all, Newman scored over 1500 runs during the 1968 season, including 1428 runs in Saturday and Sunday matches alone.

1969 saw a turn around in the first eleven batting averages with Roy Morley topping the table after scoring 526 runs at an average of 32.8. Ken Newman came a close second with 479 runs, averaging 25.2. Morley also topped the bowling averages with 15.1, taking 31 wickets, although Newman took most wickets with 34.

1960

Saturday 14th May – Westinghouse v. Wagon Works

A splendid stand for the eighth wicket between Graham Hale and Roy Morley averted a Wagon Works' collapse in their game against Westinghouse at Chippenham, and enabled the visitors to build up the respectable total of 156.

Westinghouse were quickly in trouble against the accurate Works attack, Tony Salter, in particular, posing them numerous problems, and when stumps were drawn their last wicket pair were in possession.

WAGON WORKS					WESTINGHOUSE	
N Barker	b	Miles		1		
W Lodge	c	Newman	b	Vizer	26	83 for 9	
B Cummings	st	Isaacs	b	Newman	9	A Salter	5 for 18
G Farmer	c	Pearce	b	Vizer	10	J Corbett	2 for 10
S Phelps	lbw		b	Vizer	5	R Morey	1 for 22
G Hale	not out				48	D Yearsley	1 for 22
E Stephens	c	Newman	b	Day	3	**MATCH DRAWN**	
R Morley	c	Isaacs	b	Vizer	24		
A Salter	run out				8		
J Corbett	c	Day	b	Newman	0		
D Yearsley	c	Day	b	Newman	13		
EXTRAS					9		
TOTAL					156		

Wagon Works 'A' v. Westinghouse

Veteran Charlie Newman, head groundsman at the Wagon Works Sports Ground, hit an undefeated century for the Works 'A' side against Westinghouse 'A', sharing in a third wicket stand with Tony Webb of 172.

At the tea interval Wagon Works 'A' declared at 197 for 2, Newman hitting 107 not out which included a 6 and 13 boundaries, and Webb 61 not out.

Westinghouse 'A' compiled 125 for 5 at close of play with George Woodridge (3-38) being the best of the Works' bowlers.

Powell Lane v. Wagon Works 'B'

Powell Lane defeated Wagon Works 'B' by 39 runs after being dismissed for 105, of which Doug Edgeworth hit 28 and Arthur Bray 24. Another veteran, Bill Tandy, was the only home batsman to offer any real resistance as Wagon Works 'B' were shot out for 66, Tandy contributing a fighting 17.

Saturday 2nd July – Wagon Works v. Hoffmans

Given an excellent start by their captain Mike Gough who hit a stylish 60, Wagon Works' batting showed a marked improvement in the game at the Sports Ground against Hoffmans, who made a disappointing reply and were decisively beaten by 84 runs.

Giving their skipper excellent support were Nigel Barker (20), Brian Cummings (21) and Graham Hale (20). Wagon Works were able to declare at 165 for 9. Ray Brown, Rodney Cale and Reg Stephens shared the wickets equally for the visitors.

Hoffmans began disastrously, losing two wickets without a run on the board, and although skipper Rodney Cale played an invaluable innings of 28, none of the other batsmen stayed long against the bowling of Roy Morley (4-34), Mike Gough (2-7) and Tony Salter (2 for 14), and the team were all out for 81.

Tuesday 12th July – Gloucester K.O. Final Rotol v. Wagon Works

The eventual result will be forgotten long before the vicissitudes of the game and a controversial run-out decision.

For the record, Rotol batted first and compiled 72, thanks mainly to a belligerent contribution from Fred Merrett who thumped 19 off one over from Jackie Corbett. With Dennis Jones adding a useful 14, Rotol reached their total after being 48 for 9.

Yet the uncertainties that attend cricket by no means ended there! Wagon Works started, no doubt full of confidence, and lost two wickets in their first over. One, that of big hitter Eric Stephens from a run out as the result of a remarkable direct throw in, the other from a peach of a ball that swung in from the off and hit the leg stump.

From there Doug Nourse took over, completed a brilliant 'Hat Trick', and Wagon Works were staggered at 14 for 7. Veteran Graham Terrett and young Tony Salter rescued their side from the depths of despair and added 34 runs before the controversial run out decision ended the stand. Terrett was given out, but eventually recalled after both batsmen had been anchored at the same end. But it made comparatively little difference; Wagon Works were all out for 58, Nourse finishing with an analysis of 7 – 24.

Saturday 23rd July - Lydney Have Little Trouble In Beating Off-Form Works Side

Ineffective batting by Gloucester Wagon Works, combined with some finely taken catches by the Lydney slip fielders, led to their defeat by six wickets on the Lydney ground.

Wagon Works   C. Newman 1, W. Lodge 4, N. Barker 6, G. Farmer 0, R. Morley 28, G. Hale 15,
                       N. Tyson 8, E. Stephens 3, A. Salter 16, J. Corbett 4, D. Yearsley 10, Extras 2.
                       Total 97

Lydney   D.Brown 6, R. Nicholas 14, J. Morgans 40, D. Thomas 10, J. Wiltshire not out 8,
                       G. Taylor not out 17, Extras 3. Total for 4 wickets 98

                       Bowling: Salter 1-22, Morley 2-49, Corbett 1-12.

Saturday 20th August - Works Win Last Minute Thriller

In an exciting finish, Wagon Works beat Swindon B.R.W.R. at Swindon by the hair's breadth margin of two runs.

Wagon Works   S. Phelps 7, E. Stephens 23, R. Morley 4, G. Hale 21, A. Webb 12, G. Woodridge not out 17, N. Tyson
                       3, R. Carr 5, A. Salter 9, D. Yearsley 10, J. Corbett 0, Extras 6, Total 117.

Swindon B.R.W.R. 115 all out Bowling: - Yearsley 6-45, Corbett 0-11, Salter 4-27, Morley 0-28.

A section of the crowd, waiting with anticipation at the County Cricket Festival in the early 1960s.

1961

Saturday 20th May - Wagon Works Beat Thornbury

A steady, but invaluable innings by opening batsman Stan Phelps, given excellent support by Eric Stephens and Graham Hale, helped Wagon Works to gain a splendid and exciting win, their first of the season over the strong Thornbury side at the Sports Ground by three wickets.

Thornbury: 146. Corbett 2-30, Yearsley 5-37, Morley 0-23, Salter 3-27, Pugh 0-19.

Wagon Works: 147 for 7. S Phelps 69, E Stephens 17, G Hale 34, R Morley 4, A Webb 1, R Carr 3, A Salter 1, D Yearsley Not Out 13, M Dickerson Not Out 1, Extras 4. J Corbett and A Pugh did not bat.

Saturday 24th June - Hale Hits 100 in Works Win

After their narrow defeat of the previous week, Wagon Works returned to form with a splendid win over Tewkesbury at the Sports Ground by 92 runs, but they owed their success mainly to a brilliant maiden century by Graham Hale, the former Gloucester and County rugby full back.

WAGON WORKS						TEWKESBURY	
S Phelps	c	Burd	b	Atwell	0	85 All Out D Bowles 28	
G Hale	c	Coutts	b	Sollis	100	Bowling: Corbett 4-19	
R Morley	c	Coutts	b	Atwell	8	Yearsley 2-19	
A Webb	c	Atwell	b	Boyce	23	Salter 2-16	
R Carr			b	Sollis	5	Morley 2-30	
N Tyson			b	Sollis	21		
F Stephens			b	Sollis	0		
A Salter	lbw		b	Burd	4		
D Yearsley	c&b		b	Burd	7		
J Corbett	not out				2		

Saturday 1st July - Lydney v. Wagon Works

Lydney opened their season with a seven wicket victory over the Wagon Works at Gloucester and cherished the hope that they would be able to repeat the dose at Lydney, but it was not to be. The game ended in a draw with the Wagon Works knocking up 192-9 and Lydney getting 153-5 in reply.

WAGON WORKS						LYDNEY					
S Phelps	c	Wintle	b	Morgans	1	D Thomas	c	Young	b	Corbett	0
E Stephens	run out				37	T Wintle	c	Carr	b	Pugh	49
G Hale			b	P James	16	M James			b	Salter	14
R Morley			b	P James	35	J Morgans	not out				56
A Webb	c	Thomas	b	Tomkins	9	J Hampton			b	Phelps	32
R Carr			b	Whereat	6	J Wiltshire			b	Phelps	0
N Tyson			b	Whereat	2	M Jarrett	not out				0
D Young	c	Morgans	b	Jarrett	15						
A Salter	not out				26						
J Corbett	c	Wiltshire	b	Jones	35						
A Pugh	not out				0						
			EXTRAS		10				EXTRAS		2
			TOTAL (for 9)		192				TOTAL (for 5)		153

Bowling: A Jones 1-29, J Morgan 1-14, M Jarrett 1-21, T Tompkins 1-43, P James 2-47, W Whereat 2-18   Bowling: J Corbett 1-23, A Salter 1-35; A Pugh 1-28, S Phelps 2-3-

Saturday 29th July J Clements Takes 10 Wickets for Wagon Works II

John Clements was in fine form for the Works second eleven at Tewkesbury, claiming all ten wickets, but even this brilliant performance was not enough to win the match, the Works losing by just six runs.

TEWKESBURY II						WAGON WORKS II						
M Hurley	b	Clements			7	R Lander	lbw		b	Gittings	3
V Caudle	c	Tandy	b	Clements	0	W Tandy	b	Gittings			0
E Martin	lbw		b	Clements	4	D Turner	b	Goodwin			20
F Courts			b	Clements	15	R Morley	b	Goodwin			15
I Winter	lbw		b	Clements	9	D Taylor	c	Caudle	b	Martin	21
M Boyle	not out				47	H James	c	Winter	b	Boyle	0
W Devereux			b	Clements	13	J Clements	c	Goodwin	b	Boyle	0
G Goodwin			b	Clements	4	J Brickell	c	Coutts	b	Martin	19
C Attwell			b	Clements	0	D Mortimore	c	Devereux	b	Martin	7
N Gittings	c&b			Clements	0	R Holl	not out				3
						R Vallender	b	Martin			0
				EXTRAS	1					EXTRAS	6
				TOTAL	100					TOTAL	94

Bowling: R Morley 0-25, J Clements 10 for 45, Mortimore 0-29

Bowling: Martin 4-15, Gittings 2-31, Boyle 2-18, Goodwin 2-15

Saturday 19th August - Wagon Works Thwarted

A brief hold up through rain and a dogged eighth wicket stand by the home side thwarted Wagon Works in their bid for victory over Swindon British Rail at Shrivenham Road.

The visitors, declaring at 180 for 7, scored their runs at a brisk rate. They owed much to a splendid half century by Tony Webb, who hit seven fours, good supporting contributions from Stan Phelps and Norman Tyson and an exhilarating unbroken partnership of 45 for the eighth wicket between Tony Salter and skipper Jack Corbett.

Wagon Works: 180 for 7 dec (S Phelps 22, R Morley 12, A Webb 52, N Tyson 22, A Salter n.o. 33, J Corbett n.o. 19)
British Rail Swindon 132 for 7 (Morley 3-37, Pugh 2-15, Corbett 1-29, Salter 1-21, Stepehns 0-14)

Saturday 2nd September - Wagon Works' Easy Win Over Hereford

Although meeting spirited resistance from the visitors' seventh and eight wicket pairs, Wagon Works gained a comfortable victory over Hereford at the Sports Ground by six wickets.

After a promising start, Hereford wickets tumbled in remarkable fashion against the hostile attack of skipper Jack Corbett and Tony Salter, until six men were out for only 33 runs. Then determined batting by Smith, Allesbrook and Lewis added substance to the innings, which eventually closed at 106.

Works lost an early wicket but Stan Phelps and Graham Hale put them in a sound position. Roy Morley also batted steadily, though there was a danger of the home side falling behind the clock until an exhilarating knock by Ken Newman, whose undefeated 21 contained four boundaries, put the issue beyond doubt.

Hereford: 106 All Out. (B Smith 32, Allesbrook 20, Lewis 15) Bowling: Corbett 3-30, Salter 6-34, Morley 0-33, K Newman 0-2, F Stephens 1-0.

Wagon Works: 109 for 4. (S Phelps 21, G Hale 31, Morley 21, K Newman 21 not out) Bowling: Chadd 3-29, Standford 1-33

Saturday 16th September - Wagon Works v. Gloucester Nondescripts

On the Works Sports Ground
Nondescripts 202 for 6 Dec (T W Halls 100, J Moore 51, G Farmer 15, J Mansell 11) Bowling: Stephens 4-52, Yearsley 1-40. Wagon Works: 166 for 2 (Stephens 62, G Hale 17, R Morley not out 39, K Newman not out 35) Bowling: Dwyer 1-58, Gough 1-42

1962

Saturday 2nd June - Late Stand Thwarts Wagon Works

An unbeaten seventh wicket partnership robbed Wagon Works of victory against Westinghouse (Chippenham) at the Sports Ground after their pace bowlers had broken the back of the visitors' batting.

The Works' innings was dominated by the stylish batting of opener Stan Phelps who shared in a productive partnership with Eric Stephens. But, with the latter's dismissal, three further wickets fell cheaply and it was left to the tail-end batsmen to give Phelps the necessary support.

Phelps was eventually caught for a polished 78, but Tony Smith, Tony Webb, Tony Salter and skipper Jack Corbett batted to such purpose that Works reached 184 in 134 minutes.

Corbett was quickly on the mark when Westinghouse replied, clean bowling three batsmen while conceding but three runs, and the visitors were 10-3. Six wickets had gone for only 53, but Day and Newman defied the Works' attack and held out to the close.

Wagon Works:	S. Phelps 78, Stephens 19, G. S. Hale 0, K. C. Newman 3, R. G. Morley 0, A. Smith 12, A. Webb 23, A. B. Salter 17, J. J. Corbett 17, G. Phelps not out 5, A. Pugh 0; extras 10, Total 184.
Westinghouse	118-6 (E. Day not out 41, J. Newman not out 27; Corbett 4-16, G. Phelps 1-21, Morley 1-49, Salter 0-4, A. Pugh 0-3, Stephens 0-11).

Wagon Works 'A' Collapse

Wagon Works "A" collapsed badly against Westinghouse "A" at Chippenham and were beaten by 99 runs, despite a fighting innings from Dave Taylor.

Graham Terrett and Dennis Mortimer bowled accurately for Works, but the home side were able to reach 149.

The Works lost their first two wickets without a run scored and it was only the steadying influence of Dave Taylor that saved the innings from becoming a rout. Seventh out at 44, he had scored half the runs.

Westinghouse:	"A" 149: (R. Puntis 48; G. Terrett 5-34, D. Mortimer 4-30, M. Roberts 1-67).
Wagon Works:	"A" 50: (D. Taylor 22).

Sunday 3rd June - W. Works 'A' Beaten Again

Wagon Works "A" lost their second successive match when Colwall "A" beat them by 51 runs at Colwall.

Thanks to a fine innings by Thurtle and a last wicket stand of 35, the home side were able to total 156 despite a steady bowling spell by John Clements and Dennis Mortimer.

Another sound innings from Dave Taylor with good support from Graham Terrett gave Works an encouraging start in their reply, but then wickets fell quickly, and though skipper Dick Hamblett, making his first appearance of the season, offered stubborn resistance in a brave effort to stave off defeat, the visitors were all out for 105.

Colwall:	"A" 156 (R. Thirtle 46, C. Gibbons 25 not out; J. Clements 4-52, D. Mortimer 2-22).
Wagon Works:	"A" 105 (D. Taylor 25, G. Terrett 20, R. Hamblett 15, D. James 12).

Saturday 9th June - Last Six Clean Bowled as Works Race to Victory

In the most entertaining match at the Sports Ground this season, Wagon Works accounted for visiting Colwall by 27 runs, the losers' last five wickets falling for only five runs.

The Works were given a good start by Stan Phelps and Eric Stephens, the latter hitting a six and four fours before being first out with the score at 53.

Graham Hale was soon out, but with the dismissal of Phelps, a fourth-wicket stand between Ken Newman, who hit eight fours, and Roy Morley put the home side in a commanding position and they were able to declare at 173-5, compiled in little more than two hours.

Opening batsman Pedlingham completely dominated Colwall's reply. Batting with supreme confidence he was eventually caught at the wicket for 90 – the first of skipper Jack Corbett's victims in a devastating second spell which brought about a remarkable collapse. With 140 on the board, only four wickets down and more than half-an-hour left for play, Colwall looked within sight of a comfortable victory. But Corbett and Tony Salter, who had maintained an accurate length throughout, fired out the tail with little trouble, the last six batsmen all being clean bowled.

Wagon Works:	S. Phelps lbw, b Green 27, E. J. Stephens b Clark 38; G. S. Hale lbw b Clark 1; K. C. Newman lbw b Pedlingham 48; R. G. Morley not out 43; D. Wilson b Lawrence 7; A. Webb not out 1; extras 8, total (for 5 dec) 173.
Colwall:	146 (P. Pedlingham 90; Corbett 4-36, G. Phelps 0-16, Salter 4-28, Morley 0-32, Pugh 2-27).

Sunday 10TH June - Phelps' Century in Record Second Wicket Works' Stand

In an exciting ending, Dowlais' last wicket managed to hold out and the Wagon Works Sunday XI could only draw.

The Works team did not get off to a good start and were 38-2, but then Roy Morley joined Stan Phelps and they were still together when they declared at 188-2, Phelps having batted for a very attractive 103 not out and R. Morley 59 not out.

This was a record second wicket partnership for the Sunday team.

R. William was the highest scorer for Dowlais with 57. A. Salter, 4-47, and A. Pugh, 2-5, bowled best for Wagon Works.

Wagon Works Sunday XI 188-2; *Dowlais* 153-9.

Saturday 23rd June - Morley's Match

A magnificent all-round performance by table tennis international Roy Morley, together with another splendid innings by Stan Phelps, gave the home side a resounding victory by 34 runs when Wagon Works and Nondescripts, the two strongest clubs in Gloucester, met in the long-awaited clash at the Sports Ground.

Phelps' innings, of course, laid the foundation of Works' success, yet it will long be known as "Morley's match." For after sharing in a rescue act with Phelps, after a Nondescript break-through seemed imminent, Morley took a hand in the dismissal of every one of the visiting batsmen except Dickie Etheridge.

Eric Stephens and Phelps gave Works, as is their want, another useful start but then two more important wickets fell before Morley joined Phelps. From 48-3 the pair took the score to 143-4 when Phelps had the wretched luck to be run out within sight of his second century of the season.

John Moore and Mike Sparey gave Nondescripts an encouraging start, hitting 58 in half an hour before being separated. Then Morley struck, claiming both openers in successive overs.

Bowling unchanged throughout the Nondescripts' innings, he claimed six wickets for 86 runs. In addition, he ran out two other batsmen and caught the ninth off Graham Terrett.

Nondescripts, it is true, were without their two opening batsmen, skipper Trevor Halls and David Bevan; but to offset this Wagon Works were without three of their frontline bowlers – including their two opening pace men – in skipper Jack Corbett, Gilbert Phelps and Alan Pugh. Hence the necessity of opening the bowling with leg-spinner Morley!

Wagon Works:	S. Phelps run out 84, E. J. Stephens lbw b Etheridge 27, G. S. Hale c Yardley b Etheridge 1, K. C. Newman b Lanham 3, R. G. Morley not out 54, A. Webb not out 30. Extras3. Total (for 4 wickets declared) 202. A. B. Salter, G. Terrett, D. Turner, A. Smith, and N. Tyson did not bat.
Bowling:	Etheridge 2-58. Lapham 1-54, Dwyer 0-45, Gough 0-25, Godding 0-17.
Nondescripts:	J. Moore b Morley 33, M. Sparey lbw b Morley 26, G. G. Farmer run out 37, M. Godding c Smith b Morley 6, M. G. Gough lbw b Morley 17, P. Hobbs not out 32, R. F. Etheridge b Terrett 1, E. H. Dwyer c Webb b Morley 1, R Yardley c Morley b Terrett 5, N. Lapham run out 7, T. Moore b Morley 1, extras 2. Total: 168.
Bowling:	Salter 0-36, Morley 6-86, Terrett 2-44.

Saturday 4th August - Works' Victory Bid just Fails

Left to score 163 at the rate of nearly 100 runs an hour, Wagon Works took up the challenge to such an excellent effect that they were within three runs of victory at the close of their match against Old Vigornians at the Sports Ground.

Their Worcester visitors, newcomers to their fixture list, took an unduly long time over their ponderous innings of 163-3 declared and even continued batting after the tea interval.

The Works, scorning to put up the shutters with a colourless draw in view, attacked the bowling from the start. Even the early departure of veteran Charlie Newman – returning to the game following his knee injury – and his son Ken, failed to disturb Graham Hale and Roy Morley.

Hale, who included a six and a four among his initial shots, was the senior partner in this earlier stand and had scored the bulk of the runs when he was third out at 57.

The arrival of Tony Salter to join Morley brought the highlight of the match. Hitting almost everything within reach, he raced to his fifty in 24 minutes with the help of three sixes and five fours. Morley meanwhile had also accelerated, and at the close the Works were within three of victory!

Old Vigornians: 163-3 dec. (T. Senter 94 not out; G. Terrett 1-14, R. G. Morley 1-73, J. Corbett 0-30, A. B. Salter 0-30, A. Pugh 0-21).

Wagon Works: G. S. Hale c. Cook b Wadley 38; C. Newman b Brain 1; K. C. Newman b Brain 9, R. G. Morley not out 45, R. Carr b O'Neill 9; A. B. Salter not out 57, Extras 2. Total 161 for 4 wkts.

Gloucester 20 over Knockout X1 1962
O.Hepburn G.Phelps A.Smith A.Salter K.Newman R.Morley
G.Hale E.Stephens J.Corbett S.Phelps H.Webb

1963

Saturday 25th May - Hopson's 50 for Engineers in Draw

Terry Hopson, the Gloucester and County rugby outside half, was in brilliant form with the bat for Gloucester Engineers who had much the better of a drawn game with Old Elizabethans at Worcester.

Engineers had lost the three valuable wickets of Stan Phelps, Eric Stephens and Graham Hale for only 37 runs when Hopson joined Morley, the newcomer striking an immediate offensive. Hopson dominated the partnership which added 69 runs before he was out for a stylish, aggressive half century, his powerful driving bringing him two sixes and five fours compiled in only 34 minutes.

Morley went steadily on and was unlucky to miss his fifty by seven runs.

The home side began their reply confidently and passed the half-century mark without loss, but then Roy Morley's leg spinners caused a minor collapse, and at the close, Old Elizabethans were struggling to avoid defeat.

Engineers: R. G. Morley 43, T. Hopson 50, K. C. Newman 27, A. Webb not out 20, total for 6 dec 173.
Old Elizabethans: D. Hodges 43, R. G. Payne 30, total for 7, 141.
Bowling: Morley 5-58, Terrett 2-17, Pugh 0-15, Salter 0-15, Corbett 0-24.

Saturday 8th June - Ken Newman's Brilliant 100

A brilliant unbeaten century by Ken Newman was the highlight of Gloucester Engineers' away match with Monmouth, where the dogged batting of the home side saved them from a heavy defeat.

Both Graham Hale and Terry Hopson had gone for 56 runs when Newman joined Stan Phelps and immediately dominated the batting with a splendid array of shots all round the wicket.

Phelps was unluckily run out when going well, but Roy Morley joined Newman and the pair added 120 for the fourth wicket without being separated. With eleven fours and two sixes as his chief hits, Newman raced to his century in only 83 minutes.

Gloucester Engineers: S. Phelps 32, G. Hale 13, T. Hopson 11, K. Newman not out 103, R. Morley not out 37, extras 7, total for 3 dec' 203.
Monmouth: B. Harris 56, K. Barnikel 27, total for 7, 116.
Bowling: A. Salter 5 –16, J. Corbett 2-20, G. Phelps 0-13, A. Smith 0-23, R. Morley 0-31.

Saturday 10th August - Newman's Second Century of the Season against Monmouth

A magnificent century by Ken Newman who shared in a huge unbroken partnership for the third wicket with Roy Morley was the highlight of Gloucester Engineers' drawn match against Monmouth on the Sports Ground.

Both opening batsman had gone with only nine runs on the board when Newman joined Morley. Slightly less than two hours later the pair were still together when a declaration was made with Newman, always the dominant partner, having completed a brilliant 108 which included 2 sixes and 14 fours.

Morley, if overshadowed by his enterprising partner, played an invaluable innings of 60 not out.

Though never able to match the home side's scoring rate, Monmouth found the pitch still easy paced and had little difficulty in forcing a draw, though Graham Terrett returned the creditable figures of 2-28.

Engineers: 184 for 2
Monmouth: 147 for 4
Bowling: G. Terrett 2-28, A. Smith 1-15

1963 AVERAGES

FIRST XI

	In	N.O.	BATTING Runs	Aver'		Overs	BOWLING Runs	Wkt	Aver'
Morley	15	6	476	52.89	Terrett	44	137	11	12.45
Phelps	16	4	444	37.00	Morley	150	525	37	14.19
Newman	15	3	423	35.25	Phelps	48.3	137	9	15.22
Hopson	7	0	158	21.67	Smith	65	184	11	16.73
Terrett	3	1	40	20.00	Salter	143.4	355	21	16.91

SUNDAY

	In	N.O.	BATTING Runs	Aver'		Overs	BOWLING Runs	Wkt	Aver'
Morley	14	6	492	61.50	Morley	105.3	369	44	8.39
Newman	16	6	425	42.50	Pugh	70.2	208	23	9.04
Phelps	16	2	524	37.43	Terrett	109.2	288	25	11.52
Hale	15	2	455	35.00	Smith	95.3	239	18	13.27
Terrett	3	2	24	24.00	Salter	177.5	464	21	17.19

"A" XI

George Woodridge topped both the batting averages (25.50) and the bowling (11.25) for the "A" XI.

1964

Saturday May 23rd

Old Elizabethans of Worcester played Gloucester Engineers on the Sports Ground. Batting first, the visitors made 155 for 8 declared, Engineers replying with 144 for 6 with Phelps making 76 not out.

Terry Hopson, the Gloucester and County rugby outside-half who was injured near the close of the last rugby season, makes his first appearance on the cricket field this weekend when he plays for Gloucester Engineers II against Old Elizabethans II at Worcester. He is also included in the side to meet Old Richians at the Sports Ground on Sunday.

Saturday June 13th - Exciting Draw for Engineers

The Gloucester Engineers team shared a draw with Old Elizabethians at Worcester, but it was by no means a tame affair for the visitors' last pair was at the wicket when stumps were drawn with only four runs separating the teams!

The highlight of the match was a magnificent innings by the Engineers' skipper Graham Hale who rescued his side from a threatened collapse.

Opening the innings, he alone of the recognised batsmen faced the home attack with confidence as Engineers chased a total of 136. Half the side were out for a mere 35 runs but first Tony Salter, then Jack Corbett, stayed with Hale who was last out with only 9 runs needed for victory.

Earlier, Salter and Graham Terrett had proved the most effective of the Engineers' bowlers and the home side were only saved from a rout by their middle order batting.

Old Elizabethians 136 (Hawkins 31, Brant 24) Corbett 2 - 21, Salter 4 - 25, Terrett 3 - 30.
Enginners 132 for 9 (Hale 71, Corbett 27, Salter 13)

Sunday June 14th - Gloucester Engineers' Six-a-Side Tournament

The scene: three deserted wickets at the Gloucester Wagon Works Ground, Tuffley. The time: yesterday. Suddenly, the quiet is broken. Onto the ground pours an army of cricketers and cricket followers, ready to joust in the annual six-a-side knockout tournament organised by the Gloucester Engineers Sports and Social Club.

Over 194 cricketers and a large crowd gathered to see some rare sport, despite the threatening clouds and the odd drop of rain. There were 32 teams in a conflict that was ultimately won by Carsons of Bristol, who narrowly beat Gloucester Co-Op in the final.

Early in the day the three pitches were alive with the clicking of bat on ball and ball on stumps, with each team member hoping that the ball just bowled didn't - to use an old army proverb - have their number on it.

In the 31 matches played, a total of 4,017 runs were scored and 255 wickets taken at an average of nearly 16 runs a wicket. This was cricket with a difference and the attitude of most of the players was, "if you can't get any runs yourself, get out and let someone else have a bash".

The above report was written by the late Arthur Russell who was the sports correspondent for the Gloucester Citizen newspaper. He was well known in local cricket and rugby circles having played both sports himself - a great character and sadly missed.

The six-a-side tournament ran for over 10 years and was well known and supported by cricket clubs throughout the county and a good number from further afield. There were over 30 presentations given in 1964, from overall winners to best batting and bowling figures to highest individual scores, wickets etc and also the following:

Best stand, bowler taking a hat trick, best all rounder, best bowling analysis, highest score by a left hander, highest by a right hander and numerous others - a great tournament.

Saturday June 27th - Engineers let Lydney off the hook

At one time it looked for all the world as though Lydney would come to grief against Gloucester Engineers, for they were stuggling at 30-4 against their visitors' total of 202-8 declared.

Witney had been dismissed without scoring. John Morris had been clean bowled for 1, and when opener D.A.L.Thomas was beaten by a good ball from Corbett for 16, Lydney were on the rack.

They were rescued however by M.J. James and David Imm who defied the Engineers' attack to take Lydney out of the toils and make a draw an almost certain conclusion.

When the pair were separated at 119 there were only 15 minutes left for play, James having hit 46 and Imm 44.

Earlier in the afternoon there had been some attractive batting from the Gloucester team, openers S. Phelps (36) and G. Hale (28) featuring in an opening stand of 70.

Gilbert Phelps hit a fast 43, but top scorer for the Engineers was anchor man G. Woodridge who carried his bat for 48 and was rather unlucky in not getting his half century.

On a wicket that gave very little assistance, no bowler had good figures.

Engineers 202 for 8 declared (S. Phelps 36, G. Hale 28, G. Woodridge 48 N.O., G. Phelps 43) Bowling: P. James 5-72, J. Morris 2-60.

Lydney 131 for 6 (M. James 46, D. Imm 44) Bowling: J. Corbett 2-24, Salter 2-23, Pugh 1-17, Newman 1-18)

Saturday August 15th - Engineers beat rain to win

Gloucester Engineers had a comfortable win over British Railways (Swindon) at the Sports Ground, but they met stern resistance from their visitors' tail-end batsmen and when the last wicket fell, the drizzle had turned to heavy rain.

Despite the early loss of skipper Graham Hale, the home side scored at a cracking pace and their total of 191-6 declared came in 143 minutes.

Stan Phelps, who played another invaluable innings, figured in productive partnerships with Roy Morley and the Gloucester R F C winger, Bob Smith.

Apart from opener Don Howie, the visitors' recognised batsmen failed against the varied Engineers' attack and six wickets were down for only 67. The last four batsmen, however, more than doubled the score.

Engineers 191 for 6 declared (S. Phelps 63, R. Morley 26, R. Smith 46, A. Salter 26 N.O.)

British Railways 148 (D. Howie 40) Bowling Salter 2-27, G. Phelps 3-33, Morley 3-48, Holl 0-13, Newman 2-21.

Saturday August 29th - Engineers have to declare with Phelps on 99

Even more frustrating than being dismissed for 99 is to be within one of the century when a declaration is made - that was the lot of opening batsman Stan Phelps at the Sports Ground, where Gloucester Engineers had the better of a drawn game with their old rivals, Gloucester Nondescripts.

Phelps, though partly responsible for three of his colleagues being run out, was the backbone of the Engineers' innings. He figured in a valuable second wicket stand with Bob Smith, the Gloucester rugby winger, but then rapidly ran out of partners until the tail-enders came along to render commendable support.

At the tea interval when Engineers were forced to declare, Phelps was still one short of the coveted century. His patient, but valuable contribution, included 10 fours.

The most successful Nondescripts' bowlers were Willie Jones, the former Glamorgan all-rounder, making one of his now rare appearances on the cricket field, and John Goodman.

Joe Stubbs and Mike Gough gave the visitors an excellent start to their reply before both were caught at the wicket. Willie Jones, another victim of skipper Graham Hale failed to get going, but his son Allen was in great form and at the close had hit 4 fours in an unbeaten half century.

Engineers					Nondescripts					
S. G. Phelps -	not out			99	R. Stubbs	c	Hale	b	Salter	40
G.S. Hale	c	Stubbs	b	Goodman	3	M.G. Gough	c	Hale	b	Salter	16
R.C. Smith	c	A.Jones	b	W. Jones	19	A. Jones -			not out		50
G. Woodridge -	run out			0	M. Godding	c	Carr	b	Salter	1
K. C. Newman -	run out			8	W. E. Jones	st	Hale	b	Newman	14
G.G. Farmer	c	Godding	b	W. Jones	3	K. Turner	c	Hale	b	Newman	4
M. Roberts	b	W. Jones		10	D. Hutchinson	b	Salter			21
R. Carr	b	Goodman		15	R. Holl	b	Salter			1
A. B. Salter -	run out			14	P. Bennett -	not out				0
J. J. Corbett -	not out			2						
		EXTRAS		4			EXTRAS			9
		TOTAL (for 8 declared)		177			TOTAL (for 7)			156

G. F. Terrett did not bat.

Bowling: Godding 0-41, Goodman 2-58 W. Jones 3-47, Gough 0-27.

J. Goodman and D. Turner did not bat.

Bowling: Salter 5-43, Terrett 0-52, Newman 2-43, Corbett 0-9.

1965

Saturday 15th May - Engineers Win, Thanks To Phelps

A splendid innings by their opening batsman Stan Phelps, who figured in a productive third wicket partnership with Graham Hale, helped Gloucester Engineers to gain a comfortable victory over S. Smith and Sons (Bishops Cleeve) at the Sports Ground by six wickets.

The visitors recovered from an indifferent start and thanks mainly to an undefeated half-century by Cooper batting at No 6, were able to declare at the tea interval.

Engineers lost two early wickets, but the stand between Phelps and Hale realised 80 and dashed all hopes of victory the visitors may have cherished. Hale was dismissed shortly before the century was hoisted and with the score at 123, Phelps was caught for a stylish and invaluable 70 which included eight boundaries. Skipper Roy Morley and Terry Yearsley safely steered Engineers to victory without further loss.

S. Smith and Sons 147 for 7dec (E. Cooper not out 51, C Ballinger 33). Bowling: Corbett 10-1-21-1, Salter 18-3-24-2, Holl 10-4-21-2, Newman 7-0-23-1, Morley 6-0-42-1.

Engineers 149 for 4 (S.G. Phelps 70, K.C. Newman 3, E.J. Stephens 2, G.S. Hale 32, R.G. Morley not out 18, T Yearsley not out, 9 extras 15). D Evans, J.J Corbett, A.B. Salter, B. Holl did not bat.

Saturday 12th June - Engineers v Gloucestershire Club and Ground: Procter Hits 100 in 69 minutes

What tremendous assets those two young South Africans Mike Procter and Barry Richards will be to Gloucestershire if they do eventually qualify. They have given countless examples of their potential and at the Sports Ground they again gave impressive displays for Gloucestershire Club and Ground against Gloucester Engineers.

This time it was Procter in particular who left his opponents and the spectators gasping with a magnificent and chanceless century, after the Club and Ground had lost three fairly cheap wickets.

He raced to his hundred in just 69 minutes and in all hit 2 sixes and 14 fours with a series of gloriously fluent shots. David Shepherd too punished the home attack with a splendid half -century and mainly due to this pair the whole innings of 263 took only 140 minutes.

Engineers were quickly in trouble in their reply and after Ken Newman, who hit all but four of the 25 runs scored at that point had been run out, wickets fell with bewildering rapidity. Fortunately, some sound batting by tail-enders Bob Deane and Tony Salter enabled them to hold out to a draw, though Engineers were still 158 runs behind with their last pair at the crease when stumps were drawn.

Gloucester Club and Ground

T.M. Riley	c	Hale	b	Smith	27
D. Bevan	c	Deane	b	Smith	4
B. Richards	b	Smith			18
R.Etheridge	c& b	Morley			18
M.J. Procter	b	Salter			119
D. Shepherd	c	Farmer	b	Salter	56
J. Sullivan			b	Salter	13
M. Haynes	Not out				6
EXTRAS					2
TOTAL (for 7)					263

Engineers

S.G. Phelps	c	Hillmen	b	Procter	0
K.Newman	run out				21
G.S. Hale	b	Procter			0
R.G. Morley	b	Richards			5
G. Farmer	b	Mustoe			6
T. Yearsley	c	Haynes	b	Mustoe	9
E. Stephens	b	Richards			12
R.L. Deane	not out				23
J.J. Corbett	b	Wiltshire			7
A.B. Salter	c	Mustoe	b	Richards	20
A. Smith	Not out				1
EXTRAS					1
TOTAL (for 9)					105

Sunday 13th June - Engineers' six-a-side Tournament

Gloucester Engineers' six-a-side cricket tournament has never been won by the host club, but they came within an ace or, to be exact, one ball and three byes, of winning this year's competition.

For on the Sports Ground they succumbed to a Swansea Team in the final over, as exciting a finish as anyone could wish to see! 32 Teams took part in the competition using three pitches and included teams from the Gloucester area, Witney, Stroud, and Swansea. Final:

Gloucester Engineers 'A'

E. Stephens	b	Foster	5
K. Newman	b	Jerimiah	0
R.G. Morley	run out		10
G.S. Hale	b	Bevan	28
A.B. Salter	not out		0
	EXTRAS		7
	TOTAL (for 4)		50

J.J. Corbett did not bat.

Swansea

J. Foster	c	Hale	b	Morley	19
P. Jenkins			not out		3
E. Bevan	b	Morley			6
T. Jerimiah			not out		16
			EXTRAS		7
			TOTAL (for 2)		51

Bowling: Morley 2 for 9

The trophies for the winners and runners up and the numerous other prizes awarded throughout the tournament, were presented after the final by David Allen, the Gloucestershire and England off-spinner.
An autographed bat raffled in aid of John Mortimore's benefit fund realised £17 12s.

Saturday 19th June - Newman In Form For Engineers

All–rounder Ken Newman has played numerous fine innings for Gloucester Engineers, but in their away match with Tewkesbury, it was as a bowler that he shone and returned the best figures of his career.

Tewkesbury 152 all out.   Salter (14-7-29-2), Terrett (9-1-23-0), Morley (15-1-55-1), Newman (18-2-1-42-7).
Engineers 123 for 7.   K. Newman 18, E. Stephens 23, R. Morley 26 not out.

Engineers 'A' 169.   G Farmer 44, R. Hill 42, R.J. Lander 29, A.E. Webb 25, R. Holl 11 not out, L Berryman 5 for 51.

Tewkesbury 'A' 136.   P Fox 31, R. Holl 4 for 43, M.J. Roberts 3 for 0, S Karadia 2 for 31.

Match played at the Sport Ground. M.J. Roberts took the ball with Tewkesbury on 137 for 7 and in two overs he captured the last three wickets without a run being scored off him.

Sunday 20th June - Engineers Beat City By 27 Runs

In an interesting game at the Sports Ground yesterday, Gloucester Engineers' Sunday X1 beat Gloucester City by 27 runs. After a useful start Engineers lost quick wickets, but some spirited hitting from Graham Terrett and Tony Salter helped them to recover and make a declaration.

Engineers 159 for 8 dec   Newman 21, Phelps 17, Hale 17, Morley 4, Farmer 23, Yearsley 1, Deane 28, Terrett 23, Salter not out 22, Carr not out 1, G. Curtis did not bat.

Gloucester City 132 all out   T. Smith 24, W. Shaw 32. Bowling: - Salter 1 for 27, Terrett 1 for 35, Newman 3 for 42, Morley 5 for 22.Friday 16th July **Engineers Win Cup With Ease**

There need be no further talk of Gremlins, Leprechauns or Bogeys as far as Gloucester Engineers are concerned. That modicum of fortune that has so often – some ten years or more, I suppose – deserted them when they appeared at the Spa in the semi final or final of the Gloucester Cricket Knockout Cup Competition, was not lacking today. Indeed, in accounting for Gloucester Nondescripts with almost consummate ease by seven wickets before nearly 3000 enthusiasts at the Spa, they won the Lee Williams Cup for the first time in their history.

Saturday 31st July - Engineers Owe It To Morley

Roy Morley was not content to play a skipper's innings for Gloucester Engineers, he also turned in a splendid bowling performance. His prowess with both bat and ball virtually assured his side of victory over Old Vigornians, their Worcester visitors, by 19 runs.

Engineers: (SG Phelps 32, K.C. Newman 10, G.S. Hale 52, R.G. Morley 59, T. Yearsley 17) 180 for 7 dec.

Old Vigornians: (A Mackie 40) 161 all out. Bowling: Corbett 9-1-30-2, Salter 7-2-17-0, Smith 4-0-9-0 Morley 15-2-52-7, Newman 12-1-47-1.

Saturday 28th August Century Stand By Engineers' Pair

Despite numerous interruptions due to rain, Gloucester Engineers scored at a rapid rate in their local derby against Gloucester Nondescripts at the Sports Ground.

Engineers 185 for 5 dec: S Phelps 79, K Newman 57, G. Hale 8, R Morley 17, G Farmer not out 1, E Stephens run out 15, A. Salter not out 2. M. Roberts, J. Corbett, G. Curtis and E. Lane did not bat.

Nondescripts 127 for 5:   A Jones 26, *W Jones 61, Dunkley 15. Bowling: Corbett 9-4-13-1, Salter 11-2-38-1, Morley 9-1-39-3, Newman 7-0-27-0.

*W.E. Jones played cricket for Glamorgan and was a well known Gloucester Rugby Player.
Also on this date, Dave Howe, who has since played for the Winget club, scored 51 for his old club Robinswood Hill against Frocester.

1966

Sat 28 Sun 29 Mon May - Engineers' Bowlers On Top

After Brian Worrall had met with such success in Saturday's match against Westinghouse, off spinner Ken Newman played a major role in dismissing Dowlais for 157 on Sunday, while Tony Salter finished with 7-31 in their Monday match against South Gloucester, also at the Sports Ground.

Gloucester Engineers	199 (K. Newman 40, L. Smart 33, C.Pugh 8-32).
Dowlais	157, (P. Williams 35, K. Newman 6-41, G. Curtis 2-35, M. Roberts 2-39).
Gloucester Engineers	122 (K. Jones 44, G. Hale 29, A. Hopkins 5-19).
South Gloucester	89 (G. Austin 36, A. Salter 7-31, B. Worrall 2-25).

Saturday 4th June - Second Ton For Newman

Despite another brilliant century by Ken Newman, his second this season, Gloucester Engineers lost an exciting, high scoring game against S. Smith and Sons at Witney by four wickets, more than 400 runs being scored in four-and-a-half hours play.
Newman dominated the Engineers' batting, his 101 out of 163 containing 2 sixes and 11 fours. He shared in an opening stand of 95 with Stan Phelps and with Roy Morley adding a useful unbeaten 22, Engineers had topped the double century at the tea interval when they declared.
Smiths scored at an even quicker rate thanks mainly to a splendid innings by their wicket-keeper and opening bat, Geoff Souch, who was run out when in sight of his century.
Newman displayed his versatility by being the visitors' most successful bowler. His off-spinners brought him a wicket with his first ball as he broke the home side's promising opening stand, and he was the only bowler to send down a maiden.

Engineers:	204 for 5 Dec' (K. Newman 101, S. Phelps 35).
Smith's:	207 for 6 (G. Souch 87, Newman 3-38).

Saturday 11th June - Easy For Engineers

A splendid partnership of 76 for the ninth wicket between table tennis international Roy Morley and Brian Worrall saved Gloucester Engineers from threatened collapse and led the way to an easy victory over Gloucester Nondescripts at the Sports Ground by 63 runs.
After Stan Phelps and Ken Newman had given Engineers a useful start, the batting fell to pieces in the face of some accurate bowling by the medium paced Peter Barnes.
Roy Morley however, stood firm, and was joined by Worrall with the Engineers' score in the gloomy regions of 84 for 9. It was the introduction into the Nondescripts' attack of Mike Ashwin that eventually broke the partnership.

Engineers:	172 (R. Morley 71, B. Worrall 36, P. Barnes 17-7-26-6).
Nondescripts:	109 (J. Moore not out 47, Salter 14-1-35-4, B. Worrall 5-3-15-4).

Saturday 9th July - Worrall's Hostile Bowling

An accurate and hostile bowling spell by the medium paced Brian Worrall paved the way for Gloucester Engineers' victory over S. Smith and Sons, their Bishop's Cleeve visitors, at the Sports Ground by three wickets.
None of the visitors' batsmen displayed real confidence or enthusiasm, against Worrall who had good support from his opening partner, Tony Salter, and only some spirited hitting by the middle order brought an air of respectability to their innings.

Smith's:	119, (L. Cooper 32, Worrall 5-29).
Engineers:	121 for 7, (S. Phelps 31, K. Newman 41, Webb 3-35, Hyde 3-35).

Tuesday 19th July -Engineers' Easy Win To Retain K.O. Trophy

In a somewhat uneven struggle at the Spa, Gloucester Engineers - the holders, retained the 'Lee Williams's' trophy when they defeated Churchdown in the final of the Gloucester and District cricket knockout competition by the resounding margin of 80 runs.

Engineers: 140 for 4, (G. Hale 14, K. Newman 26, R. Morley 23, L. Smart not out 52, Allen 2-36).
Churchdown: 60 for 9, (B. Smith 30, Salter 2-5, Newman 4-24).

Saturday 30th July to 5th August - Engineers give Lesson in Spin Bowling

As the Ventnor batsmen groped against the spin attack of Ken Newman and Tony Webb in the first match of Gloucester Engineers' Isle of Wight tour, it became increasingly obvious to the tourists that the islanders were not familiar with this kind of bowling.
The fact was confirmed when Tony Webb bowled a ball that turned a great deal and saw the Ventnor umpire signal a wide.

Results: Ventnor: 125 for 9 Dec (K. Newman 3-27).
           Engineers: 129 for 4 (S. Phelps 50, K. Newman 46).
           Shanklin: 133 for 6 Dec (A. Salter 3-25).
           Engineers: 102 for 3 (K. Newman 50).
           Engineers: 67 (G. Hale 21).
           Wembley Park: 60 (A. Salter 5-19, A. Webb 2-3).

Saturday 30th July - Forceful Fifty by Smart

With the majority of their 1st XI players touring the Isle of Wight, weakened Gloucester Engineers acquitted themselves admirably in having rather the better of a drawn game at the Sports Ground against the strong Tewkesbury side.
Jim Hindle and acting skipper Graham Farmer were associated in an opening partnership of 48 and though Roy Morley failed, according to his own standards this season, another productive stand between Les Smart and Bob Deane added 64 for the fourth wicket.
Deane reached the boundary five times, while Smart hit a six and six fours and was still unbeaten with a forceful half century to his credit when Engineers declared.
With Brian Worrall and Morley as the only recognised front line bowlers in their side, Engineers rarely looked capable of dismissing Tewkesbury, although it was left to Cliff Burd and Tony Attwell to steer the visitors to safety.
Both reached their respective half-centuries before falling to the persistent Morley, and at the close, Tewkesbury still needed 30 runs for victory.

Engineers: 188 for 5 Dec, (Smart n.o. 38, Farmer 37, Burd 2-48, Green 2-21).
Tewkesbury: 159 for 5, (Burd 53, Attwell 58, Morley 2-52, Bingham 1-26).

Soccer World Cup '66 – England win World Cup Final beating West Germany 4-2.

Saturday 13th August - Morley Magic

After Winget had lost seven wickets for 118 runs, Tony Salter added a sting to the tail and together with Ron Thomas took the score to 147 without further loss, a score at which Winget declared at tea against Marle Hill at the Sports Ground.
The visitors however, never seemed able to master the Winget attack. Seamers Brian Worrall and Tony Salter returned half the side to the pavilion for only 41 runs. Then spinners Kevin Newman and Roy Morley dismissed the remaining batsmen for a further 35 runs.
Winget: 147 for 7 Dec' (A. Salter 36, R. Thomas 12 n.o., Shaw 4-42).
Marle Hill: 76 (R. Morley 7-5-5-4).
Cheltenham Extra First: 200 for 4 Dec' (Thomas 1-10).
Winget II: 93 for 7 (C. Thomas 35, K. Hamblett 24 not out).

Saturday 20th August - Newman and Phelps in 180 Stand

A remarkable unbroken stand of 180 by Ken Newman and Stan Phelps steered Gloucester Engineers to an equally amazing victory over Winget (Rochester) at the Sports Ground by ten wickets.

The visitors can scarcely have visualised such a crushing reverse when they declared in the comforting regions of 176-6, despite some accurate bowling by Brian Worrall and Tony Salter. Newman, always the dominant partner, and Phelps, raced to their target with a galaxy of shots that the visitors' attack and fielders could do little to check.

With his 12th four (he also hit two sixes), Newman reached his brilliant unbeaten century. Phelps scored the winning single, with his main shots being six boundaries, the pair passing the Winget (Rochester) total in only 117 minutes.

Winget (Rochester):   179-6 (B. Deane 56, A. Salter 3-61).

Engineers: 180 for 0 wickets, (K. C. Newman 102 N.O., S. Phelps 71 N.O.).

1967

Saturday 20th May - Winget v Old Elizabethans

A restrained half-century by Roy Morley – the sheet-anchor of the side, and a more forceful innings from Les Smart served to bolster Winget at the Sports Ground, where they recovered from vague beginnings to respectability, and eventually had the better of a drawn game.

Winget suffered early misgivings when Ken Newman and Ken Jones went with only 9 runs scored, but Morley joined the imperturbable Stan Phelps and the batting took on a more settled appearance.

Morley displayed a neat range of shots without taking undue risks, but lost Phelps caught at short square-leg, with the score at 38. Skipper Graham Morley had made a valuable contribution even before he and Smart added 74 for a splendid fifth wicket partnership.

Winget 143 for 5 declared (R. Morley 54, L. Smart 37 n.o. Russell 3 – 25).
Old Elizabethans 120 for 8, (S. Gardner 25, A. Salter 3 – 27, J. Bingham 2 – 18).

Old Elizabethans II 46, (R. Thomas 3 – 12, J. Corbett 2 – 6, R. Holl 2 – 25).
Winget II 48 for 3 (D. Taylor 16, M. Roberts 10 n.o.). Played at Worcester.

Saturday 10th June - 48 For Last Wicket – Then Winget II Lose

Splendid bowling by Jackie Corbett and Bob Holl shattered the early order Naunton Park batsmen and the visitors slumped to 29 – 6.

Then came a series of short but resolute innings to reach 61-9 before Ken Calthrop and Alan Mourton took the score to 107 when the innings was closed with the former falling lbw to Holl.

George Woodridge, Dave Taylor and Holl offered resistance to the consistent bowling of Naunton Park, but generally the visitors held the upper hand throughout and the Winget innings, in a nail-biting finish, closed three runs short of its target.

*Winget II 104 (*G Woodrige 30, R.Holl 31 not out, D. Taylor 16, J Bingham 10: R Freebury 4-20, R. Cavell 4-21, A. Amourton 1-26, J Wiggins 1-30)

Naunton Park 107 (J Calthrop 33, A. Mourton 25 not, C Cripps 11, Corbett 5-26, Hill 3-29).

Sunday 11th June - Thrilling win In final of Winget Sixes

After accounting for C.E. Baker's strong team in an exciting finish in the second semi-final, the Welsh VI from the Swansea area beat the host club's 'A' side – off the last ball of the game – in the final to win this year's Winget Cricket Club's six-a-side tournament, held at the Sports Ground.

Few of the large crowd could have envisaged such exciting matches, particularly in the final where the Welsh VI, who gave a remarkably consistent performance throughout the day, required five runs off the last over bowled by Ken Newman.

But, if the Welshmen were the star performers collectively, it was Winget's Newman who carried off the most awards, from cricket bats and a lighter to a share in a four-and-a-half gallon barrel of beer.

The trophies and awards were presented by Winget directors Messrs Peter Brown, John Barber and Max Puckridge.

With Smith's of Witney withdrawing at a late hour, 31 teams, some from a long distance away, took part in the tournament which enjoyed the best weather since it was inaugurated.

The Results

First Round: Winget 'B' 61-2, Westbury-on-Severn 'A' 43-2: Down Hatherley 36-1, Kingsholdm 'B' 23-4: Robinswood Hill 'A' 13-0 South Gloucester 'A' 11 Gloucester Post Office 53-5, Highnam 36-5, Elmore 48-1, Gloucester Co-Op 'A' 45-2 *Winget 'A' 44-2, Kingsholm 'A' 43-;3* Marie Hill 50-2, Stonehouse 34-1, Naunton Park 'B' 46-5, Gloucester West Indians 41-1. Naunton Park 'A 45-4, Sperry's 'A' 43-3 Robinswood Hill 'B' 42-1, Gloucester Co-Op B, 41-2, C.E. Baker's VI 44-3, Cultha College 35-3, Grange Court 54-1, St Paul's 41-3, Longlevens Walk-over, against S Mith and Sons,(Witney): Vallindre Sports (Swansea) 38-0 Sperry's B 35-5 Frampton-on-Severn 38-1 Bristol Snidely (Cardiff) 37-3
Second Round: Winget 'B' 58-0, Down Hatherley 42-2: Robinswood Hill 'A' 33-0, Gloucester Post Office 32-3: *Winget 'A' 63-1 Elmore 37*, Marley Hill 51-3, Naunton Park B 23-3 Robinswood Hill 'B' 35-4, Naunton Park 'A' 33-5, C.E. Bakers Vi 42-2, Grange Court 41-2, Vallindre Sports 49-2, Longlevens 34-5L Welsh VI 27-0, Frompton—on-Severn 25-4.

Third Round: Robinswood Hill A 41-2, *Winget B 40-0 Winget A 55-2,* Marie Hill 45-5, C.E. Baker's VI 51-1, Robinswood Hill B 50-2, Welsh VI 50-1 Vallindre Sports 43-1.

Semi Finals

Winget 'A' 57-1, Robinwood Hill A 44-3.
Welsh VI 47-1, C.E.Baker's 46-2.

The Final

Winget 'A' (batted first) 43-2, Welsh VI (Swansea) 44-2.

Saturday 17th June - Morley's Day

It was all-rounder Roy Morley's day at the Sports Ground on Sunday when he played the leading part in dismissing visiting Leicester for 221, then had the wretched luck to miss his century by only four runs in Winget's reply. Despite his remarkable performance however, Winget only just managed to save the day, their last wicket pair being together at the close.
Morley captured half the visitors' wickets for 98 runs. Morley and Newman put on 68 runs in 47 minutes for their first wicket partnership, and a change in the batting order brought in the hard-hitting Les Smart, followed by Tony Salter.
The move failed, however, and when Morley was caught for 96, including 11 fours, Winget dropped behind the clock.

Took Four Wickets In One Over.

In an evening match last week, Sperry's were shot out for nine runs against a Winget XI at the Sports Ground. It must have given them considerable satisfaction, therefore, to reach 107-4 against Winget 11 on Saturday afternoon.
But then, John Bingham produced a devastating spell of bowling to take four wickets in one over, Tony Webb captured the remaining two in his next over, and Sperry's had suddenly slumped to 107 all out, their last six wickets falling without a run being scored.
The only two batsmen to offer any real resistance to the home attack were Ron Tyler and Terry Baker, who added 55 for the fourth wicket.
Dave Taylor left early in Winget's reply, but George Woodridge and Dave Wood took the score to 94 before the latter was lbw, one run short of his half-century. Woodridge was unbeaten with 51 as the home side cruised to a convincing victory by seven wickets.
Sperry's 107 (R.Tyler 39, T. Baker 34, J Bingham 6-24, A E Webb 3-22)
Winget II 105-5 (G H Woodridge 51 not, D Wood 49).

Saturday 1st July - Winget Top 200 In 140 Minutes

With their batsmen on full production, Winget gained an overwhelming victory at Chippenham where they hit 205-3 declared, before dismissing Westinghouse for 99.
Ken Newman and Stan Phelps set the tempo with an opening stand of 98 at well over a run a minute. Newman, always the more aggressive, was the first to be dismissed. His 65 included 4 sixes and 6 fours.
Phelps was out shortly afterwards, but Roy Morley and Ken Jones stepped up the scoring rate to such an extent that they added exactly 100 in 50 minutes before Morley was bowled. At the end of the same over, Winget declared having topped the double century in 140 minutes.
Westinghouse could never match the speed or skill of the visitors and at one period had lost seven wickets for only 35 runs against the bowling of Newman and Brian Worrall.A desperate fling by their No. 8 batsman Thomas, who hit 9 fours in an unbeaten 53 however, boosted their final score to 99.

Monday 3rd July - Sperry's K.O. Cup Holders Winget

In the "shock" result of the season in the Gloucester cricket knock-out cup competition, Sperry's defeated strong favourites Winget, winners of the trophy for the past two years, in the third quarter-final match at Fieldings' Ground last night by 19 runs.
It was a game of tremendous hitting with the respective opening batsmen, Phillip Whettell and Ken Newman, stealing most of the honours.
Sperry's owed their imposing total of 134 in the allotted 20 overs almost entirely to Whettell and his opening partner Bob Baker, who was content to play a supporting role.

Whettell, indeed, batted throughout the innings for an unbeaten 75 which included three sixes and six fours and forced the withdrawal of the Winget pacemen from the firing line. It was not until spinners Ken Newman and Roy Morley were introduced into the attack that the holders began to make inroads.

Newman began the Winget reply in such brilliant form that a total of 135 for victory looked comparatively easy.

He raced to 53 out of 63 in six overs with the aid of four sixes and three fours, but on his dismissal, only Tony Salter with four fours in an unbeaten 28 kept Winget's dwindling hopes alive. As it was, they fell behind the clock, lost quick wickets and the game.

Sperry's 134-8: (P Whettell 75 not out, R Baker 26, K.C. Newman 4-28, R.G. Morely 2-33.
Winget 115-7: (K.C. Newman 53, A.B. Salter 28 not out, R Pennington 5-31.

Saturday 15th July - Newman Stars As Winget Beat Malmesbury

As though to vindicate his father, head groundsman Charlie Newman, and to show Derbyshire that there is little wrong with the pitches at the Sports Ground, opening batsman Ken Newman hit a faultless 68 to put Winget on the road to victory over visiting Malmesbury, who last week accounted for Stroud.

Hitting a six and eight fours, Newman shared in stands of 45 with fellow opener Stan Phelps and 71 with Roy Morley. When he left at 116 several wickets fell quickly, but a bustling unbeaten 31 from Tony Salter boosted the score to 184 before a declaration was made.

Malmesbury began their reply confidently against the Winget pace attack, but the introduction of Newman and Morley, the spinners, began the visitors' slide.

They maintained their challenge sportingly however, and in an exciting finish, Winget gained the verdict by eight runs.

Sunday 16th July -Century Follows His 68

Ken Newman followed his 68 on Saturday by completing a brilliant unbeaten century for Winget on Sunday when they gained an overwhelming victory over St. Fagan's, the strong Welsh side, by eight wickets.
St Fagan's scarcely found it a chore to get runs either for they accumulated them freely enough to be able to declare at tea despite some more accurate bowling by Winget's spinners Roy Morley and Ken Newman, who is in remarkable form with both bat and ball this season.
Winget scored even faster than their visitors, Newman and Morley figuring in a stand of 111 for the first wicket in 93 minutes. Newman's innings included two sixes and 15 fours and he completely dominated the unbroken third wicket stand with Phelps, who scored only 13 of the 60 runs added.
St Fagan's 170-9 dec: (D Williams 45, C.M. Cox 29, D. Ireland 21, (Salter 12-3-34-1: Worrall 8-1-17-0: Morely 18-1-65-4, Newman 14-3-24-4).
Winget K.C. Newman not out 104, R.G. Morley C Kimberley by Helsall 48 L Smart c and b Kimbley 0 SG Phelps not out 13 Extras 7 Total for 2 Wickets 171.

Saturday & Sunday 26th 27th August - Victory Weekend For Winget

Following their crushing defeat of Cirencester on Saturday, Winget completed a hat trick of holiday victories by accounting for Almondsbury on their opponent's ground on Sunday and then gained a thrilling verdict over Old Cryptians at the Sports Ground yesterday.

Winget: K.C. Newman lbw Webb 49, R.G. Morley c Brewer b Allen 12: G.S. Hale b Edgeworth 23: L. Smart not out 53: G.H. Farmer b Edgeworth 32: R.W. Thomas b Allen 6; M. J. Roberts b Edgeworth 0; A.B. Salter not out 1: Extras 11, Total (for 6 wkts dec) 187 .Almondsbury: 146 (Robbins 57, Taylor 37; Worrall 11-2-22-1 Salter 9-1-20-1, Morley 8-0-49-0, Newman 9-3-27-5, Thomas 2-0-16-2).

Yesterday's game provided remarkable changes of fortunes, Winget losing their first six wickets for only 46 runs, but another splendid innings by Newman, with tail-end support from Tony Salter and Brian Worrall the two opening bowlers, sent the total soaring to 183-9 before the home side declared.

Mick Roberts went to hospital after being hit by a ball from Bob Bevan. He was later found to have chipped a bone in his elbow. Old Cryptians too met with misfortune when spinner Peter Lewis split a finger trying to make a catch.

In their reply, Old Cryptians, thanks to the sparkling batting of two Gloucester RFC players Eric Stephens and Terry Hopson, seemed set for an overwhelming victory for, with Derek Howell also adding valuable runs, they were 156-3. Their last seven wickets fell for only 23 runs however, to give Winget an exciting victory by four runs.

Winget: K.C. Newman not out 81, G.S. Hale b Bevan 2, R.G.Morley c Howker by Bevan 0, K.Jones b Bevan 4, J Hindle b Lewis 8, L Smart b Lewis 0, G.H. Farmer c Hopson b Bevan 9 A.B. Salter lbw b Rose 29, M.J. Roberts c and b Bevan 6, B.W. Worrall b Meadows 34, Extras 10: Total for 9 wkts dec 185. G.I. Curtis did not bat.
Bowling: Meadows 6-0-44-1, Bevan 15-3-43-5; Lewis 11-2-38-2, Rose 8-0-33-1, Hopson 3-0-15-0.

Old Cryptians: E.J. Stephens c Newman b Salter 64, M.Rose c Newman b Salter 1, K.H. Michael c Morley b Salter 17, J.T. Hopson c Worrall b Morley 41, D. Howell c Farmer b Curtis 32, K. Turner c Worrall b Morley 0, L. Bridgemout st Hale b Curtis 9, A. Howker c and b Morley 1, P.D. Meadows run out 10, R. Bevan c Newman B Morley 2 P. Lewis not out 0, Extras 2 Total 179.
Bowling: Salter 12-4-40-3, Worrall 8-0-61-0, Newman 5-0-23-0, Morley 9-0-41-4, Curtis 5-1-12-2.

Saturday 2nd September - Record Match For Winget

A car breakdown indirectly led to a new record being set in the history of Winget Cricket Club. Arriving at Oxford to play Pressed Steel on Sunday, the visitors found that the mishap had left them without several of their recognized batsmen, and it was not known how long they would be delayed.

With the scanty resources at their immediate disposal, it was decided to send in fast bowler Tony Salter, originally due to bat at No. 8, at the fall of the first wicket. He duly joined Roy Morley when Winget appeared to be in further trouble with the dismissal of Ken Newman, who has been in such splendid form this season, with only 10 runs scored.

Not until the total had reached exactly 200, however, was this remarkable partnership broken and they had added 190 runs in 90 minutes, also the time of course for Salter's century.

When he was bowled for 103, Salter had hit a six and 10 fours, Morley went on to complete his century shortly after his partner's dismissal, his main hits being 14 fours, and he was still unbeaten when a declaration was made.

The amazement of the other players when they eventually arrived is understandable, for Morley and Salter had achieved a Winget record – two centuries in the same innings.

Winget

Winget 222 for 2 dec (K. C Newman b Morgan 1, R.G. Morley not out 109, A.B. Salter b Morgan 103, B.W. Worrall not out 7, Extras 2.)
Pressed Steel 123 (M. Sweeney 66 not out, D. Taylor 18, G. Parley 16, P. Wiggins 10). Bowling: Worrall 4-1-12-0: Curtis 7-1-13-1: Newman 10-1-50-1 Morley 9-1-39-3: Salter 6-3-5-2: Thomas 3-2-2-1

1st X1 1967

K.Jones G.Farmer S.Phelps L.Smart B.Worrall A.Salter
D.Carr R.Morley G.Hale (capt) K.Newman R.Thomas

1968

Saturday 10th May - Winget Robbed by Rain

Pathetically slow batting by visiting Colwall and rain after the tea interval robbed Winget of victory at the Sports Ground. So uninspired were the Worcestershire side against the medium paced Brian Worrall and the spin of Ken Newman that they resumed their innings after tea, eventually making a declaration with their last pair at the wicket. With only 117 on the board at tea, Colwall added a further 12 runs in 26 minutes before declaring. Winget were quickly in the hunt for runs in their reply, but a stoppage through rain for nearly 20 minutes killed all hopes of victory.

Colwall 129 for 9 Dec' (R.J. Stainton 52)
Worrall 14-4-25-4, Salter 12-3-23-4, Morley 5-0-12-0, M. Roberts 1-0-2-1.

Winget 93 for 4 (S. Phelps N.O. 45, K. Newman 19, G. Hale 11, K. Jones 8, R. Morley 3, L. Smart N.O. 3)

Sunday 11th May - Newman Takes 7, Hits 62

Ken Newman routed the Westinghouse innings by taking 7 for 47 and then hammered their attack by hitting a brisk 62 that included ten boundaries. The Westinghouse opening partnership of Frank Day and Alan Rumble put on 78 before Newman had Rumble caught at third slip. The off-spinner continued to wreck the visitors' innings with Roy Morley giving him excellent support from the other end. The Westinghouse innings eventually closed for 139. Winget suffered an early loss when Stan Phelps fell to paceman Smart with only 23 runs scored, but then Newman and Morley took the score to 84 before Morley was run out. Les Smart and skipper Tony Salter were called upon to hit out for their victory.

Westinghouse 139 all out (F. Day 62, A. Rumble 42, Newman 7-47, Morley 2-48)
Winget 141 for 7 (K. Newman 62, R. Morley 21, A. Salter 18)

Saturday 1st June - Six wins it for Winget

It was left to Tony Salter to hit the winning six off the last but one ball of the day to gain Winget their victory over Thornbury at the Sports Ground for, although the winners had ample batting left, they slipped behind the clock and only two successive sixes by Ken Jones off paceman Brian Loveridge brought them within sight of victory.
At one stage Thornbury were 89-7, but an eighth wicket stand added 38. Another wicket fell without addition to the score, but a last wicket partnership between Curtis and Len Gullwell took the total to 154. Winget got off to a sound start with Ken Newman and Stan Phelps putting on 112, before Phelps was caught off opener Gullwell in the paceman's third spell. Newman was run out with only one more run being added, but Winget had slipped behind the clock. Ken Jones, hitting 18 in level time and Tony Salter, hitting eight in two minutes, swung the game back in Winget's favour. Salter's second shot – a six high over mid wicket – brought victory.

Winget 158 for 4 (S. G Phelps c Vizard b Gullwell 47; K. C. Newman run out 64; R.G Morley c Vizard b Poole 16; K. Jones c Gullwell b Loveridge 18; A. B. Salter not out 8; D.A. Taylor not out 1, Extras 4.)
Thornbury 154 (J. Curtis 33, D Hawkins 30, J. Harbottle 16, R. Vizard 25 not, B. Loveridge 15, R. Waterhouse 13)
Bowling: Salter 14-4-29-3: Worrall 16-2-45-2; Carr 4-1-8-0; Morley 9-0-45-2; Newman 7-2-22-2.

Saturday 8th June - Newman hits 90 off Cardiff

Ken Newman, displaying the full range of his repertoire of shots, lashed the Cardiff attack at the Sports Ground in the first ever fixture between the two clubs. He cut, drove and hooked with immeasurable skill, and played a major role in Winget's declared total of 162-6 at tea.
With his opening partner Stan Phelps dropped in the order to second wicket down, Newman put on 55 for the first wicket with Roy Morley, before the latter fell lbw to Alan Priday in the paceman's 11th over. Morley's contribution to this total was 13 with Newman generally receiving far more of the bowling. The second wicket stand with Ken Jones took the score to 100 before off-spinner Ray Thomas had Jones stumped. Phelps then came together with Newman and the score reached 131 before Thomas' second victim. Newman then fell to second change bowler Ken Williams without addition, having scored 90 of the 131 runs scored. His total included two sixes, both off one over from Williams, and eight fours. Both Graham Hale and Graham Farmer were dismissed before Winget closed their innings at 162-6.

Winget's opening attack of Tony Salter and Brian Worrall gained early successes as Cardiff lost their final four wickets for 41 runs, but former Cardiff rugby full-back Alun Priday came together in a fifth wicket stand with Howard Williams that took the score to 129 before Priday was run out in attempting a quick single. Fourth change Archie Carr gained a further wicket before the end of the day when Cardiff were 133-6.

Sunday 9th June - Winget win their own "Sixes"

With a series of convincing displays throughout the day, Winget 'A' won their own popular six-a-side cricket tournament at the Sports Ground, Tuffley Avenue, with victory in the final over Gloucester Police. It was also a splendid performance by the Police who had never before entered the competition. They too gained several resounding victories, and in Dick Griffiths had a prolific and consistent scorer who hit an unbeaten half-century in the second-round game with Elmore. The final brought its misfortunes for the Police, however, for all-rounder Peter Day was forced to retire hurt with a badly pulled back muscle. They made a disastrous start when Winston Morris was bowled without scoring, followed by the retirement of Dave Griffiths, who had previously only been dismissed once during the day. He appeared to be on his way to another big score when he was caught and bowled by Roy Morley. Arthur Cooke gallantly tried to step up the rate of scoring, but at the end of their allotted five overs the Police had only reached 35-3. Winget, who had been disposing of their opponents in summary fashion in nearly every round, again made light work of their task with Ken Newman and Tony Salter hitting off the necessary runs without being separated. Watched by a large crowd who had basked in the sunshine all day, Mr. Peter Brown of the Winget management presented the trophies and numerous prizes.

Saturday 29th June

Newman passes his 1,000 in K.O run feast

Sunday 30th June - Winget just foiled

Winget were just foiled of victory in their game against Bath Civil Service at the Sports Ground, the visitors hanging on grimly to draw with their last wicket pair together. Ken Newman again stole the batting honours for Winget, sharing in a century opening partnership with Stan Phelps before he was second out at 141, his stylish 79 containing two sixes and five fours.

Winget: 193 for 3 dec (S. G. Phelps b Fordham 40; K. C. Newman c Twyman b Hayter 79; R.G. Morley not out 37; G. H Farmer c-b Fordham 29; Extras 8)
G.S. Hale, H Reed, M. J. Roberts, R. Hayes, A.B. Salter, B.W. Worrall and P. Lamb did not bat.
Bath CS: 108-9 (Worrall 11-3-12-2, Salter 11-6-18-0, Morley 14-2-48-3, Newman 12-2-27-3).

Saturday 15th August Morley Magic

After Winget had lost seven wickets for just 118 runs, Tony Salter added a sting to the tail and together with Ron Thomas took the score to 147 without further loss – a score at which Winget declared at tea against Marle Hill at the Sports Ground.
The visitors, however, never seemed able to master the Winget attack. Seamers Salter and Brian Worrall returned half the side to the pavilion for 41 runs, with Worrall bowling exceptionally well. Then spinners Ken Newman and Roy Morley dismissed the remaining batsmen for 35, with Morley taking 4-5 in 7.5 overs.
Winget 147 for 7 dec (G. S. Hale c Richards b Godwin 22; K.C. Newman c Holder b Shaw 26; R.G. Morley lbw b Shaw 6; G.H Farmer st Holder b Shaw 13; L. Smart b Godwin 1; K. Jones c Richards b Lowe 24; R. Deane b Shaw 4; A.B Salter not out 36; R.W. Thomas not out 12. Extras 3) Godwin 2-67, Shaw 4-42, Lowe 1-35.
Marle Hill 76 (C. Gibbons 15, B. Green 14, D. Richards 12, Worrall 16-3-25-4; Salter 14-4-22-1; Newman 9-3-14-1; Morley 7.5-5-5-4)

Playing Records and Averages for 1968 Season

First XI record: Played 29, won 8, drew 12, lost 7 and cancelled 2.
Ken Newman topped the batting average, scoring 698 runs for an average of 30. R. Morley was second, scoring 410 runs with an average of 27.3. Top of the bowling average was Brian Worrall, taking 40 wickets for an average of 14.1, second was A. Salter, taking 35 wickets for an average of 15.5.
The second team played 14, won 7, lost 2 and drew 5. Top of the batting averages was R. Thomas 21.8, second J. Corbett 21.5, and third Clifford Thomas 16.7. In the bowling, D.A. G. Carr topped the averages with 20 wickets for an average of 5.5 and R. Thomas was second with 14 wickets for an average of 14.3.

The Sunday XI played 21 games, won 7, drew 7 and lost 4, three being cancelled. Top of the averages was R. Morley (580 runs for an average of 72). K. Newman was second scoring 730 runs for an average of 45.

In the bowling, K. Newman was top, taking 55 wickets for an average of 7.33. A. Salter, the captain, was second with 20 wickets for an average of 15.5.

1969

Saturday 8th June - Winget Winners again

Winget, the holders, won their own six-a-side cricket tournament at the Sports Ground yesterday when their 'A' team accounted for Gloucester Police in one of the most exciting finals in the history of the competition. Graham Hale and Roy Morley, after the early loss of Ken Newman, steered Winget to a commanding total of 53 in their allotted five overs, helped considerably by 10 extras.

But, though Winston Morris also went early in the quest for runs, Ken Daun and Tony Pockett looked as though they would steer Police to victory. There were two balls remaining – and six runs required. But Daun thought it was the last ball, tried to hit for six, just failed in the attempt and was subsequently run out in the scamper for runs. Dickie Williams valiantly tried to hit a six off the last ball, but missed it completely.

In the semi-finals, Police defeated Westbury-on-Severn "B" who made a marked impression in the tournament and Winget "A" accounted for Robinswood Hill "A".

Saturday 14th June Sixth Wicket of 99 Leads to Victory

Les Smart and Cliff Thomas shared a sixth wicket stand of 99 at Rochester to enable Winget (Gloucester) to win the Winget Cup in their annual match with their sister firm in Kent. The pair came together when the visitors were 83-5, and in a whirlwind stand lasting just 43 minutes they added a match winning partnership with Smart hitting one six and three fours and Thomas hitting three sixes and four fours.

Winget (Rochester) were in trouble immediately. Tony Salter took a return catch to dismiss Alan Dykes in his first over and when Brian Worrall took two wickets in his second over the home side were 3-3. Salter claimed another wicket in his third over as the home side slid to 8-4, but then Mike Clarke shared a 94 partnership with John Munday that saw the former hit 11 boundaries in his 99 minutes at the wicket. Roy Morley eventually bowled Clarke and then, in his next over, took four wickets to shatter the Winget (Rochester) innings.

Winget (Gloucester)

K.C. Newman c Munday b Chandler	26
S G Phelps c Fox b Kingswell	17
R.G. Morley c Ambrose b Chandler	18
G S Hale c Munday b Chandler	16
K. Jones c Munday b Chandler	6
L Smart st Munday b Hayward	41
C. Thomas not out	55
Extras	5
Total (for 6 Dec.)	182

D. Wood A.B. Salter B.W. Worrall and C. Matthews did not bat.

Winget (Rochester)

J. Fox b Worrall	2
A Dykes c& b Salter	0
L Ward b Worrall	0
M Clarke b Morley	83
F. Mcleod b Salter	2
J Munday b Salter	17
C. Ambrose st Hale b Morley	2
L Hayward st Hale b Morley	2
M. Candler Not out	1
A Silcock st Hale b Morley	0
A. Kingswell c Hale b Morley	15
Extras	**3**
Total (all out)	**138**

Bowling: Worrall 2-13: Salter 3-14: Wood 0-32: Morley 5-31: Newman 0-29: Matthews 0-16.

Saturday 2nd August - Winget come off best in run crawl

Winget travelled to Cardiff and gained victory by six runs in a slow scoring match with St. Fagans. The visitors compiled 112 runs off 49.5 overs and then dismissed the home side for 106 off 44.2 overs.

Winget lost wickets at regular intervals on a pitch that was proving awkward to the batsmen and only an unbeaten 25, which included five boundaries from No 10 Brian Worrall enabled Winget to pass the hundred mark. Stan Phelps batted well for his contribution before falling lbw to a ball from Bob Campbell, who bowled unchanged for 24 overs and conceded only 27 runs.

The home team were immediately in trouble when they replied. After 12 overs the Winget opening attack of Tony Salter and Roy Morley had claimed four wickets for only 18 runs. Two further wickets fell for the addition of a further 21 runs.

Richard Harris and Harold Morgan then came together in a seventh wicket stand that realised 63, before Harris was run out. With only 13 minutes left, St. Fagans needed 11 runs with three wickets standing and the game was finely balanced, liable to go either way. Salter returned to the attack for a second spell and in five balls took the remaining three wickets to give Winget victory with one minute to spare.

Winget: S.G. Phelps lbw b Campbell 28: K Jones b Campbell 6; R G Morley b Campbell 0: K C Newman b Morgan 13; G S Hale st Loosemore b Morgan 8: Smart c Smart b Campbell 5; C Thomas b Morgan 0; A B Salter c and b Campbell 12: R W Thomas b Morgan 1 : B W Worrall not out 25 : C Matthews c Hamlett b Smart 5. Extras 9. Total 112.

St. Fagans: J. Short b Salter 4: K J Hamlett c Smart b Salter 1: J Loosemore b Morley 11: N Williams c Morley 11: N Williams c Morley b Thomas 0: J Bristow c Salter b Morley 0: R Harris run out 30: C Brain c Thomas b Morley 5: N W Morgan b Salter 44; A Muir b Salter 3; R Campbell b Salter 0; J Smart not out 0. Extras 8 Total 106.

Salter 11.2-4-17-5: Morley 14-2-28-3: Thomas (R) 6-2-14-1; Newman 8-0-25-0: Worrall 5-1-14-0.

Saturday 16th August - Reed Gets the Vital Wicket

Following his splendid all-round performance last weekend, Harold Reed stepped into the Winget attack at Oxford and gained the vital breakthrough. He was third change and with the second ball of his second over he had Mike Ball caught by Stan Phelps, just as the Pressed Steel batsman looked as if he might have revived the home side's fortunes.

Then their remaining wickets fell rapidly and Winget gained victory by 19 runs.

Winget: SG Phelps c Hookham b Spicer 41; G S Hale c Hookham b Langford 11; R G Morley not out 64, K C Newman c Carter b Spicer 0; L Smart b Carter 5; H E Reed lbw Spicer 16 R Hill not out 4, Extras 3. Total 144 for 5 wkts dec.

Pressed Steel (Oxford): D Carter c Worrall b Salter 13; D Webb b Wood 10; M Sweeney c Worrall b Salter 0; M V Ball c Phelps b Reed 55; T Williams b Wood 10; C Spicer b Wood 4; R Finch c and b Reed 10; A Mitchell b Wood 5; T Hookham b Reed 5; B Langford not out 0; T Franklin c Hale b Morley 8. Extras 5, Total 125.

Worrall 7-4-6-0; Salter 12-5-22-2; Wood 11-0-39-4; Newman 7-0-27-0: Reed 7-0-26-3; Morley 2-0-0-1.

Winget first XI Averages 1969

Batting Averages

	Inns	N/O	Runs	Average	Catches
R. Morley	22	6	526	32.8	14
K. Newman	22	3	479	25.2	4
S. Phelps	17	2	303	20.2	4
G. Hale	18	3	289	19.2	10
A. Salter	12	3	171	19.0	10
H. Reed	5	-	72	18.2	1
L. Smart	16	3	233	17.9	7
C. Thomas	8	1	108	15.4	6
R. Thomas	4	3	12	12.0	5
G. Farmer	6	-	68	11.3	4
K. Jones	13	2	72	6.5	4
C. Matthews	4	-	20	5.0	4

Bowling Averages

	Overs	Maidens	Runs	Wkts	Average
R. Morley	126	8	469	31	15.1
A. Salter	207	54	527	34	15.5
K. Newman	147	12	503	23	21.8
B. Worrall	175	34	449	20	22.4
D. Wood	92	13	314	11	28.5
R. Thomas	30	8	77	6	12.8
D. Carr	44	3	173	7	24.7
H. Reed	12	-	55	3	18.3
K. Jones	14	3	53	2	26.5

Winners Winget six- a-side Tournament 1969
A Salter K Newman E Stephens C Matthews
G Pellant Mr P Brown R Morley B Worrall

1970

Saturday 23rd May - 30-7 But Defeat Averted

Winget, who have still to win a Severn Counties' League match, will rarely find victory closer than in the game at the Sports Ground where they had Tewkesbury reeling at 30-7. They then allowed left-hander Francis Stillwell and captain Tony Attwell to pull the game out of the fire with an unbeaten eighth wicket partnership that enabled them to reach 103-7 at the end of their allotted overs.
Winget's innings had started in a cloud of uncertainty as both Newman and Ken Jones were returned to the pavilion for only 15, but a left-handed third wicket partnership between Geoff Pellant and Graham Hale laid foundations which Morley, Les Smart, Dave Taylor and Harold Reed happily built on to take Winget to 157 with three balls of their 45 overs remaining.

Winget: KC Newman c Page c Caudle 11; K Jones c Attwell b Caudle 1; G Pellant c Page b Green 29; G S Hale c Martin b Attwell 40; R G Morley c Page b Attwell 16: L Smart c Stillwell b Attwell 13; D Taylor run out 15; H E Reed c Page b Caudle 10; AN Salter c Page b Attwell 1; BW Worrall c Pearson b Attwell 6; DAJ Carr not out 2. Extras 3. Total 157 (44.3 overs).

Tewkesbury: L Berryman c Smart b Worrall 9; G Haines c Morley b Salter 0; C Burd b Worrall 0; A Collins c Morley b Salter 2; G Page lbw b Worrall 2; R Pearson c Reed b Salter 6; F Stillwell not out 52; J Martin b Worrall 2; A Attwell not out 25. Extras 5. Total 103 for 7 wkts.
Worrall 19-3-33-4, Salter 15-7-17-3, Newman 4-0-21-0, Morley 2-0-5-0, Carr 2-0-6-0.

Winget II Defeated

In reply to Tewkesbury's 117, Winget II were 61-1 and then 78-2, but the introduction of spinners Frank Lewis and Graham Goodwin signalled a complete collapse and their innings closed at 113 – just four runs short!
Stan Phelps and Alan Causon got the innings off to a sound start before Phelps was bowled after a 67-minute innings which brought him 43 runs.
John Bingham bowled exceptionally well for Winget and dismissed half of the Tewkesbury side for just 35 runs off 16 overs.

Tewkesbury: 117-8 (40 overs) (T. Crisp 54, N Walford 16; Bingham 5035, Corbett 2-28, Webb (A.E) 1-23).

Winget II 113 (S.G. Phelps 43; A. Causon 18, J. Bingham 10; Lewis 6-12, Goodwin 4-31).

Sunday 24th May -Pellant Century

Geoff Pellant hit a magnificent unbeaten century to help set the stage for an exciting Bank Holiday encounter against Headington – a new team on Winget's list who stepped into the gap caused by Oxford's cancellation on Friday evening. At the close the visitors were 179-8, only nine runs short of victory. Batting first, Winget soon lost the wicket of Ken Newman who was caught, but fellow opener Stan Phelps and Pellant proceeded to put the 50 up in 58 minutes until at 59, Phelps was bowled. Skipper Roy Morley joined Pellant and they added 128 before Morley was dismissed – the signal for the declaration and tea. Pellant cracked eight boundaries in his century, which arrived in 124 minutes.
The visitors replied in quick time and put the half-century up without loss in 25 minutes. At 65, Alan Bowerman stepped back on his stumps to a ball from Ken Newman – the first of the spinner's six wickets. At 81, Newman took two wickets and spin contained the Headington batsmen until Roger Smith and Mike Crook came together with the score at 138-7.
The pair added 38 before Smith 'left' a ball from Newman that bowled him, but the clock beat them when they were within sight of victory.

Winget 187 for 3 dec (K C Newman c Goodyear b Bishop 2; S G Phelps b Summers 30; G Pellant not out 101; R G Morley c Smith b Goodyear 46, Extras 8, Bishop 9-1-28-1.

Headington 179-8 (A. Bowerman 40, J Smith 37, J Hatwell 17, R Smith 33, M Crook 22, Salter 12-0-42-0, Carr 6-0-24-0, Newman 19-3-47-6, Read 7-0-27-0, Morley 5-0-29-2).

Saturday 31st May - Morley in form for Winget

With their first five batsmen back in the pavilion for 99, skipper Roy Morley and Jones cracked 81 runs in an unbeaten sixth wicket stand for Winget at the Sports Ground, 81 of the runs coming in just 39 minutes. Morley, who had earlier shared a third wicket stand with Geoff Pellant which added 37 runs, hit three boundaries and Jones hit four, but the two batsmen ran well between the wickets to keep the runs flowing freely. When Thornbury replied Tony Salter struck two early blows, but then a defiant third wicket stand between Graham Parks and Dave Grace added 50 before Parks became the first of Morley's three victims. Newman shared the attack at the other end, and between them they spun the Thornbury innings to a close.

Saturday 4th July - Winget win off last ball

It could be coincidence, but each time Cheltenham are involved in a Severn Counties' League encounter, a controversy rages over a decision. The game at the Sports Ground was no exception. Skipper Roy Morley was adjudged lbw at a vital stage when he and Ken Jones were set to lead their team to victory, though justice was finally done and the win shot Winget up into third place in the league below Gloucester and Hereford.

Off the last over Winget needed five to win. Jones hit the second ball for three and Brian Worrall hammered the last ball of the game for four, to gain Winget their first Severn Counties victory.

Cheltenham: D W J Brown b Corbett 35; R S Midway c Jones b Worrall 50; N C Furlet c Pellant b Corbett 0; C Smith c Phelps b Salter 18; M Adams b Salter 2; S K Hansford b Salter 14; CJK Coley not out 24; M Finch b Salter 6; D F Locke c Pellant b Salter 0; B J Edrich not out 1; extras 15; total (for 8 wickets) 165. A D Lawrie did not bat. Fall of wickets: 75, 81, 105, 108, 132, 143, 159, 159. Worrall 14-1-64-1, Salter 22-5-46-5, Corbett 9-0-40-2.

Winget: S G Phelps run out 23; EJF Stephens c Coley b Finch 29; G Pellant c Hansford b Locke 9; R G Morley lbw b Finch 37; G S Hale c Finch b Locke 7; K C Newman c Adams b Brown 1; K Jones not out 39; L Smart c Adams b Lawrie 13; A B Salter c Coley b Finch 0; W B Worrall not out 8; extras 11; total (for 8 wkts) 168. J J Corbett did not bat. Fall of wickets: 29, 54, 54, 66, 73, 124, 130, 157.

Monday 3rd August - Newman and Pellant get half centuries

Ken Newman and Geoff Pellant each hit a half-century for Winget in their annual match against touring Surrey Oakers. They came together with the score at 31-2 and added 88 for the third wicket, the stand being dominated by the hard-hitting innings of Pellant who cracked seven boundaries in his score.

It was insufficient for victory however, and Winget had to be content with a draw after Newman had anchored the innings in his knock which took him 106 minutes.

The tourists had generally enjoyed success against the Winget attack until Brian Worrall returned for a second spell which brought him three wickets in nine balls including the vital fifth wicket of Peter Jones which halted a partnership that had added 53 with Dave Astle.
Surrey Oakers 164 for 8 dec
Worrall 9-0-35-3; Salter 8-2-21-1; Newman 16-1-49-0; Morley 17-2-49-4
Winget 142 for 6

Monday 31st August

On this day, Gary Sobers, who in later years was to become Sir Garfield Sobers, arguably the world's finest all-rounder, hit six sixes in one over to create a world record. Playing for Nottinghamshire against Glamorgan at Swansea, he hit Malcolm Nash, the Glamorgan spin bowler, for six consecutive sixes.

*In the late 1970's Winget 'A' defeated Winget 'B' in the semi final of the
Gloucester six a side competition, and went on to win the final.
Winget 'A': A Salter E Stephens C Thomas M Jones J Taylor K Newman
Winget 'B': T Shaw R Hopkins A Hawkes C Mills C Matthews R Allen*

1971

Saturday 12th June - Less Than A Run An Over

Old Cryptians bowled 59 overs in 135 minutes at the Sports Ground and the Winget innings closed five minutes before tea for just 58 runs.

After 18 overs Winget were 5-1 and Ian Arthurs' nine overs had been bowled without a run being conceded. He finished with the amazing return of 29-17-20-5.

Roy Morley batted throughout the innings and scored over half of Winget's total as wickets fell regularly at the other end.

Eric Stephens was caught at deep extra cover off Morley's first over, but although losing two further wickets, Old Cryptians hit off the required runs in 45 minutes.

Winget							Old Cryptians						
S G Phelps	c	Knights	b	Arthurs		2	E J Stephens	c	Hale	b	Morley		2
R G Morley	NO					30	A H Jones	c	Phelps	b	Newman		26
G S Hale	st	Howell	b	Lewis		0	J A Bayliss	c	Gurney	b	Salter		17
A Causon	c	Howell	b	Lewis		11	D L Howell	NO					4
A B Salter	c	Lewis	b	Arthurs		4	A Cheeseman	NO					4
K C Newman	c	Jones	b	Arthurs		1							
C Thomas	c	Knights	b	Arthurs		2							
B W Worrall	st	Howell	b	Arthurs		3							
M J Roberts	c	Howell	b	Lewis		0							
C Matthews	c	Jones	b	Lewis		0							
J Gurney	st	Howell	b	Lewis		0							
		Extras		Lewis		5			**Extras**				6
		Total				58			**Total**				59

Howell
Lewis 30-11-33-5
Arthurs 29-17-20-5

Newman 13-4-16-1
Morley 8-2-27-1
Salter 4.1-1-11-1

Saturday 3rd July

Clifford Thomas sees Winget II to League Win

An unbeaten 74 by young Clifford Thomas steered Winget II to their Severn Counties victory at the Sports Ground, where they maintained their 100% record by defeating Cheltenham II by four wickets with three overs to spare.

The young batsman came to the crease after Winget had lost their two openers, John Mansell and Jack Corbett for only 35 runs, but after early indecision over running and calling with Corbett, Thomas settled down to add 72 for the third wicket with Dave Taylor and continued through for an unbeaten contribution that eased Winget II to victory.

Winget were chasing a target of 172 to win and with the score at 18, Mansell was run out to a good return direct throw by John Russ. With the score at 35, Corbett was bowled by off-spinner David Sewell who had been called up to share the attack with opener Derek Sollars, the former Birdlip and Brimpsfield paceman.

Seventy two runs were then added for the third wicket by Thomas and Taylor. Taylor cracked three boundaries before offering a return chance to Sollars in the paceman's first over of his second spell. New batsman Ron Thomas was particularly harsh on Sollars' next over and he was taken off, but the two Thomas's added 28 before Ron was given lbw to Sollars who was brought back two overs later at the other end.

With victory in sight, Glenn Curtis and Tony Webb firmly placed ball to bat as Thomas continued to dominate the innings and the winning runs came with three overs to spare.Thomashaving taken one six and six fours off the attack and finishing with two boundaries off Sewell's last over.

Cheltenham's total was a carefully acquired one with the runs being shared. Ron Johnson and Frank Sewell realised 36 for the first wicket before Johnson, the senior partner, was caught in the slips off Ron Thomas, and then Derek Sollars, displaying his skills with the bat, took the score to 70 before Sewell was run out.

After 20 overs Cheltenham had scored 100 runs for the loss of four wickets, but effective bowling changes by skipper Tony Webb never allowed the opposition to build on this good start and the innings closed with Winget just unable to gain their third bowling point and with Cheltenham four runs short of a third batting point.

Cheltenham II

R Johnson	c	Mansell	b	Thomas	24
F J Sewell	run out				22
D Sollars	lbw			Thomas	34
J T Russ			b	Thomas	0
K Eaglestone	c	Thomas	b	Thomas	49
G Massey	c	Webb	b	Bingham	10
R Self	c	Gurney	b	Bingham	6
D Allan	c	Thomas	b	Curtis	8
F Toughey	not out				11
D Sewell	not out				1
Extras					**6**
Total					**171**

Winget II

J Mansell	run out				10
J J Corbett			b	Sewell	18
D W Taylor	c & b			Sollars	37
C Thomas	not out				74
R W Thomas	lbw			Sollars	15
G I Curtis			b	Sewell	3
A E Webb	run out				9
C Matthews	not out				2
Extras					**8**
Total					**174**

B Bevan did not bat
Fall of wickets 36, 70, 70, 90, 113, 129, 144, 163
Corbett 8-0-22-0
Ablett 4-1-20-0
Thomas (R) 13-2-30-4
Webb 6-1-22-0
Bingham 9-0-35-2
Curtis 7-0-36-1

J Bingham, J Gurney and H Ablett did not bat
Fall of wickets 18, 35, 107, 135, 138, 159
Sollars 15-1-41-2
Bevan 11-0-50-0
Sewell (D) 13-2-56-2
Toughey 3-0-19-0

Winget II (14 pts) beat Cheltenham II (4 pts) by four wickets.

Saturday 10th July - Newman 61 fails to save Winget

Winget's debut in the Gloucestershire 40 over Knock Out competition ended at the Sports Ground yesterday when they were set a target of 212 for victory by the North Gloucestershire club, Bourton Vale. As four wickets fell for 58 runs, Ken Newman and Tony Salter came together in a stand that added 73 for the fifth wicket, but it failed to steer Winget into the semi-final.
Bourton Vale 211 for 5 (D. Essenhigh 49)
Bowling: James 8-0-31-1, Salter 8-0-40-1, Worrall 8-0-31-1, Newman 8-0-38-1, Morley 8-0-50-0
Winget 179 all out (K. Newman 61 NO, A. Salter run out 41, A. Causon 29)
Bowling: Bandiera 8-1-19-3, Hitchman 7.5-0-36-5, Moulder 8-0-37-0, Stevens 8-0-40-1, Essenhigh 7-0-43-0.

Saturday 14th August - Hale steers Winget to victory

After Gloucester City had been dismissed for 80 when choosing to bat at the Sports Ground yesterday, Graham Hale, in defiant mood, resisted the visitors' attack to steer Winget home with an unbeaten half-century.
Howard Ablett shared Winget's opening attack with Tony Salter and together they tied down Gloucester's opening pair of Howard Morgan and Doug Hutchinson. In the eighth over Ablett bowled Hutchinson and five overs later with only three runs added, Gulam Musa was taken at the wicket. In the next over Morgan was caught at second slip and Gloucester were 20-3.
Salter, who had bowled five maidens in his opening ten over spell, was relieved in favour of Archie Carr. The next over brought a further bowling change with Salter returning from the other end. With the score at 36, John Melton was bowled by Ablett and with the wickets of Mike Ashwin and John Davis falling, Joe Stubbs who batted soundly for his contribution, lacked support and the innings closed for 80 off 37 overs.
Left 15 minutes batting before tea, Winget lost Stan Phelps in Roy Bonell's second over, but Graham Hale joined Roy Morley and tea was taken at 3-1. After the break, Gloucester resumed with Bonell and Lapham and Morley fell to a leg-side catch at the wicket off Lapham with the score at 12.
Ken Jones, never looking happy against the pace attack, was bowled round his legs and skipper Ken Newman offered a simple chance to mid on. Winget were 26-4.
In Charlie Matthews, however, Hale found a resolute partner and a partnership of 52 set Winget on the victory path. Matthews, who

was missed twice and survived a difficult leg-side chance at the wicket, was out at 78 and Tony Salter joined Hale in time for the left hander to firmly drive Lapham to the boundary for his half-century and victory.

Saturday 28th August
Unfortunate

Gloucester

Hutchison			b	Ablett	8
Morgan	C	Phelps	b	Ablett	11
Musa	C	Gurney	b	Salter	1
Ashwin	C	Morley	b	Carr	7
Melton			b	Ablett	10
Stubbs			b	Newman	15
Davis	C	Salter	b	Newman	6
Wray	C	Morley	b	Salter	4
Lapham	C	Newman	b	Salter	0
Kibble		Not Out			11
Bonell	C	Salter	b	Newman	3
Extras					**4**
Total					**80**

Winget

Phelps	C	Melton	b	Bonell	2
Morley	C	Davis	b	Lapham	2
Hale		Not Out			53
Jones			b	Bonell	8
Newman	C	Kibble	b	Lapham	0
Matthews			b	Lapham	17
Salter		Not Out			0
Extras					**2**
Total					**84**

Controversy raged at the weekend after a match at the Sports Ground resulted in Hereford losing all chance of depriving Cheltenham of the Severn Counties league title.

The respective captains, Roy Morley of Winget and Hereford's Keith Edwards defended their actions, but nevertheless it was on an extremely unfortunate note that the league season finished.

Hereford needed victory and five batting points to clinch the title as Cheltenham, their programme completed, sat at the top of the table with a 14 point lead.

When Winget won the toss and chose to bat, they had to score sufficient runs to make a 125 total but as the first five wickets fell for 50 runs, the chances became remote.

Impressive sixth and seventh wicket stands between Jack Corbett and Cliff Thomas, and Corbett and Tony Salter, hoisted the score to 111 at which stage both Corbett and Salter, the latter out to a dubious lbw, were dismissed.

Then Winget set a determined path to last out their overs and ignored runs in the process. Contriving to get the necessary runs on the board, Mike Rose delivered four wides and then threatened to bowl underarm. As James was subjected to a doubtful run out, Winget's captain Roy Morley declared at 118-9, denying Hereford any chance of even tying for the title by robbing them of a fourth batting point.

Hereford got the runs with four wickets to spare and five overs remaining, but as both captains argue their particular angle of events, it is hoped that this finish does not impair club relations.

Winget

E J Stephens		b Rose	1
A Causon	c Davies	b Rose	33
R G Morley	c Symonds	b Davies	7
G S Hale		b Rose	2
J J Corbett		b Rose	25
K Jones	c Symonds	b Rose	4
C Thomas	c / lbw Hayward	b Rose	13
A B Salter		b Rose	23
B W Worrall		Jenkins	2
M James		Not Out	0
J Gurney		Run Out	0
		Not Out	
Extras			**8**
Total			**118**

Hereford

A Powell	c Gurney	b Salter	12
E Morgan		b Worrall	14
M Peek		b Worrall	17
E Jenkins		Run Out	37
M Hayward	c Gurney	Worrall	8
M Rose		Morley	18
T Goodwin		Not Out	4
R Jenkins		Not Out	1
Extras			**8**
Total			**119**

Davies 11-2-22-1
Rose 20.3-4-42-7
Edwards 1-0-0-0
Goodwin 3-0-22-0
E Jenkins 4-0-24-0
R Jenkins 2-2-0-1

Worrall 15-5-39-3
Salter 10-3-33-1
Morley 10-0-21-1
James 5-0-18-0

Hereford (13 pts): Winget (2 pts)

The outcome of this match was that later, the league committee decided to award Hereford the batting points and so win the league. For the record, had the Hereford side played in the right spirit playing orthodox cricket and not bowling underarm etc., theymay well have won the match legitimately.

Gary Sobers and Mike Procter meet Gloucestershire supporter Mrs Edith Haverson of Churchdown at the County Festival in 1971

Winget CC. 1st X1 1971
Standing: T.Salter C.Thomas A.Causon K.Jones K.Newman A.Salter L.Smart R.Holl
Sitting: B.Worrall G.Hale R.Morley (capt) E.Stephens Mrs.D.Salter

Winget C.C. 2nd X1 1971
J.Corbett D.Carr H.Ablett R.Hayes D.Wilson G.Curtis Mrs.V.Holl M.Turner
M.Roberts J.Gurney A.Webb (capt) P.Lamb J.Mansell

1972

Saturday 1st July

Winget II trounce Lydney II

Dave Taylor and Ken Jones set up a good win for Winget II at Lydney, where they maintained their leadership of Division Two of the Three Counties League.

After skipper Archie Carr and Alan Causon had both been dismissed at 31 runs, Dave Taylor became associated with Ken Jones in a partnership that reached three figures before Lydney gained their first bowling point.

The pair added 69 with Taylor dominating the stand as he made his way towards a splendid half-century. He was eventually sixth out, but had eased Winget within sight of their second batting point at 143. With Steve Miel taking two wickets with successive balls in his last over, Lydney gained a third bowling point before the 45 overs were complete.

The dismissal of veteran Bill Stone gave Winget early joy, but Nigel Hooks and Ken Pugh added 33 runs before being parted. Having gained the breakthrough, Winget maintained control and Lydney's remaining wickets fell for just 38 runs.

Winget II 161-9 – D W Taylor 54, K Jones 29, M Lay 12 not out; Hart 2-24, Miel 4-28, Gifford 2-4.
Lydney II 78 – K Pugh 26, N Hooks 19, A Jones 13; Jones 1-19, Carr 3-21, Causon 1-4, Featherstone 1-20, Wilson 4-2.

Saturday 8th July - Winget 19 runs short of target

Winget were given 91 minutes and a churned-up pitch to get 136 runs for victory over Cheltenham at the Sports Ground on Saturday. But time ran out on them and, by the close, they were 19 runs short. The start was delayed for an hour while the pitch dried and Cheltenham, winning the toss, decided to make first use of it.

Cheltenham: D Brown 1, J Goode 3, R Falconer 73 not out, L Edrich 4, M Adams 19, P Knight 2, C Coley 27 not out., Extras 6. Total 135 for 5 dec.
Worrall 14-5-32-3, Salter 11-3-37-1, Wray 8-2-31-1, Morley 5-0-29-0.
Winget: S Phelps 0, K Newman 3, G Hale 17, J Corbett 33, R Morley 33 A Sadler 15, K Jones 11 not out, A Salter 2, L Wray 1 not out, Extras 2. Total 117 for 7.
Rutter 10-3-23-2, Finch 5-1-19-0, Brown 7-1-31-3, Edmunds 5-0-30-0, James 2-1-12-1.

Match drawn.

Saturday 29th July - Sadler hits 77

All season Winget have searched for an opening batsman, and in Tony Sadler they seemed to have found their man. After hitting a splendid innings against Knebworth Park during the week, he was again in form against Tewkesbury at the Sports Ground.

He lost his opening partner Stan Phelps off the first ball of the innings when Phelps was caught at the wicket, but he saw the half-century up in a second wicket stand with Jack Corbett. He added considerably to Winget's efforts in partnerships with Eric Stephens and skipper Roy Morley, steering Winget to two batting bonus points before being run out within three runs of a third.

Winget 186-7 – A Sadler 77 not out, J Corbett 35, E Stephens 20, R Morley 25, K Newman 16 not out.
Tewkesbury 169-6 – C Burd 36, L Berryman 28 not out
Bowling: - Worrall 16-5-21-1, Wray 12-1-33-2, Newman 10-1-41-0, Morley 7-0-58-1.

Winget II knocked off top

Winget II were knocked from the top of the second division of the Three Counties League when they failed to meet the 205 target set by Tewkesbury, whose innings was built on an opening stand of 121 between Francis Stilwell and Geoff Haines.

Tewkesbury II

F Stilwell	c Reed	b Ablett	92
G Haines		b Taylor	68
G Goodwin	c Taylor	b Ablett	14
J Doran		Not Out	20
V Foster	c Karadia	Ablett	0
R Blakeman		Not Out	4
Extras			6
Total			204

Winget II

D A J Carr	c Martin	b Lewis	34
H E Reed	c Price	b Lewis	33
C Matthews	St Cartwright	b Lewis	13
D W J Taylor	c Haines	b Lewis	15
J Taylor		Not Out	22
D Wilson		Run Out	18
P Holford		b Goodwin	0
L Karadia		Not Out	0
Extras			5
Total			130

Ablett 9-0-43-3
Karadia 14-3-45-0
Carr 8-0-38-0
J Taylor 11-1-49-1
Wilson 3-0-23-0

Green 9-2-18-0
Price 6-0-24-0
Martin 10-1-22-0
Lewis 14-0-46-4
Foster 3-0-9-0
Goodwin 3-1-6-1

Monday 7th August

Shock for Winget before victory

After dismissing the touring Surrey Oakers for 55, Winget's task at the Sports Ground yesterday seemed little more than a formality, but their innings started in sensational manner with the Oakers' opening paceman on a hat-trick with his first three deliveries.

Peter Smith the Robinswood Hill captain, who has now joined Winget for his Saturday cricket, opened with John Mansell, and without offering a stroke Smith was bowled by the first ball. New batsman Roy Morley was lbw to the first ball he received, putting Mike Richardson on a hat-trick.

Eric Stephens joined Mansell and was lucky to survive a chance at slip off his first ball preventing the hat-trick. Having done so, however, he shared a half-century partnership with Mansell and Winget were within four runs of victory when Stephens was out.

Surrey Oakers

K Thomas	c Mansell	b Worrall	4
A Giles	c Smith	b Salter	0
K Berrington	c Stephens	b Webb	35
P P Jones	c Shaw	b Salter	0
P Smith		b Worrall	1
N Turk	c Morley	b Wray	6
G Charman	c Smith	b Wray	6
M Richardson	Smith	Wray	1
E Wood	Run Out		0
D Stacey	Run Out		0
T Scannell	Not Out		0
Extras			2
Total			55

Winget

P J Smith			b Richardson
J Mansell		Not Out	
R G Morley	lbw		b Richardson
E J F Stephens	c Thomas	Smith	
G S Hale		Not Out	
Extras			
Total			

SUNDAY XI AVERAGES 1972

PLAYED 19: WON 9, LOST 4, DRAWN 3, ABANDONED 3

BATTING

	Inns	Not out	Highest Score	Total	Average
R Morley	17	5	70*	573	46.92
A Salter	16	2	93	422	30.14
S Phelps	16	3	53	381	29.31
G Hale	15	1	54	290	20.71
K Newman	17	2	65	272	18.13
C Matthews	9	1	30	93	11.63
B Worrall	10	4	25*	66	11.00
A Webb	11	3	18	79	9.88
L Wray	9	1	7	19	2.38

BOWLING

	Overs	Maidens	Runs	Wkts	Average
A Salter	114.5	33	253	23	11.00
L Wray	57	14	125	10	12.50
B Worrall	101	25	339	24	14.13
R Morley	75	7	302	21	14.38
A Webb	73	5	295	19	15.53
K Newman	81.3	6	323	17	19.00

CATCHES

K Newman 9, J Gurney 8 + 4 stumpings, G Hale 8 + 2 stumpings, A Salter 8, S Phelps 7, R Morley 6, A Webb 4, K Jones 4, L Wray 3, A Causon 2, B Worrall 2, M Lay 2, C Matthews 1, S Karadia 1.

1973

Saturday 5th May - Winget v. Hatherley & Reddings

Stan Phelps and Roy Morley shared a century stand for the second wicket at the Sports Ground against Hatherley and Reddings. Filling the breach for Hatherley, who were without a couple of their established players were two youngsters, Richard Stuart and David Stanton, but neither posed Winget's batsmen any problems although Stuart initially contained the run rate reasonably well.

After just 10 overs the left arm spinner Chris Sumner, who claimed the two wickets to fall, came on to bowl. After being hit for 6 by Ken Jones, Sumner bowled him the next ball with the score at 47, while his second wicket came in the first over of his second spell when he bowled opener Phelps to end a second wicket stand that had added 128 runs. Phelps hit 2 fours in his 140-minute innings, whilst Morley hit one 6 and 6 fours.

Winget called on seven bowlers in their bid for victory, but although Hatherley never threatened to get in reach of their target, they held on to finish at 111-9 to deny the home side a win.

Saturday 15th May - Winget II v. Thornbury II

Taking 7 for 24 off 15.4 overs, Levi Wray was mainly responsible for the dismissal of Thornbury II at the Sports Ground, but Winget II suffered several stormy moments before they inched to a 3 wicket win with Wray hammering a fine unbeaten 32 to get them home. Openers Alan Park (21) and John Gillespie (15), together with Ted Wilde (15) and No. 10 Dave Browning (19 not out), were the visitors' main contributors while Keith Featherstone with his slow left arm spin took 2-39 and Harold Reed 1-14.

With Eric Stephens in his usual aggressive mood, the opening partnership with Alan Causon put on 31 runs off the first 3 overs before Stephens was out for 17. Causon 11, Reed 8 and Dave Taylor then progressed cautiously before victory came in the 30th over.

Saturday 5th June - Pressed Steel Oxford II v. Winget II

In a game that produced nearly 400 runs, Winget II drew at Pressed Steel. The home side had declared at 217 for 3 off 47 overs - and at 4.5 runs an over it was a giant challenge for the visitors. Against an attack without the recognised front line partnership, seven bowlers toiled as Tony Mitchell and Alan Parsons shared in a century opening stand, the onslaught continuing even after they were dismissed.

In their reply, Winget lost Charlie Matthews with only 21 runs scored, but undeterred they kept their eyes firmly fixed on their target with Cliff Thomas in resounding form and determined mood. He hit 3 sixes and 9 fours in a splendid innings that ended in the penultimate over, though even if Thomas had remained, the target would eventually have proved too great for the Gloucester side.

Pressed Steel   217 for 3   Winget   172 for 5.

Monday 14th June --Gloucester Citizen Report

Gloucestershire start their County Cricket Championship match against Essex on Saturday to open their Gloucester Cricket Festival Week, and it will be the fiftieth year that they have been playing on the ground. Winget Sports Ground's records show it was in early June 1923 that the County played their last match on the Gloucester Spa Ground and immediately moved for their next game to the ground, then known as the Wagon Works, where Lancashire were the visitors.

Saturday 26th June - Winget II Share Fifth Place

With John Mansell hitting a splendid unbeaten 66, Winget II beat Worcester II by seven wickets to topple the Midlanders from top spot in the 2nd Division of the Three Counties League and move up to share 5th place. Mansell hit six boundaries in his total and shared in an opening stand with Charlie Matthews that added 34. Winget hit the runs off in 35.1 overs. Previously Worcester II had fallen for 104 with Tony Webb taking 5-26. Howard Ablett 2-15, D Witter 2-16 and Archie Carr 1-14 claimed the other wickets. The second wicket, that of Peter Rushforth, fell in amazing fashion. Pulling a ball to leg, the ball struck Winget skipper Archie Carr on the head and rebounded for wicket keeper Dave Taylor to hold the catch.

Saturday 3rd July - Winget II Move Into 2nd Place

Lydney II have been clinging to the top of the 2nd division of the Three Counties League all season, but at the Sports Ground on Saturday they had their championship hopes rudely shattered when they were dismissed by Winget II for 136, the Gloucester side going on to win by 8 wickets. Winget have now clipped into second place behind Panteg. Two wickets fell for 10 runs in Lydney's innings and the pattern was set, but at 78 for 5 Keith Davler and Cyril Gifford became associated in a partnership that added 37 runs, the batsmen contributing 24 and 45 respectively. Howard Abblet took 4 for 28 and D Witter 3-25, both achieving early breakthroughs before returning to each take two wickets in their second spells.

John Mansell (66) and Charlie Matthews (59) took Winget to within 5 runs of victory before being parted. Mansell hit 7 fours and Matthews reached the boundary 4 times, both batsmen falling to Dave Tunnicliffe who, at fifth change, took 2 for 16 in 3 overs. Winget's win came in 32 overs.

Saturday 21st July - First Win In The League For Winget

In a rain affected game at the Sports Ground where the overs were reduced to 30 each side, Winget gained their first Three Counties League win of the season, successfully chasing a target of 130 with 9 balls to spare.

Winget 133-8; Ross 129-8.

Saturday 25th August Winget Draw At Cirencester

After the pendulum had swung unbelievably against them, youngsters Glyn Worrall and Andy Hawkes saw out 3 overs that enabled Winget to cling on for a draw at the Park against title seeking Cirencester.
With Hereford and Lydney setting a hot pace at the top Cirencester needed a win, but after Tony Frape and Trevor Telling had each claimed a victim with the score at 6, Roy Morley shouldered the responsibility to hold the innings together. Progress was somewhat slow, but at 100-4, there was adequate cause for optimism.
Cirencester recalled Frape to the attack in a bid to contain, but his recall signalled a slump and 5 wickets fell for 8 runs, with Roy Morley caught at the wicket with three overs remaining.
It was then that Worrall and Hawkes faced their test, and came through it well to earn a draw.

Winget   108 for 9 Wickets
Cirencester   140 (Wray 21-6-68-6; Salter 16-1-39-2; Taylor 5-0-24-1).

1974

Saturday 4th May - Winget v Hatherley and Reddings

With 5 wickets for their last 20 Overs in hand, Winget gained a 4 wicket win over Hatherley and Reddings at the Sports Ground after being asked to chase a mammoth target of 205 to win.

Opener Stan Phelps quickly warmed to the task and when he was out after dragging the ball on to his stumps with the score at 29, he had scored all but 6 of the runs. The backbone of Hatherley's innings was provided by Nigel Mills, who was 6th out at 190 after hitting a polished 87 that included seven fours.

Hatherley & Reddings	204 for 7 wickets declared
Winget	205 for 6

Saturday 18th May - Winget Beat Lydney

At the Sports Ground Winget gained victory over Lydney in the Three Counties League Match.

Winget	180 for 9
Lydney	130 for 9

Saturday 15th June - Witney Mills v. Winget

Winget batsman Eric Stephens raced to the fastest century of the season when he hammered 133 against Witney Mills. He was in occupation for 88 minutes and received 72 balls, his century coming in 70 minutes off 58 deliveries. He hit 6 sixes and 13 fours and shared in 3 stands that lifted the score from 24 for 2 to 211 for 5 when he was out.

Winget were in the comfortable position of declaring 20 minutes early with 262 on the board after 130 minutes batting.

Witney Mills were left 135 minutes to get the runs and received 50 overs, but they were 118 for 4 at the close, with Graham Hale using 8 bowlers and seriously contemplating giving the groundsman a bowl.

Winget   263 for 6 declared. Witney Millls 118 for 4. *Match Drawn.*

Saturday 22nd June - Winget win and then lose

Champs for a day. On Saturday night, Winget were top of the league, deserved reward for victory over Worcester the leaders, but after losing to Abergavenny at home on Sunday, Winget slipped back into 3rd position.

Levi Wray ripped through the Worcester innings and had it not been for a determined 4th wicket stand between Terry Rone and Steve Lennox that added 79 runs, the Midlanders would have been humiliated. The other nine batsmen contributed just 22 runs between them and the last six wickets tumbled for just 13.

Worcester were replying to Winget's total of 177, but after losing 5 wickets for 74 runs they relied heavily on their tailenders, particularly Graham Hale and John Taylor who shared a 7th wicket stand of 46.

On Sunday, the boot was on the other foot and Winget were put out for 110 after Abergavenny had reached 182 for 7. Although perhaps they were never up with the clock, Winget started soundly, only to lose their last 6 wickets for the addition of only 37 runs.

Gloucester 20 over Knockout Winners 1974

standing: Mrs D Salter, A Salter, K Jones, K. Newman, D Taylor, J Taylor, S Phelps
kneeling: L Wray, A Webb, G Hale, (Capt), C Matthews, T Shaw

Winget

S G Phelps	c	Istan	b	Aston	8
L Jones		Run Out			13
K C Newman			b	Lennox	0
E J Stephens		Run Out			38
C G Matthews	c	Ridings	b	Istan	13
C Thomas			b	Astan	1
J Taylor	st	Ridings	b	Bertman	36
G S Hale		Run Out			32
A E Webb	c	Ridings	b	Lennox	13
A B Salter		Not Out			17
L Wray		L.B.W.	b	Aston	0
		Extras			**7**
		Total			**177**

Worcester 109
Wray 20-5-51-6
Salter 16-3-21-4
Newman 4-0-29-0

Saturday 29th June - Winget v. Lydney

Skipper Graham Hale, veteran of so many tight situations, faced one of his stiffest tests at the Sports Ground against Lydney - but with a nerve of steel, defied the combined pace of Gordon Sargent and John Morris to inch Winget to a one wicket victory.
Winget were only chasing 91 to win, but in the face of some competitive fielding and accurate bowling on a pitch beginning to dry, they were 62 for 7 when Hale and Tony Webb came together. Fifteen runs were added before Webb gave a chance and with 8 further runs added, Tony Salter offered a chance. Levi Wray, having bowled unchanged with Salter to dismiss Lydney, was left to see things through and the pair put on the requisite runs with Hale striking Sargent to the boundary for the winning hit.

Winget:- S G Phelps (10), K Jones (14), K Newman (0), E Stephens (22), C Matthews (0), C Thomas (8), J Taylor (6), G Hale (17 N.O), A Webb (12), A Salter (1), L Wray (3 N.O).

Lydney:- 90 All Out

Saturday 6th July - Winget v. Colwall

After their 24 hours at the top of the table of the Three Counties League the previous week Winget, with another competent display against Colwall at the Sports Ground, regained top spot. They made only 131 for 9 off their allotted overs, but with tight bowling and an efficient display in the field, they dismissed Colwall for 81.
The feature of Winget's total was another fine innings by Ken Newman. He hit only 3 boundaries, but looking for his shots well, he stretched the field and took intelligent singles to keep the score moving. He was the backbone of 7 partnerships before being 8th out at the score of 115.

Colwall's innings lasted just 36.4 overs with Tony Salter, including 3 L.B.W. decisions, taking 5 wickets in his 19 over spell.

Winget 131 for 9   Colwall 81 All Out

Monday 15th July - Winget Knockout Champions

Winget were restored as Gloucester City knockout champions last night when they beat Stinchcombe Stragglers in the final of the Gloucester Club Cricket Federation Knockout at The Spa. It was a title that they won 2 years ago and previously held in 1965 and 1966. In a nutshell, Winget proved the more competent side in every department - their fielding was sharper, their batting showed more depth and their bowling was more decisive.

Tony Salter took the wickets to win the Man of the Match award, but Levi Wray contributed tremendously to affairs. He found that extra pace from what is a notoriously slow pitch and pegged the batsmen down.
Nevertheless, the issue was inevitably decided by the toss. It was the first time that the Stragglers had been required to bat second, and although only chasing 100 to win they looked strangely out of things after only 4 overs.
They started slowly and left the lower order batsmen too much to do and seeking quick runs, wickets fell. The innings closed with 1 ball remaining and Stinchcombe 20 runs short of victory.

Winget

S Phelps		b	Aston	1
K Jones	c Phillips	b	Smith	18
K Newman		b	Cowley	20
C Matthews	Run Out			23
A Salter		b	Cowley	0
J Taylor		b	Cowley	5
G Hale	Not Out			12
D Taylor	Retired Hurt			3
A Webb		b	Cowley	5
T Shaw	Not Out			1
Extras				**11**
Total for 7 wkts				**99**

Stinchcombe
Stragglers
All Out 80

Saturday 20th July - Winget v. Ross

Apart from a few moments of concern when their early batting temporarily faltered, Winget never relaxed their grip on affairs in the Three Counties League match with Ross, though the visitors fought back doggedly to force a draw.

The workmanlike approach of Ken Jones and skipper Graham Hale produced an encouraging start to the Winget innings, but when they and Ken Newman departed with the total on 41, more forthright remedial measures were demanded.

Fortunately in Eric Stephens, they have the ideal batsman for such occasions. Taking the offensive in the company of Charlie Matthews, Stephens dealt with the situation in his own inimitable style, hitting 3 huge sixes on his way to a scorching half-century. A little less ambitious, Matthews led some valuable middle order contributions that took Winget to the encouraging total of 199.

It was a target that Ross, after initial reserves, had little hope of achieving. Dave Hodges retaliated admirably in the face of adversity, and was distinctively unlucky to be run out when offering some minor threat to Winget's security.

Ross earned 6 points with Winget taking 11.
Winget 199.
Ross 123 for 8.

Monday 29th July

With consummate almost contemptuous ease, Winget added to their honours this season by defeating Cainscross Exiles, the Stroud Area Trophy Winners, by nine wickets to win the Gloucester Strollers Memorial Cup.

The trophy was presented to Graham Hale, the Winget captain, by Bob Madeley, a Vice President of the Gloucester Strollers Cricket Club.

Phelps had six boundaries as his main shots, while Newman, making the winning hit with his third 4, also included a huge straight driven six in his innings.

Cainscross: 86 for 9

Winget:				
	S Phelps		Not out	44
	K Jones	lbw	b Cripps	0
	K Newman		Not Out	39
	Extras			**7**
	Total (for 1 wkt)			**90**

C Matthews, G Hale, C Thomas, J Taylor, A Salter, T Shaw, A Hawkes and L Wray did not bat.

1975

Saturday July 5th - Winget v Colwall

After being nudged off the top of the Three Counties League several weeks ago,Winget regained their first place at Colwall when they successfully bowled out their hosts who have drawn 6 out of 8 games played this term.

At 71-5 after 15 overs , Winget batting first were not in a very comfortable position but thanks to disciplined batting from their middle order,including a patient innings from Eric Stephens, Winget compiled a winning total of 188.

After an early success from John Taylor ,Colwall added runs assiduously and it was only when the off spin of Ken Newman was brought to bear on things that the second break through and important one was gained.Never the less a 4th wicket stand between Ron Godsall and Alan Berry threatened Winget's progress adding 44, but once the stand was broken with the return of Levi Wray to the attack, wickets then started tumbling and Colwall were dismissed for 168.

Phelps	c Berry (J)	b Flint	6	Taylor c - b Berry (A)		30
Jones	c Berry (J)	b Flint	1	Reed c Peddingham	b Flint	23
Newman	c Berry (A)	b Flint	11	Hale lbw	b Berry(A)	13
Matthews lbw		b Hewitt	0	Webb not out		12
Thomas	lbw	b Flint	14	Wray	b Hewitt	3
Stephens c Godsall		b Hewitt	44.	**Extras 21**	**Total**	**188**

Wray 15 - 6 – 39 - 4   Taylor 11 - 1 - 55 - 3   Newman 8 - 1 - 29 - 2

Sunday July 6th   Incredible but true

John Mansell local cricketing veteran scored his maiden century when he reached an unbeaten 102 for Winget II in their run chase against Malmesbury II at the sports ground.

1976

Saturday June 26th - Lydney v Winget

Winget won the battle of tactics in a thrilling finish against Lydney at the Recreation Ground

The result was in the balance until the last over though Lydney had let the opportunity o victory slip away earlier in the game.

Chasing a Winget total of 182 for 6,Lydney played themselves into an excellent position and were well on top of the required run rate.But a change of tactics and the reintroduction of pace bowlers Wray and Pandor brought the home teams downfall.

Lydney,s tail-end batsmen anxious to make the game safe ,played and missed at deliveries and Winget recorded their second success of the season over Lydney .

Winget had found runs difficult to aquire and had scored only 103 in 37 overs But in a final flourish Tony Salter hit 43 not out in 25 balls including a six and six fours .

He was well supported by Cliff Thomas(38)while the early batting had been dominated by Ken Newman(37)and Alan Causon(22)

.

Saturday August 17th - Easy for Winget

Colwall reached 73 and were beaten by 6 wickets.

It was Pandor who was responsible for destroying Colwall .He took 5 for 15 off 11 overs and other wickets fell to the off spin of John Halliday and Ken Newman .John Taylor hit off the required runs without further loss.

Causon	9	Matthews		4
K Jones	7	A Hawkes		5
K C Newman not out	25	J Taylor not out	20
Extras	10	Total for 4 wickets	80

1977

Monday June 27th - Winget v Worcester City

Winget despit losing their opening batsman Allan Causon off the first ballof the match made a good recovery.

Cliff Thomas gave a splendid display of batting and severely punishing anything short of a length .He reached his 50 in 76 minutes which included five boundary strokes .After the mandatory 45 overs Winget reached the respectable total of 187.

Worcester City in their reply after losing their first four wickets for 30 runs made a partial recovery but splendid pace bowling from Jacob Pandor and ASalter effectively stopped the batsmen from securing the run rate per over.

Despite a valiant eighth wicket stand,Winget secured a splendid victory by 73 runs.

A Causon lbw b Rone 0, K Jones b Cole 15 , S Phelps c Rentch b Cole 10, C Thomas run out 54, A Hawkes lbw b Rone 4, DCarr b Copson 6, J Taylor c Pugh b Davies 44, G Hale c Cole b Davies 6, ASalter c Butterworth b Davies 13, Y Pandor not out, J Holliday not out 0. Extras 24 Total(for 9) 187

Y Pandor 18 -5 - 41- 4 ASalter 19 - 8 - 46 - 4 J Halliday 6 - 1 - 0 1 J Taylor 2 - 1 - 7 - 0

Worcester 114 (45 overs)

Winget won by 73 runs

Saturday July 4th - Winget v Lydney

Lydney got off to a good start against Winget at the County Ground

Winget in their reply made light of their task.Ken Jones and G Hale treating the medium pace bowling of Henderson and Tomkins with scant respect and after Hale went, Stan Phielps carried on with some delightful strokes ,being particularly severe on the few loose balls that were offered.

With the dismissal of opener Ken Jones who made 36 runs the highlight of the game was the batting of C Thomas who made a sparkling performance.With Ken Newman in support he went on to an unbeaten 44 which included 3 fours and a six.

The Lydney bowlers toiled hard to contain the Winget batsmen and only Henderson met with any success.

K Jones lbw b Henderson 36, G Hale b Henderson 8, S Phelps lbw b Tomkins 30, C Thomas not out 44, K Newman not out 7. Extras 13

Winget 138 (Total for 3) Y Pandor 8 - 0 - 27 - 0   T Salter 15 - 4 - 37 - 2   J Halliday 14 - 5 - 2- 46 - 4 J Taylor 7- 2 -7- 2

Lydney 136

1978

Saturday 2nd June - Winget finished best

Winget entertaining Abergavenny at the Sports Ground found the playing conditions favourable and they made an excellent start with Ken Jones displaying some fine strokes,and he reached his 50 after only 87 minutes play. He was ably assisted by John Dowdeswell and they put on over 100 for the second wicket.

After Jones had been dismissed for 65 the later batsmen made useful contributions and aftr they compiled the useful total of 166 runs.

Despite Abergavenny being without two of their best bowlers they stuck to their task.

They made a steady start but Y Pandor with his fast medium deliveries played havoc with the first four batsmen and they were soon struggling ,and falling short of the run rate required for victory.The later batsmen fell easy victims to the spin bowling of John Taylor and Winget were well worthy of a winning draw.

K Jones 65, A Hawkes 1, J Dowdeswell 45, J Taylor 17, C Thomas 7, K Newman 0, S Phelps 18,A Salter 4, G Hale not out 1, Y Pandor not out 1.   Extras 8

Winget   166 for 8

Abergavenny 117 for 9

Saturday July 19th - Winget v Tewkesbury

Tewkesbury belied their lowly placed position in the Three Counties League table when they met Winget at the Sports Ground. Winget started shakily but a 3rd wicket stand by Ken Jones and Ken Newman producing 60 runs ,paved the way for a winning total but on their dismissal they fell behind in the run rate required.

C Thomas was unfortunately run out when batting confidently and it was left to to D Carr who set about bowling with good effect ably assisted by Y Pandor and the winning hit was made in the last over.

J Mansell 6, E Stephens 16, K Jones 34, K Newman 33, G Hale 6, C Thomas 11, J Taylor 5, D Carr 37, Y Pandor 9, J Gurney did not bat.   Extras 8

Tewkesbury 164

Winget   165

1979

Saturday 30th June - Winget v Lydney

Winget showed improved form and beat Lydney convincingly at the sports ground by 6 wickets.
They made light work of the task and except for losing Stan Phelps and Robert Hopkins cheaply Ken Newman took charge and runs flowed from his bat.Eric Stephens entertained with a whirlwind display ,for in the space of 6 overs which included 3 boundary strokes and 2 sixes reached 35 runs.
Ken Newman was undefeated with 77 runs to his credit at close of play and Winget were victors by 6 wickets.
S Phelps 5, K Newman 77, R Hopkins.6, E Stephens 35, J Dowdeswell 18, A Hawkes 10, Extras 7
Y Pandor 18 - 2 - 38 - 0, M Jones 16 - 4 - 39 - 3, K Newman 6 - 0 -35 - 1, L Wray 5 - 0 - 33 – 4.
Winget 158 for 4 wickets
Lydney 154 for 9 wickets

Saturday July 7th - Winget v Colwall

After asking Colwall to bat Winget successfully chased their target with 4 balls to spare and 2 wickets in hand.
Wingets opening attack of Pandor and Jones struck two early blows before openers Alan Terry and Roger Crump blunted the attack with a third wicket stand that added 37.
From then Winget maintained the whip hand as Ken Newman and Levi Wray supplemented the attack.
Newman and Levi Wraysupplemented the attack . Newman in particular bowled well and conceded only 26 runs off 9 overs.
Winget lost openers for one but gradually the innings built upinto a challenging total through some challenging middle order batting.With John Mansell providing the backing after the loss of two quick wickets,Winget crept to victory with 4 balls remaining.

Colwall 163 for 6
Winget 166 for 8

Saturday July 21st - Winget v Ross

Wlinget showed the true depth of their batting with a score of 237-5 and the feature of the total was an innings of 79 from Cliff Thomas .He came to the crease after the opening stand between Stan Phelps and Ken Newman had added 64 and proceeded to demoralise the attack with a series of powerful shots all round the wicket,bringing him seven foursand three sixes.
Phelps fell at 78 and without addition Eric Stephens was run out.It was then Alan Hawkes who picked up the theme and revelled in the spirit of the thing ,adding 112 for the fourth wicket before falling. Thomas went on 211 and Winget surged forward ,taking every run available to reach a formidable total.
It was Newman who then plotted Ross's defeat .Bowling unchanged, he picked up seven wickets as the home side were dismissed for 183. Winget however had some rather anxious moments before victory was their's and Ross,s captain became Newman's sixth victim.

S G Phelps 34, K Newman 36, C Thomas 79, E Stephens 0, A Hawkes 49, R Hopkins 19, C Mansell 8
Extras 12

Pandor 13 - 3 - 45 – 1, Newman 21.5 - 2 - 79 – 7   Wray 5 -1- 23 – 2   Jones 5 – 0 - 25 – 0
Winget   237 for 5 wickets (innings closed)
Ross   183

1980-89

The 1980s proved to be a very significant and exciting period in the club's history.

The flow of players from the Works was reducing alarmingly, coinciding with the uncertain employment situation. Apprenticeships were a thing of the past, so young players were not forthcoming from that source. The players who had served the club during the 1960s and 1970s were either coming to the end of their careers, or were moving away to seek alternative employment. The club that had been virtually a closed shop for Works' employees now needed to find new blood in order to survive.

Winget had enjoyed only moderate success in the Three Counties League during the 1970s and apart from finishing runners up in the first division in 1972 and 1974, never really threatened the dominance of Hereford and Worcester City who monopolised the league in terms of championships won.

Some very talented players such as Ken Newman, Tony Salter, Ken Jones, Stan Phelps, Roy Morley and Graham Hale had served the club well for many years, but new young blood was needed to support the likes of John Taylor, Charlie Matthews, Cliff Thomas, Andy Hawkes, John Dowdeswell and Mark Jones who were now the backbone of the side.

The decade opened disastrously with both first and second teams finishing bottom of their respective divisions in the league. Respectability was achieved in 1981 with both sides finishing mid table. Winget also had its first local cup success for some time, winning the Gloucester six a side competition. Tony Salter had taken on the first team captaincy with Graham Hale leading the seconds.

New players started to arrive at the club in 1982 and 1983 and mid table league positions were maintained. Paul Carter was a notable new young arrival and he quickly showed signs of the talent that was to establish him as an all rounder feared by all other clubs in the area. Other new arrivals at this time included Tony Tetley, Tony Sadler, Bob Owen, Dave Page, Roger Nicholls, Mike Powell, the Tegg family and the self-styled "Prince" of Zanzibar – Mustapha Nasser. Love him or loathe him (and many people did both), you could not deny his cricketing ability. You certainly could not fail to notice he was around! He arrived with his talented sibling, Noorali, who was not quite as vociferous a character as his older brother!

The Gloucester 20 over knockout and six-a-side competitions were both won in 1983 and also at the first attempt, the Peter Richards Cup. This was a fifteen, eight ball over evening knockout competition played in regional rounds, followed by semi finals between the winners of the Gloucester, Stroud, Cheltenham and Tewkesbury areas. Slad Exiles were defeated at Stroud, then in an exciting and tense final played at Cheltenham Cricket Club, a hard fought last over victory against Cirencester was secured to win a superb trophy and a much welcomed cash prize.

On the 23 August,the Gloucester Citizen reported :

Another trophy for Winget as...
Salter lifts the gloom

Winget overcame the gathering gloom, a collapse in the excitable 80's and Cirencester's total of 107– 7 to climax a wonderful season of cup hunting with the Peter Richards Cup last night. They added the Richards overall title to the Gloucester area title, the Jaco Twenty Over Knockout Cup and the Western Trust six-a-side trophy. The only cup to elude them this season was the Three Counties six-a-side where they could only manage the runners-up spot! Before a slightly disappointing crowd at Cheltenham's Victoria Ground, Cirencester captain Dick Tugwell won the toss and chose to bat first in this all Three Counties League clash. Their approach was slow but steady against an accurate attack and keen fielding. Tugwell reached a painstaking 54 in the last over before he was out off the last ball and none of his colleagues were able to take the bowling by the scruff of the neck. Levi Wray claimed 2-38, Dave Page 1-15, Paul Carter 1-24 and John Taylor 1-24 in a good all round display.

Winget's reply began in rapidly deteriorating light as heavy storm clouds gathered. And they made the worst possible start, as spinner Essenhigh had Tony Sadler brilliantly stumped down the leg side in the first over. Despite some quicksilver fielding by the young Cirencester fielders, Eric Stephens, with some belligerent and characteristic hitting, and the more fluent Cliff Thomas began to push the score along. Stephens fell at 29, but Mustapha Nasser joined Thomas in a prolific stand which ended when Thomas fell for a well composed 38. The big hitting John Taylor departed at 85-4 and the 12th over proved to be the most dramatic of the match, after a vital *missed* catch off the first ball *faced* by Tony Salter. The rangy Montague had Mustapha Nasser caught for 21 at 87. Andy Hawkes played all round one and was bowled one run later, and the promising Carter had his stumps moved by a ball that clipped the top of his leg on the way through. This left Winget reeling at 88-7, the light getting worse and only three overs left to get 21. Salter threw caution aside as easily as he threw his bat, and with 18 not out, won the game with two boundaries in the last over. In Roger Allen, he found an unflustered partner who held things together after the collapse. Winget took the handsome trophy plus the £600 prize with £300 going to the losers. Gloucestershire chairman Don Perry gave the man of the match award to Tugwell for his patient innings. The competition was a huge success with more than 100 clubs taking part in the four regional competitions.

Peter Richards Cup Final 1983

Cirencester

D Durston	c Carter	b Page		5
R Tugwell	c Allen	b Wray		54
P Sykes	b Carter			7
D Essenhigh	run out			15
J Turton	b Taylor			0
M Greener	run out			5
D Frape	c Hawkes	b Wray		4
A Lockey	not out			10

Extras 6   Total for 7 wickets   107

Winget

A Sadler	s	Frape	b	Essenhigh	0
E Stephens	c	Montague	b	Essenhigh	18
C Thomas	c	Tugwell	b	Darsley	38
M Nasser	c	Frape	b	Montague	3
J Taylor		v	b	Frape	3
N Salter		not out			18
PCarter			b	Montague	0
R Allen		not out			4

Extras 9   Total for 7 wickets   111

1984 saw Winget back in The Three Counties honours when the second eleven finished runners up.The first eleven finished sixth . The Gloucester six- a- side was retained, though there was defeat in the overall semi final of the Peter Richards Cup ,having once again winning the Gloucester area final.

 John Taylor was captain of the first eleven in 1985 and Eric Stephens took over the seconds.Both sides finished runners up in their respective leagues,with each failing by less than half a point average to take top spot.The end of season league averages had their fair share of Winget names in them with Carter,Sadler and Nasser prominent in the first eleven batting and Salter high up in the bowling.Paul Carter took a hat trick against Corsham.Steve Tegg Ken Jones and Roger Nicholls showed well in the second eleven batting and Charlie Matthews,Bob Hopkins and Levi Wray were well up in the bowling.The first eleven finished runners up in theGloucester 20 over knockout competition and once again the Peter Richards cup, now renamed the Knightsbridge cup .was won .The overall final was played at Tuffley Avenue against Stinchcombe Stragglers and a young Colin Tetley featured in an exciting victory that once again increased the bank balance.

1986 saw both sides slip back to mid table league positions and Tony Sadler had now taken on the first eleven captaincy. Phil Smith had joined the club and quickly established a reputation for hard hitting and deadly throwing.He scored a massive 132 Usk against Usk seconds and an unbeaten 122 a week later against Panteg.
He went on to finish top of the Three Counties second division batting averages .

The 20 over knockout was won and Winget supplied both sides in the final of the six-a-side competition.Alan Pugh stepped down as club secretary ,a post he had held since1974,but continued as fixture secretary for another season .He had served in this position with only a two year break since 1961.

With playing membership soaring ,a third eleven was formed under the captaincy of Mike Powell in 1987.This was to prove a significant factor in the second eleven becoming Three Counties second division champions and contributed to the overall club success during the following years by supplying good players during heavy holiday periods.The first eleven finished fourth in division one with Tony Tetley taking fifty four wickets with his looping,bewildering leg spin .Bob Owen benefited tremendously from Tetley's guile and fight with 12 stumpings,most of which were taken while the batsmen were pondering whether to hit the ball for six or four !

The second team success in winning the league was achieved with only one defeat and the emerging talent of Jon Tegg was significant. Scoring five hundred runs and claiming fifteen victims behind the wicket, he showed signs of things to come. Fast approaching veteran status, Cliff Thomas topped the batting averages, while new arrival Andy Adams showed much promise and Colin Lewis, another new face, led the bowling. The newly formed third eleven finished a creditable fifth in division three of the GCCF League. The twenty over knockout competition was retained with the first eleven defeating the second eleven in the final. This was also the case in the six-a-side final and the club was now dominating the local cricket scene.

Under the guidance of new secretary Bob Owen, the club organised a highly successful cricket week in July and played a game every day against touring and local representative teams. The playing side of the club was backed by a very successful and hard-working ladies' committee and Winget quickly gained a reputation for supplying one of the best teas in the league. The end of season presentation evenings at this time were always well supported, with well over a hundred guests attending on an annual basis.

The momentum was maintained during the 1988 season. The first eleven came agonisingly close to winning the first division under new captain Nasser, eventually finishing as runners up and it appeared that the side was destined to always be the bridesmaid, never the bride! The seconds retained their champion status and the thirds did well, continuing to supply the senior sides with able replacements such as Clive Pattenden, John Dix and Steve Wilson. The local cup success was restricted to runners up in the six-a-side competition, while the cricket week continued to flourish. In September the club entertained a Gloucestershire County side in aid of Andy Brassington's benefit. Well known names such as Graveney, Lawrence and Russell mingled with the likes of Nasser, Owen, Hawkes and Carter, an honour for them indeed. The decade came to a close with a complete turnaround from the way it opened and the reward for years of hard work finally arrived in 1989.

The 1st eleven captaincy reverted back to the cunning and sometimes extrovert John Taylor. He was never afraid to try the unexpected and nearly always had the opposition wondering what he was thinking and what he would do next. His own players even found themselves in that position sometimes! His reward came with the side winning its first ever league division one title by the massive margin of 2.5 average points. The league averages that year read like a "who's who" of Winget Cricket Club with no less than six batsmen and five bowlers in the honours list.

The second team, under new captain Cliff Thomas, made it a club double with their third consecutive title. Andy Adams, Clive Pattenden and Thomas himself were the top three players in the league batting statistics, all averaging over fifty. Pattenden scored a massive 967 runs and was very unlucky not to be given the Second Division Player of the Year award. Dave Carter, younger brother of Paul, topped the league bowling averages as for the third year running, Winget pushed Frocester's 2nd XI into second place. At the league presentation evening, held at Hatherley Cricket Club, Winget's large attendance at the event was remarked upon by league President John Chadd, when he thanked the club for allowing others present to attend their celebration. It was a wonderful sight to see John Taylor and Cliff Thomas holding the trophies aloft, backed by so many players and supporters. The third eleven finished near the top of their league but were just unable to gain promotion and local cup success returned when the twenty over knockout was won and once again both finalists in the six-a-side competition were from Winget CC.

So, quite a decade! It started with the club at rock bottom, and finished with Winget sitting proudly at the top of the Three Counties Leagues and dominating the local cup competitions. It was an amazing change in fortunes that left everyone at the club looking forward with hope and anticipation to the nineties.

Head Groundsman John Taylor and Mark Jones preparing for another
Gloucester Cricket Festival at Tuffley Avenue in the early 1980's.

1981

Saturday 6th June Winget v Panteg

	Played on the sports ground
Panteg:	122 for 4
Winget:	126 for 7 (Eric Stephens 46)

Saturday 13 June Winget v Colwell

	At Colwell
Winget:	148 all out (Ken Newman 64)
Colwall:	149 for 7 (Ken Newman 4-43)

Saturday 20 June Winget v Usk

	Played on the sportsground
Usk:	102 for 9 (Salter 5-32)
Winget:	107 for 4

Saturday 27 June Hatherley and Reddings v Winget

	At Hatherley and Reddings
Hatherley:	187 for 9
Winget:	153

	At the sports ground
Winget II:	108
Hatherley II:	89

Saturday 4 July Winget v Abergavenny

	At the sports ground
Abergavenny:	120 for 9
Winget:	121 for 7 (John Taylor 30)

Saturday 11 July Winget v Stinchcombe Stragglers

	At the sports ground
Winget:	169 for 8
Stinchcombe:	109 for 7

Saturday 25 July Lydney v Winget

Winget chased 214 for 6 at Lydney. Ken Newman opened with 48, though Eric Stephens was soon back in the pavilion. Trevor Shaw and Cliff Thomas came together for a 100 partnership, Thomas hitting an unbeaten 84 and Shaw 51. Winget totalled 216 for 2, victory arriving in the 43rd over.

Saturday 15 August Winget v Colwall   Played on the sports ground

Colwall:	167 for 9 (J. Taylor 3 for 25)
Winget:	169 for 7 (C. Thomas 73, G. Shaw 30)

Saturday 22 August Winget v Usk

	At Usk
Usk:	155 for 7
Winget:	128
	At the sports ground
Winget II:	269 for 5
Usk II:	153 for 8

1982

Saturday 15th May Usk v Winget

Played at Usk

Usk: 201 for 5

Winget 152 all out (Eric Stephens 40,
                        Cliff Thomas 40).

Saturday 22nd May Winget v Heref

At the sports ground

Winget: 118 (Tony Sadler 20

Hereford: 118 (Y Pandor 3-57, T Salter 2-2
                    C Mills 2-16, T.Sadler 2-1).

Winget C.C. 1st X1 1982
T.Salter G.Pandor J.Taylor P.Carter A.Sadler Y.Pandor Mrs.D.Salter
F.Bhaiyat A.Hawkes T.Shaw A.Salter (capt) J.Gurney C.Thomas

Saturday 29th May Winget v Cirencester

At Cirencester

Winget: 135 (E Stephens 27, J Dowdeswell 18)

Cirencester: 139 for 9

Saturday 12th June Winget v Ross

At the sports ground

Winget: 100 all out (C Thomas 20)

Ross: 126, (M Jones 5 for 30,

            T Salter 2-26, Y Pandor 2-42)

Saturday 19th June Winget II v Hatherley II

At the sports ground

Winget II: 80

Hatherley II: 79

Saturday 3rd July Winget v Corsham

At Corsham

Winget: 115 (Mark Jones 29)

Corsham: 116 for 4

Saturday 31st July Winget v Cirencester

At Cirencester

Winget: 169 (F Baiyat 66)

Cirencester: 144 for 9

During the match, Mark Jones required three stitches to his hand

Saturday 22nd August Winget v Panteg

At Panteg

Panteg: 121

Winget: 113

Saturday 22nd August

Winget pace bowler Tony Salter took 6 for 39 in the Three Counties League match at Abergavenny, but the club still lost by 13 runs. Winget were left to chase a total of 140, a modest target which should have been made comfortably. An early collapse upset their plans however, and only Yak Pandor (47) and Tony Salter (31) made any impression as Winget were tumbled out for 127.

Peter Richards Cup Final Winners 1983
L.Wray A.Hawkes P.Carter M.Nasser D.Page A.Pugh (sec)
A.Sadler R.Allen C.Thomas A.Salter (capt) N.Nasser J.Taylor E.Stephens

Ist XI 1984
R.Owen R.Hopkins P.Carter E.Stephens A.Tetley A.Manns G.Embling
M.Nasser A.Sadler J.Taylor C.Thomas N.Nasser A.Salter

1984

Saturday 26th May - Tetley spins a winning spell

The cunning leg spin of Tony Tetley helped Winget to another fine victory in the Beach Villas League.
His baffling mixture bamboozled Chepstow, who started the day on top of the league with four wins out of four.
The Beaufort teacher finished with 4 – 23 off 6.3 overs to take his wicket tally in four matches to 17.
Chepstow collapsed to 65 all out with Tetley and Tony Salter (4 – 23 off 15) shining, in reply to Winget's 185 for 7.
The wet afternoon ruled out play in most league games and affected Winget's innings. After 13 overs they had scored only 13 runs, then a magnificent knock by Tony Sadler (73), supported by Paul Carter and John Taylor (26 each), lifted the side to a useful total.
But it was Tetley's day and his performance brought praise from Taylor, the club captain.
"He became available just when we needed a spinner and is bound to make a big difference this season" he said.

Saturday 16th June - Nasser skill turns tide for Winget

Winget found a hero in the nick of time to turn the tables on Lydney in the Beach Villas derby.
A fine spell of gentle medium pace from Noorali Nasser succeeded, where the Gloucester club's main strike bowlers had failed.
He tore through the middle order of Lydney's deep batting line up and helped turn the game with a magnificent 5 – 25.
The opponent's captain Bob Brain, who had taken the innings to within sight of a huge total, then watched in disbelief as six wickets toppled for 35. Winget were set a target of 172 to win and the first wicket pair, Tony Sadler (76) and the bowler's brother Mustapha Nasser (44), built a solid foundation.
The final runs were scored in the 44th over, strengthening further the winner's bid for the league championship.

Saturday 30th June

Hatherley	151 for 9 (Wilson 35, Palmer 35)
Bowling:	Carter 4 – 24, Nasser 4 – 36.
Winget	145 for 8 (M. Nasser 25, P. Carter 31)
Bowling:	Palmer 2 – 39, Bonell 4 – 24.

Saturday 21st July - Winget v Stinchcombe

The consistent batting of Mustapha Nasser (70) and the guile of leg spinner Tony Tetley (5-36), helped Winget to a fairly easy win over Stinchcombe.
Winget were faced with 145 to win and after a huge opening stand between Nasser and Tony Sadler (40), they won in the 38th over.

Saturday 28th July Winget v Chepstow

At Tuffley Park
Winget 209 for 8 (M. Nasser 96)
Chepstow 167 for 9 (J. Taylor 4-43).

Division II at Cirencester

Winget II 159 for 9 (A. Frape 5-44)
Cirencester II 98 all out (M. Jones 6-65)

Combined 1st X1 and 2nd XI 1985

C.Thomas A.Tetley S.Tegg D.Tetley R.Owen P.Burrows
J.Carter R.Tait K.Jones R.Nicholls P.Carter A.Salter G.Embling J.Gurney A.Pugh(sec)
A.Sadler R.Hopkins J.Taylor S.Phelps(chairman) E.Stephens M.Nasser C.Tetley J.Tegg

1988

Saturday 4th June - Winget lifted by ton

Winget's Charlie Matthews was among the runs in Division Three of the C and G League. He flayed the Dowty Ashchurch attack for 151, with Dave Smart (52) and John Dix (21) helping to build a mammoth total of 271-6. Top Dowty bowler was L Gibbons with 2-66. Dowty were all out for 101 in reply with Steve Wilson taking 6 for 10.

Winget II had an easy victory over Abergavenny, scoring 181 for 9, with Cliff Thomas hitting 35 not out and Ian Parish 32. Abergavenny were skittled out for a mere 72, Tony Salter taking 8 for 34.

Saturday 11th July - Two Wicket Win for Winget

Paul Carter hit a fine 86 in the Winget reply and with good support from Sadler (41) and Smith (32) saw Winget to 204-8, the winning runs coming with just four balls remaining.

	TEWKESBURY		
Tibbles		b Ellinor	0
Kilminster		b Salter	20
Piesse	st Owen	b Taylor	96
Lane	c Nasser	b Salter	9
Burn	c Taylor	b Tetley	28
Hayes	c Owen	b Tetley	0
Brown		b Taylor	27
Burd	st Owen	b Tetley	8
Caudle	not out		7
Gledhill	not out		1

Extras 6	**Total** (9 wkts)	**203**

	WINGET		
Nasser		b Brown	10
Sadler		c and b Burd	41
Carter	c Brown	b Caudle	86
Adams	st Piesse	b Burd	4
Smith		b Hayes	32
Salter	lbw	b Caudle	0
Taylor	c Burd	b Hayes	15
Lewis	c Lane	b Caudle	0
Ellinor	not out		6
Tetley	not out		0

Extras 10	**Total** (8 wkts)	**204**

J Ellinor 5-2-16-1; A Salter 14-4-55-2;
P Carter 7-0-46-0; A Tetley 14-1-53-4;
J Taylor 5-0-29-2.

C Hayes 10-0-41-2; T Brown 7-2-22-1;
G Caudle 10-2-0-43-3; P Lane 9-1-40-0;
C Burd 5-0-29-2; R Gledhill 3-0-21-0.

Winget returned to winning ways and maintained their lead in the Beach Villas League with a two-wicket victory over Tewkesbury in a tense finish at Tuffley Avenue.

Put in to bat on a green strip, Tewkesbury batsman Graham Piesse, helped by some wayward bowling and slack fielding, fell just four runs short of what would have been an excellent century as the visitors rattled up a useful 203-9, Tony Tetley picking up 4-53 in 14 overs.

Winget II stayed top of Division Two after a 9-wicket win at Tewkesbury. The home side struggled to 136-4 in their 45 overs while Winget strolled home with plenty of overs to spare, Adrian Farnell hitting 65 not out and Clive Pattenden 56.

Saturday 18 July - Two wins for Winget

Winget held on to top spot in the League with a 37-point haul over the weekend. Captain Mustapha Nasser played a vital role in both games, hitting a superb century on Saturday at Usk and 60 against Panteg on Sunday.

Usk totalled 209-9 in Saturday's match, Tony Kear hitting 55 after they had slumped to 100-6 and Paul Carter claiming 4-68. In reply Nasser dominated the Winget innings, hitting 20 boundaries before being run out for 134. Gwyn Williams took 4-92.

On Sunday, Winget scored 199-7 from their 45 overs with Nasser (66) again top scoring and gaining useful support from Smith (42) and Carter (30). Kevin Murphy (51) and Keith Miles (48) launched the Panteg reply, but Tony Salter's 4-45 saw them finish 19 runs short.

Winget II maintained their hundred per cent record with a brace of victories in Division Two. Andy Adams hit his maiden century as Winget made 228-4 against Usk II, Clive Pattenden supporting well with 47 before Usk were restricted to 135-8.

On Sunday, Cliff Thomas scored 96 and Andy Hawkes 61 not out as Winget again topped two hundred at Panteg. Colin Lewis (5-24) and Neil Willerton (4-42) claimed the wickets as Panteg were bowled out for 130.

Saturday 25th June - Lydney Torn Apart by Dynamic Duo

Winget openers Mustapha Nasser and Tony Sadler, blasted Lydney with a brilliant partnership of 141 on a perfect batting strip at the Recreation Ground.

Lydney's opening attack was treated with disdain by the Winget pair. The aggressive Nasser opened up from the start, taking three fours off the first over from young Lydney pace bowler Paul Morris and they never looked back in the chase to overtake Lydney's total of 179 for 9.

The score had moved to 141 and Lydney were sliding to an overwhelming defeat when Winget's concentration wavered against a frail Lydney attack. Tim Stone, who rarely bowls, had anchorman Sadler smartly stumped by Hale for 40 and then Nasser, attempting to drive a six over long-on was caught on the boundary. He had scored an outstanding 98.

Three more wickets tumbled as Winget made hard work of scoring the remaining runs required to pick up 19 points and extend their lead at the top of the Beach Villas Three Counties league.

Lydney's innings had started well enough with Robert Mills and Andy Kear sharing a 57 run opening stand. Mills went on to score 40, though Lydney's top scorer was Tim Stone who looked in good form for his 61.

For Winget, Colin Lewis picked up four wickets for 29 and Paul Carter 4 for 63, but on such a good strip nothing short of 200 was going to present the Winget batsmen with any great problems.

Cheltenham and Gloucester Division III

Winget won by six wickets against Newent. Joe Williams 30 not out, Mike Powell 31 not out and Dave Smart 28 led Winget to 112, after Newent had been dismissed for 111 with Steve Wilson taking 5 for 17.

Monday 18 July - Teenage Ace Leads Winget

Teenager John Tegg led Winget 'B' to a thoroughly deserved victory in last night's Gloucester Cricket Federation 20 Over Knockout Cup semi-final against Arcadians at Tuffley Park.

Tegg scored 59 not out in Winget's impressive total of 124 for two, a total that proved far too many for Arcadians.

By the end Arcadians had made 96 for nine, and they had not really ever been in the hunt after losing opener Neil Eley to a sharp catch by Ian Parish off Tony Salter in the second over.

Winget batted first and made good progress, with openers Tegg and Dave Carter (33) putting on 95. Tegg was then joined by Parish who hit 22 before he was run out off the last ball of the innings.

That looked an impressive total and it looked even more daunting when Arcadians began to lose wickets to Neil Willerton, and Tony Salter who finished with six wickets.

They were 38 for four after ten overs, 64 for six after 15 and never really looked capable of making Winget too nervous.

Winget now play Gloucester City or Witcombe, who clash at Tuffley Park tonight, in Friday's 20 Over Cup final.

WINGET 'B'		ARCADIANS	
D Carter b Hayward	33	N Eley c Parish b Salter	1
J Tegg not out	59	R Payne b Willerton	4
I Parish run out	22	R Smart c Adams b Salter	6
Extras 10 total (2 wkts)	124	C Peacey c Thomas b Salter	17
Bowling: N Hayward 10-0-51-1;		D Williams c Carter b Willerton	4
P Gale 10-0-64-0.		S Eamer b Willerton	11
		N Hayward b Salter	7
		P Gale not out	20
		C Godding b Salter	10
		T Boakes b Salter	2
		S Base not out	0
		Extras 16, **Total (9 wkts)**	**96**
		Bowling: N Willerton 10-0-39-3;	
		A Salter 10-1-42-6.	

Saturday 23rd July - Winget tighten Grip on Title

Winget snatched another 16 points, beating Frocester and the weather to tighten their grip on the Beach Villas Three Counties League title.

A slow wicket worked against the batsmen who were forced to struggle for runs, and Frocester seemed worst affected as they lost the toss and were put in to bat.

They were pinned down by accurate Winget bowling, especially from left arm medium pacer Neil Willerton. He did not take a wicket, but his 15 over spell included four maidens and he conceded just 21 runs.

Frocester lost two early wickets and struggled to work up a scoring partnership. It was not until the final seven overs that they started to hit out, but by then they had already lost too much ground to build up a respectable score and at the close of the 45 overs, had scored only 137 for the loss of seven wickets.

Top Winget wicket taker was leg spinner Tony Tetley who took four for 29 off eight overs. Paul Carter claimed the other three, conceding 50 runs off 18 overs.

Winget's batsmen also struggled and Frocester lost close fielder Eric Woodmason, who was hit in the face and taken to hospital with a fractured cheekbone as his team attempted to put the City side under pressure.

Winget lost their first wicket with the score at 31, but Mustapha Nasser worked hard for his team's top score of 32 as they passed Frocester's total for the lost of six wickets.

FROCESTER			WINGET	
G Hudd	b Carter	14	M Nasser c Pearce b Hudd	32
D Wincup	c Sadler b Carter	1	A Sadler b Little	14
J Evans	c A Tetley b Carter	22	C Thomas c and b Little	1
R Spyvee	c Farnell b Tetley	19	A Farnell b Woodmason	0
I Smith	b Tetley	37	P Carter st Pearce b Woodmason	21
P Field	c Owen b Tetley	26	C Tetley c Smith b Hudd	16
C Partridge	st Owen b Tetley	7	C Lewis not out	18
D Poultney	not out	1	J Taylor not out	12
Extras	**10**	**Total** (7 wkts) **137**	**Extras 24**	**Total (6 wkts) 138**

N Willerton 15-4-21-0; P Carter 18-4-50-3;
A Tetley 8-2-29-4; J Taylor 2-1-6-0;
C Lewis 2-0-21-0.

P Field 7-2-24-0; S Little 12.3-4-34-2;
E Woodmason 10-1-28-2; G Hudd 9-2-29-2.

Saturday 20 and 21 August Winget hopes fading

Ecstasy followed by agony, that was the tale of Winget's fading bid to capture the Beach Villas Three Counties League title over the weekend.

A competent all round team performance easily accounted for Usk on Saturday, but it was a different story at Panteg on Sunday where a resounding thrashing left them with the slim hope that Hereford, with a game in hand, will throw points away in their final games.

Winget's 19-point haul against Usk put them briefly back on top, and it was the work of seam bowlers Paul Carter and Tony Salter who destroyed the Welshmen. They bowled unchanged to skittle out Usk for 120, with Salter picking up five wickets and Carter four. Salter's 19 over spell included seven maidens and conceded just 56 runs. Carter bowled 20 overs and conceded only 54 runs, bowling three maidens. The tables were turned at Panteg, however, where Winget were all out for 121, victims of some accurate bowling. Only Farnell (49) and M Nasser (23) really got to grips with the Panteg attack, the hosts making the required runs and picking up 19 points for the loss of only four wickets.

Andy Adams scored an unbeaten 59 in Winget second string's total of 118 for three, chasing an Usk total of 117 on Saturday.

Saturday 27th August - Cheltenham and Gloucester Division III

Newent 180 for 4
Winget 183 for 1 (C Pattenden 54, C Matthews 88 not out)

The only Division II match played on this day due to rain.

1989

Saturday 3rd June - Cirencester v Winget

Cirencester 203 for 8
Winget 152 for 8 (A Sadler 46, P. Smith 39)

Winget II 252 for 4 (C Pattenden 110, R. Nicholls 79)
Cirencester II 132 for 9 (P. Carter 4-68)

Winget III 227 for 7 (C. Thomas 48, D. Smart 112)
Charfield 110- 8

Wednesday 5th July - County Bid For Winget

Winget clinched the Eggletons under 13 Gloucester Cricket Championship, with a narrow 14 run victory over challengers Upton St Leonards.
Put in to bat, second placed Upton looked like setting Winget a big total after reaching 231 without loss in the first four of their 16 overs.
But Winget hit back in the closing stages to snap up five Upton wickets, including two run outs, to see the Upton challenge finish on 223.
In reply, Winget scraped home to finish on 237 for the loss of two wickets, after a shaky start to their innings and tremors at the end.
Winget could only manage 211 at the halfway stage, but a calm display by Winget's third pair meant that the last duo of Tom Williams and Harper went to the crease needing three runs without loss to guarantee the championship

2nd XI - Three Counties League Div. 2 Champions 1989
*R.Wheatley R.Nicholls D.Carter J.Ellinor R.Owen I.Parrish
A.Adams A.Farnell C.Thomas (capt) C.Pattenden A.Hawkes*

Tuesday 11th July - The B's Knees

Winget B beat their first team club mates to take the Gloucester Cricket Federation 'Sportlink' outdoor sixes competition last night.
Batting first, Winget B made 78 for four in their eight overs – reduced from 12 because of a late start.
Ian Parish was 25 not out and Dave Carter hit an unbeaten 22. Winget A bowlers who inflicted the damage were Phil Smith who took two for 11 and Bob Hopkins who grabbed two for 19.
In reply, Winget A managed only 63 for five with their best score being the 20 from Mustapha Nasser; Tony Sadler taking two for 13.
The second semi-final was played before the final with Winget B qualifying at the expense of Gloucester City.
Winget B made 130 for five (Sadler 44, Parish 27, Carter 20), while City reached 117 all out (Tony Robinson 41, John Hooper 20.)

Tuesday 18th July - Classy Tim Steers Winget 'A' To Final

Former Gloucester City batsman Tim Williams, lined up a clash with his old club mates when he steered Winget A to victory in last night's Gloucester Cricket Federation "Mellor Finn" 20 Over Knockout Cup semi-final
Williams scored 42 including three fours, in a quality 33 minute, 33 ball innings, which proved the key to Winget's success against their own B team.
Winget A now face Gloucester City in Friday's final, again at the Winget ground in Tuffley Avenue.
Winget B batted first and scored 123 for six, with Andy Adams making 27, Adrian Farnell 23, and Andy Hawkes 22.
In reply, Winget A suffered two early blows when Tony Sadler and Colin Tetley were out, leaving them on 19 for two.
But Mustapha Nasser, who scored a steady 21, and Williams, who dominated the partnership with some outstanding strokes, put on 67 runs for the third wicket.
That proved crucial as Winget A reached 124 for six in 18.4 overs.
Now Winget A take on Gloucester City who field a mixture of their top three teams in this competition.
City skipper Dave Collinson believes it will be a hard game and says:
"Winget are a good side and we need to be at our best if we are to win."
Gloucester City are the holders, having beaten Winget A on their way to last season's final and Winget B to lift the trophy.

Friday 21st July - Ridley On Song For Winget

Winget's Kevin Ridley was the hero at Tuffley Park last night as he steered his side to a 17 run victory over Gloucester City in the Mellor Finn 20 over knockout final Ridley snapped up the vital wickets as City went in chase of a modest Winget innings of 125 for five.

Though Gloucester set about the task slowly - losing opener Mark Collinson in the fifth over with the score on 15 – incoming batsman Alex Robinson looked set to swing the match in Gloucester's favour.

Robinson had shared in a third wicket stand worth 31 when he was caught by Tegg off the bowling of Ridley and when Paul Baker departed in the following over, again falling victim to Ridley, this time forcing a catch out near the boundary from Colin Tetley, Gloucester's challenge was all but finished.

Going into the final three overs they still needed 36 runs for victory and such pressure inevitably led to a rapid fall of wickets. Five went down for the addition of only 19 runs.

2nd X1 Gloucester 20 over Knockout 1989
S.Phelps G.Watts J.Ellinor R.Nicholls D.Carter I.Parrish Miss R.Thomas
A.Hawkes R.Wheatley C.Thomas (capt) R.Hopkins E.Stephens

Ridley finished with figures of five for 39, with his bowling partner Stuart Wilshaw claiming two for 60.

Winget's innings had benefited from the fifth wicket partnership of Phil Smith and John Taylor. These two provided vital acceleration at the tailend of the Winget innings, Taylor going on to clout 34 runs before finally departing in the final over, bowled by Jason Hooper who finished with figures of four for 51. Smith finished unbeaten on 22.

Sadler	c M Collinson b Hooper	8	M Collinson	b Ridley	8	
Nasser	b Hooper	12	Martyn	Run Out	20	
Tetley	b Hooper	12	Robinson	c Tegg b Ridley	21	
Williams	Run Out	20	Baker	c Tetley b Ridley	11	
Smith	Not Out	14	D Collinson	c Tetley b Wilshaw	10	
Taylor	b Hooper	34	I Collinson	b Wilshaw	2	
Lewis	Not Out	34	Hooper	c Smith b Ridley	10	
Extras 3			Moody	b Ridley	4	
			Cooper	Run Out	0	
			Loughlin	Not Out	0	
			Extras		23	

Total (5 wkts)	**125**		**Total (9 wkts)**	**109**	
Baker 0-64; Hooper 4-51.			Ridley 5-39; Wilshaw 2-60.		

Saturday 22nd July Winget Charge Goes On

Winget took a massive step towards the Beach Villas Cricket League Division One title, beating reigning champions and nearest rivals Hereford by 66 runs at the Racecourse ground.

A half-century from Mustapha Nasser laid the foundations for Winget's 208 for seven, while Colin Tetley (41) and Phil Smith (38 not out) provided the middle order impetus.

Phil Hunt hit 51 in the Hereford reply of 142 for seven and Henderson Broome 32 not out, but the home side finished well short. Kevin Ridley claimed two for 36, Stuart Wilshaw two for 28 and Colin Lewis bowled 14 overs for only 14 runs.

Winget seconds went on the rampage in their Division Two game against Hereford seconds at Tuffley Park, hitting 256 for five before holding the visitors to 129 for nine. Andy Adams cracked 92 and skipper Cliff Thomas 72 in the Winget total, the pair adding 121 for the third wicket. Jim Ellinor, Tony Salter and Dave Carter each claimed two wickets as Hereford slipped from 86 for two to 110 for nine, Ernie Morgan striking 52.

Easy Victory for Winget III

Winget 264 (R. Nicholls 56, Eric Stephens 56)
Newent 41 (J Dix 4-5, R Hopkins 3-7)

Saturday 12th August - Two Victories For Winget

Winget consolidated their lead at the top of the league with a convincing 87 run victory over Abergavenny at Tuffley Park.
Winget lost both openers early on, but the middle order batted steadily before John Taylor (42) and Chris Worgan (33 not out) ended the innings with a flourish.
The visitors were dismissed for 118, with Colin Lewis continuing his recent run of wickets, bowling unchanged for seven for 43 from 21 overs.
Clive Pattenden's 86 not out took him past 800 runs for the season, smashing the Division Two aggregate scoring record in the process as Winget seconds cruised to a nine wicket win at Abergavenny.
Pattenden received solid support from Roger Nicholls (28) and Andy Adams (31 not out) as Winget hit 156 for one in reply to the home side's 153 all out.
Ian Parish bowled unchanged for seven for 73 and John Dix claimed three for 31 in the Avergavenny innings.

Saturday 2nd September - Winget Clinch Title

Winget have clinched the Beach Villas Cricket League championship for the first time.
Their 120 run victory against Chepstow on Sunday made sure of the Division One Title. The Gloucester club are set to make it a double, for their seconds are top of Division Two and require only seven points to ensure they are also champions.
Winget slipped up on Saturday when they lost by ten wickets against Lydney. Bob Brain took five wickets as Winget crashed to 113 all out, with Lydney racing to 114 for nought. Glamorgan batsman Steve James hit 58 not out and Australian Ben Armstrong 47 not out.
But yesterday Winget amassed 276 from their 45 overs with Colin Tetley scoring 90, Paul Carter 46 and John Taylor 42.
Chepstow were all out for 156, Stuart Wilshaw securing four for 26 and Taylor three for 28.

Saturday 9th September - Winget Title

Winget II clinched the Beach Villas Cricket League Division Two Championship for the third successive season with an eight-wicket victory over Colwall II at Tuffley Park.
Needing only five points to clinch the title, the City club saw Colwall reach 75-0 after 25 overs before spinner John Dix was introduced.
Dix claimed six for 45 as the visitors slumped to 153 all out, with three wickets falling in the final over and the decisive fifth point coming off the final ball.
With the title won, Winget easily reached their target with Andy Adams (80 not out) and Cliff Thomas (42 not out) hitting the winning runs with six overs to spare.

1989 saw the 1st X1 win the Three Counties League first division for the first time, and the 2nd XI win the second division for the third consecutive year. The photo shows the combined teams celebrating at the presentation evening.

1990-2002

The 1990s proved to be the most successful decade in the long and varied history of Winget Cricket Club. 3 Three Counties League 1st XI titles, a Three Counties Cup triumph, a Tetley Bitter Cup victory, two County Cup Final appearances, four Gloucester KO Cup and five GCCF 6-a-Side successes. There was also a 2nd XI league title, three runners up places and three 2nd XI Cup Final appearances, while a good number of individual records were also established during this time.

The decade began with the 1st XI successfully defending their Three Counties League title, though first place was not confirmed until the season's final game after a neck and neck tussle with Frocester went right to the wire. With the league's main sponsors changing from Beach Villas to WG Cricket that season, the club became inaugural winners of the re-named silverware, during which time Paul Carter established a new record by becoming the first batsman to pass a thousand runs in a League season, recording a staggering 1,194 (average 62.84). Not surprisingly, Paul was voted the Three Counties League Player of the Year – the first time a Winget player had achieved this accolade. No doubt Panteg cast a favourable vote in Carter's direction – his 1990 run record against them read 2 innings, 236 runs, not out twice. Also to the fore in that successful 1990 team were bowlers Colin Lewis (54 wickets at 15) and Stuart Wilshaw (30 wickets, also at 15), proving that the two extremes of speed through the air really do work well in tandem. The 2nd XI, looking to extend their winning streak to four successive titles, had to be content with runners up spot after Hereford just hung on to a lead established early in the season. Andy Adams struck two unbeaten 2nd XI centuries early in the campaign to achieve immediate promotion to the 1st XI, while the two Tony's – Salter and Tetley – both claimed over forty wickets apiece.

It was a case of *deja-vu* the following season with Winget again champions, Frocester again runners up and Carter again TCL Player of the Year. The all rounder added another 944 runs to his fast blossoming career tally and claimed 34 wickets into the bargain. 1991 was the year in which the TCL changed their format with the number of league fixtures being reduced to 15 due to the introduction of the League Cup, a competition that proved fruitful for Winget until they reached the final. Meeting Clevedon at Lydney CC, the club were bowled out for little more than 100, with future England opening bowler Andrew Caddick claiming eight wickets including a hat trick.

Not to be outdone, WCC's Kevin Ridley went one better in the league encounter at Tewkesbury when he notched 9-41, the first – though not the last time – a Winget bowler has enjoyed a 90% innings return. The 2nd XI again ended in second spot with Panteg taking the honours on this occasion. One notable happening was the total of 317-5 recorded against Ross on 10th August – the third highest team total recorded in a TCL 2nd XI fixture, with Steve Tegg scoring 147.

1992 saw the 2nd XI reverse the trend of the previous two seasons as they claimed top spot with a narrow victory over the previous season's winners, Panteg. Mustapha Nasser led the batting with 565 runs at 37, though unfortunately this was the last time this colourful character featured prominently in the club's statistics, as he was soon to depart in order to pursue his business activities elsewhere. Jon Andrews and Tony Salter averaged 14 and 15 runs per wicket respectively to end the season occupying the two leading places in the league bowling averages.

1992 proved to be a disappointing campaign for the 1st XI, however, with a third of the scheduled games being cancelled due to bad weather and a final TCL placing of sixth. Jon Tegg ended the season with a highly creditable 557 runs scored at an average of just over 50, while Colin Lewis grabbed 38 wickets in the season. One bowler who gave an inkling that he might be able to swing matters in the 1st XI's favour, however, was John Dix, who received a late call up for the away fixture at Kington. Coming into the attack as second change, Dix returned 8-31 to win the game against ever lengthening odds, only to find he was back in the 2nd XI the following week. The selectors' decision was based on the premise that John's presence did not give balance to the attack, though at several stones over the optimum cricketer's weight, one wonders what type of balance was forthcoming – or indeed who was bowling at the other end – when he was eventually reinstated into the side.

The 1993 season was again dominated by the 2nd XI who at first glance won the league and cup double, with Chepstow ostensibly runners up in both competitions. Phil Smith's belligerent half century led Winget to a well deserved seven wicket cup success, though the end of season Presentation Evening was disrupted by the news that the league committee had upheld an appeal by Hatherley and Reddings regarding an abandoned game in August and, penalising the club by adding a one game penalty to their season's average, relegated them to runners up spot. Suffice to say, Chepstow, despite being awarded the title, duly apologised for the 'honour'. Winget's efforts were recognised by the league committee, however, with Tony Tetley receiving the 2nd XI Player of the Year award after taking 44 wickets at 11 apiece. Bob Owen setting a new league record with 33 wicket keeping dismissals in the season and Dave Edwards topping both the scoring charts (558 at 39) and the dress stakes.

Chepstow deservedly took the 1st XI honours with Winget again finishing in 6th spot, despite Colin Tetley's 825 runs at 55 – an excellent performance and confirmation of a real talent. The team lifted the Plate KO trophy thanks to victory over Clevedon in the final to salvage some consolation from the campaign.

Unfortunately, the 1993 season will also be remembered for the sad loss of Jim Stephens, who in over 60 years association with the club was player, Chairman and President. There is now a trophy presented each season to the first eleven player of the season in his memory.

The TCL changed again in the 1994 season with four new clubs – Malpas, Bredon, Dumbleton and Brockhampton joining the League to increase the complement to 20 – though for the first time in eight seasons, neither Winget side finished in a top two position. Both 1st and 2nd XI's ended in sixth place, yet some solace was found in a first ever County Cup Final appearance, even though the game plan did not quite come to fruition – Bristol West Indians triumphing by some 158 runs.

Jon Tegg again excelled with the bat averaging 62, while Colin Lewis placed another 33 wickets in his ever-expanding locker. Things did not go all Lewis's way during the summer however – during one of his less fruitful outings in north west Herefordshire at Kington, he was struck for a second six over long on by home batsman Clive Scott. Unlike the first boundary, which nestled comfortably in an adjoining thicket, the second soared upwards – then downwards – straight into the forehead of a passing spectator, who, at the time, was pushing a young child around the ground in her pram. Preferring to let the nearest fielders examine the injured party, the batsman stood his ground, only to later discover that the lady who had retired hurt was indeed his wife!

Adrian Farnell completed three highly successful years with the bat by leading the 2nd XI charts with an average close to 50, though Dave Edwards ended top scorer with 576 runs to his credit – and he counted every one! Dave, a great character during his time at the club, moved back to his native Kent at the end of the season, and has spent the years since comparing batting averages to a minimum of three decimal places with his previous Garden of England team mates.

Veterans Tony Salter and Tony Tetley proved that if you're good enough you're young enough by bagging a remarkable 99 wickets between them, while Owen reset the TCL 2nd XI wicket keeping record in claiming 36 victims. Defeat in a classic League Cup Final against arch rivals Chepstow was enlivened by the collapse half way through a third run of No11 batsman Steve Wilson who, on one of his brief batting forays to extend into double figures, fell to the ground – not through faulty spikes as first thought – but due to exhaustion brought about by the rare excursion into the necessity of running a three. Despite his prone position, the resulting overthrows added a welcome few runs to the WCC total.

The 1st XI campaign lost its direction in 1995, in much the same way as Jon Andrews lost his during the home encounter versus Colwall. When the opposing batsman hit a straight drive back into the stumps at the bowler's end, knocking off the bails in the process and set off for a run, Andrews plucked out one of the remaining stumps and began chasing the ball frantically across the outfield. Obviously he had only understood half the run out rule referring to a broken wicket – though possibly Law No 38 reads somewhat differently at Carrickfergus Cricket Club.

With only Tetley's 656 runs which included a swashbuckling 130 at Hatherley and Reddings and Carter's 44 wicket haul standing out in the individual statistic department, it was left to Abergavenny's Anil Kapoor to set a new TCL batting record, amassing no fewer than 1,416 league and cup runs. It is worth noting, however, that the Indian International made only 12 of those runs (c Dix b Carter), against Winget.

The 2nd XI also struggled to an eighth placed finish, despite another 60 victims for skipper Tetley and the appearance of one Martin McLean who arrived late, failed to trouble the scorers, adjourned the ground following the season's opener and has never been seen since.

Two seemingly unconnected changes occurred at the outset of the 1996 season – Pershore replaced Stinchcombe in the TLC, while Andy Hawkes replaced Tony Tetley after seven years as chairman of WCC. These separate happenings, though, each had a similar effect – all Winget v Pershore 2nd XI matches ended approximately an hour after most similar games due to the incessant ball-by-ball ramblings of the Wiltshire club's wonderfully named batsman Sidney Fudger, while the Gloucester club's Presentation Evenings also went into added time due to the Chairman's somewhat longer than usual seasonal reviews.

Maybe these recollections were in celebration of a more successful showing by the Winget teams, with both 1st and 2nd XI's improving their performances to finish in 3rd position in their respective divisions. The successes of 1996 were based on some excellent performances with the ball – Neil Salter giving notice of things to come by topping the League bowling averages returning 44 wickets at just 12 apiece, while Jon Andrews (27 at 14) and Colin Lewis (41 at 15) both also finished in the League's top five.

Tony Tetley took over the Chairmanship of the Three Counties League in 1997 as the competition split into two divisions, based on relative positions the previous season. The 1st XI First Division was won by Chepstow at a canter, with Winget again finishing a comfortable third as Tim Williams returned for a third spell as first team captain. Jon Tegg topped the League's batting averages with 747 at an average of 57 which included a score of 177 not out at local rivals Hatherley. This effort was only two short of Kapoor's League record individual score set two years earlier and helped Winget register 335-4 – a total which remains the third highest team score in TCL history.

Also writing another personal entry into the record books was Paul Carter, who claimed 9-8 from 12 overs in the victory at Cirencester, while Neil Salter ended in second place in the TCL averages after taking 31 wickets, again at just over 12 apiece. The 2nd XI ended their campaign in 5th spot with Tony Sadler (392 runs at 39) and Luke Townsend (25 wickets at 13.64) topping the batting and bowling listings.

With the structure of local cricket beginning to undergo rapid change as the sport followed in the by now well worn boot steps of both football and rugby, the ECB's new pyramid system brought about fresh importance for the club's teams to do as well as possible, as quickly as possible. Responding to this dictum in some style, the 1st XI walked away with the Three Counties League Division One title – their only league defeat coming at the hands of Pershore in the season's final fixture in what, as it turned out, was Winget's last ever TCL encounter. Tegg (734 runs at 45), Carter (604 runs and 40 wickets) and Salter (50 wickets at 15) were again to the fore as the team's successes continued with the cup competitions, though several tight finishes had to be negotiated in the process.
After slipping to 140-7 in reply to Chepstow's League Cup semi final challenge of 193-9, Lewis, Hawkes and Dix, with a boundary off the game's penultimate delivery, saw Winget edge home by 2 wickets. In the final itself, chasing Usk's 169-7, WCC had slumped to 83-7 off 32 overs before Chris Wayman (34), Salter (37no) and Lewis (13no) turned the tables to lift the trophy by a 2 wicket margin. This was not the first occasion on which Wayman had come to his side's salvation that season – two months earlier with his team reeling at 63-5, he had struck a 37 minute 76 to help Winget to victory at Pershore.

More success was achieved when the side lifted the Tetley Bitter KO Cup following a 12 run victory over Winterbourne. A return to the County Ground in Bristol was achieved after victories over Winterbourne and Knowle and a 5 run semi final margin against Thornbury, though the County Cup continued to prove elusive as Brislington emerged victors by 21 runs in the final.

The 2nd XI reached their third TCL Cup Final of the decade due to excellent victories at Kington and Hatherley following qualification from the group stage, but a talented Abergavenny side proved too strong as Winget eventually fell at the last hurdle. With a comfortable 2nd XI mid-table league position again attained, the club could look back at probably its most successful season ever as a fitting tribute to the behind the scenes work of Andy Hawkes in particular, who doubled up the duties of both Chairman and Secretary at a time when committee volunteers were in particularly short supply.

Thanks to the success of the 1st XI during 1998, Winget took their place in the Western League for the first time the following year, though this new experience concluded in somewhat disappointing circumstances. Needing one win from their final two matches to secure a top half finish and a place in the West of England Premier 2 Division the following year, the side suffered heavy defeats at the hands of both Cheltenham and Swindon, and despite a playing record of 9 victories and only 6 defeats ended just below half way in sixth position.

There were several more close encounters of the cricketing kind that season, including a 1 run success at Wootton Basset, a 2 run loss at Cheltenham, a 1 wicket defeat at Cirencester and, in possibly the most remarkable encounter of all, an 8 run reversal against Old Bristolians Westbury. With Winget down and seemingly out at 78-8 and 117-9 chasing the visitor's 214-4, Chris Wayman and Gary Watts (23no) added 89 for the last wicket – a club record – before Wayman was caught on the boundary for 66 in the final over. Appearing for Old Bristolians and scoring 51 not out that day was one Chris Bassano who, less than two years later in May 2001, became the first ever batsman to accumulate two separate centuries on his first class debut. Bassano was playing his first County Championship match for Derbyshire at the time – and the side on the receiving end of those record-breaking runs was – Gloucestershire!

Sixth place was achieved by the 2nd XI following a season of some fine victories, coupled with some disappointing losses – the major 'up' being the defeat of Cheltenham who, set a mere 104 runs for victory, were bowled out for just 63 –Tony Salter's match winning 5-26 being the last of many, many five wicket hauls recorded by one of Winget's greatest stalwarts during more than 40 years of 1st and 2nd XI action.

The loss of the potential League slot meant that the 2000 season was spent in the newly-formed Gloucestershire/Wiltshire Division One, though the ongoing restructuring of the by now fast-rising pyramid saw the sad demise of the Three Counties League, just one year short of what would have been its 30th anniversary, while the Western League's similar existence was also brought to a premature conclusion.

Now only top spot would suffice if Winget was to gain the status it had so narrowly missed out on during the previous campaign. With Neil Salter at the helm of the 1st XI, the side was locked in a four-way battle for the title with Frocester, Dumbleton, and the late emergence of Malmesbury making for a tense, yet ultimately successful, final few weeks to the season. Carter (442 runs at 63) and Salter (39 wickets at 11) once more led the averages, though Mike Wildy, following promotion from the 2nd XI and a number of visits to the Glamorgan CCC nets whilst at university in Cardiff, made some valuable contributions with both bat and ball towards the end of the campaignFar less tense was the progress of the 2nd XI, who ended the campaign in sixth position, having won 7 and lost 8 of its 15 games played. Cliff Thomas was again the leading batsman with 311 runs at 31, while Ben Williams was beginning to show signs of fulfilling his undoubted potential, averaging 26. Tony Tetley and Steve Wilson, with 27 and 22 wickets respectively, were again the side's leading bowlers as Wilson completed his two year stretch as 2nd XI captain, having led the side to two comfortable mid-table finishes. One player who found the going far from comfortable however, was part-time bowler Damien Hatch, whose frustration at seeing a catch dropped off one of his better deliveries during a game at The Spa resulted in a broken bone in his hand and a substantial indentation in the Park End popping crease.

Winget began 2001 with the aim of establishing themselves in the Premier League, though it was events off the field for which the season will best be remembered. Inside the boundary rope, the 1st XI acquitted itself well and between the rains which saw five games cancelled, won six and lost seven to finish in a mid-table position. The 2nd XI found things more difficult in the higher echelons, though still managed to end the campaign clear of both Corsham and Stroud in eighth place.

Jon Tegg and Paul Carter each finished in the top ten of the league batting statistics, while Jon Newton repeated the achievement in the bowling stakes, a performance which included the season's top bowling figures – 7-44 against Frenchay. With Cliff Thomas and Bob Owen also finding their way into the League 2nd XI's top ten, the initial objective of consolidation had been achieved.

However, rumours that the club would face relegation from the Premier League due to the lack of a youth set up gained momentum during the latter weeks of the campaign, though the translation of hearsay into reality still hit the members hard. The committee were under the impression throughout that Winget would have two to three years to put a youth system into place – after all there had been no youth set up when the club had been accepted into the Premier Division less than twelve months previously, yet, despite a series of meetings and appeals, the relegation ruling was upheld.

As if that disappointment wasn't enough, the club suffered a sudden loss of players during the close season, with no fewer than twelve established 1st and 2nd XI cricketers either moving from the area or retiring from the game altogether. Talk was now not of the enforced relegation, but of whether the club would survive at all. The committee and remaining players however, were determined that Winget must continue in what was its 125th anniversary year, and a pre-season players' reunion was held at Hucclecote RFC. While this event proved to be an enjoyable and sociable function at which many ex-players relived past matches and estimable cricketing feats, it failed to persuade any of the more recently retired to re-don their whites and resurrect their cricketing careers. As such, the 3rd XI was disbanded and all remaining players pushed into second team action, while a number of 2nd XI regulars of previous seasons were promoted to the 1st XI.

It was against this background of relegation and uncertainty that 2002 opened with the club now operating in Gloucestershire / Wiltshire Division One. The 1st XI began with a single run victory over Hatherley & Reddings, followed by a two run loss at Apperley – this despite Jon Tegg's 121 – an innings which began a year that not only saw him top the club's batting averages, but also the league's (674 runs at 61). After six fixtures, however, it seemed that the side might face a relegation battle, but centuries from Tegg and Carter set up a big win over Swindon in their seventh outing, and began a run of seven wins from their final eight fixtures to end in third place.

No such run for the 2nd XI, however, who struggled with player availability from day one. A first career century from Greg Newman which gave the team their first victory at Apperley at the beginning of July, was a brief ray of sunshine in an otherwise difficult campaign which yielded just one more win and a second successive relegation was confirmed well before the season drew to a close.

1993

Saturday 1st Sunday 2nd Monday 3rd May - Cup atones for league setback

Winget lost out in their opening Three Counties League match, but made amends by picking up two League Cup victories.
In the league, Usk provided the opposition, and in a thrilling finish won a low-scoring game by four runs.
Usk batted first and scored 102 all out with Jim Ellinor taking four for 12 and Paul Carter three for 30.
A lacklustre batting display by Winget saw them crash to 98 all out, only Colin Lewis (33 no), Jon Tegg and John Dix reaching double figures.

Victory was snatched from Winget when a last wicket stand of 22 was ended with Kevin Ridley trapped leg before, leaving Usk victors.

Tewkesbury provided the first League Cup opposition and it turned out to be as thrilling as the previous day, with Winget winning by two wickets with two balls to spare.
Tewkesbury batted first with openers Baker (74) and Ashby (50) laying the foundations for a total of 197 for four. In reply, Winget lost both openers for 32, but a third wicket stand of 53 between Tim Williams (36) and Colin Tetley retrieved the situation before Williams was bowled.

Andy Adams joined Teltley and added 57 before Tetley fell for 38. While wickets fell steadily in the latter stages, a maiden first XI 50 by Adams who made 57 not out saw Winget through to victory.

On Bank Holiday Monday, Winget travelled to Cirencester in a rearranged League Cup match and produced a five-wicket victory.
Cirencester were put in to bat and useful contributions from skipper Guy Partridge (42), Jason Huxtable (49) and a wonderful 52 by J Partridge helped towards a total of 173 for eight.

The Winget reply started badly, with both openers out with only 14 on the board.
A third wicket stand of 103 between Tim Williams and Jon Tegg put Winget back in charge. Williams was first to go for 65, including five sixes, while Tegg also reached 65 before being trapped leg before.

Colin Tetley, with 27 not out, saw Winget through to a comfortable victory at 174 for five. Winget Second XI showed they are still a force to be reckoned with after two good wins at the weekend. Veteran Tony Salter skittled Usk out for 70, taking eight for 23 and Winget won by nine wickets before tea.

On Sunday at Tewkesbury it was the batsmen who showed their strength as Winget amassed 270 for four off 45 overs. Andy Hawkes scored his maiden league century with 127 not out and Tony Sadler hit 93. Tewkesbury struggled to 74 for nine in reply, John Knight taking two for 20 and Colin Spencer three for 15.

Saturday 8th May Carter leads Winget charge

Paul Carter hit an unbeaten century and took four wickets to help Winget to a seven run victory over Abergavenny in the Three Counties League.
Winget won the toss and elected to bat and first to go was Steve Tegg. He was followed by Tim Williams who retired hurt and Jon Tegg for a duck.
Opener Carter was joined by Colin Tetley who set about the bowling, including Worcestershire player Chris Tolley, with some venom. The pair added a superb 157 for the third wicket before Tetley was out for 68.
Williams made a brief return before falling to Tolley, but Carter finished unbeaten on 105, a welcome return to form as Winget established a final total of 212 for four.
Abergavenny's reply got off to a flyer before John Dix and Carter helped stem the flow of runs.
But the chase continued and with three overs left, 26 runs were required with three wickets in hand.
Ian Parish went for 10 in the 43rd over, but Carter picked up the vital wicket of Beaumont and some useful fielding enabled Winget to hold out for victory.

Saturday 15th May - Winget On Top In Cup

Winget continued their winning run in the League Cup with a convincing six-wicket victory over Stinchcombe.
Stinchcombe were invited to bat and, against accurate opening spells from Paul Carter and Kevin Ridley, struggled to 37 for four from 18 overs.
Greg Newman (30) and Dave Howe (34) led a revival with a stand of 59 for the fifth wicket, but both went in quick succession, leav-

ing Mike Watkins (34) to lead the innings to a respectable 140 all out. Winget skipper Ian Parish picked up four wickets for 31.

In reply, Steve Tegg was first out with the score on 36; he was quickly followed by Carter for 32, leaving Winget 39 for two off 14 overs.

Tim Williams fell for 15 giving Esterhuizen his third wicket. Then, Jon Tegg and Colin Tetley led an assault on the Stinchcombe bowling, adding 56 in just under 30 minutes for the fourth wicket.

Tegg finally fell for 43, leaving Tetley to see Winget through to victory with a hard-hit 45 not out.

Saturday 19th June

Winget in top form

Winget, playing their third Three Counties Cricket League match of the season, entertained previously unbeaten Kington, the Gloucester club emerged winners by seven wickets.

Kington were put in to bat, and after 22 overs were 72 for two.

Jim Ellinor was introduced into the attack, and bowling against a strong wind soon put his mark on the game, taking two quick wickets leaving Kington 79 for four.

He continued to pick up wickets throughout, finishing with six for 63 from 13 overs; Paul Carter (2-54) also played his part as Kington were held to 183 for nine.

Winget had a bad start, Steve Tegg being caught for nought.

Paul Carter and Tim Williams recovered the innings, adding 124 in 29 overs for the second wicket before Williams was caught for 54. Jon Tegg joined Carter and added 47 before Carter finally fell for 84. Colin Tetley and Tegg (24 not out) saw Winget through to victory by seven wickets.

Saturday 3rd Sunday 4th July - Tegg And Tetley Lead Winget Race

Winget Cricket Club had mixed fortunes, winning convincingly against Ross-on-Wye in the WG Three Counties League, but failing to qualify for the League Cup quarter-finals after losing to Colwall.

Winget won the toss against Ross and elected to bat, a decision that proved correct after they amassed 235 for four from 45 overs. They lost Paul Carter early in the innings, but Tim Williams then joined Steve Tegg and they added 47 runs before Williams fell for 27.

Tegg was the next wicket to fall for 53, but he had put on 44 with his brother Jon to put Winget in a strong position.

The stand of the innings followed as Tegg and Colin Tetley put on 138 in less than an hour. Tetley fell for 78, but an unbeaten 66 from Tegg gave Winget their formidable total.

The Ross reply began well, with three boundaries coming from the first three deliveries, but the Winget bowlers got on top after this and restricted Ross to 131 for nine.

Kev Ridley took three for 38, Carter two for 22 and Colin Lewis two for 31.

Winget could not repeat their form against Colwall the following day, allowing them to make 219 for five in their innings.

In reply Winget struggled to 118 for nine. Andy Adams top scoring with 20.

Saturday 11th September - County cup final place for Winget

Winget entertained Western Cricket League side Brislington in the County Cup semi-final, and won a pulsating match by two wickets Brislington won the toss and elected to bat on a green, hard pitch, but two quick wickets for Kevin Ridley left them struggling at 14 for two.

Gregson, who the previous day scored 100 against Stroud, was next to go, bowled by John Dix for 11.

Wickets continued to fall at regular intervals with all the Winget bowlers producing useful figures.

The only resistance came from Hamblin, who batted steadily through the Brislington innings and was rewarded with a century, which he reached off the last ball of the innings as Brislington finished on 159 for nine.

Winget's reply started with a 57 stand between Paul Carter (32) and Andy Adams (24).

The in-form Colin Tetley added 26 with Steve Tegg before falling for 28, Tegg followed soon after for 13.

However, steady batting by Tim Williams and Phil Smith took the score to 130, but disaster hit Winget at this point as they lost four wickets with the score on 130.

However, Colin Lewis was joined by John Dix, and with sensible batting plus a little luck they saw Winget through to victory by two wickets with eight balls to spare.

Winget now face Downend on September 19th at the Phoenix County Ground Bristol

Sunday 19th September - Winget fail to build on promising start

Winget became Gloucestershire County Cricket Cup runners-up for the second time when they lost to Downend by 94 runs.

The last time they reached the final, in 1991, they also lost heavily to the Bristol West Indians.

Batting first, Downend, who play in the Famous Grouse Western League, started slowly and had only reached 60 for two after 25 overs.

Paul Carter bowled well for Winget, taking one for 16 from his nine overs. He was well backed up by Colin Lewis who took one for 32 from his nine overs.

Unfortunately for Winget, Downend's top batsmen Jason Louch was again on his best form and he was able to turn the game around for the Bristol club.

Louch was eventually run out for 97 off the last ball of the innings, but he had already done the damage as far as Winget were concerned, taking his side to 218 for six from their 45 overs.

The Winget reply began well with 40 runs coming from the first 12 overs. Unfortunately, the loss of Carter started a slump in the Winget innings from which they never recovered.

Andy Adams was the best of the Winget batsmen, but he was eventually caught on the boundary for 38 as Winget faltered to 124 for seven.

1999

Saturday 1st May - Winget Open Campaign With Victory

Winget 216-8

Wootton Bassett 162-8

Winget opened up their Merchants Investors Western Division campaign with a comfortable 54 run victory over Wootton Bassett at Tuffley Park.

Winget were inserted on a slow, green pitch and Rob Sterling was first to go for a single with the score on nine.

Jon Tegg and Colin Tetley added 92 in 18 overs, before Tetley (44) became one of four victims for Drew (four for 66).

Neil Burton was next out for two, leaving Winget 110 for three off 26 overs. Tim Williams (30) helped Tegg, who made 66, add a further 54 before both fell in quick succession.

Andy Adams (21 not out) and Greg Newman (14), assisted by Chris Wayman and Neil Salter, helped Winget reach 216 for eight off 50 overs.

Wootton Bassett's reply started well before Twin (16) and Poulton (one) departed, leaving the score on 49 for two off 16 overs.

Chahall (40) and Ratcliffe (26) looked to be well set, until spin duo Colin Lewis (three for 41) and Sterling (one for 40), slammed on the brakes.

Skipper Smith (28 not out) was the only remaining batsman to look comfortable as Salter returned to finish with four for 40.

Saturday 5th June Winget Win County Cup Derby Match

Neil Salter had a superb opening spell of seven overs, sending back City's top four with just 20 on the board.

Damien Cummins (36) and Dave Collinson (23) added 35, before Cummins fell to a catch in the deep by Jon Andrews off Ben Lambert.

Ian Collinson (3) joined his brother in adding a further 23 before both fell in quick succession. City made just 114 all out.

Winget's emergency opener Colin Lewis (22), Colin Tetley (37) and Ben Lambert (32) not out) saw them through to a comfortable five-wicket win1

Winget won by five wickets.

Saturday 12th June - Winget edged out in two run thriller

Winget made the short trip to Cheltenham, and came away with a two run defeat in a nail biting finish in Western League Division One.

Rob Hall won the toss and elected to bat on a firm but slow pitch, although openers Edwards and Elliott-Sware both found the bowling of Salter and Lewis hard to get away.

Salter made the breakthrough by bowling Edwards (two), and Elliott-Sware (12) was out soon after, run out by Tegg.
Salter then picked up the wicket of Walton (five) and Cheltenham were struggling on 43 for three off 19 overs. Cowley and Hall steadied the ship, adding 61 before Cowley (50) was out trying to force the tempo. Stanton (10) fell to a diving catch at backward square by Salter in the 37th over with the score on 121 for five.

Veteran Nick Price joined skipper Hall and both started to dominate, adding a priceless 72 in 11 overs before the return of Salter saw the demise of Price (46).

Cheltenham's innings closed with the loss of Gomm (two) with Hall 51 not out from a final score of 201 for seven. Salter with three for 47 and Sterling, who took two for 43, were the leading bowlers.
Winget's reply saw Tegg (28) begin in aggressive fashion, dominating an opening stand of 47 with Sterling (13) before both perished. Tetley and Lambert continued to look positive by putting on 40 before Lambert (10) was caught behind, leaving Winget 97 for three off 24 overs. Cheltenham then started to come back as Winget lost wickets at regular intervals, including that of Tetley, run out for 56, as they slumped to 178 for nine off 45 overs.
Last man Andrews joined Wayman who was looking in good form as they added 21 important runs in four overs, leaving three runs off the last over.
Wayman (34) perished first ball to Bailey, leaving Cheltenham victors by two runs, Elliott-Squire's four for 42 making him the top bowler.

Saturday 19th June - Winget In Derby victory

Winget celebrated a victory in their West of England Club Championship Western Division derby match against Gloucester City at The Spa.
Mark Collinson won the toss and inserted Winget on a pitch that offered help to the bowlers.
Sterling was first out to a stunning slip catch by Mark Collinson off O'Dell.
Paul Barker picked up three wickets for 15 runs as Winget slipped to 62 for four off 17 overs. Lambert fell soon after, before Andy Adams (68) and Paul Carter set about repairing the innings.
With sensible running and some late aggression, they added 65 valuable runs before Carter was caught by Nawaz Mucadam off the bowling of Ian Collinson.

Gloucester City		Winget	
M Collinson b Salter	4	Lewis c R Taylor b Bonnell	22
Dawe c Lewis b Salter	1	Tegg c I Collinson b Steadman	0
Newton lbw b Salter	9	Tetley c N Collinson b Bonnell	37
Steadman c Tegg b Salter	0	Lambert not out	32
Cummins c Andrews b Lambert	36	Harrington run out	1
D Collinson b Lewis	23	Wayman b Steadman	6
I Collinson c Lewis b Wayman	3	Salter not out	11
N Collinson c Williams b Wayman	1	Extras	7
P Taylor c&b Lambert	4	Total (5 wkts 30.5 overs)	**116**
B Taylor b Wayman	26		
Bonnell not out	2		
Extras	5		
Total (all out 41.2 overs)	**114**		

Bowling Salter 9-3-27-4; Andrews 9-0-26-0; Lambert 6.3-0-37-2; Lewis 9-4-11-1; Wayman 7-2-11-3

Bowling Steadman 9-1-31-2; Taylor 3-0-20-0; Bonnell 9-5-18-2; N Collinson 5-0-26-0; I Collinson 3-5-0-15-0; Cummins 1-0-2-0

Wayman joined Adams and they added a further 34 runs in five overs. Wayman eventually fell to a catch behind by White and after this, Winget lost their final four wickets for 16 runs, closing on 189 all out with Adams top scoring with 68.
The City reply started well with Lee and Mark Collinson putting on 27 before the former was trapped leg before by Neil Salter. Gwyn Griffiths joined Collinson before the introduction of Carter brought about Collinson's downfall.
Newton and Mucadam soon followed as City slumped to 60 for four. Griffiths was eventually out when he fell to a neat catch behind by Jon Tegg off the bowling of Sterling.
City finally succumbed to 137 all out with only brothers Ian and Dave Collinson looking in any sort of form, Sterling finishing as Winget's leading bowler, giving Winget victory by 52 runs.

Saturday 26th June - Tegg Century fires Winget to victory

Jon Tegg blasted an unbeaten century as Winget overwhelmed Malmesbury by nine wickets in the Western Division of the West of England Club Championship on Saturday.

The Winget opening batsman was in superlative form, striking 102 as Tim Williams' men easily overhauled the 155 they needed for victory.

Spin duo Lewis, with three for 38 and Sterling (three for 46) were the chief destroyers of the Malmesbury batting as only Jeremy Newman with 43 offered any resistance.

The early work was done by Salter who captured one for 23 and Carter one for 44 with a useful opening burst.

Sterling and Tegg were in devastating form as they added 109 in just 24 overs before Sterling was out for 40.

But that did not deter Tegg, who hit 16 boundaries in his unbeaten 102.

Saturday 3rd July - Winget Victory

Winget's excellent run of success continued when they beat Brislington by 10 runs on Saturday.

Tim Williams' men had first use of a good batting wicket. Jon Tegg with 40 and Tetley with 14 added 71, a stand that proved to be the backbone of their innings of 169 for nine, with Scott capturing four for 38.

Brislington's reply was in disarray at five for three, and Salter with four for 38 and Carter three for 20 chipped away as Brislington were reduced to 63 for seven.

Last pair Iles and Tripp were required to get 70 from 10 overs and they made a good fist of it, striking 52 before Lewis took a return catch to give Winget the victory.

Thursday 15th July

Winget retained the Barnwood Shop Fitting Six-a-Side Knockout competition after a 19 run win over Arcadians.

Andy Wilshaw gave Arcadians the perfect start, capturing a hat-trick as Winget were sent reeling to 34 for five.

The match then swung back Winget's way when Jon Andrews smashed 79 not out as the holders finished on 115.

Rob Smart gave Arcadians the perfect start with an unbeaten 26 and Mike Foster increased the tempo with 27, but Arcadians fell just short of the total on 96 as Winget retained the trophy.

Six-A-Side Mayhem

On a beautiful sunny July evening, a very strong (on paper anyway) Winget six took the field for the final of the outdoor 6s against an equally strong Arcadians side on the Spa.

Confidently led by Neil Salter, Winget had no hesitation in batting first. After all, both openers had yet to be 'out' in the competition and the rest, except for Jon Andrews, were well capable of dealing with the Arcadians' attack, or so Neil thought.

Chaos, though. Both openers out in the third over, a third wicket falling in the fourth and another half way through the fifth, the score 30-4 and only Colin Tetley and Jon Andrews left. Neil was pacing the boundary – "What's going on?" We might as well go home….!"

But the voice of reason came from Chris Wayman.

"Look – as long as Colin's batting we've got a chance. Jon will bat sensibly and give Colin the strike. Don't worry!"

Next ball – Colin blocks it and shouts 'NO', but what's this? – Jon hasn't heard, his head is down, his arms pumping like pistons, he sprints past a head bowed Tetley – "What are you doing?" cries Tetley

"Bet he heard that"! shouts a happy Arcadians fan. Tetley run out for 8.

Neil disappears into the pavilion. He's going home.

The score is 34-5 and now it's the last man stand.

The evening is now getting even better for Mr. Tetley, for he now has to stay in the middle and bat with Mr. Andrews (a volatile situation).

What happened next is probably the reason we have all played sport.

Jon, who apart from a few runs in touring fixtures and friendlies, had never shown any inclination that he could score runs in a competitive situation. He took the game, and Mr. Tetley, by the scruff of the neck and launched a blistering attack of pulls, drives, cuts and even hooks on the Arcadians' bowlers.

Suddenly, the game was turning in Winget's favour. The crowd (such as it was) was definitely a little partisan and was getting a bit fed up with Neil's "I told you he could bat!" and "Didn't they know I reversed the order?"

As can be seen from the scorecards, Jon Andrews finished with a marvellous 79 not out, Winget won the match and Arcadians left very early.

Saturday 24th July - Tetley Flows To Ton As Winget Trumph

Colin Tetley hammered a century as Winget's great run continued in the Merchant Investors Western Division game against Midsomer Norton.

Tetley blasted 15 fours and two sixes in his 110 and was the backbone of Winget's 252 for six.
Winget were struggling on 26 for two before Tetley started his assault and he was assisted by Adams' unbeaten 49 as Winget scampered 52 runs from the last six overs.

Midsomer's reply was always behind the clock after Carter and Sterling had made early inroads.
However, Chakrawarti cut loose as he pushed the score on to 188 for five from 40 overs.

But the return of Lambert, who bagged four for 44, accounted for Chakrawarti for 93 as the final five wickets fell for 51 runs.
Winget's victory was tempered by the loss of influential batsman Jon Tegg with a broken thumb and skipper Tim Williams with a dislocated finger.

Winget 1st XI 1999
Mrs E Phelps C Lewis J Newton C Tetley N Burton S Tegg A Hawkes
L Harrington P Carter N Salter J Tegg A Adams

2000

Saturday 13th May - Four wicket success for Winget

Winget eased to a commendable four-wicket success over Hereford to continue their unbeaten start to the season in Gloucestershire and Wiltshire Division One.
Paul Carter struck a match-winning 80 as Winget made it two wins out of two.
Travelling to Hereford, Winget kept the pressure on in the field, restricting the home side to just 196 for nine in their 50 overs with all the bowlers chipping in with wickets.
In reply, the Tuffley Park outfit were never seriously threatened thanks to Carter's knock and Colin Lewis, who chipped in with an unbeaten 40 as Winget reached their total for the loss of four wickets.

Saturday 10th June

Winget collected maximum points over Dumbleton with an ominous display.
At eight for two after three overs Winget were facing problems, but Colin Tetley's 75 and Neil Burton's later order fireworks that produced an unbeaten 70 set Dumbleton the challenging target of 246 to win.
They were never in it and slumped to 74 all out with skipper Neil Salter, Paul Carter and Stuart Wilshaw all collecting three wickets.
"It was a good win and good to collect maximum points" said Salter. "It was not the easiest track to bat on early on, but Colin Tetley played well for 70 and we managed to score 78 runs from the last nine overs. Neil Burton smashed it to all parts of the ground in his 70, hit ting through the line and just took on the bowlers. We bowled well and had them at 27 for four, and Stuart Wilshaw came on and mopped up the tail". Salter added.

Saturday 17th June - Five Star Lewis is Winget hero

Winget became outright leaders of Glos/Wilts Division One with a thumping 10-wicket success over Hatherley and Reddings.
Neil Salter's men continued their challenge at the top of the table after Colin Lewis ripped Hatherley apart with a five-wicket burst as they slipped to 114 all out.
Salter had initially feared the worst when the home side won the toss, but Paul Carter's two for 18 from 15 overs and Salter's two or 17 from 10 pegged Hatherley back.
Lewis then came on and ripped out the lower order to finish with five for 23.
"It was very comfortable" Salter said. "Another 24 points keeps us right up there and I am delighted. There was a bit of grass on the pitch, and if I had won the toss I might have stuck them in, but it was very hot. We kept it tight all the way through and Lewis came on then and ripped out the middle order."
Winget wasted little time in chasing their victory target, racing to 115 in just 14 overs.
Carter continued his impressive form with an unbeaten 47.
"They just basically smashed it from ball one. I thought Hatherley might have given a bit more resistance than they did because they didn't appear to put too much into their bowling" Salter added.

Saturday 15th July - Carter's century brings success

Paul Carter underlined his value to the Winget side with 114 as they bounced back from defeat at Malmesbury last weekend.
Carter's knock formed the backbone of their 233 for nine against Hereford, while Colin Tetley added 58.
In reply, Hereford were dismissed for 183 despite 70 from Dean Mockler.
It left Winget skipper Neil Salter delighted: "It was hard work, but nice to get back to winning ways after losing two games we should have won.
They won the toss and put us in, but the pleasing thing was that we got 22 points and it's still all to play for.
We didn't get the best of starts – Jon Tegg went second ball, but then Paul Carter and Colin Tetley put on 104 for the second wicket. Everybody else chipped in and I was pleased with the total.
We fielded well and bowled well and I think it will go down to the wire," he said.

Saturday 22nd July - Salter and Carter destroy City

Neil Salter and Paul Carter bowled Winget back into championship contention with a five wicket humbling of neighbours Gloucester City on Saturday.

The Winget skipper grabbed five for 32 Paul Carter five for 23 as City were hustled out for just 56.

City won the toss and elected to bat first on a greenish looking pitch, but never came to terms with Salter and Carter. They slumped to 21 for five after 10 overs and only Billy Dawe with 17 and number six Jon Newton who struck 11, reached double figures.

"We started with a vengeance and we did not really expect it to be that easy," said Salter. "They elected to bat first and if I had won the toss, I would have put them in anyway. It was a really good result and it's always nice to take five wickets.

It was unfortunate for City, but it sets us up now for next weekend's game against Frocester. We needed those 23 points and it was nice to get them," Salter added.

Tetley Ensures Winget double

Winget 2nd XI made it a club double, defeating City II by 33 runs at Tuffley Park. Cliff Thomas was the mainstay of the hosts innings with a well made 60, while Tony Sadler struck a patient 35. Radcliffe, Bhaiyat and Robinson claimed 2 wickets apiece for the City, though when the visitors batted it was veteran leg spinner Tony Tetley who wreaked havoc, returning 6-47 from 12 overs. Steve Collinson (34) and Robinson (33) were the mainstays of a Gloucester innings which subsided to 138 all out in the 45th over.
Winget: A.Sadler lbw b Taylor 35, B.Williams b Radcliffe 0, L.Harrington b Radcliffe 1, C.Thomas c Blake b Bhaiyat 60, G.Watts Run Out 23, D.Howe b Robinson 1, P.Newbury b Bhaiyat 0, M.Wildy Run Out 11, R.Owen b Robinson 8, S.Wilson b Ganny 0, A.Tetley Not Out 8. Extras 24, Total 171.
Gloucester City: S.Collinson c Wilson b Tetley 34, S.Patel st Owen b Wildy 0, P.Taylor b Howe 8, A.Robinson c Harrington b Tetley 34, A.May lbw b Tetley 0, W.Radcliffe b Wilson 5, M.Musa c & b Tetley 24, C.Dodds st Owen b Tetley 4, T.Dodswell c Owen b Tetley 11, R.Bhaiyat Not Out 4, W.Ganny b Newbury 1. Extras 14, Total 138.

Saturday 29th July - Winget Slaughter dismal Frocester.

Winget moved a step nearer promotion when they thrashed nearest rivals Frocester at Tuffley Park on Saturday
They are now clear at the top of the Glos/Wilts Division and should win a place in Premier Two of The Stroud and Swindon Building Society League.
Frocester would have been happy when Neil Easto took seven for 41 to bowl out Winget for 175, but the Gloucester side stormed back into the match, bolting out their opponents for 67.

Saturday 12th August - Winget on course for title

Winget remain top of the Gloucester and Wiltshire Division One table after their 38 run victory over Colwall.
The Gloucester side posted a respectable 191 for eight which proved too much for Colwall.
Paul Carter with 38 and Jon Tegg with 20 gave Winget a flying start, while Andy Adams weighed in with 35.
The Colwall spinners put Winget under pressure by slowing down their scoring rate, but captain Neil Salter went on the attack at the end of the innings.
Salter smashed an unbeaten 48, putting on 71 off 10 overs with Stuart Wilshaw who made 15.
Colwall put up some stern resistance but were bowled out for 153, despite 52 from Tim Riley.
Paul Lambert was the pick of the Winget bowlers with four for 39, but there were also good efforts from Wilshaw who took three for 27 and Salter with three for 33.

Saturday 26th August - Williams sees Winget II to Victory

A fine unbeaten half century from Ben Williams and a solid 44 from Dave Howe helped Winget II to a 6 wicket victory over Wootton Bassett at Tuffley Park. Howe and Tony Sadler (20) put together a half century opening stand and though both were dismissed in quick succession, Williams wasted little time in seeing his side home. Earlier, John Knight (3-11), Paul Newbury (2-11), Howe (2-26) and Steve Wilson (2-35) had all been among the wickets as the visitors were dismissed for 143.
Wootton Bassett: D.Ponting b Knight 68, D.Griffin b Howe 5, J.Barnes c Thomas b Howe 0, H.Griffin b Salter 10, C.Cooper b Wilson 6, M.Davies b Wilson 9, N.Smith c Owen b Newbury 15, M.Hill c Thomas b Knight 4, D.Yeoman c Owen b Knight 0, K.Pamphilon c Thomas b Newbury 0, G.King Not Out 0. Extras 22, Total 143
Winget : A Sadler c Griffin b King 20, D Howe c Hill b Griffin 44 , B Williams not out 56 , C Thomas c King b Griffin 2
J.Ellinor c & b Barnes 5, A.Fadden Not Out 8. Extras 9, Total (4 wkts) 147.

2001

Saturday 5th May - Tegg and Newton give Winget brilliant start

Newly promoted Winget began their season in the West of England Premier Two with a 22 run victory over Frenchay.

Jon Tegg led the way with a superb 122 as Winget scored 252 for six batting first.

Frenchay were bowled out for 212 in reply with A. Seymour scoring 51, Jon Newton taking seven for 44 on his debut to snatch the bowling honours

Winget's second XI however was unable to match the success of their senior team.

They scored 150 for eight against Frenchay, but the Bristol club reached the target for the loss of four wickets.

Saturday 12th May - Winget II fall to 6 wicket defeat against Swindon

A total of only 138 was never going to be enough to prevent Winget II sliding to defeat against Swindon's 2nd XI at Tuffley Park. Bob Owen (30) and John Goodchild (25) staged a recovery from 31-5 and though Ben Williams returned 2-26, Swindon eased home with 15 balls to spare.

Winget II: D.Howe c Hayward b Norridge 11, A.Fadden c Howe b Norridge 2, B.Williams b Norridge 0, C.Thomas Run Out 5, J.Goodchild Run Out 25, P.Thomas b Brabazon 4, R.Owen c Rahman b Hayward 30, C.Matthews b Hayward 8, J.Knight lbw b Norridge 9, I.Thomas b Hayward 7, A.Tetley Not Out 0. Extras 38, Total 138.

Swindon II: M.Rahman c Thomas b Williams 10, A.Compton c Owen b Williams 32, D.Baker Not Out 39, M.Hopington st Owen b Tetley 36, D.Howe st Owen b Goodchild 2, C.Iles Not Out 7. Extras 14, Total (4 wkts) 140.

Saturday 26th May - Carter in great form

A superb all round performance by Paul Carter helped Winget thrash Stroud by 222 runs in Premier Two of the West of England Premier League.

On winning the toss, Winget captain Neil Salter had no hesitation in electing to bat, and rewards were immediate as Carter and Jon Tegg set about the Stroud bowling attack.

They scored 120 off the first 20 overs before Tegg (64) was caught behind by Matthew Watts off the bowling of Chris Defelice. Carter was then joined by Steve Tegg (six) and he took the score to 146 before being caught by Keith Daniels, again off the bowling of Defelice.

Colin Tetley joined Carter and added 53 for the third wicket before Tetley (34) was caught behind by Watts off the bowling of Leighton Collins.

Carter continued to destroy the Stroud attack and was joined by Neil Burton (15) and Salter (11) as the score was taken past the 300 mark.

Carter was finally run out for 159 as Winget finished on 316 for seven from their 50 overs.

In reply, Carter and Salter skittled out the top order as Stroud were reduced to 46 for seven.

The only resistance came from Daniels (25) and Collins, who came to the crease and added a gritty 29 before being caught by Andy Hawkes off the bowling of Jon Newton. Stroud were finally bowled out for 94.

Carter capped off a great game with figures of 10-3-26-3, while Salter finished with figures of 11-4-17-4.

Saturday 28th July - Winget double over local rivals.

Winget completed the double over rivals Stroud in their Stroud and Swindon West of England Premier Two Clash.

The Gloucester side had completed a comfortable win over their adversaries on May 26, and Neil Salter's men put in another convincing display to make certain of their triumph.

Salter admitted a four-wicket victory at Tuffley Park was a much-needed boost after a string of recent setbacks.

"We have had three or four defeats, so we needed to get back on to the winning trail" said Salter. "What pleased me most was that it was a fine all round performance by all the lads, which could set us up well for the rest of the season. I was particularly pleased with the performances of our spinners, Colin Lewis and Jon Newton. They bowled a good line on what I think was a pretty good pitch, and caused their batsmen a few problems"

Medium pace bowlers Paul Carter and Salter kept it tight at the start of Stroud's innings. Salter struck an early blow when he bowled opener Cook for three, leaving Stroud on 17 for one. Daniels and Davis held things together for Stroud, taking the score to 55 before the spinners took over.

Lewis grabbed two quick wickets, removing Daniels for 25 and Davis for 18, leaving the visitors' score at 61 for three.
Overseas professional Brett Williams repaired the innings with Martin Kimber.

The South African struck a six and four fours in his 37, while Kimber contributed 19 with both players falling to Newton.
The rest of the Stroud batting put up little resistance, apart from Collins who was run out for 21, and they were bowled out for 161.
Lewis had excellent figures of four for 44, while Newton took three for 27.

Paul Carter dominated the strike in the reply for Winget, putting on 56 for the first wicket with Jon Tegg who was trapped leg before for 11.

Tetley, Englebrecht and Adams kept Carter company for short periods, but his main support came from Lewis who made 24, including four boundaries.

But it was Carter's fine knock that steered Winget towards their victory as he hit 77 in a score of 162 for six.
Carter showed an excellent array of shots with two fine sixes and nine fours.

The best bowling for Stroud came from Williams with two wickets for 12 from 12 overs, while Collins returned two for 45.

Howe and Wilshaw Lead Seconds Home

Winget Second XI also had a resounding success over Stroud, who were skittled out for 73.
Only tailender Clive Mills reached double figures as Wilshaw claimed four for 13 from 10 overs, Dave Howe four for 28 from 12, and Mike Wildy two for 17.

Winget reached their target for the loss of one wicket, with Cliff Thomas hitting an unbeaten 32 and Andy Hawkes 15 not out for a 21-point haul.

Stroud II: T.Chancellor c Tetley b Wilshaw 0, T.Hill b Wildy 3, C.Dutton b Wilshaw 0, S.Cook c Thomas b Howe 7, S.Hewitt c Owen b Wilshaw 6, B.Jeffries b Wilshaw 6, T.Medcroft b Howe 1, S.Whittenbury b Howe 0, I.Butcher b Howe 0, CS Mills Not Out 17, CW Mills c & b Wildy 8. Extras 21, Total 73.

Winget II: C.Thomas Not Out 32, R.Owen c Hewitt b Dutton 10, A.Hawkes Not Out 15, Extras 16, Total (1 wkt) 74.

Saturday 12th August - Last over thriller

Championship chasing Winget kept up their relentless surge towards the Glos/Wilts One Title with a four-wicket success over Dumbleton in a last over thriller.

Winget, who headed the division after their defeat of nearest rivals Frocester a fortnight ago, were indebted a to a superb bowling spell from Colin Lewis who collected six for 43 to deny the home side reaching Winget's 216 for eight.

Dumbleton needed just six runs from the final two overs, but skipper Neil Salter secured a wicket maiden with the final ball of the penultimate over, and he dived in to take the winning catch from Lewis's bowling with just two balls to spare.

Andy Hawkes was the backbone of Winget's total with a stubborn 50 and was the only player to make real use of a flat pitch with a nicely paced innings. He guided Winget to a total of over 200, along with 37 from Paul Carter and 34 from Steve Tegg.

2002

1st XI 2002

R Sterling M Wildy J Newton P Carter C Lewis A Hawkes
N Burton J Tegg L Harrington S Tegg J Tegg snr

Sunday May 19th - Winget v Frocester County Cup

In the County Cup,Frocester got the better of Winget on Sunday in a keenly contested game at Pounds Close.
The Tuffley Park side batted first and thanks to a fine opening stand between Paul Carter who made 67 and Jon Tegg ,looked set for a total in excess of 200 .A tight spell of five for 24 from Trainor and two for 27 from Eric Woodmason restricted Winget to 198 all out.
Frocester effort was evenly with Whincup striking 26 and John Evans 48 ,but Winget battled back ,pegging Frocester back to 94 for 5 after25 overs .
With Trainors 73 not out and Alastair Downey's unbeaten 25,Frocester reached their target in the 43rd over.

Saturday June 15th - Winget v Malmesbury

Winget enjoyed a fine success over Malmesbury.
Opener John Tegg proved the mainstay of their innings with a fine 79,as they made 214 for 7.
Malmesbury were never in the hunt in reply as Winget shared the wickets around to bowl them out for only 136.

Saturday 30th June - Swindon swept aside by devastating Winget

Winget produced a devastating batting display to record a thumping Gloucestershire/Wiltshire One victory over Swindon.
Centuries from John Tegg and Paul Carter enabled the Tuffley Park club to amass an imposing 303 for 6.
Tegg and John Newton startedslaughter with an opening partnership of 75 before Carter joined in the fun following Newton's dismissal for 22.
The pair added 188 in 26 overs and made superb centuries.

Swindon werenever really in the hunt thanks to three wickets from Ben Lambert and Newton and two each for Carter and Colin Lewis,completing a magnificient victory for the Gloucester club who bundled Swindon out for 167.

Saturday July 6th - Tegg steers Winget to a six wicket triumph

Jon Tegg guided Winget to a thoroughly deserved Gloucestershire /Wiltshire One victory on Saturday with his second successive half century.

Hatherley and Reddings were on the receiving end of his effort at North Park as Tegg followed up his century against Swindon the previous week with a match winning 67 to guide the Tuffley Park club to a six wicket triumph.

Paul Carter led the Winget effort in the field with a fine spell of bowling and the removal of the prolific Mark Bray put the skids under Hatherley.

They were eventually dismissed for 187 before Teggs knock secured victory.

It was a fine all-round effort from everybody said club spokesman Cliff Thomas.We have got an experienced side now and Ben Lambert is also showing good form and beating Hatherley is very pleasing.

Obviosly we would like to win every game but we would consolidate in mid table.

Saturday July 20th - Winget v Devizes

Winget's 4th successive win away to Devizes has catapulted them to 4th

The home side batted first but were made to struggle against accurate opening bursts from Paul Carter and Ben Lambert. .Jon Wenton was then introduced and proceeded to take 4 for 59 as Devizes were restricted to 161 for 9.

It has been the bat of Jon Tegg in recent weeks that has proved to be so productive and he and Lambert got Winget off to a flying start with 63 for the first wicket.

Lambert reached his half century and an unbeated 39 from Steve Tegg saw Winget home.

The 126th Season

The 1st XI's hopes of improving on the previous year's third place finish seemed unfounded as the team began 2003 with heavy reversals against Swindon and Trowbridge, and following an abandoned fixture against Goatacre, it was not until 31st May that the first victory was achieved.

Carter – as he had so often proved to be in the past – was the architect of that initial success at Wootton Bassett, returning 5-9 and initiating a run of four straight wins. Progress was pegged back by Dumbleton however, as Winget, requiring seven from the final over could manage only three, but forthcoming encounters with Devizes and Trowbridge eventually proved decisive. Both teams were genuine title contenders when arriving at Tuffley Park, where a rare outing by Neil Salter ended with the former skipper switching ends to claim 5-33 to help dismiss Devizes for just 92, while Trowbridge were shot our for only 59 – Carter this time weaving his magic to record 7-27.

After pegging back their major title rivals, three wins frm the final four games would make it mathematically certain of top spot. The run-in began well – Colin Tetley's explosive 87 from just 43 balls helping his side to a narrow success over Bredon, though reverses at Colwall and at home to Hatherley, coupled with wins for the teams around them, meant Winget would need to defeat Dumbleton while requiring a helping hand from Colwall at Devizes in the final round of matches.

Tetley, in slightly more restrained mood (76 off 49 balls), starred again in a fine all round team performance that yielded a 20 run victory at Dairy Lane, while news that Colwall had won at Devizes sparked off the victory celebrations. Tetley's return to the fold proved to be a great fillip to the side and following his late season heroics, he easily topped the team batting lists with an average of 41, while Carter claimed 36 wickets at an average of below 10 – a championship return if ever there was one.

The 2nd XI proved to be a much more competitive outfit in Division Two, and under the leadership of Tony Fadden claimed six wins from their fifteen completed fixtures. Ultimately there was little to choose between their eighth place finish and all bar Lydney and Hinton Charterhouse, who ended the season well ahead of the chasing pack. Newman, Hatch and Owen totalled almost a thousand runs between them – the team's best batting performance for several years – while Ben Williams, Hatch, and the ever-improving Scott Jones were the side's leading bowlers.

2003

Saturday 31st May

Carter Inspires Winget

Paul Carter produced a superb spell of bowling to inspire Winget to a 10-wicket win over Wootton Bassett.

The stand in skipper, who replaced the unavailable Lloyd Harrington, ripped apart the Bassett batting to capture five for 19 from 11 overs to set Winget on their way to their second Gloucestershire/Wiltshire One victory of the season.

Having been asked to field, Winget immediately took the initiative with opening bowlers Mike Wildy and Carter putting Wootton under pressure on a wicket that showed signs of variable bounce from the outset.

Carter, with his extra height, exploited the bounce well, and backed up by some excellent catching, took the first five wickets to fall to leave Wootton struggling at 38 for five.

It was then left to the spin twins, Colin Lewis and Rob Sterling, to finish off the innings.
Both bowlers enjoyed the sun on their backs and bowled with great control.

They were again supported with excellent ground fielding. The Wootton Bassett batsmen could not free themselves from the stranglehold and were dismissed for 71 in 35 overs.

Lewis claimed figures of two for 21 from 11 overs and Sterling three for 10 from seven.
For Wootton, only Barton showed any form and was the only batsman into double figures – driving well through mid-on and mid-off to score 24 - before becoming Sterling's first victim.

Winget openers Carter and Steve Tegg, after a cautious start, took the attack to the Wootton bowlers.

Tegg, in particular, dealt savagely with anything short of a length and with the support of his captain, Winget raced to their target of 71 in 13 overs with Carter on 26 and Tegg on 38 not out.

Saturday 7th June - Nine wicket Victory for Winget

Winget consolidated their top place position in Gloucestershire / Wiltshire One with a crushing nine-wicket success over Bredon.
It was the third success of the season and left them narrowly clear of Dumbleton following their latest triumph.

Paul Carter retained the captain's armband following their thumping victory over Wootton Bassett and when he won the toss, he invited Bredon skipper Tim Young to bat on a green wicket, juiced up by overnight rain.

Carter opened the bowling with Ben Lambert. Both got the ball to swing and seam off the damp pitch and Bredon wickets soon began to fall.

Backed up again by excellent catching, Bredon slipped to 24 for five, former Gloucester City goalkeeper Lambert proving once again what a valuable all rounder he is by picking up three for 16 in his 11 over spell.

Winget's lack of a third seam bowler was exposed slightly as they had to turn to the spin duo of Colin Lewis and Rob Sterling for the bulk of the remaining overs.

Lewis took two for 33 from 11 and Sterling had one for 27 from 15 as Bredon's lower order of Young (15) Dunn (27), Bridge (19), and Dudfield (16) battled away against the slower bowling and tried to repair the early damage.
But with overs running out Carter returned to the attack to pick up the last two wickets, finishing with four for 28 from 12 and leaving Bredon with a hard earned total of 108.

"Our outfielding, as in previous weeks, was of a good standard, but wicket keeper Jon Tegg's performance behind the stumps on a lively seamers' wicket was of a particularly high standard," said Carter.
After the interval, with the wicket having dried considerably, Winget openers Carter and Steve Tegg attacked from the outset.
Carter hit 23 before being caught at slip with the score on 35. Sterling arrived at number three and he and Steve Tegg set about their target in determined fashion and with the left hand, right hand batting combination making it difficult for the Bredon bowlers to get a consistent line, the two batsmen were always able to keep the scoreboard moving.
Young made regular bowling changes, but he was unable to find a combination to really trouble the two batsmen.
Steve Tegg showed excellent form to finish with a controlled and stylish 46, and Sterling a flamboyant 19 as Winget completed their victory in the 29th over, picking up 21 points.

Saturday 14th June - Sterling Impresses

Winget maintained their grip on top spot in the Gloucestershire / Wiltshire One table with a commanding, but hard-earned victory over Hatherley and Reddings.

A fine all-round contribution from Rob Sterling, who was outstanding with the ball and then made a defiant unbeaten 50, saw Winget home by eight wickets.

He was supported well by Jon Tegg, who struck 63 not out in his first Saturday innings since the first game of the season against Swindon.

Lloyd Harrington won the toss and despite the wicket looking in good condition, asked Hatherley to bat hoping to exploit their lack of runs in recent weeks.

But it was Hatherley who made the better start, with opening batsmen Mark Nally and Hutter playing the Winget opening bowling with confidence.

Harrington then quickly made a bowling change – turning to the left arm spin of Sterling - and he immediately bowled Nally for 21 with the score on 40.

The Hatherley batting started to falter, with Sterling and his spin partner Colin Lewis bowling well in unison.

As the scoring rate slowed, wickets began to fall with only Hutter showing any pedigree in the Hatherley opening order with a score of 67.

The arrival of West Indian Tony Mayer to the crease at number six introduced much needed momentum to the innings as he made Winget pay for a Burton dropped catch at mid-wicket by scoring 24 off one Lewis over – hitting three huge successive sixes.

But when he was run out for a hard hit 37, Hatherley were quickly dismissed for 166. Paul Carter picked up two for 49 and Lewis four for 61, but it was Sterling who was the best of the bowlers, bowling 15 overs and picking up three for 25.

Winget openers Carter and Steve Tegg set about the task of chasing 167 to win but were put under pressure by a fine bowling display by Mayer.

Bowling at a lively pace, he had both batsmen in trouble and accounted for the in-form Steve Tegg for six, deceived by a slower ball with the score on 20. Carter fell the same way for 19, and the game was in the balance with Winget on 50 for two.

Sterling, batting at three, was then joined by Jon Tegg and having battled to see Mayer out of the attack, the two batsmen settled to their task and proceeded to accumulate, without too much trouble, the runs required from the rest of the Hatherley attack.

The pair put on 117 for the third wicket with Sterling capping an excellent game with a fine 50, but playing second fiddle to an excellent and dismissive knock of 63 from Tegg.

Saturday 21 June - Seven Wickets for Carter

Paul Carter produced one of the most devastating bowling spells of the summer to inspire Winget to a crushing victory over Trowbridge.

The all-rounder, who has been suffering from a leg injury, conjured seven for 27 to dismiss Trowbridge for only 59 and get Winget's Gloucestershire / Wiltshire One title dreams back on track.

Carter has taken 28 wickets this season, but was some way short of his career best – nine for eight against Cirencester in 1997.

Bowling off a limited run-up, Carter struck immediately to trap Gingell leg before for one.

Mike Wildy then took a stunning catch to dismiss Edginton for two and Goddard edged his first ball behind for a duck.

Trowbridge then slipped to 18 for four when Edgington was stumped by Jon Tegg off the bowling of Ben Lambert.

Dangerman Burger was lucky to survive another stumping chance off Lambert, but Carter got his man when Steve Tegg took a straightforward slip catch to remove him for 10.

Whitting was the third batsman in the game to be out first ball when he was brilliantly caught by Lambert, again off Carter, and Trowbridge were reeling at 29 for six.

There was no stopping the seamer now, and Carter struck again when Lloyd Harrington held on to a catch from Heel for eight.

Jon Newton replaced Lambert, and immediately struck when Whitting was leg before for 11.

But Carter was in superb form, taking a return catch from Russell and when Newton picked up his second wicket, Trowbridge had been blitzed for 59 – Carter picking up seven wickets.

Earlier Winget had been asked to bat first, and after a solid start from Steve Tegg and Robin Sterling, the innings begin to slip away. South African Burger bowled at a lively pace and forced Jon Tegg and Lambert on to the defensive.

Lambert was the first to fall and Neil Burton's miserable season continued when he was leg before for a solitary run. Burger then had Jon Tegg caught at second slip.

Winget were in trouble at 68 for five, but Colin Tetley was then joined by Newton and the pair tried to rebuild the innings.

With the score at a precarious 89 for six and with 21 overs remaining, Carter came in to bat with Newton. The pair began cautiously, conscious of the time left in their innings, but they slowly built up momentum and put on 43 runs in nine overs before Newton was dismissed for 21.

Harrington was unluckily caught next ball at point off the same bowler and Winget were again struggling at 132 for eight.

At 143 for nine they were desperate to get the extra batting point on offer available at 150 but easily achieved their target as the Trowbridge bowlers lost their length and direction.

With Carter finding the gaps in the field and last man Mike Wildy prepared to block, the pair put on 29 runs for the last wicket before Carter was caught for a top score of 36, Winget finished on 172 before Carter's outstanding spell of bowling fired his team to glory.

Saturday 5th July - Knight Inspires Winget II to victory at Box

Winget II notched up only their second victory of the season as a fine all round performance from John Knight saw them to a 45 run win at Box. Coming in at No 9, Knight (35) and the consistent Greig Newman (28 not out) added 45 for the 8th wicket to hoist the visitors to 182-9. An excellent opening spell from Scott Jones (3-25) put the hosts on the back foot before Knight (3-20) administered the last rites.

Winget II R.Owen c Mead b Lilley 17, R.Bennett c Gray b McClounan 28, D.Hatch c Patterson b Lilley 10, J.Trigg b Gray 7, A.Fadden c & b Hope 11, M.Hussein b Lilley 3, G.Newman Not Out 28, S.Jones st Mead b Hope 4, J.Knight c Lilley b McClounan 35, J.Dando b Lilley 0. Extras 39, Total 182.

Box II M.Hope st Owen b Jones 15, D.Cogwell c Bennett b Jones, M.Saunders c Bennett b Jones 0, C.Carmody Run Out 25, N.Millward b Bennett 0, R.Gray b Knight 14, M.Lilley st Owen b Knight 7, D.Mead c Knight b Bennett 2, P.Patterson Not Out 11, C.McClounan b Hatch 5, S.McClounan c Hatch b Knight 2. Extras 24, Total 137.

Saturday 2nd August - Victory Carries Winget Closer To Title

Winget's ruthless home efficiency ensured another comfortable victory on Saturday - and moved them a step closer to the Gloucestershire / Wiltshire One title.

While they begin a tortuous run-in next weekend that will culminate at their nearest rivals Dumbleton, Winget were far too strong for Wootton Bassett.

Their six-wicket victory was every bit as emphatic as the margin suggests and the only concern was a leg injury to all rounder Paul Carter that required hospital treatment

Before his collision with team-mate Andy Hawkes Carter was in the thick of the action, collecting a wicket in the first over after Lloyd Harrington had won the toss and elected to field.

Carter then proceeded to take the next three wickets to leave Bassett in dire straits on 24 for four after 17 overs.

It was left to the youngster Lukens and his senior partner Smith to repair the innings and unlike several sides who have visited Tuffley Park this season, the two batsmen dug in and batted well against both seam and spin.

Having taken the score to 94 in a stand of 70 in 25 overs, both batsmen looked set to launch a final assault before Carter's injury.

Following a long break in play Lukens lost his concentration and was trapped leg before by Colin Lewis for an excellent 30.

With only seven overs remaining and Winget in a desperate search of the five remaining wickets, it was left to the spinning duo of Robin Sterling and Colin Lewis to remove the remaining batsmen.

Backed up by some excellent catching, wickets fell at regular intervals and the Wootton innings finished in the final over with the score on 132 when Smith was last out, bowled by Sterling for a hard-fought 47.

The pick of the bowlers was Carter with four for 19 from 15 overs, Lewis with three for 46 from 10 and Sterling with three for 31 from 12. Steve Tegg and Robin Sterling put on 21 for the first wicket before Tegg was adjudged leg before for nine.

Ben Lambert managed only two before he also fell to a leg before and the Wiltshire side sensed the possibility of an upset with the score at 30 for two in the 11th over.

Sterling went for 29 after a brilliant slip catch by Leach left Winget at 54 for three.

Jon Newton was in fine form for his 35 before he became the third batsman to be dismissed leg before.

Harrington joined Jon Tegg in search of the required 40 runs and despite a couple of alarms, the pair led the Gloucester side home with Tegg in his usual bullish fashion, dismissing the bowling in an unbeaten 32.

"It was an excellent performance from us and we deserved the win" Harrington said. "Wootton Bassett, to their credit, fought hard but we were just too strong for them. It was good to see Jon Newton battling with such confidence and for the first time in Winget colours he showed with the bat what I know he is capable of"

Saturday 9th August - Batsmen lead seconds to victory

Winget II were indebted to local club Highnam who provided three players at short notice to offset availability problems caused by the holiday season. A big opening stand between Tony Fadden and Bob Owen and some fine middle order hitting from Damien Hatch set up the opportunity of a victory against Apperley, who eventually ended 58 runs short of the home side's 253-5. Brian Leeke (46) batted well for the visitors but John Goodchild's 3-33 from 12 overs helped Winget home.

Winget II: R.Owen c Greenaway b Taylor 38, A.Fadden b Griffiths 48, S.Jones c Taylor b Griffiths 7, B.Williams b Taylor 18, D.Hatch Not Out 69, M.Loughlin b Leeke 25, J.Goodchild Not Out 9. Extras 37 Total (5 wkts) 253.

Apperley II: M.Macpherson c Owen b Hathaway 6, B.Leeke b Williams 46, S.Best b Hathaway 0, J.Davison b Goodchild 21, M.Griffiths b Goodchild 20, S.Greenaway b Goodchild 22, C.Chatham Not Out 32, R.Taylor b Jones 5, N.Wallace Not Out 5. Extras 29 Total (7 wkts) 195.

Saturday 16th August - Winget II Blown Away At The Spa

Gloucester City II strolled to a 9-wicket victory over Winget II at The Spa. Bob Taylor took 4-24 and Greig Newman hit 62 not out as the visitors laboured to 156-6, a total passed by City with 9 wickets and 10 overs to spare. Jeremy Evans (57) was the only home wicket to fall as Ian Collingwood (42no) and Howard Johnson (43no) eased their team to victory.

Winget II: R.Owen c Dawe b Price 7, A.Fadden b Taylor 12, G.Newman Not Out 62, B.Williams c & b Evans 34, D.Hatch b Taylor 24, M.Jones b Taylor 3, M.Haines c Morse b Taylor 2, S.Jones Not Out 2. Extras 12, Total (6 wkts) 156.
Gloucester City II: I.Collingwood Not Out 42, J.Evans c Newman b Hatch 57, H.Johnson Not Out 43. Extras 14, Total (1 wkt) 157.

Saturday 30th August - Winget Take League Title

The Tuffley Park club produced one of their best results of recent times to finish top of Gloucestershire / Wiltshire One, after a high scoring clash against Dumbleton.

Going into their fixture, Wiltshire side Devizes seemed certain to land the title and promotion into Premier Two, if they could beat third placed Colwall.

Winget needed to hope not only that Colwall won, but that they could also secure a large points haul at Dairy Lane.
Batting first, Lloyd Harrington's side made an imposing 243 all out before restricting Dumbleton to 223 for nine.

That left them sweating on the result at Devizes where Colwall posted 187 for nine before bowling their opponents out for 172.
It meant Winget were crowned champions – but they were unable to take their place in the higher division because their structure did not meet league requirements.

Winget CC – 1st XI Averages 2003

Batting Averages

Player	Matches	Inns	N/Out	Runs	H/Score	Average
Colin Tetley	8	7	0	287	87	41.0
Jon Tegg	13	11	2	286	63*	31.7
Steve Tegg	14	14	2	279	53	23.2
Paul Carter	13	12	1	249	66	22.6
Rob Sterling	15	14	2	256	50*	21.3
Ben Lambert	14	12	0	238	55	19.8
John Newton	10	7	1	108	35	18.0
Lloyd Harrington	14	12	2	149	44	14.9
Colin Lewis	14	10	4	68	25*	11.3
Andy Hawkes	14	10	2	90	37	11.2
Neil Buton	11	8	0	57	21	7.1
Mike Wildy	12	7	2	20	11	4.0

Also Batted

F. Salim 13; S. Jones 6, 0; H. Mohammed 5*; P. Douse 20; D. Hatch 0; N. Salter 5; J. Tegg snr 0,1,7*; J. Trigg 3; A. Fadden 0*; Y. Pandon 0,8,9.

Bowling Averages

	Overs	Mdns	Runs	Wkts	Best	Average
Paul Carter	148	45	340	36	7-27	9.44
John Newton	32	1	148	10	3-46	14.80
Ben Lambert	133	37	398	21	4-23	18.95
Colin Lewis	127	12	539	24	4-61	22.46
Rob Sterling	159	28	483	21	3-10	23.00
Mike Wildy	75	8	336	10	3-29	33.60

Also Bowled

N. Salter 15-5-33-5; Y. Pandor 9-0-41-1; S. Jones 16-0-73-1; F. Salim 7-1-29-1.

Fielding

16:	Jon Tegg
9:	Lloyd Harrington
8:	Paul Carter
7:	Ben Lambert, Steve Tegg
6:	Colin Lewis
5:	Rob Sterling
4:	Andy Hawkes, Mike Wildy, John Newton
2:	Cliff Thomas, Colin Tetley, Scott Jones
1:	Damien Hatch

Winget CC –2nd XI Averages 2003

Batting Averages

Player	Matches	Inns	N/Out	Runs	H/Score	Average
Greig Newman	8	8	3	325	72	65.00
Mike Haines	8	6	2	111	35*	27.75
Bob Owen	15	15	3	330	60*	27.50
Damien Hatch	15	15	3	310	95	25.80
Russ Bennett	6	5	0	66	33	13.20
Tony Fadden	16	16	0	200	48	12.50
Scot Jones	13	12	1	137	29	12.45
Ben Williams	12	12	0	143	34	11.90
John Knight	9	6	1	55	35	11.00
Jason Trigg	7	6	1	52	28*	10.40
Eddie Hyde	13	8	5	30	14*	10.00
Mo Hasnain	7	4	0	25	10	6.25

Also Batted

A. Watkins 4, 10, 0, 1, 0, 0; A. Salter 0,0; L. Harrington 64; M. Blackford 2*; C. Thomas 4, 12; I. Holl 9, 0, 1, 4; A. Hawkes 52*; M. Jones 3; T. Sanders 0*; J. Dando 0; Salim 5*

Bowling Averages

	Overs	Mdns	Runs	Wkts	Best	Average
Ben Williams	45	3	279	16	3-10	17.4
Mike Haines	51	3	257	11	5-43	23.4
Jason Trigg	13	0	75	3	2-39	25.0
Mo Pandor	14	0	53	2	2-19	26.5
Damien Hatch	99	5	498	16	3-31	31.1
Scott Jones	126	17	447	14	3-25	31.9
Russ Bennett	50	10	169	5	2-32	33.8
John Knight	61	3	265	7	3-54	37.9
Wally Watkins	46	6	184	4	2-48	46.0

Also Bowled

A. Salter 6-0-31-0; L. Harrington 10-0-45-2; Omar 7-0-26-0; P. Collins 12-2-24-4; Teddy 2-0-11-1; S. Wilson 12-2-37-3; Salim 8-2-25-3; A. Davis 4-0-40-1; A. Hathaway 7-1-27-2; J. Goodchild 12-2-33-3; G. Newman 2-0-15-0

Fielding

16:     Bob Owen
5:     Ben Williams
4:     Damien Hatch
3:     Greg Newman, Mike Haines, John Knight
2:     Jason Trigg, Cliff Thomas, Russ Bennett
1:     A. Salter, E. Hyde, M. Blackford

The Last Rites

The 127th and final season in the long and often illustrious history of Winget Cricket Club began in disastrous fashion as the 1st XI, fielding a largely inexperienced side due to injury and unavailability, began with five straight defeats, an opening from which they never fully recovered. New captain Ben Lambert was the first high-profile name on the injured list, the all rounder breaking his leg playing 5-a-side football shortly before the start of the season and his absence proved to be a key factor in the team's struggles to find any sort of consistency.

May – and a 10-wicket drubbing by Stroud and a 185-run loss at Trowbridge tell their own story, but wicketkeeper-batsman Jon Tegg was in the form of his life, hitting two unbeaten centuries and a 91 not out in the opening four matches, his eventual season's aggregate of 771 runs at 70 being his best ever return.

The first victory on 19th June coincided with the return after injury of Paul Carter, though it was another Tegg century and four wickets from Colin Lewis that were the biggest factors in a 61 run success over fellow strugglers Dumbleton at Tuffley Park. Lewis went on to top the 1st XI bowling averages with 32 wickets at 17 apiece, though the fact that no other bowler even threatened to reach the 20-wicket mark is symptomatic of the team's struggles to dismiss the opposition over the course of the summer.

One other player to impress however was the mercurial Rob Sterling who struck over 500 runs, a total that included an unbeaten century in the return victory over Dumbleton. Indeed, four wins and a narrow 2-wicket defeat at the hands of Colwall from the last five games was title-chasing form, but with only that earlier victory over Dumbleton from the previous ten outings, a bottom-but-one finish could not be avoided.

Player availability was a problem throughout, with the 1st XI calling on 34 different individuals during the campaign, while the 2nd XI team sheet included no fewer than 41 different players and the disappointing results reflected this. Yakub Pandor was forced to stand down as second team captain at the very beginning of the campaign due to illness, so Tony Fadden continued to perform a sterling role at the helm for the third consecutive season.

Bob Owen and Ben Williams contributed over 700 runs between them, with Williams' unbeaten century at Marlborough being one of the few statistical highlights of the campaign. On this occasion, an eighth wicket stand with John Knight which looked as if it might force an unlikely victory was ended when Knight top edged a delivery into his face, resulting not only in the spinner being forced into a premature departure, but also the enforced absence for some time thereafter of the only bowler likely to support the wicket taking efforts of Steve Wilson, who claimed 34 scalps at an average of barely 14 – a return which accounted for nearly 40% of his side's wickets.

The condition of both the square and the outfield at Tuffley Park had been giving concern from day one, but despite a series of representations to the City Council, no improvements were forthcoming. The situation regarding playing strength in terms of both numbers and quality was becoming desparate and with no youth section to provide back-up or hope for future seasons, it seemed as if 2004 would see the end of Winget CC competing in the senior leagues for the foreseeable future.

Several ideas were banded regarding the direction in which the future might lie and to what it might hold, but at the beginning of August an approach was made by Gloucester City CC as to the possibility of a merger between the city's two largest clubs. This possibility had been muted several seasons previously and explored again in some depth in 2002, but this new proposal was backed up by realistic ideas and provided real potential benefits for both parties. Initial meetings at both Winget and The Spa realised a positive response towards the idea, so the West of England Premier League committee was informed of the proposal that Gloucester City and Winget merge for entry into the Gloucester / Wiltshire League in 2005.

Things had to move fast now, for applications to the WEPL structure had to be received by mid-September. Further committee meetings at each club were held and a joint meeting of the two committees on 7th September agreed on further details for the proposed amalgamation. At 7.30pm on Friday 10th September, Extraordinary General Meetings of both Winget and Gloucester City Cricket Clubs took place at Tuffley Park and The Spa respectively, and by 9.00 that evening both clubs declared overwhelming support for the merger.

Six days later Winget secretary Ivor Thomas, who played a leading role in the negotiations throughout, presented up-to-date details of the merger to WEPL and on 27th September, the incumbent committees of Winget and Gloucester City met to begin to thrash out the smaller details of the amalgamation.

On Tuesday 12th October the final committee meeting of Winget Cricket Club was held at Tuffley Park and on Friday 29th October, Winget members were invited to and attended Gloucester City's 175th Anniversary Dinner at the New County Hotel, where City chairman Colin Dodds talked enthusiastically of the merger.

The inaugural AGM of the new 'Gloucester City Winget Cricket Club' was held on Friday 12th November at The Spa and a new committee was appointed. It was agreed that the 1st and 2nd XI's of the new club will play their home matches at The Spa, while the 3rd and 4th XI's will stage their home fixtures at Tuffley Park. The two senior sides will compete in the Gloucestershire / Wiltshire League, while the 3rd XI will enter the C & G competition with the 4th XI playing in the '2nd XI' County League competition.

Considering that less than ten years ago Gloucester City were a strong Western League side and just four years previously, in 2001, Winget were holding their own in the West of England Premier League Division Two, the respective league placings of the newly formed GCWCC for 2005 may seem fairly modest. Yet this really is a large part of the justification for a merger from the point of view of both Gloucester City and Winget and the hope that the joint playing strength created by this amalgamation, backed by the youth set-up that has been carefully developed over the past decade at The Spa, will see Gloucester having a cricket club that can return to a position of former glories and foster a sporting institution of which the city itself can be justifiably proud.

And so for Winget Cricket Club as we know it, the end has come. But for senior cricket in the city of Gloucester, a new era has dawned. Two clubs with over 300 years of history become one and while 'From Wagon Works to Winget – the story of a Cricket Club' is now complete, a new tale of sporting folk and the club that binds them together, is just beginning.

Winget CC – 1st XI Averages 2004

Batting Averages

Player	Matches	Inns	N/Out	Runs	H/Score	Average
Jon Tegg	15	15	4	771	127*	70.1
Paul Carter	10	9	2	273	82	39.0
Rob Sterling	15	15	1	532	112*	38.0
Lloyd Harrington	13	12	5	192	70*	27.4
Abu Saleh	5	5	1	80	38	20.0
Greig Newman	12	10	0	140	41	14.0
Steve Tegg	7	6	2	55	17*	13.7
Mike Wildy	13	8	4	47	26*	11.8
Neil Burton	6	5	0	39	14	7.8
Colin Lewis	14	8	1	20	10	2.9

Also Batted

C.Wayman: 3, 42, 9. A.Hawkes: 1, 1. J.Newton: 16, 0, 0, 11. T.Sheikh: 0. S.Jones: 0. 4*, 10. S.Fourie: 7. C.Thomas: 1*. M.Loughlin: 13*. A.Fadden: 14. A.Adams: 3, 0, 0. C.Tetley: 4. B.Lambert: 3, 0, 7, 4*, 10. R.Francis: 33. I.Thomas: 0*.M.Nell: 4.

Bowling Averages

	Overs	Mdns	Runs	Wkts	Best	Average
Ben Lambert	42	7	148	9	3-21	16.44
Colin Lewis	135	19	548	32	5-31	17.12
Paul Carter	122	27	370	14	2-29	26.43
Scott Jones	33	1	165	6	2-11	27.50
Rob Sterling	143	25	465	15	3-35	31.00
Mike Wildy	122	17	473	14	3-44	33.79
Jon Newton	22	0	120	3	1-18	60.00

Also Bowled

A.Saleh: 38-3-188-0; T.Sheikh: 5-0-52-0; S.Fourie: 6-0-22-0; M.Davies: 6-0-33-1; N.Burton: 1-0-21-1; R.Francis: 6-0-36-0; A.Adams: 3-0-18-0; S.Tegg: 1-0-8-0; J.Goodchild: 4-0-34-1.

Fielding

14:	Lloyd Harrington
12:	Jon Tegg, Colin Lewis
6:	B.Lambert
5:	Rob Sterling
3:	Greig Newman
2:	Abu Saleh, Andy Adams, Steve Tegg, Scott Jones, Mike Wildy
1:	Cliff Thomas, Neil Burton, Paul Carter, R.Francis, Martin Loughlin

Winget CC –2nd XI Averages 2004

Batting Averages

Player	Matches	Inns	N/Out	Runs	H/Score	Average
Bob Owen	14	14	3	406	61*	36.9
Ben Williams	10	10	1	331	103*	36.7
Tony Fadden	12	12	0	232	58	19.3
Damien Hatch	8	8	0	132	36	16.5
John Knight	5	5	2	40	18*	13.3
Eddie Hyde	7	7	2	32	9	6.4
Andy Sharpe	5	4	1	18	13	6.0
Tahir Sheikh	8	7	2	25	10*	5.0
Ivor Thomas	10	7	3	18	14	4.5
Steve Wilson	12	11	2	38	15*	4.2
Mo Pandor	8	7	2	16	5	3.2
Scott Jones	4	4	0	12	5	3.0

Also Batted

T.Sanders: 0, 5, 0, 0, 1; J.Trigg: 0, 4, 0, 1, 0; R.Hussain: 2; J.Faulkener: 18; G.Weekes: 0; A.Hussain: 0*; S.Fourie: 5; G.Newman: 4; M.Patel: 20; Salim: 21; Khan: 0; M.Hussain: 4; R.Bennett: 2; P.Carter: 54; I.Dessai: 17*, 0, 0; A.Hawkes: 10, 1; Aziz: 17; B.Lambert: 20; M.Jones: 0; G.Watts: 5, 1; K.Pepperell: 0; I.Holl: 0, 22; C.Thomas: 24; J.Goodchild: 12; J.Andrews: 15; J.Ellinor: 5; C.Collinson: 0.

Bowling Averages

	Overs	Mdns	Runs	Wkts	Best	Average
Steve Wilson	148	30	499	34	7-36	14.7
Scott Jones	25	7	77	5	3-44	15.4
John Knight	54	7	200	12	4-37	16.7
Jason Trigg	23	0	144	4	2-56	36.0
Ivor Thomas	79	9	262	6	3-43	43.7
Mo Pandor	34	1	180	3	1-22	60.0
Damien Hatch	73	8	354	5	3-20	70.8
Tahir Sheikh	49	3	232	3	1-16	77.3

Also Bowled

S.Fourie: 13-1-59-3; A.Fadden: 8-0-66-1; Salim: 11-3-21-0; R.Bennett: 11-0-37-0; A.Sharpe: 12-0-83-1; M.Patel: 3-0-21-0; G.Newman: 1-0-17-0; M.Hussein: 1-0-6-0; A.Veshmia: 13-1-35-5; P.Carter: 13-2-27-4; I.Dessai: 2-0-10-0; B.Lambert: 9-1-30-2; M.Jones: 5-0-52-0; B.Williams: 4-0-25-0; J.Goodchild: 13-3-61-2.

Fielding

14:	Bob Owen
4:	Tony Fadden, Steve Wilson, Paul Carter
3:	Ben Williams
2:	Jason Trigg, Tim Sanders, Damien Hatch, Mo Pandor
1:	Andy Sharpe, I.Dessai, A.Veshmia, Ian Holl, John Knight, Gary Watts, Eddie Hyde

GLOUCESTERSHIRE COUNTY CRICKET CLUB

AND THE WAGON WORKS

Gloucestershire played their first championship match on the ground on the 2nd, 3rd and 4th June 1923 against Lancashire, who won the match by 75 runs. In all, 155 matches have been played on the ground with Gloucestershire winning 43, 55 being drawn, 57 lost and 4 abandoned.

W R Hammond's highest score for Gloucestershire was made on this ground, 317 against Nottinghamshire in 1936; in addition 5 scores of 200 and 60 scores of 100 were made between 1923-1992.

Gloucestershire's record 4th wicket partnership of 321 (W R Hammond and W L Neale) was also made on this ground against Leicestershire in 1937 and Zaheer Abbas equalled W R Hammond's world record of 7 centuries in each innings of a match when scoring 162* and 107 against Lancashire in 1982.

The county has played against overseas touring sides, namely New Zealand and India, and the South West of England Ladies played Australia Ladies in the early 1970s. On the 12th June 1965 a County Club and Ground side played against the Works team and included the following players:

TEAM

B Richards	M Procter	D Shepherd	D Bevan	R Etheridge	G Wiltshire
T Riley	W Mustoe	J Sullivan	P Hillman	M Haynes	

TEST AND COUNTY PLAYERS WHO HAVE PLAYED ON THE GROUND

Below is a list of some of the great players who have graced the Works Ground.

T M Alderman	R C Russell	D V Lawrence	E R Dexter	J A Snow	D I Gower
R Illingworth	D L Underwood	W R Hammond	M J Procter	I T Botham	W J Edrich
C Washbrook	K R Miller	D A Allen	J B Mortimore	R E S Wyatt	G A R Lock
J C Laker	B D Wells	G Emmett	C A Milton	A E Wilson	L B Fishlock
G E Lambert	A E Wilson	C Cook	T W Graveney	T W Goddard	D M Young
B Richards	C J Barnett	C W L Parker	B D'Oliviera	P M Walker	A R Lewis
C Milburn	D Amiss	K F Barrington	Zaheer Abbas	Sadiq Mohammad	D M Green
G S T Sobers	B Bolus	R M Prideaux	Mushtaq Mohammad	D S Steele	H M Ackerman
F J Titmus	M W Gatting	P H Edmonds	G Boycott	C Walsh	K R Fletcher
D C S Compton	M Marshall	P May	Kapil Dev	S Gavaskar	F Engineer
D W Randall	B S Bedi	B S Chandreskhar	M C Cowdrey	H Larwood	JS Hobbs
K S Duleepsinhji					

The list is endless and I am sure that you can think of others, indeed it would make a good topic for conversation. One statistic that seems to be lost is that of Mike Procter's batting average on the Works ground, which was his highest at any first class ground on which he regularly played (1357 runs at 43.77 including 4 centuries).

For what it's worth, I have chosen a Gloucestershire 'Dream Team' from County players that have played on the Wagon Works Ground. Alongside is an all stars team of non-Gloucestershire players who have also appeared.

	Gloucestershire XI	All Stars XI
1	C J Barnett	S Gavaskar
2	Sadiq Mohammed	J S Hobbs
3	Zaheer Abbas	P May (Capt)
4	W R Hammond	M C Cowdrey
5	T W Graveney	D C S Compton
6	M J Procter (Capt)	G A Sobers
7	J C Russell (Wkt)	K R Miller
8	D A Allen	I T Botham
9	T W Goddard	F M Engineer (Wkt)
10	G E Lambert	H Larwood
11	C Walsh	M Marshall

I have chosen Mike Procter as the Gloucestershire skipper for his all round ability and because I found him a player who put back into the game what he took out. I remember after one County match at the ground where Procter, as captain, dressed in blazer and tie, was last to leave the pavilion. After a short conversation with the groundsman, John Taylor, he enquired from a steward how many young autograph hunters there were. When told, he pulled up a chair and told the youngsters to form an orderly queue and then stayed until he had signed everyone's autograph book.

This I admired as I have witnessed many so-called stars who begrudge the youngsters who help make them stars in the first place. Also included is T W Goddard to represent the Works team and Courtney Walsh who has taken well over 400 test wickets. I am sure it would be a game to delight us all and it would be of interest to add up all the Test appearances made by these players.

I am sure that there are many who, having watched the County play on the ground, have stories to tell of individual feats of play over the years. In the early seasons of County Cricket, spectators' main form of transport was usually a bicycle and I am told that during their lunch breaks and after work, hundreds of employees from local industries cycled to the ground to watch their heroes. Many paid at the gate, sometimes at reduced rates, but Wagon Works' employees gained access with their sports and social club cards. There were also those, especially youngsters, who chose to view from over the wall at the Tuffley Avenue end standing on their bicycle saddles.

I had the opportunity many years ago to speak to Mr G A Edrich, the ex Lancashire player and brother of Bill Edrich. Winget had just completed a game against C E Baker's XI from Cheltenham and Geoff had turned out for them. He told us the story of his first County match which was played against Gloucestershire on the Works ground. He had opened the batting and during the first over edged a ball from Lambert to the wicket keeper. As the appeal was turned down, Geoff, being keen to impress, did not walk. At the end of the over Wally Hammond walked past him and without pausing said to Geoff, "Your brother would have walked." "Needless to say", Geoff explained, "those few words were enough to unnerve me and I was out shortly afterwards."

I was also involved in a conversation with Sadiq Mohammed, the County opener, during a match in the 1970s. A spectator asked Sadiq what he thought of Alastair Hignall's batting. His short but concise reply was, "Alastair bats like a rugby player". Alastair, of course, played rugby for England.

MATCHES PLAYED AT THE TUFFLEY AVENUE GROUND

ALSO KNOWN AS WAGON WORKS GROUND

1923 – 1992

Derbyshire	1924 1927 1934 1951 1957 1961 1967 1969 1978 1982 1984 1986 1991
Essex	1925 1929 1934 1938 1939 1946 1954 1973 1978 1980
Glamorgan	1933 1950 1952 1953 1954 1966
Hampshire	1926 1930 1932 1933 1948 1951 1956 1972 1979 1987 1988 1990
Kent	1928 1936 1938 1948 1954 1955 1959 1979 1986
Lancashire	1923 1924 1926 1930 1935 1937 1939 1946 1950 1959 1982
Leicestershire	1925 1935 1936 1937 1947 1957 1964 1977 1988 1990
Middlesex	1929 1934 1946 1952 1956 1957 1961 1963 1971 1976
Northants	1927 1947 1952 1955 1958 1960 1965 1968
Nottinghamshire	1928 1936 1953 1958 1967 1971 1989 1991
Somerset	1992
Surrey	1925 1932 1939 1951 1956 1959 1962 1964 1970
Sussex	1926 1930 1933 1938 1949 1972 1974 1976 1989
Warwickshire	1931 1932 1934 1935 1937 1949 1950 1963 1965 1970 1981
Worcestershire	1929 1931 1936 1947 1948 1949 1955 1958 1962 1966 1984 1985 1987 1992
Yorkshire	1924 1927 1933 1935 1938 1953 1960 1969 1973 1985
Indians	1974
New Zealand	1931
Cambridge University	1946
Combined Services	1948

Tuffley Park, Gloucester

Playing Record (1923-1992):	Played	Won	Lost	Drawn	Abandoned
County Championship	151	41	56	54	4
Other First Class	4	2	1	1	0
Total	155	43	57	55	4

First Match	June 2, 4, 5 1923		v Lancashire	
Last Match	May 23, 25, 26 1992		v Somerset	

Highest Innings Total:	Gloucs:	529		v Glamorgan	1933
	Opponents	553		- Essex	1938
Lowest Innings Total:	Gloucs:	42		v Yorkshire	1924
	Opponents	34		- Cambridge Univ.	1946
Highest Individual Score:	Gloucs:	317	W.R Hammond	v Nottinghamshire	1936
	Opponents	263*	H.T.W. Hardinge	- Kent	1928
Best Bowling in an Innings:	Gloucs:	9-44	C.W.L Parker	v Essex	1925
	Opponents	9-37	M.S. Nichols	- Essex	1938
Best Bowling in a Match:	Gloucs:	17-56	C.W.L Parker	v Essex	1925
	Opponents	15-165	M.S. Nichols	- Essex	1938

Most Matches:		62	T.W.J. Goddard	
Most Runs:		3549	W.R. Hammond	
Hundreds:	Total:	135	(Gloucs 65, Opponents 70)	
	Most:	13	W.R. Hammond	
Most Wickets:		343	T.W.J. Goddard	

First Class Highest Wicket Partnerships – Gloucestershire

1st	144	C.A. Milton & R.B. Nicholls	v Nottinghamshire	1967
2nd	195	R.A. Sinfield & B.H. Lyon	v Esssex	1929
3rd	213	C.W.J. Athey & P. Bainbridge	v Yorkshire	1985
4th	321	W.R. Hammond & W.L. Neale	v Leicestershire	1937
5th	219	M.J. Procter & J.C. Foat	v Essex	1978
6th	140	W.R Hammond & H. Smith	v Northamptonshire	1927
7th	151	B.O. Allen & G.W. Parker	v Hampshire	1932
8th	120	W.R. Hammond & C.W.L. Parker	v Yorkshire	1927
9th	133	W.R. Hammond & V. Hopkins	v Nottinghamshire	1936
10th	89	R.C. Russell & A.M. Smith	v Somerset	1992

First Class Highest Wicket Partnerships – Opponents

1st	274	P. Holmes & H. Sutcliffe	- Yorkshire	1927
2nd	231	T.S. Curtis & G.A. Hick	- Worcestershire	1987
3rd	311	C.G. Greenidge & D.R. Turner	- Hampshire	1987
4th	211	M. Azharuddin & T.J.G. O'Gorman	- Derbyshire	1991
5th	214	P.H. Parfitt & H.J. Featherstone	- Middlesex	1971
6th	145	J.W. Hearnne &H.J. Enthoven	- Middlesex	1934
7th	132	C.H. Taylor & J.C. Bradshaw	- Leicestershire	1925
8th	134	M.S. Nichols & C.S.R. Boswell	- Essex	1934
9th	93	H. Larwood & S.J. Staples	- Nottinghamshire	1928
10th	66*	P.I. Bedford & M.O.C. Sturt	- Middlesex	1961

Limited-over Records	Played	Won	Lost	No Result	Abandoned
Gillette / Natwest (1990)	1	1	0	0	0
Sunday League (1969-1992)	24	11	11	2	2
Benson & Hedges (1981-1983)	2	0	1	1	0
Total	27	12	12	3	2

Highest Innings Total:	Gloucs:	325-4	(NW)	V Lincolnshire	1990
	Opponents	272-4	(SL)	- Derbyshire	1984
Lowest Innings Total:	Gloucs:	107	(SL)	V Kent	1979
	Opponents	86	(SL)	- Middlesex	1977
Highest Individual Score:	Gloucs:	103	B.F. Davison	V Yorkshire	1985
	Opponents	109*	B. Dudleston	- Leicestershire	1974
Best Bowling	Gloucs:	5-8	M.J. Procter	V Middlesex	1977
	Opponents	5-27	I.T. Botham	-Worcestershire	1987

Limited Overs Highest Wicket Partnerships – Gloucestershire

1st	113	G.D. Hodgson & A.J. Wright	(NW)	v Lincolnshire	1990
	113	A.W. Stovold & B.C. Broad	(SL)	v Sussex	1982
2nd	76*	Sadiq Mohammad & R.D.V. Knight	(SL)	vNottinghamshire	1974
3rd	104	Sadiq Mohammad & M.J. Procter	(SL)	v Essex	1980
4th	77	P. Bainbridge & P.W. Romaines	(SL)	v Leicestershire	1988
5th	147*	C.W.J. Athey & J.W. Lloyds	(NW)	v Lincolnshire	1990
6th	51	D.M. Green & A.S. Brown	(SL)	v Yorkshire	1970
7th	18	R.C. Russell & M.W. Alleyne	(SL)	v Worcestershire	1987
8th	56*	R.W. Phillips & D.A. Allen	(SL)	v Yorkshire	1969
9th	33*	D.A. Gravened & R. Swetman	(SL)	v Essex	1973
10th	6	S.A. Westley & J. Davey	(SL)	v Worcestershire	1971

Limited Overs Highest Wicket Partnerships – Opponents

1st	132	J.G. Wright & B. Wood	(SL)	- Derbyshire	1981
2nd	119	B. Dudleston & R. W. Tolchard	(SL)	- Leicestershire	1974
3rd	88	M.E.J.C. Norman & B.F. Davison	(SL)	- Leicestershire	1972
4th	165	M.E.J.C. Morris & G. Miller	(SL)	- Derbyshire	1984
5th	92	A.G.E. Earlham & J.N. Shepherd	SL)	- Kent	1979
6th	54	C.E.B. Rice & J.D. Birch	(BH)	- Nottinghamshire	1981
7th	54*	J.D. Love & A. Sidebottom	(SL)	- Yorkshire	1985
8th	35	J. Abrahams & J. Lyon	(SL)	- Lancashire	1975
9th	43*	E.E. Hemmings & K.E. Cooper	(SL)	- Nottinghamshire	1989
10th	13	P.D. McKeown & D. Marshall	(NW)	- Lincolnshire	1990

SOME FIRST CLASS PLAYERS' COMMENTS

David Allen
Gloucestershire and England

I have many happy memories of the Wagon Works ground where the pitches were conducive to good cricket.

Charlie Newman, the head groundsman, made good pitches and near the match he would put on a little marl. With good timing, the pitches encouraged all bowlers, while batsmen were able to play entertaining innings.

In my first full season in 1959 we played Lancashire and Kent in what was a good summer. I had wickets in both matches and was presented by the committee with the match ball, suitably mounted, for taking 7 for 66 versus Lancashire.

At the end of the season we were challenging for the championship and we played Surrey in what became a famous match.

I believe Charlie was asked to take the 'grass off the pitch', but none of us reckoned on the dust bowl that resulted.

Incredibly the first day saw two innings completed and Surrey batting again that night. If a catch had been held close to the wicket they would have finished that evening on 0 runs and lost 3 wickets. Needless to say, with Lock and Bedser, Surrey won.

In 1961 Gloucestershire fought back against a first innings deficit and played well to leave Middlesex to score 241 in their last innings.

At 150 for 7 wickets the opposition looked dead and buried, when a dolly catch from Ian Bedford went to mid-off to our best catcher, Arthur Milton, who dropped it. We couldn't believe it because Arthur could catch 'sparrows'. We didn't believe it would be too costly as Ian Bedford was not the greatest player, but he went on to slog himself a match winning score of 75 not out.

There were many great innings and feats of bowling, Ken Barrington always at ease on the challenging pitches, as was Colin Cowdrey; he was a wonderful player and a great timer of the ball. On the Wagon Works he picked up a ball from me and was caught at deep mid wicket near the clubhouse by a fielder who had his back against the fence.

Colin let out an expletive, which was unusual for him and later I asked him why. He replied, "I must be timing the ball well as I only meant to chip it over the mid-fielder for one run"

Perhaps one of my worst moments was being asked to pick up David Shepherd and Jack Davey at the motorway service station on my way to Gloucester. Due to an unfortunate mistake -and neither party will admit guilt to this day, we never made contact. I arrived at the ground ready for the start, a special car was sent to pick up the other two and they arrived on the field late, much to my embarrassment.

Off the field that great off-spinner Tom Goddard was a spectator and we always had good support from Ted Warner, a well known businessman; they were both great characters.

Mike Procter
Gloucestershire and South Africa

I always enjoyed playing cricket at Gloucester on the Winget ground, even though the pitch was usually on the slow side and favoured the spinners more than the fast bowlers.

The one game I will always remember is when we played Yorkshire who were captained at the time by Brian Close. He declared and set us a smallish total of 151 runs in 105 minutes to chase. I came to the crease after we had lost a couple of wickets and early in my innings I hit a ball straight to mid-off who caught it. When I hit the ball, I hit the ground very hard and, for some reason, stood my ground and was given not out. I think the umpire was Tom Spencer.

The Yorkshire players were astonished at the decision and before I faced the next ball, I realised that it couldn't have been a bump ball, so feeling rather guilty, I had a huge slog at the next delivery, connecting perfectly and it went for six. The look on Don Wilson's face is one I will never forget. I ended up scoring a few runs and we won the match. The Yorkshire team was not very happy.

Norman Walters
President GCCC, 1998, 1999 & 2000

My recollections of the Winget (Wagon Works) ground come under three headings – as a Journalist, as a Shop Keeper and as the Club's Honorary Treasurer for 12 years.

As a Bristol newspaper executive keen on cricket, I 'helped out' from time to time by reporting a Saturday match. When I did so at Gloucester it always seemed to be rainy or cold, or both! We were in a draughty marquee (with the scorers) in days when there was only one telephone in the 'Press Box', and that for the exclusive use of a national agency. So we lesser mortals had to compete for the only public phone available – across the ground in the clubhouse. Or to be more precise in my case, my wife competed; she regularly trudged across and tried to decipher my scrawled copy! As a Shop Keeper, it was with the Club Shop, which my wife and I looked after for some 20 years. Sometimes we were able to have our caravan/shop from Bristol brought to Winget: sometimes it was a wooden hut supported by a wigwam tent. Business was not exceptional, except in cigarettes! We never seemed able to get enough.

Right against the trend from my reporting days, there was one Gloucester Festival in a heat wave! We had started using the tent as a sweetshop and literally found chocolate running out from under the flap. That was the year we introduced the sale of soft drinks – tepid ones, as we had no fridge!

As Treasurer it was always a worry, especially in the hard up early days as to whether the Gloucester Festival could be sustained. Apart from one year it always was, but the profit and loss accounts invariably made gloomy reading. Timing of the event and the huge success of nearby Cheltenham were major factors. Indeed, they still are at the present venue.

Finally, an amusing memory; we arrived very early for a Sunday League Match, having stayed overnight at Rodborough and settled down to read the papers. For once we had NO commitments, or so we thought! Then an exceedingly harassed-looking County Secretary (the late Graham Parker) appeared at my elbow. Most of the gate stewards had failed to turn up and there were queues waiting to come in.

We manned the main gate in from Tuffley Avenue with one steward to deal with cars and for the next two hours we grabbed money and handed over tickets like wild things. The tally didn't balance (we had cash over!) and a few spectators were doubtless short-changed. Most couldn't care – they had got in on time! For us it was an un-nerving experience, and of course, Sod's law and all that, it was a boiling hot summer's day! By the time we had sorted things out and changed out of our perspiration-sodden clothes, it was the tea interval!

David Shepherd
GCCC, 1965 -1978

The ground at the Wagon Works in Tuffley Avenue brings back many memories, some good, some not so good. I remember it was where I scored my first championship century against our near neighbours Worcestershire, but it was also the ground where I suffered the indignity of a "King Pair" against Derbyshire, caught at the wicket first ball off Brian Jackson and caught short leg first ball off Derek Morgan. Understandably, I was dropped for the next match!

We used to have a week long festival which was usually opened with a civic reception. It was special to come to the city of Gloucester to play a couple of matches to fly the flag in the north of the county. We always received a warm welcome. Most of the county team was based in Bristol, so it meant quite a journey each morning and evening to and from Gloucester. Rather than each player driving his car, we used to take it in turns and share transport. I used to drive the kit wagon and would travel around Bristol picking up various players.

One of my most embarrassing memories of the Wagon Works was when David Allen picked up Jack Davey and me to transport us to Gloucester where the county were playing Hampshire. On reaching the motorway, David noticed that the ignition light remained on so we pulled into the Michaelwood Service Station where we discovered the fan belt had parted. Jack and I went back down the slip road to try to attract the attention of other players, all to no avail. David had replaced the fan belt and not being able to see Jack or me, he drove on to Gloucester, unknowingly leaving us stranded.

Time was now pressing and 'phone calls were hastily made to the ground and a car was detailed to fetch us, but this would take time! We eventually arrived at the ground about an hour late. Many felt that the two Devonians didn't fancy fielding! Substitutes had been arranged with the Hampshire players. Barry Richards volunteered and stuffed an extra sweater under his own, and explained "OK I'll be Shep!" What a cheek, but thanks mate.

That was an example of the friendliness and camaraderie which existed in the county game then. I have since been back to Tuffley Avenue as an umpire, but sadly no more!

Yes, the Wagon Works has many happy memories for me.

David Green
GCCC 1968-71

I had many enjoyable days at the Winget Ground, both as a player and in my later incarnation as a cricket writer. It was a characterful ground with an interesting pitch that generally helped bowlers, particularly spinners, without making batting so difficult that reasonable scoring was impossible.

I remember, particularly, four days in July 1969 when the championship match against Yorkshire on the Saturday, Monday and Tuesday straddled the Sunday John Player league game – this was the first year of the Sunday League.

In the championship game we bowled Yorkshire out fairly cheaply on the Saturday, got a useful lead by tea on the second day and had them in trouble again. They battled their way out of it, their skipper Brian Close playing a big part and shortly after tea on the third day they had saved the match being now 150 runs ahead with 5 wickets still standing. At this point Closey, who was nothing if not positive as a Captain, declared, setting us a target of 151 runs in 105 minutes.

We started well, reaching 61 before we lost a wicket, then wobbled to 84 for three, at which point Yorkshire were beginning to fancy their chances. Mike Procter, batting at 5, had only just come in when he drove at Don Wilson, their slow left armer, hitting him throat high to mid-off. The Yorkshire lads were delighted and had gathered together in jubilant little groups, when someone noticed that Proc was still standing there – he had actually hit turf with the toe of the bat as he struck the ball and was under the impression that he had hit it into the ground, producing a 'bump ball' (though one would hardly expect a flat carry of 45 yards to have resulted if that had been the case!)

Anyway, the Yorkies, looking red-faced and indignant, then appealed. Umpire Tommy Spencer was the only man on the ground who saw it Proccy's way and gave him not out. There was consternation among the Tykes. Don Wilson's prominent blue eyes were bulging out of his head, and bulged out even further when Proc hit his next ball over mid-wicket for six! In the end Proc made a rapid unbeaten 51 and we won by 5 wickets.

This was a double blow for the Yorkies for on the Sunday they had lost a game they had looked like winning easily. There was a very big crowd. Wisden records that over 8000 spectators crammed into the ground with a good many more perched on the roofs of the houses in Tuffley Avenue. We batted first and began horribly, Ron Nicholls and I opening, and both making ducks. David Shepherd made a defiant 49, but when he was seventh out the score was only 90. Wycliffe Phillips and David Allen did really well with an unbroken stand of 56, but even so, Yorkshire only needed 151 for victory.

They set off with a confident opening stand of 43. John Woodford made a solid 56 and though we kept it pretty tight, Tony Brown taking three wickets in an excellent spell, they came into the final straight needing only 13 runs from 16 balls and they still had 4 wickets standing. However, they did not score another run. Proccy and David Smith, both wicketless up to this point, came back and cut them down.

The crowd roared and bellowed as each wicket fell and when Proc bowled their last man, Peter Stringer, they poured onto the field surrounding us and thumping us vigorously about the back and shoulders. One bloke, still looking dazed said, "That's the best day's cricket I've ever seen". Certainly, fortunes shifted bewilderingly throughout the contest, and it was a terrific game to have played in.

CLOSE OF PLAY

Although compiling this book has been thoroughly enjoyable and hugely interesting, it was disappointing not to find more information on earlier games in the 1870s and the 1880s, but I suppose 120 years is a long time.

We are of course indebted to the local newspapers, namely the Gloucester Citizen and Journal and those members who took the time to send reports of matches to them.

Whether it is Gloucester Railway Carriage and Wagon Co. or just Winget, the club has a great tradition of loyalty, players turning out season after season. At the turn of the century we see L V Huggins and H E Perkins as stalwarts of the side.

In the 1920s the names of Brown and Hopcroft emerged. The 1930s, again Hopcroft, Goddard (when County duties allowed), Frank and Jim Stephens with team mates A H Evans, H Banks and Charlie Poolman. The war, of course, took its toll, but 1945 onwards saw the names of Frank Barber, Brian Cummings, Charlie Newman, Doug Swift, Vic Beamish, Tom Salter, Alan Pugh and others appear season after season.

Today we have Tony Salter and Eric Stephens who have played for the club for nearly, believe it or not, 50 seasons. Cliff Thomas and myself, for over 30 years have made the annual trek to play cricket on The Works ground. Others have played so often that they don't really need to "take guard" when batting.

Even Andy Hawkes has been a permanent fixture for over 20 years, and the 2004 players – the likes of Paul Carter, Jon Tegg, Colin Lewis, Bob Owen, Steve Wilson and others have themselves been around for many years.

Winget today still fields two Saturday teams, and although the ground is not in the condition it was when Arthur Paish, Charlie Newman and John Taylor tended it, the club still has a nucleus of strong cricketers at its core.

I believe that in recent years local cricket has seen a downturn. Ground conditions are not as good, and quietly, but worryingly, we have lost a number of clubs like Gloucester Bohemians, Gloucester Strollers, Robinswood Hill and Gloucester West Indians. The authorities need to identify the problems and find answers, otherwise the great traditions of cricket will die forever and that is a thought I dread to contemplate.

As for the Works ground, although now owned by the Council, I'm sure we could, at some point in the future, see the return of a "Golden Age". If more time and money were to be spent on its upkeep, we might even see the return of County Cricket one day. I would dearly love, like many others, to see this work done. I believe that the ground, with its historic background deserves this input, and I also believe like Brian (Bomber) Wells in his Foreword, that it also deserves a more appropriate name. My choice would simply be, as we all know it, "The Wagon Works".

As time drifts on, another season comes to a close with the final match. Players, after a pint or several, say their goodbyes, some to take up the games of rugby or soccer, skittles, or a visit or two to Kingsholm. The leaves from the plane trees start to gather on the outfield and the sound of the distant chimes from what seems to be the ever-present Ice Cream Van mark the conclusion of another sporting summer.

ACKNOWLEDGEMENTS

I would like to thank the following people for their help and support in compiling this book.

Firstly, to my sister Valerie Weaver who spent many hours at Gloucester Library searching archives, photographs and information. To Kathy Hartigan, who spent much time typing the majority of the text, also Charlotte Easterbrook, Theresa Powell, Angie Hopkins Jane Gee, Eileen Thompson and Tara Perkins who each helped in this way.

To Gloucestershire C.C.C's historian Mr Bert Avery for information regarding players and statistics and to Mr Jack Russell for his wonderful sketch for use on the cover. Messier Dowty I thank for their support, without which the format of the book could not have been achieved.

My thanks to the Editor of the Gloucester Citizen who gave his permission for the use of a large number of match reports from the Citizen and Journal.

Thanks too to former members Peter Smith, Gil Roberts, Doug Swift and others who have loaned team photographs and information. Thanks go too to Winget Cricket Club's President Stan Phelps and club members Bob Owen and Cliff Thomas for their much appreciated input.

I am very grateful to Mr Brian (Bomber) Wells for his delightful foreword, and to the county players who gave us some of their memories of the ground.

Finally, thank you to my daugher Alanna, without whose help I would have finished the book a year or two earlier!

Charlie Matthews

 Publisher's note: *Since this was written numerous people have donated funds towards the publication of this book. and we extend to them our heartfelt thanks. Finally a last word from Charlie's sister Valerie Weaver:*

To Charlie

***Cliff and I have finished off your book for you to the best of our ability…..even with
Alanna's help!
So it wasn't all in vain.
We hope you would have approved
God bless! Little brother
Val   xxx***